CONTESTED TREASURE

 **IBERIAN ENCOUNTER AND EXCHANGE 475–1755 | VOL. I**

SERIES EDITORS
*Erin Kathleen Rowe
and Michael A. Ryan*

THE PENNSYLVANIA STATE
UNIVERSITY PRESS

ADVISORY BOARD
*Paul H. Freedman
Richard Kagan
Marie Kelleher
Ricardo Padrón
Teofilo F. Ruiz
Marta V. Vicente*

The Iberian Peninsula has historically been an area of the world that fostered encounters and exchanges among peoples from different societies. For centuries, Iberia acted as a nexus for the circulation of ideas, people, objects, and technology around the premodern western Mediterranean, Atlantic, and eventually the Pacific. Iberian Encounter and Exchange, 475–1755 combines a broad thematic scope with the territorial limits of the Iberian Peninsula and its global contacts. In doing so, works in this series will juxtapose previously disparate areas of study and challenge scholars to rethink the role of encounter and exchange in the formation of the modern world.

CONTESTED TREASURE

JEWS AND AUTHORITY IN THE CROWN OF ARAGON

THOMAS W. BARTON

THE PENNSYLVANIA STATE UNIVERSITY PRESS
UNIVERSITY PARK, PENNSYLVANIA

Library of Congress Cataloging-in-Publication Data

Barton, Thomas W., 1976– , author.
 Contested treasure : Jews and authority in the crown of Aragon / Thomas W. Barton.
     pages   cm — (Iberian encounter and exchange, 475–1755)
Summary: "Examines how the Jews in the Crown of Aragon in the twelfth through fourteenth centuries negotiated the overlapping jurisdictions and power relations of local lords and the crown"—Provided by publisher.
Includes bibliographical references and index.
ISBN 978-0-271-06472-7 (cloth : alk. paper)
ISBN 978-0-271-06473-4 (pbk. : alk. paper)
1. Jews—Spain—Aragon—History—To 1500.
2. Jews—Legal status, laws, etc.—Spain—Aragon—History—To 1500.
3. Jews—Spain—Tortosa—History—To 1500.
4. Aragon (Spain)—Politics and government.
I. Title.

DS135.S75A7215 2015
946'.55004924—dc23
2014021730

Copyright © 2015 The Pennsylvania State University
All rights reserved
Printed in the United States of America
Published by The Pennsylvania State University Press,
University Park, PA 16802-1003

The Pennsylvania State University Press is a member of the Association of American University Presses.

It is the policy of The Pennsylvania State University Press to use acid-free paper. Publications on uncoated stock satisfy the minimum requirements of American National Standard for Information Sciences—Permanence of Paper for Printed Library Material,
ANSI Z39.48–1992.

To my parents and step-parents

Contents

ACKNOWLEDGMENTS ix
NOTE ON THE TEXT xv

Introduction 1

1 Foundations and Withdrawal 25

2 Royal Administrative Change and the Emergence of a Jewish Policy 55

3 Seigniorial Administration and Micro-convivencia 83

4 Royal Administrative Advances 120

5 Administrative Strategies and the Royal Takeover 138

6 Seigniorial Jurisdiction and the Transition to Royal Governance 161

Epilogue: Contested Treasure in Broader Context 188

NOTES 215
REFERENCES 253
INDEX 277

Acknowledgments

This study emerged as a side interest while I was transforming my dissertation on the conquest and settlement of the Ebro River Valley into a monograph. It increasingly stole time away from that initial project until it became my primary research focus. As *Contested Treasure* has evolved from a germ of a research idea to a conference paper to an article to an unwieldy book manuscript that had to be reduced, streamlined, and polished, I have benefited from the advice and support of numerous friends, colleagues, and collaborators.

I first had the opportunity to put together some of my ideas when I collaborated in an unusually synergistic session held at the delightful Sewanee Medieval Colloquium in 2009. I owe Maya Soifer Irish a debt of gratitude for inviting me to take part in that panel and for teaching me all that she has about Jewish-Christian relations, informally and as a collaborator, since then. I learned much from the stimulating contributions by Gregory Milton and Tom Burman at that gathering.

The four anonymous reviewers at *Speculum* provided vital feedback for revising the article manuscript. I thank Paul Szarmach, Ronald Musto and Eileen Gardiner, and Jacqueline Brown for their assistance and patience over the course of numerous revisions as well as their understanding when I later chose to withdraw my submission.

As always, the hosts and participants at the California Medieval Seminar at the Huntington Library provided sage advice as I was preparing to enlarge the project into a book manuscript. I would like to thank Karen Burgess for organizing the seminar as well as recognize, in particular, Piotr Górecki, Sarah Whitten, Ned Schoolman, Scott Wells, and Antonio Zaldivar for their helpful feedback on that occasion. The recurring seminar of doctoral students of the Crown of Aragon organized by Daniel Duran i Duelt and Stéphane Péquignot at the CSIC's Institució Mila i Fontanals in Barcelona was a delightful and illuminating gathering that served as a useful sounding board for some of my earlier ideas about Tortosa's urban history.

An indefatigable supporter of all things medieval and an all-around mensch, Mike Ryan alerted me to the creation of the Iberian Encounter and Exchange, 475–1755 series he would be editing with Erin Rowe. I thank them both for doing their part to find a home for the manuscript as well as to support its revision and improvement. The Pennsylvania State Press has been a delight to work with and helped, in every conceivable way, to make production as effortless as possible. Eleanor Goodman has been everything an author could hope for in an editor: open, upfront, accessible, prompt, and (above all) patient. Julie Schoelles meticulously edited the manuscript, rescuing me from all sorts of embarrassing infelicities. I thank Charlee Redman, Jennifer Norton, Brian Beer, Laura Reed-Morrisson, and Patty Mitchell for helpful assistance with logistics, as well as everyone else at the press involved in the project. The two anonymous reviewers, whom I now know were Paula Tartakoff and Jonathan Ray, provided invaluable suggestions that greatly improved the finished manuscript. I naturally take full responsibility for any and all errors that might remain in the book.

I am incredibly grateful to Paul Freedman for standing by me unfailingly as a mentor and colleague over the past fifteen years and for teaching me so much of what I know about the medieval world, Catalonia, and fine dining. Thanks also to Carlos Eire for his consistent kindness and wise advice and to Adam Kosto for his valuable constructive criticism. Peter Brown inspired me to become a professional historian and has continued to encourage me since I left Princeton. I feel fortunate to have gotten to know and learn from Teo Ruiz while working on this project. I am thankful for his advice, support, boundless warmth and compassion, and contagious passion for history. Mike McGovern's unique ability to make history come alive deeply affected me as a teenager and helped fuel my desire to pursue the study of history in college. I enjoyed getting to know Ted Melillo and Ed Watts at Yale and am grateful to have them still as good friends and colleagues on opposite coasts. I thank Matt Wranovix, Brian Noell, Paul Abelsky, Susan McDonough, and Michelle Herder for being supportive members of my medievalist cohort during my time as a doctoral student.

I feel fortunate to have such supportive colleagues at the University of San Diego (USD). I would like to recognize all of the members of my History Department family, and in particular the unflagging advocacy and mentorship of Ken Serbin during his tenure as chair. The former dean of the College of Arts and Sciences, Mary Boyd, former provost, Julie Sullivan, and outgoing president, Mary Lyons, also provided essential support, as did my current dean, Noelle Norton. I'm especially thankful for my friendships with Clara Oberle, Colin Fisher, Yi Sun, Maureen Byrnes, Avi Spiegel, and Jane Friedman. The research I have conducted in San Diego would not have been possible without the many books ordered via Interlibrary Loan by Alex Moran and the assistance of the staff at Copley Library and the Legal Research Center. The CIRCUIT system provided essential convenient access to the library collections at UCSD and San Diego State. My colleagues in the History and Religious Studies Departments, especially Len Smith, Mike Wert, and Ari Sammartino, helped make my year at Oberlin an especially fruitful one as I was first pondering what to make of this evidence concerning Tortosa's Jews.

I am also extremely thankful for the hospitality and indispensible assistance of administrators, staff members, and colleagues at a number of different archives and libraries in Catalonia. First and foremost, Albert Curto, head of the Arxiu Històric Comarcal de les Terres de l'Ebre in Tortosa, has been so helpful with my questions and countless requests and such a welcoming host over the years. Mossèn Salvador Ballester oversaw Tortosa's capitular archive when I worked there and was exceptionally kind and accommodating. I'm also grateful to the directors and helpful staff at the Archivo de la Corona de Aragón, which has come to feel like a home away from home. I would also like to acknowledge the directors and staff members at the Biblioteca de Catalunya, the library of the CSIC's Institució Mila i Fontanals, Lleida's Arxiu Capitular and Arxiu Municipal, Madrid's Archivo Histórico Nacional, and the Arxiu Montserrat Tarradellas i Macià at Poblet, which houses the Arxiu de la Casa Ducal de Medinaceli a Catalunya, for their support of my research. Laurea Pagarolas, Flocel Sabaté, Gemma Escribà, Damian Smith, and Benjy Gampel offered helpful advice during the research phase of the project.

The research for this book has been supported by funding from numerous programs and institutions, which I acknowledge with gratitude: the Andrew Mellon Graduate Fellowship, the Heckman Research Scholarship from the Hill Museum and Manuscript Library, the John Perry Miller Fellowship for Research, two separate grants from the Program for Cultural Cooperation Between Spain's Ministry of Culture and United States' Universities, a Fulbright Fellowship with extension from the Comisión Fulbright España, a dissertation writing fellowship from Yale University, a grant-in-aid research award from Oberlin College, numerous faculty research grants and international opportunity grants from USD, and a full-year fellowship from the American Council of Learned Societies that was supplemented by generous support from USD.

I would like to recognize Pere Benito Monclús for his friendship and companionship on multiple adventures during my many trips to Catalonia as well as during his own visits to New Zealand and San Diego. He has introduced me to a side of Catalonia and Catalan culture I otherwise would not have known and taught me so much about medieval history and the Spanish university system over the years. Pere's wonderful parents have provided boundless hospitality, excellent home cooking, and delightful conversation every time I've left my *quatre demonis* to visit them in Vilassar de Dalt. I am grateful to Henri Dolset and Patrick Leroy for welcoming us into their homes in Barcelona and Cherbourg and for their heartwarming kindness over the years. Other friends have been instrumental in making my time in Catalonia much more interesting and joyous as I researched this project: Xavier Sanahuja, Helena Garrigós, Marta Herreras, David Alonso, Edgar Vergara, and Teresa Julià. Marie Kelleher has been a fount of advice and humor in both Barcelona and southern California. The intrepid novelist and doctor Daniel Mason was a perfect companion during his month-long stop in Barcelona on his book tour. In addition to being fun and fascinating friends and fellow Iberian adventurers over the years, Gwen Rice and Andrew Devereux generously let me use their apartment in Madrid when I was conducting my archival work there. I have benefited from interacting with the diverse network of scholars of the Spain–North Africa Project as this book was under way. In New Zealand, many wonderful people made my research and writing much more fruitful, including Louise Waghorn, Grant Duffy, Sherryn El Bakary, Carl and Delwyn Phiskie, and Leon and Liz Walker. In San Diego, I have especially valued my friendship with Tammy and John Unikewicz and the good times I have spent with them and the extended Unikewicz-Galen family as I worked on this project.

Last but certainly not least, I should thank my family for love and support. This book is dedicated to my parents and step-parents, Brigid Barton-Robinson and Rob Robinson, and Doug and Sue Barton, who have fostered my love of history, inspired me to pursue a career in academia, and consistently helped me throughout the long and convoluted journey. My step-mom, Sue, gave me valuable comments on the *Speculum* draft, and both she and my mom, Brigid, proofed the final manuscript. Thanks also to Greg, Julie, Rachel, and Lucy Barton for camaraderie and much-needed get-togethers, and to my in-laws, Joe, Candee, and JJ, for always being willing to lend a helping hand. Ilo has been a wonderful companion throughout the writing and editing process, snoozing peacefully nearby as I've written and accompanying me on essential breaks to get fresh air in Rose Canyon, the San Elijo lagoon, and Rancho Santa Fe's horse trails. I feel lucky to have had continual support since age four from my best friend and brother from another mother, Ben Waltzer. Mele, Koa, and Nanea have grown up curiously watching me ponder difficult historical questions about the distant and mysterious places discussed in this book. Their unconditional love and spontaneity have kept me in high spirits and enabled me to persevere during the most challenging phases of the project. From New Haven to Barcelona to Paris to Waiheke Island to Oberlin to San Diego to Rancho Santa Fe, with many trips to Hawaii and Europe in between, Whitney has stood by me and encouraged me to pursue my scholarly ambitions, even if it meant sacrificing goals of her own, through thick and thin with love and patience.

Rancho Santa Fe, California
May 2014

Note on the Text

Throughout the following chapters, I have tried to be consistent and deliberate with naming and transliteration, pursuing guidelines intended to support and reinforce the book's main objectives. In order to lend a sense of the linguistic and cultural diversity of the territories of the Crown of Aragon, I have made the names of historical actors, wherever possible, reflect their places of residence or home linguistic cultures. For example, if a man originating in Catalonia appears as Petrus in a Latin document, he will be treated here as Pere, whereas a man from Aragon bearing that name will be called Pedro. Although they governed lands that spoke a range of languages and already bore a long list of titles to diverse principalities and territories by the later thirteenth century, the count-kings of Barcelona and Aragon arguably remained culturally and dynastically Catalan throughout the high medieval period. Their naming and numeration in this book reflects this orientation, with Alfons "El Cast" (r. 1154–96), for example, appearing as Alfons I rather than as Alfons II due to the earlier reign of his Aragonese predecessor Alfonso I "El Batallador" (r. 1104–34). Moreover, since she was from Castile, Alfons's queen is called Sancha rather than the Catalan Sança. For enhanced readability, I often refer to the count-kings as simply kings, comital-royal rights as simply royal rights, and the combined comital-royal government as simply the crown or monarchy. For the most part, Hebrew, Arabic, and Judeo-Arabic names of nonfamous individuals from Latin or Romance archival sources are rendered as written by the scribe without diacritical marks, although in certain cases I have regularized them or set them in their modern Catalan or Aragonese/Castilian equivalents. The names of better-known historical figures, such as al-Idrīsī or Ḥasdai ibn Shaprut, are printed in their standard form. Regions and place-names that will be familiar to the average reader, such as Aragon and Valencia, have been anglicized, whereas locations that are more obscure or do not have standard English equivalents have been put in their modern equivalents. Thus, the reader will encounter Zaragoza, Lleida, and Empúries. I have transliterated Arabic and Hebrew words based on standard academic use. Where deemed necessary, terminology such as *aljama, collecta, lleuda, prohom*, and *mudéjar* is defined at the first instance and periodically in the text or notes. Because the text employs a relatively small number of terms regularly, it does not employ a glossary.

The history of the coinage used in the Crown of Aragon is complex, and understanding its intricacies is not essential for appreciating the primary arguments of this book. It is sufficient to know that a number of distinct yet roughly equivalent silver solidus (sou) coins were in circulation in the realms. Although their values and purchasing power varied across time and place, these solidi were each subject to the original Carolingian ratio of one pound to twenty solidi to twelve denarii. By the later thirteenth century, each morabetin was worth around nine Catalonian solidi and three morabetins were roughly equivalent to five masmudines. In the mid-fourteenth century, about eleven solidi amounted to one florin. (See Balaguer 1999.)

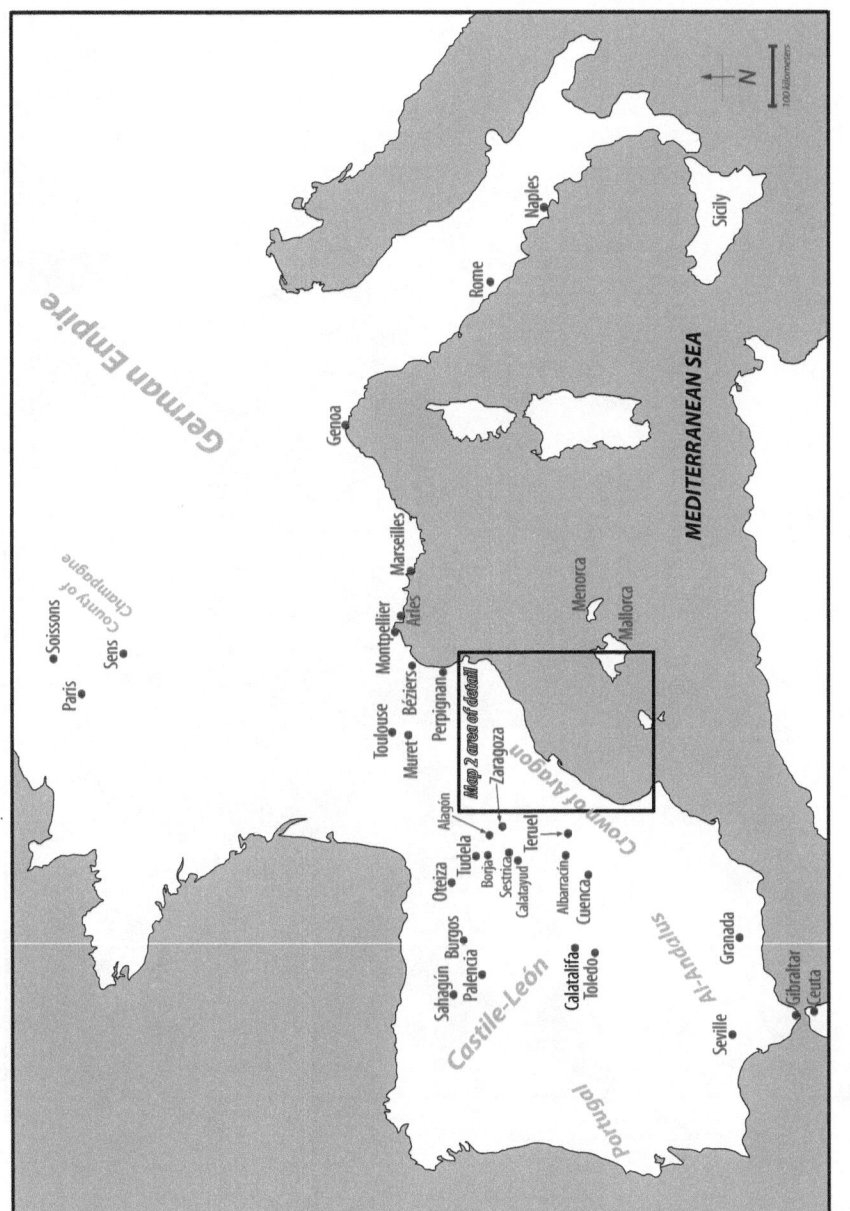

MAP 1: Relevant towns and political entities within the western Mediterranean and Europe

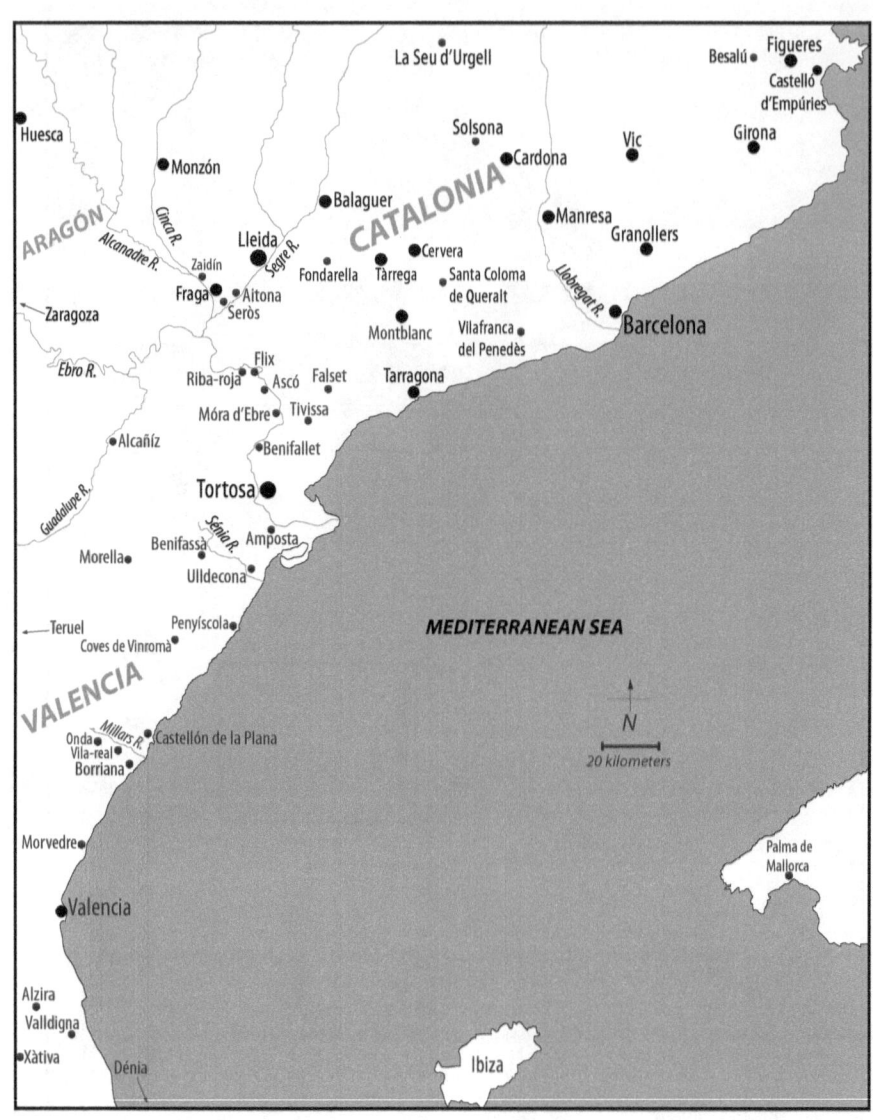

MAP 2: The eastern Crown of Aragon (detail from Map 1)

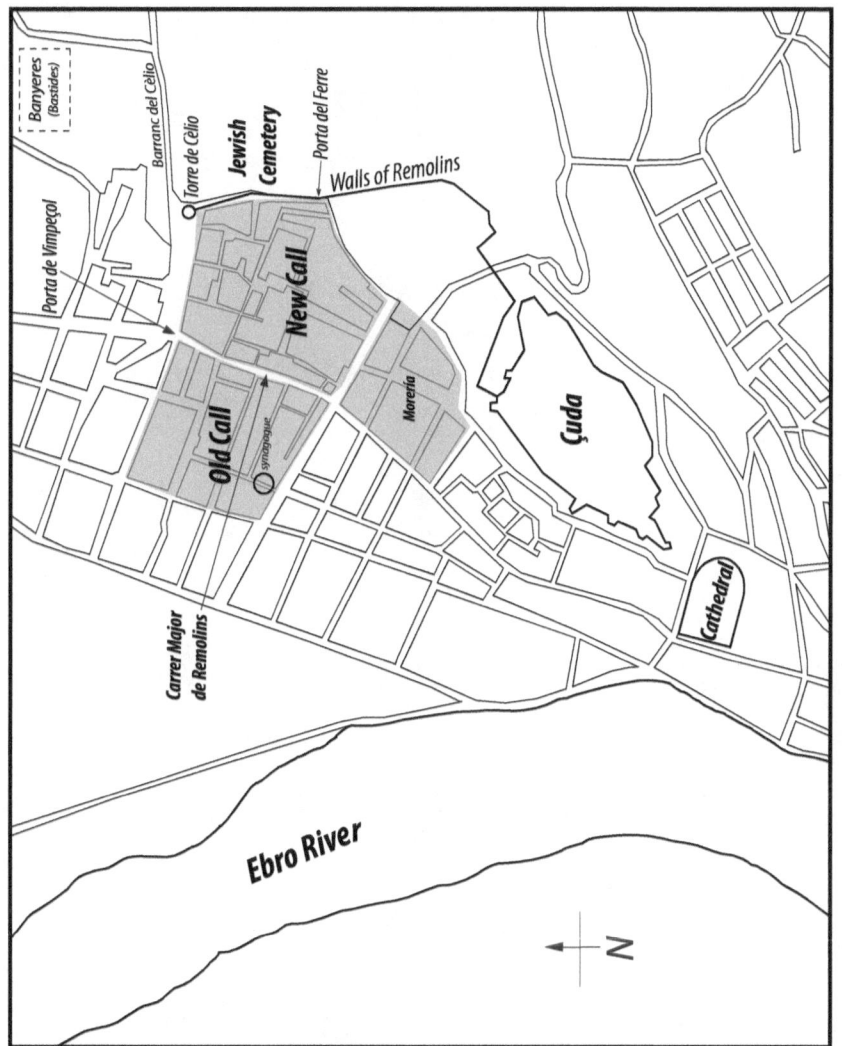

MAP 3: Approximate locations of Tortosa's twelfth- and thirteenth-century Jewish and Muslim quarters.

INTRODUCTION

In 1377, a Jewish moneylender named Abraham Açavella claimed before the royal court that he had been wrongfully imprisoned and robbed by the abbot and officers of the Cistercian monastery of Valldigna in rural Valencia. The royal procurator representing Abraham in the trial later explained that his client had visited a Muslim rural community in the Alfàndec Valley, in the monastery's domains, to pursue debt payments from several Muslims, including a certain Azmet Aeça.[1] Supposedly Azmet quickly grew hostile and tried to kill the Jew with a weapon, prompting Abraham to flee and hide in a neighboring house and Azmet to scream for help from the other Muslims in the village, claiming that Abraham had in fact attacked him. These other residents helped Azmet locate the Jew and, after giving him a severe beating, hand him over to Valldigna's abbot, who then, according to the crown's lawyer, exploited the situation to enrich himself.

The abbot allegedly incarcerated Abraham under harsh conditions until the Jew's father could arrive from their hometown of Alzira, twenty kilometers to the north, to issue the monastery a promissory note for one hundred gold florins for his release. The abbot also refused to return the sack full of silk that Abraham had been carrying at the time of the attack. The Jews later claimed it was worth more than one hundred pounds. In search of a judicial forum to overrule Valldigna, Abraham lodged a complaint with the monarchy's bailiff general in Valencia. After the officer failed to get an adequate response from the abbot, however, he referred the matter to the royal court.[2]

During the court proceedings, the jurisdictional issues raised by the case overshadowed the simple question of which party was guilty of assault. The systemic challenge the case presented to royal prerogatives likely accounts for the trial's length and the extensiveness of its extant transcripts. In keeping with the claims of Valencia's thirteenth-century territorial law, the *Furs de València*, the monarchy asserted that, because all Jews represented "the king's treasure," all cases involving Jews, no matter where they were perpetrated, necessarily fell under royal jurisdiction.[3] Given the circumstances of the dispute, Abraham obviously had a strong interest in collaborating with the monarchy's agenda, just as the Muslims who testified were motivated to support their lord. On future occasions, however, residents of Valldigna in conflict with the abbot would instead seek to use the monarchy's jurisdictional claims to escape the reach of the seigniorial court. One local Muslim in 1481 publicly ridiculed the executive authority of Valldigna's court officer, jeering that he was unable "to hang anyone [outside the valley] in the King's land, God guard him!" Proclaiming himself "a vassal of my lord the King," however, did not deter the officer from sentencing him to five hundred lashes and a five-hundred-florin fine.[4]

In the case involving Abraham, the crown aimed to expose and condemn the dangerous precedent perpetrated by the abbot of Valldigna. By universalizing the case, the royal legal experts managed to use it to broadcast the monarchy's claims of exclusive jurisdiction over such Jews. In his testimony, the governor of Valencia, who claimed responsibility to "maintain and defend royal jurisdiction," stated matter-of-factly that "usurpers and occupiers of royal jurisdiction and violators of licenses of safe passage [*guiatges*] from the king granted to this Jew and to other Jews must be punished." He based his retelling and argumentation on the assumption that the monarchy's exclusive relationship with the Jews was legally incontrovertible and universally recognized. Thus, according to the governor, when these Muslims decided to attack this lender, they naturally understood, and were choosing to defy, what was "known to all" by not "paying heed to omnipotent God and royal authority, nor observing how the said Jew and all of the other Jews are under the protection and guard of the said Lord King." As Azmet grabbed a staff to kill Abraham, the governor reasoned, he must have been "motivated by an evil spirit," since any subject in his right mind would have known not to transgress royal authority in such a fashion.[5]

In this situation, from the crown's point of view, the abbot should have known to cede the handling of the case to the king's chief officer for the kingdom of Valencia. His abuse of the judicial and executive authority he had usurped from the monarchy by finding Abraham guilty without cause and illegitimately seizing his property further emphasized why special subjects such as the Jews so depended on the effective protection that only the king could offer.[6] Even though the monarchy did not mention its parallel claims to possess all Muslims in its realms, the case obviously had important implications for the abbot's jurisdictional power over Valldigna's Muslim inhabitants. If Azmet had indeed been the victim, as he and his lord had claimed, would the monarchy have had the same right to intervene?

Valldigna, however, presented a formidable defense that asserted control over the monarchy's own claims by appealing to feudal law. Through his procurator (or legal agent), the abbot argued that, as local lord, he enjoyed the full expression of the crown's regalian prerogatives on his domains. And, unfortunately for the crown, in this instance its opponents had the documentation on hand to support their claim. According to evidence presented by the monastery, the king's predecessor, Jaume II (r. 1291–1327), had indeed invested the abbots of Valldigna with this independence by assigning them a charter of donation in 1300, later confirmed by Pere III (r. 1336–87). It had awarded them full jurisdiction over all civil and criminal cases (*merum et mixtum imperium*) as well as all other rights pertaining to "our *regalia*" over "all men and women residing or who will reside" within these domains in perpetuity.[7] The language of the *Furs de València*, the abbot's procurator continued, furthermore "provides no impediment," since it must apply only to lords who had not already been granted these powers and made into veritable micromonarchs by the crown. There is no doubt, he concluded, "that the said Lord Abbot is able to punish any delinquents in the said Valldigna, either a Jew or whomever it might be."[8]

Thus, the monks of Valldigna had little reason to challenge outright the monarchy's claims that the Jews pertained to the royal treasure because the principle undergirded their own jurisdictional rights. From their point of view, the royal donation had invested them with legal ownership of this treasure when it fell within their domains. The conflict between the principle of theoretically inalienable regalian jurisdiction over the Jews and the monarchy's chronic tendency to transfer such rights to independent lordships for varying objectives had caused numerous similar scenarios throughout the Crown of Aragon over the past generations.

This book explores the origins and expression of such controversies over the development and implementation of a policy of exclusive possession of resident Jews by the monarchy of the Crown of Aragon from the twelfth through the fourteenth centuries. By scrutinizing the case of the town of Tortosa alongside an array of comparative local studies, it will seek to document the range of responses by independent lords who contested these jurisdictional prerogatives claimed by the crown because, like the monks of Valldigna, they felt legally entitled to administer and enforce justice among the Jews and other subjects in their domains. The primary argument to be made here is that, far from a curiosity of legal history, these engagements had significant, lasting implications for the coexistence of Jews within Christian-ruled society and the development of royal and seigniorial governance. They influenced the regulatory norms for Jews that would endure until the expulsion, altered the dynamics within and between individual Jewish communities, and affected the modes of interaction between Jews and royal and seigniorial authorities. As with the court case in Valldigna, these confrontations forced rival local constituencies to confront and reconcile their conflicting interpretations about the very nature of royal power. The outcomes of these engagements would have significant implications for the interrelationships of these constituencies as well as, potentially, for the potency of the crown's regalian claims.

Jews and the Political Development of the Crown of Aragon

Occupying the northeastern sector of the Iberian Peninsula, the Crown of Aragon was home to a growing Jewish population fed by migration and territorial conquest from the eleventh century.[9] Gradually from the twelfth century, the counts of Barcelona (who later added "kings of Aragon" to their assemblage of titles) ascended in wealth, legitimacy, and authority with further conquests of Muslim lands, political gains over rebellious nobles, and administrative improvements. These so-called count-kings of Barcelona and Aragon also increasingly made moves to claim exclusive jurisdiction over the Jews resident within their domains.

This was not a phenomenon limited to this region of European society. Indeed, the possession of Jews and their property and the monopolization of punitive power over them would become a commonly claimed and highly valued regalian right in many other principalities by the middle of the thirteenth century. The Jews were not only an increasingly valuable financial resource for ambitious monarchs intent on centralizing their realms at the expense of their nobility. As a generally wealthy minority group in need of protection, they were also apt to serve as a potent symbol of the king's role in defending the public safety and common good of the realms, developed chiefly from Roman and Carolingian models, like other regalian preserves such as coinage and taxation.[10]

This informal relationship first became enshrined in official policy around 1176, when Alfons I (r. 1162–96) granted local laws and privileges (*fueros*) to the Aragonese frontier town of Teruel. Alongside other regulations promoting the local authority of the monarch, the fuero asserted that Jews "are servants of the king [*servi regis*] and always pertain to the royal treasury [*fisco*]."[11] The origins and significance of this principle within the Crown of Aragon and the wider European political landscape remain mysterious and are the subject of continued debate.[12] David Abulafia has posited that the *Fuero de Teruel* represents the earliest appearance of the servi regis formula in high medieval Europe, raising the possibility that similar provisions developed by other monarchies derived from it. He suggests that the royal ownership of Jewish property was founded chiefly on the notion of (admittedly non-Jewish) "fiscal servants" (*servi fiscales*) that was operative in Roman law and witnessed in Visigothic times.[13] Other scholarship has pointed specifically to Carolingian precedents, most importantly the tradition of granting Jews *tuitio* charters establishing "direct and mutual obligations, including that of special protection."[14] Prior rulers of the independent kingdom of Aragon, before its merger with the county of Barcelona, had granted fueros to conquered towns that regulated the Muslim and Jewish inhabitants, stipulating procedural norms essential to coexistence such as oath taking and interreligious justice. Yet, even though these laws did much to assert the king's right to a third of fines and other revenues as conqueror, they did not make any moves to eliminate the jurisdictional or ownership rights of other lords with regard to non-Christian residents.[15]

It remains unclear to what extent the ideologies and regulations promoted by centralizing monarchies such as the Crown of Aragon were influenced by the developing stance of the high medieval Church on the status of resident Jews. The considerable volume of authoritative ecclesiastical writings from the church fathers onward concerning the issue of accommodation did not inspire consistency or clarity from the papacy or other authorities throughout the high medieval period.[16] As Christianity gained the upper hand with the conversion of Constantine in the early fourth century, most church leaders, and especially the church fathers, begrudgingly permitted the presence of Jews, on the grounds that they were targets for conversion, and prescribed nonviolent means to pressure them to convert. Augustine produced the most influential writings along these lines for the policies of both late Rome and medieval society. In his view, even though the Jews were enemies of Christ and, by extension, of all Christians, they should be tolerated as witnesses to the prophesies that foretold Christ's coming until they realized their error and church and synagogue could be reunited.[17] His scriptural interpretation, expressed in numerous works including *The City of God,* that "the elder people, the Jews, should serve the younger people, the Christians," helped inspire subsequent medieval conceptions of Jewish servitude.[18]

In a letter to Spanish bishops from 1063 concerning attacks on Jews by crusaders, Alexander II largely echoed Augustine when he famously distinguished Iberian Jews as the one religious minority group deserving of protection under Christian rule. Although they had earned a condition of servitude for betraying Christ and spurning his message, Jews, unlike the bellicose Muslims, were "willing to serve Christians everywhere."[19] Calixtus II's influential *Sicut iudeis* (ca. 1120) did imply that the papacy was the ultimate guarantor of the protections offered to the Jews, but there was no clear message from ecclesiastical leaders at this time identifying which party would exercise this lordship over the Jews.[20] From the thirteenth century, certain canon lawyers and theologians did assert that local authorities represented the logical recipients of Jewish service. According to Thomas Aquinas, for instance, "rulers could [by law] receive [Jews'] property as if it were theirs" on account of the Jews' subjugation. However, because Jews were the "*servi* of the Church," Aquinas also argued that it could dispose of their property.[21] Investigations into the development and wider relevance of these positions are further complicated by the fact that no documentation has come to light demonstrating that the Crown of Aragon's Jewish policies were ever conceived or justified specifically in response to, or as a reestablishment of, Roman, Visigothic, Carolingian, or canon-legal norms.

The concept of regalian rights over Jews in the Crown of Aragon likely emerged out of a mixture of these influences. It was also clearly inspired and encouraged by the broader political objective of centralization, which was being pursued with ever-greater intensity by the monarchy from the mid-twelfth century. Indeed, an important minority of scholars has sought to examine the servi regis principle and its role in the emergence of a royal Jewish policy within the Crown of Aragon's broader institutional context—paralleling extensive scholarship on other regions of medieval Europe—as opposed to studying the administration of Jews as an isolated subset of institutional history.[22] Most notably, Elka Klein has convincingly exposed the complicated interactions between the development of the monarchy's fiscal and administrative operations and changes in the Jewish communal organization within the urban setting of Barcelona through the thirteenth century.[23] Such modes of inquiry have led Klein and others to associate the *Fuero de Teruel* and subsequent indications of an emerging Jewish policy with the count-kings' wider efforts from the mid-twelfth century to consolidate what Thomas Bisson has termed "a new feudal order."[24]

There are sound reasons for linking general efforts by the count-kings to assert control over public order throughout the realms with specific provisions reserving their jurisdiction over a tolerated minority such as the Jews. These developments were both occurring contemporaneously in the wake of the successful dynastic unification between the comital house of Barcelona and the kingdom of Aragon in 1137 and conquests of the Muslim principalities of Tortosa and Lleida (1148–53), the last of the Upper March of Al-Andalus, orchestrated by the count-prince Ramon Berenguer IV (r. 1131–62). This dynasty's territories would continue to grow southward with the advance against the Muslims and, by the later thirteenth century, come to include the kingdom of Valencia and a number of Mediterranean islands. These legitimizing and enriching conquests empowered the monarchy to introduce potent innovations in its ruling ideology and administrative apparatus.

In addition to conducting targeted surveys of his domains and developing the earliest systematic records of account, Ramon elaborated a new vision of his authority in the law code known as the *Usatges de Barcelona*, cleverly manipulated to look traditional and less controversial through its backdating to the eleventh century.[25] The code defined all subjects in the realm, irrespective of feudal contracts or jurisdictional circumstances, as subject to the overarching jurisdiction of Ramon's court and thereby responsible to serve the count or prince (*princeps*) in his defense of the realm.[26] The policies and administrative strategies of Ramon's successors, Alfons I, Pere I (r. 1196–1213), and Jaume I (r. 1213–76), built upon this vision of power with varying degrees of success. The peace assemblies and constitutions they periodically organized sought to identify and enforce specific provisions of this public peace in order to increase the local capacity of royal governance at the expense of seigniorial authority.[27] Such nonfeudal provisions for public order were paired with new administrative techniques and instruments that sought to tighten control over the crown's traditional patrimonial prerogatives, which in the past had been in danger of usurpation by assertive nobles. The most important of these new instruments was the *Liber feudorum maior*, or *Great Book of the Fiefs*, compiled by the early 1190s.[28] Alfons I also oversaw the creation of his house's first narrative genealogy, the *Gesta Comitum Barchinonensium*, or *Deeds of the Counts of Barcelona*, between 1180 and 1184, which was expanded over the following decades. According to Jaume Aurell, "re-present[ing]" the origins of the county of Barcelona "served as a powerful external validation, verifying the dynasty's claims to authority and legitimacy over political rivals . . . in the service of . . . [its] bold expansionist ambitions."[29] Such monarchy building was not unique to this region but paralleled political situations elsewhere in European society, where ascendant kings targeted seigniorial rivals. In Bisson's words, "In every other European land where the process is visible, this royal (or public) suppression of fortified lordships was a precondition for the delordified exercise of royal power."[30]

Consistent efforts by the counts and count-kings of Barcelona to assert rights of lordship over the neighboring counties and insubordinate viscounties constituting the former Carolingian Spanish March would be mostly complete by the end of the twelfth century. After the acquisition of Pallars Jussà in 1192, only Urgell, Pallars Sobirà, and Empúries maintained their full independence.[31] These remaining counties were defiantly autonomous and signaled their status by emulating some of the count-kings' administrative activity.[32] The issue of coinage, peace making, and general policy-making by the counts of Empúries, for instance, underscored their ancient county's autonomy, which was, they contended, indistinguishable from that of the counts of Barcelona.[33]

Scholars are now aware that the monarchy's campaigns to realize this vision of royal power by exploiting and policing feudal and nonfeudal prerogatives achieved only minimal progress during the remainder of the twelfth century and into the thirteenth. The early counts had been able to recover much of their lost authority and impose on the aristocracy by carefully using feudal contracts (*convenientiae*) to construct a "feudal state" tentatively founded on a hierarchy of fiefs.[34] They ostensibly orchestrated this project by drawing upon Carolingian models of public authority, which had regulated public roads, remanded private disputes to imperial justice, and monopolized the minting of coinage. One of Charlemagne's well-known capitularies had required that "fealty not be sworn to anyone except to us . . . with a view to our interest."[35] Yet, this progress did not prevent later twelfth-century aristocrats from resisting efforts by the count-kings to increase control over feudal relations while solidifying their command of public order. These lords succeeded in carving out relatively independent jurisdictions, reprising, to a certain degree, the dislocations of the eleventh century perpetrated by aristocratic uprisings.[36] Adam Kosto has shown that the ideologically potent *Usatges de Barcelona* had little local impact throughout Catalonia until well into the thirteenth century.[37] Similarly, attempts to amplify the ambitious public peace provisions promulgated by Alfons at Fondarella in 1173 were short-lived, with the result that the royal Peace and Truce was being scaled back in the early 1200s, during his son's reign. Specific safeguards for townspeople, mandates for an army of enforcement, and protections over public roads were weakened by exceptions and loopholes or removed altogether.[38] In particular, the appearance of the right of mistreatment (*ius maletractandi*) in 1202, which deprived abused peasants of the right to appeal their cases to the royal court "if not themselves commended to the king," directly conflicted with the monarchy's claims to possess pervasive jurisdiction in safeguarding public order that could not be obstructed by seigniorial feudal rights.[39] Lords now had not only de facto abilities, but also legally protected (de jure) rights to impose on their subject populations in their domains by force of arms, emanating from their castral positions, and by securing their own legally autonomous jurisdictions.

This crisis of royal authority in the face of defensive or even aggressive lordship was thus ushering in a situation of seigniorial jurisdictional autonomy paired with a system of peasant servitude that would continue to be implemented and legitimized by the passage of new laws over the course of the thirteenth century.[40] At the same time, the heavy expense of military expeditions in Occitania and against Muslims and Christian rivals in the

Peninsula was forcing the monarchy to leverage its demesne lands, shift toward indirect administration, or alienate selected lordships outright.[41] These developments served to counteract the administrative implications of the hard-won progress in imposing on the counties and viscounties of the former Spanish March.

Over the course of the thirteenth century, administrative advancements that built on the twelfth-century regnal ideology therefore did not permit the triumph of royal authority or even the full recuperation of jurisdictional rights once held by royal patrimony.[42] As Flocel Sabaté has cogently argued, in spite of a persistent discourse of royal power in which the "Barcelonan title holder did not doubt his superiority over the Catalan assemblage," vast sections of the realms remained dominated by seigniorial authority and isolated from the reach of royal administration.[43] "Powerful jurisdictional fragmentation," he notes, "converted the land into a veritable mosaic of diverse spaces, mutually impenetrable and to a great extent alien to royal representatives."[44] While the coexistence of often mutually exclusive seigniorial feudal rights and royal prerogatives may have coalesced from a "process" into a "system" from the reign of Jaume I onward as the monarchy and its legal projects institutionalized these nonroyal autonomies, the situation nevertheless remained dynamic and marked by tension.[45] Indeed, Paul Freedman has proposed that feudalism in Catalonia by the thirteenth century should be understood "according to a model of countervailing pressures, stresses, and strategies of manipulation or evasion."[46]

Regalian Rights over Jews: The State of the Question

If the jurisdictional claims of the *Fuero de Teruel* concerning the Jews shared ideological ground and were contemporaneous with these other generalized provisions about the competency of royal jurisdiction, it stands to reason that these setbacks in implementing this vision of power and the coincident growth of seigniorial autonomy would also have had potent implications for the crown's exercise of authority over its Jewish subjects. Scholarship, however, has tended not to question the dimensions of royal policy that concerned the ethnoreligious minority groups resident in the realms. In his leading study on the administrative history of the Jews of the Crown of Aragon, for instance, Yom Tov Assis claimed, without qualification, that the servi regis concept dates to the mid-twelfth century. He provided no indications that it remained a contested, controversial theory throughout this period.[47]

There seem to be several reasons for this tendency. Scholarship has infrequently integrated discussions about jurisdiction and ethnoreligious relations. This may be because of the common (and, in my opinion, misguided) view that jurisdictional constraints emerging from the dynamics of royal-seigniorial conflict did not apply to Jews and Muslims to the same degree that they influenced the diverse strata of Christian society.[48] Furthermore, the already scarce evidence resides chiefly in royal archives and thus intrinsically tends to reinforce the royal narrative of its uncontested dominance rather than counter-narratives from nonroyal competitors. A richer source base has attracted scholarship to the later Middle Ages, when the royal exercise of exclusive jurisdiction over urban Jews had gained ground and where other topics command more attention. Recent studies, in general, have been more concerned with ethnoreligious communal development and relative autonomy than with the changing circumstances of external jurisdiction and how they might have weighed upon the coexistence in a given locality.[49] Finally, not all case studies are equipped to observe these dynamics. Arguably the most important reassessment of the monarchy's authority and Jewish policies to date, Klein's study of Barcelona could not fully consider the issue of nonroyal lordship because it focused on a town that served as the crown's chief administrative center.[50] And those few studies that have dealt with nonroyal domains in the twelfth and thirteenth centuries have been broad or have tended not to consider jurisdictional issues.[51]

The interpretation put forth by Assis is problematic for several reasons. The servi regis provision of the *Fuero de Teruel* eventually appeared in a wide range of customary codes, but its diffusion was gradual and delayed by at least several decades.[52] Furthermore, clear statements in other types of documentation reserving royal jurisdiction over resident Jews only grow more prevalent in the second quarter of the mid-thirteenth century, as Jaume I sought to act on these regnal principles to increase, painstakingly, the pervasiveness of royal governance.[53] Later royal documentation can generate the illusion that these ambitious moves to expand jurisdiction had followed an unchecked trajectory, culminating in absolute authority. In 1286, for example, Jaume's successor declared, without qualification, that his chief officer for Valencia exercised authority over every subject in the realm: "Just like the Christians, so too the Jews and Muslims shall have and support you as procurator."⁵⁴ Subsequent decrees sought to portray the crown's policies and pervasive jurisdiction as static and completely consistent across the ages. When Pere III added some new laws to the *Furs de València* in 1342, for instance, he employed the formula "for all time, before the ancient *furs*, and after" to characterize his policy that the bailiff general of Valencia exercised authority over "Muslims domiciled on royal lands or other places in which the king has criminal jurisdiction [*merum imperium*]" and therefore had "jurisdiction over the Muslims of noblemen and knights" there. In an apparent effort to make these legally debatable claims seem more normative and to silence opposition, he couched the law as a confirmation of a royal privilege from a half century earlier that the Valencian lords themselves had purportedly requested.⁵⁵ Expressions in documentation from the fourteenth century onward assert plainly that the Jews as well as Muslims (known as *mudéjares*) pertained to the "royal treasure."⁵⁶ In trusting such royal perspectives and projecting them onto earlier periods, scholars have tended to overemphasize the protective and organizational roles played by the king and royal administration in Jewish communal development.⁵⁷ The dominant paradigm today has not deviated much from what Yitzhak Baer once espoused when he wrote that the "safety of the Jews could be secured *only* through the strong hand of the king and the influence of his Jewish officials."⁵⁸ In other work, Baer did acknowledge the jurisdictional rights exercised by nonroyal authorities, yet characterized them as exceptional.⁵⁹

If we accept that the servi regis provision of the *Fuero de Teruel* does date from the mid-1170s, then the Crown of Aragon would have been one of the first principalities to adopt a theory of exclusive royal possession of certain Jews.⁶⁰ Earlier candidates do exist from elsewhere in Europe. The laws attributed to Edward the Confessor (*Leges Edwardi*) asserted that the king held the Jews "as his own" (*tamquam proprium*). However, because these laws were a spurious record that did not surface until the 1130s, they are not directly reflective of either Anglo-Saxon or Anglo-Norman royal policies.⁶¹ When Alfonso VII of Castile-León (r. 1126–57) issued the *Fuero de Calatalifa* in 1141, he extended royal protection over the conquered Muslim population as well as any Jews who happened to take up residence there. Like the *Fuero de Teruel*, these laws did not apply beyond this particular municipality.

Furthermore, the wording implied that Muslims and Jews who did not reside there would not "belong to the palace."[62] Unmitigated claims that all Jews, irrespective of their place of residence, belonged to the crown would not appear in these kingdoms, and others in western Europe, until the thirteenth century. And when they did, these laws, like other regalian rights, usually proved difficult to enforce.[63]

This commonality is best illustrated through comparison with more familiar political environments. Most historians of governance now reject the traditional dichotomy holding that monarchies in Western Christendom were always unified in a way that eluded the particularistic Holy Roman Empire and thus were invariably more capable of asserting their regalian prerogatives.[64] William Chester Jordan, for instance, notes that only in England were "the claims of a paramount lord, the king, to the control and exploitation of the Jews more or less uncontested by other secular authorities or by ecclesiastics in the role of secular lords."[65] When Edward I of England set out to expel the Jews from his realms in 1290, he was able to do so by fiat, in keeping with the provisions of the Statute of the Jewry (1275), with little noticeable resistance from the lay and ecclesiastical lords. Most every baron at that time seemed to recognize that he possessed Jews only conditionally as a special grant from the king that could be revoked at will.[66]

By contrast, when Philip Augustus of France claimed to possess the Jews or issued laws such as his crown's first expulsion edict in 1182, these enactments affected only the Jews resident on his own estates. Notwithstanding important changes in the French royal Jewry law during these years, numerous barons in subsequent decades through the late thirteenth century successfully exercised their claims of *dominium* over the Jews on their lands in order to expel them using their own authority.[67] Far from asserting universal royal dominium over all Jews, when Louis IX, with the counsel of his barons, issued the Ordinance of Melun in 1230, prohibiting the migration of Jews from one lordship to another, he implicitly authorized baronial dominium over Jews, "as if they were their own servants."[68] The law, in other words, authorized lords as much as the king himself to retrieve their runaway Jews.[69]

Yet, scholars now argue that this apparent retreat by the French monarchy eventually served to increase its authority. Because the Ordinance of Melun had relied on the king's regalian right to regulate these migrations, it established the precedent that royal courts should handle all cases concerning escaped Jews and serfs. The legal rationale was that because these subjects suffered from deficient personal status, they would be subject to the king's justice regardless of their lords' condition of vassalage. This progression ultimately enabled the monarchy under Philip IV to undertake successfully a sweeping expulsion of all of the kingdom's Jews in 1305–6. This king had been encouraged to take this drastic action partly in order to repair his image of paramountcy, but also to reduce the mounting debt after suffering a humiliating and costly baronial backlash to his coinage reforms.[70] Readmitting the Jews in 1315 provided the new king, Louis X, with another vital infusion of revenue. It also enabled royal administrators and jurists to reposition the status of the Jews within the French realms as arguably more subject to regalian authority, although the political standing of the crown remained insecure at best. As "aliens, sojourners, and enemies," these returned Jews were ostensibly under firmer royal control, even if the king's license of resettlement permitted them to return to their former baronial domains.[71]

The Crown of Aragon thus does not represent an exceptional, precocious instance of claimed royal supremacy over religious minorities that would only later be followed or possibly emulated with crown "servitude," or *Kammerknechtshaft*, in other ruling contexts. Instead it represents yet another variation on this same theme of gradually emergent royal ambitions running into conflict with entrenched competitors.[72] As was also the case in thirteenth- and fourteenth-century France, developing a royal Jewish policy of universal possession and seeking to implement it as a potent regalian right throughout the realms served as a means to promote the monarchy's image of its authority.[73]

Scholars' assumption that the royal administration of non-Christians as the "royal treasure" was normative and exclusively effective in offering protection also prevents analysis of the complex dynamics shaping the varied local jurisdictional contexts in which a large subset of the Jewry lived. Seigniorial, ecclesiastical, and municipal authorities exercised what they understood to be legitimate authority over Jewish communities, sometimes in open opposition to emergent royal claims. Like the king, they increasingly took responsibility over developing modes of coexistence amenable to Jews within their jurisdictional domains by safeguarding their safety and autonomy, a phenomenon openly recognized by Jews themselves. Barcelona rabbi Salomon Ibn Adret (ca.1233– ca.1310) maintained that "every noble is like a king in his own territory, for there is no greater authority than he."[74]

Throughout Europe, these nonroyal competitors often took different forms. Nonroyal jurisdiction over Jews appears to have been primarily seigniorial in the Crown of Aragon, while in Germany, Italy, parts of France, and the rest of the Iberian Peninsula, conflicts were more often with ecclesiastical institutions, chiefly cathedral chapters and monasteries.[75] Some of the rights claimed by these religious institutions were indeed seigniorial in nature. In certain cases, they were even granted or confirmed by rulers. Yet, as we shall explore later, conflict over jurisdiction in these cases was complicated by a broader systemic challenge to secular administrative rights emanating from the later twelfth- and thirteenth-century papacy, which claimed that the Church and its courts should exercise exclusive jurisdiction over the Jews.[76]

Most historians of the Crown of Aragon have made little effort to analyze emergent local policies concerning Jews within this wider European context. Furthermore, even when they do recognize these parallel limitations and complications in the enforcement of royal ideals, scholars have tended to leave them unexplored, largely because they overestimate the growth of monarchical authority. This tendency is also shared by scholarship on Muslims, whose predominantly rural setting in fact posed an even greater threat of administrative isolation to the crown.[77] In his now classic study of fourteenth-century *mudéjares*, for example, John Boswell's assumed teleology of an ideal of "absolute" royal supremacy led him to dismiss nonroyal jurisdictional claims as an ephemeral, passing phase.[78] Some scholars, such as Miguel Motis Dolader, omit the developmental process altogether and depict the royal claims as an uncontested fait accompli: "The Jews have an *intrinsic* status that depends directly on the Christian monarchs by the right of conquest; that is to say, they are the personal property of the king. . . . One of the oldest formulations of this *unquestionable* principle comes from the fuero of Teruel."[79] Similarly, Asunción Blasco Martínez writes, without temporal distinction, that the "history of the Jews of Aragón is dependent on the key fact [*hecho clave*]" that they pertained to the king, who "directly controlled" the autonomy of each *aljama* (community) "as master and lord."[80] Although Jaume Riera i Sans's recent work is acutely aware of the hard-fought battle waged by the monarchy to make these claims a reality, it nevertheless argues that seigniorial authority over Jews sanctioned by the *Fuero de Teruel* and *Usatges de Barcelona* necessarily hinged on deliberate royal dispensation. Consequently, it supports the view that crown possession was, from the beginning, a legitimate and normative royal preserve.[81] Riera i Sans writes,

"The documented fact is that, from the mid-twelfth century, the regalia of the property of the Jews stood alongside other regalian rights exercised exclusively by the monarchs: promulgating laws, coining money, convoking courts, creating magistrates and notaries, legitimating bastards, establishing the peace, etc."[82] Recent surveys continue to treat the condition of Jews as shaped chiefly by royal and papal policies.[83]

The belief that all situations in which aljamas were administered by nonroyal potentates necessarily emerged out of deliberate royal licensing encourages scholars to underestimate the viability and autonomy of these jurisdictions. For instance, owing to the shortage of thirteenth-century jurisdictional sources, Assis relied on a fourteenth-century dispute record to characterize the seigniorial rights of the lordship of Santa Coloma de Queralt. In it, Lord Pere de Queralt sought to defend his ostensibly autonomous rights of jurisdiction against royal encroachment by claiming that his town had possessed more than fifty Jewish families since time immemorial.[84] Nowhere in the records does the king assert or the noble concede that the monarchy had ever licensed or exercised direct authority over this Jewish community. The crown's victorious effort to force Pere de Queralt to accept a royal license for up to thirty Jewish families in his lordship in 1347 effectively subjected these Jews to royal overlordship and served to standardize their living conditions by aligning their privileges with those of Barcelona. Yet, this turn of events led Assis to assert that the monarchy had been involved in the initial formation of Santa Coloma's Jewish community.[85] Such a logical leap enabled the monarchy's late victory in realizing its claim to erase any record of enduring, autonomous seigniorial lordship over these local Jews and thereby obscures this case's true historical significance.[86]

Objectives and the Case of Tortosa

From the monarchy's perspective, its possession of the Jews was normative and in keeping with centuries of legal tradition. From nonroyal perspectives, the monarchy's defense of its regalia appeared to be an illegitimate intrusion. This study's intention is to combine these distinct, often conflictive voices in order to reconstruct a more authentic historical discourse about royal authority. In so doing, this book seeks to add to the sophisticated, paradoxical vision of a deeply fragmented yet still dynamically interconnected and cohesive Mediterranean world evoked by Robert I. Burns, Shlomo Goitein, and others.[87] In Burns's view, this space consisted "less of territorial blocs or nations than of multiple small unities, loosely federated at best," held together in "larger unity by shared movements, patterns, experiences, psychology, and sets of similar institutions . . . with energies freely flowing between its separate points." He rejected the simplified scenario defined exclusively by the monolithic, monarchical perspective—"the parochially national boundaries of an older historiography."[88]

These comments serve as a reminder that other research focused on Iberia, including products of Burns's own line of research on Valencia, has directed some attention to alternative sources of authority. Generations ago, Abraham Neuman warned against laying stress on "technical royal phrases like *nostri proprii*" as signifying that the Jews were not freemen, "especially as these concepts were generally utilized by the kings to protect the Jews against the encroachments of the rival powers, such as the nobles, the municipalities, and the Church."[89] Advancing similar skepticism in his perceptive synthesis of the Jews settling along the changing frontiers of the Peninsula, Jonathan Ray notes generally that "assertions of jurisdiction over the Jews often represented a royal contention rather than an established fact, and some statements in this regard betray concerns about seigniorial opposition to royal authority."[90]

What we need to understand more fully is how these dynamics operated at the local level, where they had the potential to vary widely in accordance with jurisdictional differences. The most fundamental jurisdictional distinction to be made is between lordships that fell under some form of royal control and those that did not. Within Jewish communities under direct royal lordship, the monarchy was able to impose its developing Jewish policy with fewer complications in spite of opposition from opportunistic local lords, municipalities, and royal officials.[91] Circumstances within autonomous seigniorial domains naturally varied much more widely because individual lords and their Jewish residents had the agency to reject or adopt piecemeal royal policies as well as to develop their own.

Certain recent scholarship has already made progress in delving into these dynamics, resulting in a much more complicated, if still incomplete, picture. Ray's first monograph and subsequent work have continued to challenge scholars to appreciate both the "royal and baronial desire to enact sufficient safeguards for the Jews to attract them as settlers and to promote their economic activity."[92] Philip Daileader has shown how the king intervened, via direct action and targeted privileges governing judicial procedure, to regulate the handling of the Jews of Perpignan by nonroyal authorities, including municipal and church officials.[93] Klein's work on the Jews of Barcelona has complicated the concept of a Jewish state within a state by profiling the shifting basis of Jewish autonomy over the twelfth and thirteenth centuries and unraveling how the restructuring of the Jewish community was driven by Jewish-Christian collaboration within the comital-royal administrative context.[94] She detailed how the royal administration was able to implement a shift from Jewish communal "autonomy by default" to "autonomy by design" by restructuring institutions and leadership in collaboration with new elites in the aljama.[95] Building on Klein's work, Stephen Bensch has witnessed similar trends in the administration and communal development of the Jewish aljama under the autonomous lordship of the counts of Empúries, which was well isolated from royal management.[96]

While their methodology may depart in important respects from tradition, in essence a primary shared objective of these works, and of this present book, remains traditional: to profile the range of Jewish-Christian coexistence (rendered in Castilian as *convivencia*) and explore the extent to which it was influenced by administrative circumstances. In accordance with Burns's conception of the fractured cohesion of the premodern Mediterranean, the model of convivencia advocated here is more open to the potential for diversification and localization while maintaining an awareness of overarching jurisdictional tendencies.[97] It thus shares ground with Brian Catlos's sophisticated work on the Ebro Valley, which stresses the "complex and crisscrossing bonds of interest between Muslim and Christian parties" for understanding the dynamism of ethnoreligious relations.[98] Catlos has highlighted the importance of ad hoc, negotiated personal pacts between different authorities and non-Christians in defining enduring customary conditions that responded to the respective interests of each party:

> In some cases, if it was in its interest, seigniorial power could defend its *mudéjar* subjects against the predation and persecution of royal, municipal or ecclesiastical administrative bodies. In the same

way, *mudéjares* in conflict with their lord could appeal to royal power and find a solution, always on the condition that their support was considered of interest to the monarchy. The minority groups understood this, and this was precisely one of their strategies of survival: bringing face-to-face rival administrative, fiscal, or judicial institutions.[99]

The self-interested activity of local groups and the presence of rival authorities arguably influenced Jewish society in similar ways although, as we shall see, there are reasons to question the ability of the monarchy to intervene so effectively, even when invited by these constituencies.

In this book we will likewise explore the limitations of royal oversight and consider seriously other sources of jurisdictional authority that possessed varying degrees of power to shape the daily lives of Jews and Muslims and modes of interaction between non-Christians and Christian-ruled society. Such competition between the monarchy and rival authorities had the potential to produce locally differentiated experiences of convivencia—what I refer to as micro-convivencias. The term derives from Peter Brown's concept of "micro-Christendoms," used to describe the politically and culturally fragmented Christian units that developed and interacted over the course of the early Middle Ages. These Christian communities were distinct microcosms that were nevertheless based on shared images of what Christendom did (or should) represent.[100] Similarly, in our high medieval context, kings, lords, citizens, and ethnoreligious minorities were elaborating conditions of coexistence that built upon existing legal traditions and responded to the features of neighboring jurisdictions.

In pursuit of these objectives, this book focuses, first and foremost, on the neglected case of Tortosa, a town seated upriver from the Ebro Delta and seized from Muslim control in 1148. Ramon Berenguer IV, Count of Barcelona and Prince of Aragon, officially established a Jewish community in Tortosa shortly after the conquest. Yet, the persistence of these provisions was later cast into doubt when Ramon's successors progressively transferred jurisdiction over the town to a seigniorial regime consisting of the Templar military order and noble Montcada family.[101] Over the course of the thirteenth century, Tortosa's Jewish community thus found itself in an ambiguous jurisdictional situation and obliged to negotiate the ongoing struggle between the local lords and the monarchy. As in other localities under seigniorial authority, and far more than previous scholarship has appreciated, the lords of Tortosa did exercise prerogatives that came into conflict with the monarchy's emerging policy on the Jews and compromised to some degree the privileges promised by the Jews' royal settlement charter.[102] However, Tortosa's situation also differed from those of many other seigniorial Jewries, whose aljamas had been established de novo rather than inherited with preexisting legal traditions and infrastructure from the monarchy by their jurisdictional lords. It was also distinct from seigniorial aljamas founded, enlarged, or reestablished by conditional royal licenses, which were therefore more firmly subject to the monarchy's claimed prerogatives.

Through the thirteenth century, Tortosa's jurisdictional situation stood between these dipoles of the dominant control or complete absence of royal authority that have generally preoccupied and informed the models of prior scholarship. The monarchy had to prioritize its jurisdictional objectives. Deploying resources to establish direct administrative control over certain domains often caused the crown to lose its jurisdictional rights over other holdings to lords determined to exercise their own authority over local Jews. That this trend afflicted only specific sectors of the realms served to differentiate further the circumstances of Jewish communities; in twelfth-century Barcelona, for example, the retreat of the urban nobility facilitated the increase of the monarchy's local authority.[103]

Although focused primarily on evidence that pertains to Tortosa and a number of smaller studies of similar communities within the Crown of Aragon, this study seeks to situate these cases within the broader contexts of Iberia and wider Europe in order to avoid simply adding, as Ray has lamented, to the existing "series of microcosmic portraits of individual Jewries (the Jews of Seville, Mallorca, etc.), with no clear treatment of the commonalities and differences between such communities."[104] It is my hope that this more localized, detail-oriented work will thereby complement broader works, such as Ray's own monograph, complicating and giving nuance to their generalized models by assessing their applicability to a limited range of local environments.

The chapters that follow will seek to show that aspects of Tortosa's jurisdictional circumstances were more typical than most scholars have assumed, during, as well as subsequent to, the time frame observed here. As such, the town represents an especially useful case study for exploring how vacillations in the development of royal authority affected the interactions between rulers and the ruled. It is also ideal for observing the manner in which this dynamically shifting power balance influenced the lived conditions of subsets of royal-seigniorial subjects such as the Jews. Royal influence never completely disappeared but was tempered, manipulated, and complicated through the agency and interplay of other constituencies: most importantly, the lords, local nonroyal officials, royal officers, municipal regime, individual residents, and corporate Jewish and Muslim communities. Accordingly, the charter of security originally granted to Tortosa's Jews established conditions and privileges that interested individuals and collectives themselves reinterpreted and manipulated but did not completely reject or ignore. Thus, although our work here will uphold some of the Peninsula-wide patterns observed by Ray and other scholars, it will also present significant local deviations—grounds for a more locally variegated model of pluralistic convivencia.[105]

Sources and Approaches

The reader will notice that this study integrates certain sources that address general administrative objectives or policies or the general citizenry, yet do not target the Jewish community (or Muslim aljama) in particular. Theologians and jurists did increasingly assert that Jews and Muslims should be accommodated and protected within Christian-ruled society on distinct grounds informed by sacred and contemporary history. Furthermore, administrators were aware of the importance of permitting the continuity of distinct communal institutions and legal traditions in the Jewish and Muslim aljamas.[106] Like the concept of servi regis and other emergent principles, however, these views only came to be elaborated with clarity in canon law, royal policy, and customary law codes over the thirteenth and fourteenth centuries. These manifestations, in turn, prompted collaborative responses by the Jewish and Muslim communities alike. Jews and Muslims presented similar administrative opportunities and challenges to the monarchy, lords, and municipalities that are important to compare if we want to understand the general calculus that confronted each side.[107]

Although they exercised varying degrees of authority over their own communal affairs, Jews and Muslims were also arguably members of the wider Christian-ruled community. They resided in contiguous urban and rural spaces that were subject to similar administrative norms, some of which did explicitly extend themselves over ethnoreligious minority groups. Their livelihoods depended on the use of interconnected local economies that forced them to interact with the wider community. In Tortosa, Jews, Muslims, and Christians were obliged to use the municipal court for many if not most cases, and crucial aspects of their daily lives were governed by the same customary legal corpus.[108] The different constituencies vying for control in Tortosa, moreover, seem to have recognized that shifting relations with one ethnoreligious group could serve to enhance administrative power over the rest of the populace. These are all reasons for scholars to stay attuned to wider movements and more general sources that affected the citizenry, and the realms of the Crown of Aragon, as a whole, rather than simply focusing on the materials concerning the Jewish community in isolation. Such use of a more expansive base of documentation not only serves to de-provincialize the history of Jewish communities by helping observe its interconnectivity with broader developments of critical importance to the social history of the region during this period. It also adds detail and texture to this history of development in local environments with fragmentary documentary records that is difficult to achieve with a source base targeted exclusively at ethnoreligious minorities.

The documentation, in fact, recommends such an approach because it implies that general categories, such as *habitatores* and *homines,* were not usually exclusive of non-Christian groups. Although, juridically, non-Christians in the Crown of Aragon were not usually accorded the status of citizens (*cives*) in legal records, many of the most important administrative documents for the town did not limit their applicability to the citizenry but instead concerned themselves with the entire populace, using the term *habitatores*.[109] For instance, even though the count-king's transfer of jurisdictional rights to the Templars in 1182 never makes direct mention of the Jews, a later document indicates that these rights of lordship did in fact encompass "all men, Muslims, Christians, and Jews."[110] While some sources were limited in their application to either Christians or non-Christians, many royal, seigniorial, and municipal documents concerned the broader population, irrespective of ethnoreligious status, and yet these have tended to be ignored or dismissed by scholars. Excluding this evidence based on the anachronistic assumption that non-Christian groups were always distinct in the eyes of the law leads us to underestimate the extent to which they shared juridical conditions with the broader populace. Just as proclamations concerning a special royal relationship with non-Christians accompanied the monarchy's attempt to develop its sovereign authority, engagements between the lords and the Jews of Tortosa were part of a wider conflict between extenuating royal privileges and seigniorial jurisdiction that was contemporaneously afflicting Tortosa's entire populace. Thus, throughout this book, we will employ the principle that this wider political context, even if it did not explicitly concern itself with ethnoreligious minorities, could make a mark on the local conditions experienced by these groups.

In this respect, my methodology has been encouraged by Klein, who argued that the history of Jewish communities needs to be viewed within the context of (and in comparison to) urban Christian institutions.[111] In her monograph, she demonstrated how such comparative analysis can help us appreciate how Jewish communal organization paralleled, mimicked, or departed from coexisting foundations in other zones of this society. This model notably shares ground with patterns in "recurrent" Jewish-Christian religious dialogues throughout European society noticed by Ivan Marcus, Jonathan Elukin, and others. These scholars have recognized how moves directed at non-Christians could have wider implications or be linked to more expansive processes involving the whole of society.[112] Bensch has explored this phenomenon in his work on Empúries. In surveying a privilege granted by the local count in 1235 protecting Jewish as well as Christian inhabitants in Empúries's primary urban center of Castelló from arbitrary seizure, he linked the "sudden emergence of Jews as a collectivity . . . with the articulation of new jurisdictional rights in the context of on-going institutional experimentation."[113]

Since it is structured around the exploration of a series of local environments, this book cannot claim to revise completely the history of royal authority or of Jewish coexistence. It can, however, seek to expose and illuminate more complex historical dynamics by questioning a number of persistent assumptions within scholarship: trusting the monarchy's claims about its supremacy, accepting all too readily a teleology of absolute authority and the emergence of the modern state, and rejecting the validity of nonroyal forms of jurisdiction, particularly concerning religious minority populations, and their potential role in determining and diversifying micro-convivencias.

Tortosa may represent an exceptional and exceptionally well-documented case, but it was not an anomaly. Rather, some other urban localities and a great many rural domains shared aspects of its jurisdictional makeup. The town thus constitutes a useful laboratory for examining how jurisdictional conflicts between the monarchy and resistant lords served to challenge the exercise of royal authority over the long term and colored, persistently if not indelibly, the circumstances of local Jews and their interrelations with the greater community and realms of the Crown of Aragon.

I

FOUNDATIONS AND WITHDRAWAL

Jews had lived in Tortosa under the Visigoths and then prospered in Tortosa during the initial generations of Muslim rule, which reached its zenith under the tenth-century caliphate.[1] The community was in correspondence with the eminent Talmudic scholar Moses ben Ḥanoch, and Menaḥem ben Saruq grew up there before emigrating to pursue an illustrious career in Córdoba as a renowned philologist and chief secretary for the scholar and statesman Ḥasdai ibn Shaprut.[2] Traces of Jewish civilization in the town vanish during the eleventh century, however, likely as a result of disintegration of the caliphate and the subsequent influence of the less tolerant Almoravids and Almohads from North Africa.[3] As a result, the Jews who emigrated to Christian Tortosa were forging a new community without direct ties to earlier Jewish society there.

A year after Tortosa's capture, in December 1149, Count-Prince Ramon Berenguer IV of Barcelona and Aragon issued a charter licensing the residency of Jews in the town. Although the document is filled with particulars relating to the specific circumstances of these Jewish settlers, its primary function nevertheless resembles those of the settlement charters granted to the Muslims and Christians in Tortosa during the intervening months following the conquest. It was a transaction between Ramon, as conqueror and new territorial lord, and his subjects that outlined the basics of existence in the locality.⁴ This license would serve as a legally binding constitutional guide for generations to come and would heavily influence the customary legal development of the Jewish community.

One of the charter's most telling features is that it left unmentioned or ambiguous aspects of the Jews' jurisdictional situation and general coexistence within the town that would later become hotly contested. The reasons for these absences are not fully clear. Even though Ramon, according to Bisson, was already acting on his ambition to implement a new "theory of the principate" to expand his authority throughout Catalonia by the time of the conquest, the desirability of invoking this relationship in a charter of settlement perhaps had not yet occurred to his administrators. It may, frankly, have been impossible for contemporaries in the aftermath of Tortosa's capture to foresee the legal weight every word of these haphazard charters would exert in future years. Another possibility is that Ramon felt that his status as conqueror and distributor of the landed spoils, or his self-proclaimed title as "prince of Aragon and the march of Tortosa," had implicitly served to forge the desired inviolable bond between ruler and subject along the frontier. From the perspective of his advisors, legally labyrinthine and ingrained Old Catalonia, by contrast, may have demanded much more deliberate and cautious administrative maneuvering.⁵ Whatever their cause, the omissions in the charter would have profound implications for Tortosa's legal climate because they enabled subsequent legal instruments and other, nonroyal parties to define the juridical and jurisdictional circumstances of the town's Jewish residents in ways that ostensibly ran counter to Ramon's unwritten regalian vision.

In this chapter, we will explore the legal and material foundations of Tortosa's Jewish community and the pressures and changes they experienced as the freshly Christian town and its countryside matured over the following decades. We will be particularly interested in studying the influence of the complicated jurisdictional shift the town underwent in the later twelfth century. When Ramon's successors were obliged by financial constraints to leverage and ultimately alienate their frontier jurisdictions, including Tortosa, the new title holders inherited all of the rights and responsibilities formerly held by the crown. The lack of a clearly defined and implemented systemic royal Jewish policy in the twelfth century made possible the development of enduring localized institutional structures and customs in Tortosa. As we shall see later in the book, these local traditions would prove exceedingly difficult to eliminate or even incorporate into the developing system of realm-wide, monarchy-controlled administration of Jewish subjects.

Royal Governance and Jewish Subjects

Under what conditions was the Jewish charter produced, and what did its creators intend to accomplish with it? Drafted during the post-conquest tumult as Ramon Berenguer and his men began to consolidate their acquisitions, the charter targeted the short-term goals of outlining the privileges and material conditions necessary to attract or retain Jewish residents. The conquering regime accomplished a good part of this work by allocating the customary privileges and liabilities already held by the Jews of Barcelona, which were either not written down at the time or, more likely, have not survived. Although the circumstances of the donation emphasized a link to royal authority, its brevity and ambiguity rendered its provisions and intentions highly susceptible to later reinterpretation.

The application of Barcelona's customary laws may have been the result of more than sheer pragmatism. It likely took into account the market for settlers and intended to establish some targeted administrative precedents. Barcelona already possessed one of the region's more sizeable Jewish communities, which could have been expected to produce a good share of the migrants to populate the captured urban centers of the Ebro frontier. Replicating its privileges, which must have been familiar to Jews from throughout Catalonia, served to make the legal conditions in Tortosa a known quantity. The market for Jewish settlers was clearly distinct from those for Christian and Muslim residents although we lack data to reconstruct the precise calculus of the charter's authors. Whereas the Muslim charter of security claimed to emulate the package of privileges offered to Zaragoza when it fell to the Aragonese thirty years earlier, this offer had been in response to the explicit request of Tortosa's surrendering Muslims; encouraging Andalusi or *mudéjar* migration from other areas seems to have been, at most, a secondary objective.[6] Unlike the Christian charter of settlement, which had been fashioned from whole cloth and had offered an array of exclusive, perpetual privileges, the Jewish charter's replication of

Barcelona's general legal conditions, matched with a four-year moratorium on levies, did not try to incentivize prospective settlers in an identical way, through exemptions and other enticements, to undertake the risky venture of relocating to the insecure, war-torn frontier.[7]

It is possible that the count-prince believed that enough Jews were already sufficiently motivated to establish a presence in the frontier town without extraordinary incentives, by business interests in Andalusi lands or a greater cultural aptitude for migration, for example. When the document did make specific stipulations, they seemed to respond to features of Tortosa's environment that likely would have been cause for concern among potential Jewish settlers. It guaranteed, for example, similiar protection from jurisdiction by any Muslim to what the Muslim charter of security had awarded the surrendering Andalusis from Jewish administration, ostensibly responding to the subject group's sensitivity about its place in the societal hierarchy.[8]

Exporting the social contract held by Barcelona's Jews to the largest urban center of this conquered territory also must have reinforced the idea that the new Jewish community would similarly stand under the tight control of its conqueror. Although his predecessors had reserved control over the wealth rather than persons of Jews in Barcelona living only on their personal lordships, there are reasons to believe that Ramon was consciously taking his administration in Tortosa and throughout his realms in new directions, with the aims of protecting and expanding his authority.[9] The charter is the earliest known privilege collectively addressed to an entire community of Jews, as opposed to individuals. It used its final lines to emphasize that the present and future Jews receiving these donations, as well as their progeny, would owe fidelity to the count-prince and his successors.[10] In the license, Ramon claimed his authority as conqueror to grant laws and privileges that would limit the activity of the lay and religious lords taking possession of the spoils of conquest: "Let you not pay any service nor any custom or usage to me nor to any other lord in Tortosa or bailiff except however much you have consented to pay by your free choice."[11]

Expressing his identity as conqueror, supreme lord, and lawgiver in each of the settlement charters responded to the opportunities and challenges for royal authority offered by the captured territories.[12] Ramon had established the Andalusi principality of Tortosa as an open frontier zone (*marchio*) under his exclusive control. Within it, he retained the most strategically important fiefs, despite still honoring pre-conquest agreements to the Templars and various barons.[13] Administrative and economic dynamics in Tortosa were nevertheless complicated by independent seigniorial activity, which was not always inclined to support royal regulations or objectives in arrangements with tenants. Prominent local Jews, even those already enlisted in Ramon's administrative service, were simultaneously engaged with seigniorial patrons.[14] Surveys in Old Catalonia designed to hold officeholders accountable and remind them that their positions owed allegiance to the count-prince in the early 1150s were complemented by his strict handling of baronial abuses that threatened to encroach on royal prerogatives in Tortosa.[15]

At the time the count-prince awarded the charter of settlement, he and his administrators were already developing a mechanism to disseminate and implement this bolder vision of authority. As "propaganda" that drew on Roman legal principles to reinforce its numerous regalian claims, the *Usatges de Barcelona* sought to use the recent conquests as impetus for the recasting of greater Catalonia as a new territorial principality under the sway of a refashioned conception of royal power.[16] It is true that the reach of the *Usatges* would remain limited for some years to come.[17] Nevertheless, their objectives of promoting the principle of direct royal authority over the subjects throughout the realms based on theoretically normative conditions in Barcelona paralleled the process of modeling Jewish settlement charters in new towns such as Tortosa on the relationships in force in Barcelona.

While the code only explicitly mentions Jews a handful of times, its statutes do shed some light on the possible royal stance on jurisdiction over Jews and may even offer some clues to the content of those influential customs of Barcelona's Jewish community.[18] A number of them, in recognition of the count-prince's responsibility to dictate juridical norms for Barcelona, as well as potentially of his broader sphere of influence in Catalonia, were directed at defining judicial procedures between Christians and Jews.[19] *Usatge* 11, for instance, established that the count-prince, vaguely identified as "the ruler" or "power-holder" (*postat/potestas*), had the authority to judge anyone who beat, wounded, or killed a Jew. In the words of Gener Gonzalvo i Bou, the law "confers on the comital potestas the absolute authority of establishing the fine for aggression, expressed in a broad sense, against a Jew." While it is arguable that this statute did serve as a "very clear manifestation of comital power, of the exercise of public authority, and one of the pillars on which the feudal State was established," dictating what fines Jews themselves would receive for injury was different from the count-prince claiming compensation for himself, as if the Jew's person and livelihood were royal property.[20] Ramon was instead positioning himself as the lawgiver who had the right to claim compensation in the event that his ban was violated.

Furthermore, as Riera i Sans has pointed out, the law as written was vulnerable to a seigniorial interpretation. The ambiguous Romanist language of the *Usatges* arguably made it possible for the compensation to be claimed by whatever potestas possessed the injured or killed Jew.[21] As we shall see, this interpretation would indeed be utilized by the Templars to justify their jurisdictional control of local Jews in Tortosa in the mid-thirteenth century.[22] Nevertheless, the crown continued to employ the term *potestas* in a manner that hinged on its exercise of lordship, alongside its responsibility to defend the public peace, rather than to depend exclusively on any special protective royal relationship with the Jews.[23]

The Jews may have been subject to special regulations owing to their ethnoreligious identity, but none of these laws conferred extraordinary jurisdictional powers on the count. Far from advocating any special relationship with the Jews, *Usatges* 62 and 64 suggest that Jews were grouped with all other people who found themselves in the count-prince's realms, including "traders and merchants, pilgrims and wayfarers, friends and enemies." *Usatge* 75 threatened attempts to incite apostasy and efforts to foment interreligious violence by name-calling with fines, which were justified as payable to the "prince" because the actions violated "our ban."[24]

The *Usatges de Barcelona* thus presented a vague vision of Jewish (and Muslim) residency that was indistinguishable from that of Christian subjects aside from certain targeted judicial procedures and liabilities. They implied a social contract with the Jews that subjected them to the laws of the count-prince while also rendering them as beneficiaries of his benevolence, justice, and protection. This contract constituted, notably, a much less exclusive relationship between the ruler and his Jewish subjects than the servi regis principle that would soon appear in the *Fueros de Teruel*. On the other hand, it was significantly more explicit than the charters of population granted to Tortosa's settlers, in which Ramon neglected to enunciate clearly any extraordinary bond with their Jewish or Muslim recipients.[25]

Indeed, the Jewish charter contains no overt signs of the count-prince's ambitions for nonfeudal royal authority. Instead, it demanded fidelity from the Jews on traditional grounds, in return for his donation of property and pledges of protection, which were instrumental in providing the community with a secure, viable environment.

The Physical Environment

What did Tortosa's initial Jewish community look like, and how was it integrated into the town's broader setting? Ramon Berenguer awarded the Jews seventeen houses within an existing northern suburb soon renamed Remolins, which extended westward to the bank of the Ebro River.[26] Located just north of the zone apportioned to the retained Muslim population in the former Andalusi shipyards, this Jewish street or quarter (*call* or *juería*) sat to the northwest of the suburb's narrow principal thoroughfare.[27] Anticipating community growth, the count-prince promised to enlarge the territory if necessary and licensed the construction of up to sixty new houses, as the community saw fit.

The grant did not manifest direct concern about the physical security of the community. Archaeological remains and textual references do indicate that Remolins sat inside the existing Andalusi walls,[28] although excavations have not yet determined whether the call was completely enclosed at this point.[29] The fact that neither the Jewish nor Muslim charter of settlement mentions the presence of external town walls could reflect that the recipients were not deeply concerned about defensive infrastructure. No legal limits on Jewish property ownership have come to light. It seems likely that whatever residential segregation Tortosa experienced was de facto rather than de jure at this point.[30]

Christian migrants would only gradually establish themselves in what arguably remained an unstable frontier outpost over the early decades of Christian rule. This dearth of new residents, combined with the perceived value of local know-how, recommended the retention of the remaining lower echelons of the conquered Andalusi populace in and around Tortosa as a tolerated group. Ramon was palpably eager to maintain these residents. He even encouraged the return of exiles by guaranteeing them the restoration of their extramural property rights if they returned within four months of the conquest. The flight of the ruling class, amounting to the social and economic "decapitation" of urban Andalusi society, followed by its spatial reorganization, would engender the gradual formation of a new *mudéjar* elite. These Muslims would rise up the ranks using the institutions, regulations, and opportunities offered by Christian-ruled society, in collaboration and competition with similarly upwardly mobile Jewish settlers.[31]

The terms of the Muslim surrender treaty dictated that the remaining conquered population relocate en masse within one year to outside the town walls, where it was expected to build or occupy existing houses. This quarter, the *morería,* also sat in Remolins between the Jewish call and the former Andalusi *madīna* in what had been the suburbs of the town during Muslim rule.[32] The clustering of these two ethnoreligious minority groups on the periphery of the established urban core may have been meant to reduce the possibility of insurrection and symbolize the triumph of Christian rule. It also promoted economic continuity and integration, since this area remained the town's most active commercial and productive center.[33]

The Jewish charter devoted considerable attention to the distribution of rural lands.[34] These inclusions seem to indicate an awareness that the community's success would also depend on developing agricultural and pastoral operations to supply its members with kosher foodstuffs as well as to participate in the local commodity market. Rather than being clustered in one zone like the call, the lands were widely disseminated throughout Tortosa's countryside.

This distribution could have been a tactic by the count-prince to encourage the Jewish community to build a broader network of economic ties to the landed economy of the region. The crown's donation of conquered lands, in general, tended to be dispersed to facilitate the occupation, consolidation, and defense of the new territories. This tactic supported delegating more of the responsibilities over settlement and infrastructure building to the landlords, who were incentivized to seek out settlers and perform their own subdivisions.[35] Another possibility is that the Jews had requested the dispersal in order to diversify their agricultural holdings in terms of both location and production. This scenario would have provided insurance against loss and a wider range of agricultural products for consumption or commerce. A third possibility is that these parcels were selected from a small available subset of rural lands within traveling distance of Tortosa that had been abandoned recently or remained occupied by amenable Muslims and so were able to provide immediately the Jewish settlers with sufficient resources to support themselves. Whereas the charter awarded the "existing" buildings in Remolins without further specification, it identified many of the rural parcels by means of their current or former Muslim tenants and indicated their known agricultural output in oil, wine grapes, fruit, and cereals.[36]

The relationship of these Muslims to the donated lands is not specified, but it is possible the Jews had the option to retain the Muslims as tenants in cases where they were not obliged by the laws of *kashrut* to establish Jewish tenants.[37] What seems to be clear from the charter is that, like Christian settlers, all of these Jews would be starting with nothing beyond what the count awarded them. In contrast to his clear provisions in the Muslim surrender treaty, the count did not allow for the possibility that any of these Jewish settlers could have resided in Tortosa before the conquest. He devoted no language to the potential of Jewish property holding from Andalusi times.

The collective reception of these lands and houses by the Jewish community would have required it to parcel them or their fruits out among its present and future members. Although we lack evidence of the manner or timing of this distribution, there are no signs that the Jews managed any of these lands communally. Land-transfer documents from the early decades of Christian rule instead show that private ownership was the norm.[38] Individual Jews were also acquiring and selling their own rural properties that did not derive from the royal donation, presumably with resources they brought with them to Tortosa.[39]

Economic and Demographic Conditions

Given Ramon Berenguer's provisions and the Jews' activity during the years following the conquest, how did the community fare as a whole? The large number of houses licensed for construction suggests that the count-prince expected Tortosa to have a sizeable community. Baer once hypothesized that Tortosa's Jewish community, along with that of nearby Tarragona, "fell short of expectations held out for them at the time of their reconquest."[40] These ambitions may have been based on Ramon's awareness of Tortosa's economic strength under Andalusi rule, prosperity that had permitted its rulers to pay huge amounts of tribute over many decades.[41] The town sat at the base of the Ebro River's trade network and served as a conduit to trading with the wider

Islamic world. Al-Bakrī commented that among Andalusi Tortosa's many exported commodities, its merchants carried kohl from the town "to all lands" in the eleventh century. Al-Idrīsī lauded the "markets, buildings, ateliers, and an industry for building large ships from the timber of the [surrounding] hills." Tortosa's unequaled pine timber, he added, was "transported to all regions of the world, far and near."[42] Tortosa's renown may have attracted other Jewish merchants and traders to the freshly conquered town.

Over the coming years, however, there are signs that Tortosa's economy did not live up to its perceived potential. When the rabbi Benjamin of Tudela sailed down the Ebro River in the 1160s, he stopped at Tortosa but made no mention of a Jewish community there in his account. In contrast, he lavished considerable praise on other Mediterranean towns he visited.[43] Traffic up the Ebro was sufficient that a charter of sale for a parcel of land bordering the river in Móra d'Ebre referred to "passing boats" in 1172.[44] Yet mostly we find evidence of the crown trying to stimulate otherwise lackluster trade with concessions. In 1181, Alfons granted Tortosa's Christian and Jewish merchants an exemption from certain commerce levies on goods traded throughout his realm, including whatever passed along the Ebro River trade corridor.[45] Less than a decade later, the Count of Urgell offered exemptions from the *lleuda* and *pedatge* commerce levies to "all inhabitants of Tortosa, both Christians and Jews" bringing goods upriver from Tortosa to his lordship of Mequinenza, at the confluence of the Ebro and Segre Rivers. The Templar lords of Tortosa paid a hefty two hundred solidi for the concession.[46]

The exclusion of Muslims from the Count of Urgell's privilege may indicate that the predominantly agricultural and artisanal population of *mudéjares* was not as engaged in marketing goods along the Ebro River corridor at this time. This omission serves as another sign that the nature of this trading had changed considerably since Andalusi times in spite of the maintenance of Muslim residents and infrastructure. Evidence of *mudéjar* involvement in trading and light manufacturing under Christian rule does not predate the late thirteenth century and thus cannot be used to demonstrate the maintenance of pre-conquest patterns.[47] In his charter of security to the Muslims of Tortosa, Ramon Berenguer had guaranteed them the use of their existing trading facilities in accordance with Andalusi regulations ostensibly in hopes of reviving or sustaining their commerce but did not stipulate what products they would be trafficking.[48] Alfons did usher in a complicated system of regularized toll collection at various points along the river's course, which taxed the trade of manufactured and luxury goods with Islamic commercial centers such as Valencia, Ceuta, and Bougie. These commodities included paper, lacquer, hides, textiles, wax, various woods, dye, metals, sugar, and diverse spices.[49] Yet, the presence of trade did not signify that Tortosa or the other towns along the Ebro River and its tributaries had maintained or reestablished the economic functions of pre-conquest Andalusi society. In fact, the regulations clearly indicate that nearly all of the high-value manufactured goods were incoming, traveling up the Ebro to be deposited at trade depots, rather than outgoing, to be marketed at Muslim ports.[50]

Tolls in the document are listed as being paid in installments from Tortosa, near the river's Mediterranean delta, up through Tudela, in northern Aragon. For example, merchants transporting *brasil*, the red coloring agent for textile manufacture, had to pay twenty solidi "from Tortosa to Tudela."[51] The charter then details how that sum should be divided, listing the collection points in order from the river mouth upstream toward each successive cargo destination. Many of the taxed products were famously produced in the commercial centers of the twelfth-century Muslim world from resources that were not present in northeastern Iberia.

The regulations were trained exclusively on high-value, long-distance trade and therefore ignored the predominantly low-value, lightly processed agricultural and resource products that land-transfer documents from the time confirm were abundant along the Ebro Valley. Records from 1178 and 1198 indicate that Christians, Muslims, and Jews had to pay tithes on proceeds from salt production, gold and silver mining, hunting, and agricultural products such as olives, cereals, and wine.[52] These products must have generated the incomes to trade for the imported commodities subject to Alfons's tolls.[53]

Fifty years after the conquest, settler hardship and flight prompted action by the king as well as by Tortosa's lords, who seem to have been concerned that Tortosa's very viability as a frontier town was at stake. In 1198, Ramon de Montcada promised inhabitants that he would never again seek to impose the *tascha* levy.[54] Later that year, Pere I determined that dire economic conditions in Tortosa necessitated a reduction in the tithe obligations of its parishioners. He recognized that the concession was "contrary to written law and ecclesiastical customs," but asserted that it was justified because the settlers suffered "the utmost labor and danger to their possessions and bodies" in Tortosa "since they are on the frontier."[55] These regulations also would have applied to local Jews, who had to pay tithes on incomes from any lands that had ever had Christian owners.[56]

The king's law targeted specific sectors of the economy and restricted elites from benefiting from the reductions. Sheep products received no reduction, but chickens and pigs would be completely exempt. Neither cereal crops nor garden produce received exemption from the one-tenth and one-fortieth shares for tithes and first fruits, respectively, while small production of olives, figs, and other orchard fruit was sheltered only from first fruits. In what was apparently an attempt to reward employers and more productive operations, the law mandated that farm workers would not pay tithes on their earnings. The cultivation of olives and orchard fruit in which at least one-third of the harvest was brought to market would also be exempt.[57] The king's effort did not last long, however. By 1207, pressure from the papacy and local bishop had forced Pere to repeal it.[58]

Even before these measures were deemed necessary, there are signs that some Jewish settlers were experiencing hardship that may have motivated their exodus as the conquered landscape underwent consolidation. When the Jew Haió d'Asús bought a field in Xerta from Rotlan de Morlans and his wife, Peirona, for seven solidi in 1156, he was already a landowner in the area. The contract of sale indicated that the property bordered plots held by Rotlan himself, Christian landowners, and land already owned by Haió.[59] The Jew also purchased a field in Vilanova that had formerly belonged to Avin Ezbaballa Arraiz for sixty morabetins in 1159.[60] In February 1166, however, Haió, with his wife and son, sold the parcel to an Anglo-Norman named Osbert for a loss of five morabetins.[61] Just days later, he executed the sale of his interest in a property acquired from Rotlan de Morlans—likely the same one purchased in 1156—as well as properties in Xerta to a certain Pere Joan de Granada. In the intervening years, Haió appears to have gotten involved with an equity partner, a Jew named Choen, who decided not to sell on this occasion. With the transaction, he thus became a co-owner with the Christian, Pere Joan. Choen had purchased other property with Haió's family by this time. In addition to the 50 percent stake in Rotlan's parcel that Haió had sold to Choen, the two Jews had split the cost of a parcel from a certain Bertran. A third parcel was divided much less evenly, with Haió holding two-thirds and Choen the remainder. It may have been the subject of a *complantatio* agreement, a common agrarian contract in which one partner, in this case Choen, assumed most of the responsibilities of cultivation in return for partial ownership of the property after a set term.[62]

The apparent need to invite Choen as a partner likely could indicate that Haió was experiencing difficulty maintaining these lands. Although the sale to Pere Joan yielded Haió a sizeable sum of 124 morabetins, we lack the records of prior sales to calculate whether the Jew had lost money on these investments. The absence of further notices of buying or selling in the area could suggest that he and his family had liquidated their remaining landed assets in order to relocate to greener pastures, like many other Christian and Muslim settlers from this period.[63] Within a decade of the conquest, the presence of urban poor was already occasioning violent crime in the town center.[64] A sick house for the destitute appeared by the 1190s.[65] Within a few years, elites were making pious grants to feed the paupers of the town once a year.[66]

By the turn of the thirteenth century, Tortosa remained under serious threat of demographic crisis. It seemed unable to subsist on its own resources, necessitating support from neighboring towns as well as additional shelter from taxes and levies. In 1208, a year after Pere had revoked his tithe adjustments, he intervened again to offer Tortosa's residents a subsidized relief package:

> Since the city of Tortosa and its territory are in the frontier and in the vicinity of the Muslims, and to this point they have not been able to obtain and maintain sufficient food, we therefore give and concede to . . . all men of Tortosa, Christians, Jews, and Muslims, present and future, . . . full license and authority to import as much grain, meat, and other foodstuffs, and as many necessities from Lleida, Tarragona, Zaragoza, and Barcelona and from all the other cities and towns and other places in our lands always, whenever and however often you and they need, enfranchised and free from any *lleuda* and *pedatge* and usage and custom and seizure, existing or new.[67]

Pere's willingness to divert resources from neighboring towns and the lack of any evidence of wider food shortage afflicting the region at this time lend support to his contention that Tortosa's problems were chiefly the result of its frontier circumstances.[68]

Leveraging and Lordship Along the Ebro Valley

These indicators of Tortosa's persistent status as a costly and relatively unsuccessful frontier settlement help explain why Pere sustained Alfons's initial movement away from direct lordship over the town. Implementation of this withdrawal by these two kings took place haphazardly over the course of several decades and does not appear to have been the result of premeditated policy. Both kings sought resources from their dwindling patrimony to fund operations across the Pyrenees and against the Muslims along the southwestern frontier, leading them to reduce their direct stakes in Tortosa and other holdings in the lower Ebro Valley.

Already within the first decade of his reign, Alfons was prioritizing other holdings at the expense of his interest in Tortosa. His administrators began to transfer direct exploitation of less profitable royal domains west and south of the Llobregat River to military orders, religious houses, churches, and lay magnates, while maintaining direct control over the more profitable bailiwicks to the north.[69] These core territories of Catalonia generated more incomes and were less costly to administer and defend. The *Liber feudorum maior*, completed in 1194, seems to reflect this prioritization. As a defense of Alfons's most important feudal prerogatives and property rights, it focused chiefly on northern Catalonian and trans-Pyreneans interests.[70]

A pattern of leveraging these frontier territories first emerged in 1169 when Alfons awarded the Templar Order administration over the lower Ebro castral districts of Ascó, Riba-roja, and Seròs in return for a sizeable loan of five thousand morabetins to assist him with "great affairs and necessities." Templar personnel would administer all local functions, and all revenues deriving from royal rights and property would be allocated to defray administrative costs borne by the Order and repay the contracted loan.[71] The administration of Ascó, Riba-roja, and Seròs had thus been arranged in order for these castles to support equity lines of credit with the Templars that the crown would be able to draw down in the future. Although the Order assumed lordship over these castles, its participation in this new paradigm of demesne exploitation was chiefly fiscal. It would be reimbursed for the costs of defense, and its financial stake was insured by royal demesne possessions to the north in the event that the castles were lost to Muslim raiding. Alfons and his advisors apparently viewed this transaction as temporary, yet rendering these castral districts to the Order did amount to an administrative withdrawal that would have been difficult to reverse. These castles effectively became the property of the Templars, albeit with all of the benefits and none of the risks.

The Templars were an ideal collaborator in these leveraging operations. The Order had already built up extensive domains in the region since the conquest and served as Alfons's chief creditor since he succeeded his father in 1162. It had offered him loans that were repaid with revenues from his domains along the Ebro Valley.[72] Given this restructuring of these holdings, it is not surprising to find that Alfons continued to borrow from them. As he emerged from his minority in March 1175, he decided to increase his standing loan on Riba-roja by five hundred morabetins by assigning additional revenues from the castle of Castejón de la Puente, near Monzón, in Aragon. Basing a single pledge on frontier and inland holdings diversified the loan structure, apparently obviating the need for the king to offer other demesne possessions as a surety, as he had in 1169. Enacted in Tortosa, the loan document accounts for the destination of the received funds. Significant portions funded the purchase of horses in Lleida and Tortosa as well as the repayment of other loans. Here again, the king reiterated that these pledges meant that the Order would assume control of these castral positions. Yet, this time, instead of allocating a specific share of the revenues to cover the expenses of administration and defense, he delegated to the Order the task of calculating and deducting its expenses for the castle guard. Alfons authorized the Templars to administer and collect incomes from these districts using their own bailiffs—indicating that any and all revenues from resident Christians, Jews, and Muslims were eligible—and made no jurisdictional reservations over the lordships. Further evidence reveals how this particular arrangement endured in the future. An addendum to the charter in a different hand referred to the four years since the pledge had been established. It indicated that 225 morabetins of the loaned remained, less nonstipulated expenses incurred by the Order for maintaining foot soldiers "that the king ordered be held there."[73]

The king continued to conduct new leveraging by signing away substantial future incomes for relatively modest present payouts. Alfons assigned loan repayment from future collection of the peace tax known as the *bovatge* in the mid-1170s.[74] In 1180, in return for two good horses worth two hundred morabetins, Alfons awarded the Templars a perpetual exemption from commerce levies (the *lleuda, passatge,* or any "usage in my entire land by land or by sea") from Christians, Muslims, and Jews resident in their castral district of Miravet.[75]

We cannot rule out the possibility that the apparent imbalance of this latter transaction was offset by the fact that this was also a pious donation to a religious institution. Earlier that year, ostensibly for similar reasons, the king had exempted the well-endowed monastery of Santes Creus from various levies. Normally imposed by "my vicar, bailiff, or *saig* [porter]," these exemptions included redemptions for military service and required payments for maintaining the town's infrastructure and walls, on its considerable property in Tortosa.[76] The following year, rather than pledging future revenues to support further borrowing, Alfons piously assigned Santes Creus 140 morabetins from the incomes collected in the castle and town of Seròs.[77]

Alfons's willingness to reduce his taxation rights in Tortosa for the benefit of Santes Creus was unusual, however. In contrast to these other royal holdings along the Ebro-Segre corridor that were subject to multiple pledges over the first two decades of Alfons's reign, the king appears to have resisted reducing incomes or leveraging his stake in Tortosa during this period. This delay may indicate that Alfons remained reluctant to deviate from the patrimonial policies elaborated during his father's reign.

The Templars had acted as silent minority lords in Tortosa alongside the Montcada family until March 1182 when Alfons granted the Order full administrative responsibility over the town and Ascó and complete ownership of the castle of Riba-roja. The king's grant suggested that the Templars' rights would displace what remained of royal administration: "I transfer everything to their lordship [*dominium*] and control [*potestatem*]."[78] Unlike the feudal agreements carefully crafted by Alfons's predecessors that had reserved access to transferred holdings and restricted the recipients' autonomy and judicial authority, this transaction was a perpetual donation lacking any terminology to limit the Order's rights of possession.[79]

While clearly influenced by earlier credit transactions with the Order, this arrangement featured some significant differences with important implications for the future. Rather than set up lines of credit, in this case the king sold the Order permanent shares of these holdings. The Templars purchased dominium over all three holdings as free allods "in perpetuity" for a sum of five thousand morabetins. Riba-roja was now their castle. In Ascó and Tortosa, the Templars would have to render the crown half of all administrative revenues.

This income division would apply to any additional property acquired by either party in Tortosa and Ascó following this transaction. As with the castral pledges made in 1169, Alfons agreed to subsidize the Order's administrative expenses. Although the parties would share costs for maintaining mills, ovens, and other obligations in Ascó, the king gave the Templars a one-time payment of four hundred masmudines to cover the expense of future work in Tortosa. The contract made it clear that administration was solely the Order's responsibility: "The [Templar] brothers should have their bailiff in the city . . . , who should faithfully collect all of the incomes of the city and its district both from everything that I am accustomed to receive in incomes."[80] This scenario satisfied Alfons's fiscal needs by providing steady income while displacing ongoing liabilities.

Even though the king had assigned the Order dominium over the city and its district, he nevertheless withheld regalia (*dominicaturas*), which the Templars were obliged to respect. According to their agreement, the king retained "ecclesiastical rights which pertain to the royal majesty" as well as half of the proceeds from hunting and fishing only when he or the queen was in residence.[81] We can further reconstruct the nature of these retained rights with help from two subsequent memorials from May 1182 and January 1184, which were necessitated by conflicts between the king and the Templars over the nature of these *dominicaturas*. Although the crown retained little property—just a few select parcels—it enjoyed an impressive list of prerogatives. While in town, for example, the king and queen could take as much firewood as they needed, and the royal bailiff could collect a shipload of wood on their behalf once a year. The monarchs could also continue to sell the local Muslims vegetables and other produce from royal lands at a "just price."[82]

Over the coming decades, the monarchy would sporadically engage with affairs in Tortosa due to its residual rights. Alfons even made modest attempts to de-leverage his interest in the town by drawing on resources in zones that had not supported such dramatic borrowing. In 1194, for example, he exchanged some houses in Lleida in order to recuperate annual incomes of 120 solidi that he had given the see of Tortosa to maintain a candle at the cathedral altar.[83] A charter drafted several years after this administrative transfer confirms that the monarchy retained some of its general levying prerogatives within the town, which were not subject to this new division of revenues from the lordship. A concord forged between the see of Tortosa and the Templars in 1185 over tithes dictated that the Order would receive just one-fifth of any levies (such as the *lleuda*) collected within the town, in accordance with the "custom of Tortosa," which in turn would be exempt from tithes. The king was entitled to the remaining four-fifths share but would owe the see full tithes from it.[84]

Implications for the Jewish Community

To what extent did these alterations influence the lives of Tortosa's Jewish residents? In order to begin to deal with this question, we first need to explore the jurisdictional changes carried out by the 1182 transfer. The financial responsibilities of the arrangement seemed to require that the Templars assume the crown's quotidian jurisdictional lordship in the town. The authority associated with that role, however, remains unclear. The root cause of the ambiguity, for contemporaries and historians alike, was that the king had not ever sufficiently defined the nature of his lordship over the town's diverse population before the transfer in 1182. Twenty years earlier, for instance, he had received the homage of 106 Christian heads of household in Tortosa when he conducted his first itinerary. Although they submitted to Alfons traditionally as they would to any lord, they also swore to be his *fideles* and to aid him in the defense of his property in an apparent invocation of the nonfeudal provisions of the *Usatges*.[85] This event seemed to be unscripted, however. It is possible that the king did not plan or intend for his authority over the town to be expressed in this manner. Since other towns in Catalonia and Aragon visited by the king on this trip did not feature similar ceremonies, Tortosa's beleaguered residents may have taken the initiative to emphasize their support of the king in hopes of soliciting his favor.[86] Furthermore, because local Jews did not number among these "men of Tortosa" listed by name on the charter, and no similar concords survive involving the non-Christian residents, this profession cannot shed light on the crown's relationship with Tortosa's Jewish community.

Further complicating the situation following the transfer is evidence of at least one instance when the king appeared to sidestep the dominium held by the Order in order to reserve influence over individual elite Jews. Alfons granted to Dona, widow of "Azac" ("my Jew of Tortosa"), a privilege of exemption (*franquitas*) in 1185. In recognition of her payment of a disputed sum of four hundred morabetins to the crown, Alfons released Dona and her children from all services and financial obligations as well as any rights of administration by other parties: "Let you be under my support and maintenance alone" (*sola mea imparancia et manutinencia*).[87] These terms were common in this period for extending royal protection over persons as well as property.[88] The tie of dependence between Dona's family and the king was perpetuated by an ongoing commitment of service—in this case, her pledge to pay him an annual tribute of ten morabetins, which he forgave for the first two years following the contract. The full exemption appears to have concerned all taxation and services beyond those imposed by the aljama, half of which the king's bailiff was collecting from the Order.

Because the Templars shared these fiscal rights and possessed dominium over Tortosa's residents, the king's unilateral enfranchisement of these Jews, without any confirmation by the Order, seems illegitimate. Furthermore, in providing for the enforcement of the agreement, Alfons ignored the presence of seigniorial administration. He referred only to royal officers, ordering "all of my bailiffs, present and future," and "the inhabitants of the city of Tortosa" to maintain "all of [Dona's] possessions just as if they were my property and right of lordship [*dominicaturam*]." Nevertheless, the grant's guarantee of a level of protection to a Jew's property "as if" it belonged to the king was different from the servi regis provision of the *Fueros de Teruel*.[89] Although the relationship was based on service, the act did not stipulate actual royal ownership or equate it to possession of the Jew herself. Moreover, the individual focus of the grant seems to demonstrate that the king was not yet relying on such an overarching principle regarding the general Jewish populace in this setting.

Other documentation relating to this exemption reveals that the king's bestowal of favor to Dona and her family did not, in fact, establish a precedent for impinging on the dominium of the Templars. An earlier charter directed at "all our men from all our land, both Christians and Jews," indicates that Dona's deceased husband, whose full name was Azac avi Cogdez, had in fact originally received a sweeping exemption from all conceivable levies and taxes, as well as freedom of movement throughout all the realms, from Ramon Berenguer IV just years after the conquest, in 1156.[90] The wording of that document indicates that even though Azac was an elite Jew who enjoyed a privileged status at royal court and needed to travel for personal and likely royal business, he was a resident of Tortosa, possibly serving the count-prince as a local liaison.[91] He may, in fact, have been the unnamed *alfaquim* of Tortosa who visited Ramon's court later in 1156 to render an accounting of local affairs in the captured town.[92] These exemptions had designated Azac as the count-prince's operative and equipped him to attend to royal affairs without having to worry about reprisals from competitive royal officers or fellow Jews—hence, the grant's warning that "both Christians and Jews" respect Azac's privileges.

Alfons had observed his father's presentation of the privileges to Azac in 1156, when he subscribed the charter of enfranchisement, and the Jew must have continued to serve him faithfully in Tortosa in subsequent years. This record of service appears to have inclined the king to assist Dona and her children, "with love and prayers for my esteemed and successful *alfaquim*," although the fact that the family owed the king money likely also served as a motivator.[93] Another source from 1196 reveals that the arrangement was still in effect a decade later, despite Dona's death. Two years earlier, the document indicates, Alfons had conferred the annual tribute then paid by Azac's sons on the see of Tortosa as a pious donation.[94] Newly ascended to the throne, Pere confirmed this arrangement with the see in this charter and made arrangements for the annual payment of the ten morabetins from other sources if the two Jews were unable to pay.

A special service relationship with the crown thus had awarded this family a heritable enfranchisement that survived significant administrative changes to the town.[95] The fact that the status was only reconfirmed rather than created by the king may explain why the seigniorial administrators were not invoked by Alfons in 1185. Azac's *franquitas* was ostensibly only heritable because it had been established before the transfer of administration to the Templars. As a result, the case does not confirm that Alfons or Pere was intervening to carve out patronage relationships with wealthy Jews in Tortosa at the expense of the lords' dominium and did not establish a precedent for royal intervention.

If Alfons was respectful of the seigniorial regime's administrative rights and responsibilities in Tortosa, he did not intend to give the lords free reign to disrupt jurisdictional norms that could potentially harm the crown's stake in the town. The king made this stance clear in a renewal of the Jews' immunities and other privileges early in 1182 that bore the explicit consent of minority lord Ramon de Montcada. Emphasizing that the noble lord was bound to respect these mandates, the scribe invoked him and his bailiff by name with every guarantee and exemption detailed in the document.[96] Given its timing, less than a month before Alfons's transfer of the town to the Templars, the agreement may have been intended to emphasize to Ramon de Montcada, whose relationship with the crown positioned him as a check on Templar aggrandizement, that these privileges were to be respected even when the king lacked direct jurisdictional rights over the town.

In spite of these ambitions, however, evidence has not surfaced to indicate whether the king could have intervened to create new exemptions for local Jews. A silence in the sources could suggest that Alfons and Pere were disinclined or legally unable to interfere with the seigniorial jurisdiction they had established. Elite and non-elite Jews in Tortosa alike who had never forged protective relationships with the crown before the transfer seem to have been subject exclusively to Templar-Montcada lordship and, for the time being, not to have access to the crown for exemptions or assistance.

Scholars focusing on other kingdoms, however, have made the opposite point that such royal donations of jurisdiction over Jews could have served to "underscore royal control, emphasizing that such rights were the crown's to grant as it pleased."[97] We do, indeed, have numerous examples of other monarchs making explicit transfers of Jewish tax revenues or fidelity. Before Aragon's assumption by the counts of Barcelona, for example, Pedro I (1068–1104) donated to the monastery of Leire half of the "*lezda* [equivalent to the *lleuda*] of the Jews."[98] To the west, the monarchy of Castile-León was promoting similar principles of a special royal relationship with the Jews; the Castilian *Fueros de Cuenca* (ca. 1190), possibly borrowing language from the *Fueros de Teruel*, also asserted that Jews were servi regis.[99] These kings were prepared to grant both income entitlements as well as, much less frequently, full rights of jurisdiction over whole communities to predominantly ecclesiastical lords. Alfonso VII of Castile-León, for instance, donated to the cathedral of Zaragoza tithes from commerce levies from Muslims and tribute payments by Jews.[100] Then, in 1152, the same king donated to the monastery of Sahagún thirty local Jewish families, who henceforth would serve as "vassals of the abbot."[101] The bishop of Palencia received a similar transfer of Jews and Muslims as "vassals" from Alfonso VIII in 1177.[102]

Such scholars have not been able to demonstrate, however, that these monarchs were able to exercise overarching authority over such transferred Jewish individuals or retain any ability to reclaim these rights upon demand. Instead, we discover instances of both ecclesiastical and lay lords defending their control of Jews they had "obtained," sometimes under mysterious or poorly documented circumstances, from the monarchy's attempt to regain possession of them.[103] Tortosa's situation was analogous. In subsequent years, further modifications and exchanges confused and complicated the straightforward arrangement with the Templars. As we will see in later chapters, the lack of a clear record of the seigniorial regime's receipt of prerogatives of lordship, combined with the crown's reduction of property rights and local officers, would impede the monarchy's efforts to restore its jurisdictional rights in the thirteenth century.

Administrative Complexities and the Making of Seigniorial Tortosa

While Tortosa was exceptional in certain ways, the scenario through which its seigniorial regime obtained its Jews would remain common in the Crown of Aragon for generations to come. As we saw with the fourteenth-century case concerning Valldigna at the outset of this study, the monarchy frequently undermined its ability to exercise regalian prerogatives through unrestricted donations to seigniorial parties that enabled them to contest the idea that the Jews innately represented royal treasure on their personal domains. The dominium over Tortosa granted by Alfons was not only ill-defined and therefore easier for the seigniorial regime to aggrandize, but it also antedated the full elaboration of the concept of regalian rights over the Jews. To make matters worse for the crown, royal administrative complications in the decades surrounding the turn of the thirteenth century appear to have nullified that original donation and brought about the transfer of the town's ambiguous jurisdictional rights via intermediaries rather than directly from the monarchy.

A principal cause of this administrative turmoil was the crown's growing fiscal crisis, which emerged during Alfons's reign and persisted through the rule of his successor. When Alfons married Sancha of Castile in 1174, he assigned her a dower backed, in part, by his stake in Tortosa and other holdings along the Ebro Valley frontier.[104] These arrangements were subsequently strained by Alfons's transferal of jurisdiction and leveraging of many of these holdings, resulting in an extended conflict with the queen over her dower's integrity that would persist for the rest of her life.[105] Apart from the operations discussed earlier, over the winter of 1189–90 the king contracted further borrowing of 4,500 solidi and 700 morabetins in two separate charters, assigning repayment using his revenues from Tortosa and Ascó.[106]

The Templars apparently retained their administrative responsibilities in Tortosa and up the Ebro Valley until the late 1190s. In 1199, furthermore, a dispute between the citizens and the Templars over court jurisdiction adjudicated by Pere and his barons identified the Templars as the "Lords of Tortosa," indicating that the provisions of Alfons's transfer of the town remained in force at this point.[107] This scenario facilitated the king's use of these incomes as a line of credit. Additional loans based on Alfons's share merely decreased the annual portion payable to the royal fisc.

Alfons's will from 1194 continued to rely on property assigned to the dower. It appointed for debts to be repaid after his death from "my revenues" from Ascó and Tortosa.[108] In the document, the king also noted that the queen was entitled "without contradiction, [to] her dower that I made, gave, and conceded to her just as is contained in the charter granted and confirmed by me." After establishing these contradictory mandates, Alfons left the working out of the details to his heir. Pere, he indicated, would have to "restore to her the aforementioned property of her dower," appropriating "my other incomes" as necessary, so long as the queen remained unmarried.[109]

These provisions, combined with pressure from the queen, forced Pere to concede to Sancha direct control of Tortosa and Ascó in 1200.[110] This shift must have disrupted the standing arrangement with the Templars. The enactment stipulated that Sancha would have to respect the Order's (unfortunately unspecified) "right" in both Ascó and Tortosa, as well as miscellaneous obligations owed from the royal incomes from Tortosa, "all of which the Lord Queen would have to pay" while she held the town.[111] There are signs that Sancha possessed some administrative capacity in the town although the nature of her lordship remains uncertain. In 1202, the local Templar commander acknowledged her lieutenant, Arnau de Siscar, "who at that time held the place of the lord-queen [*domina*] in Tortosa."[112] With the consent of Ramon de Montcada, her bailiff appointed the *alcaydus* of the Muslim aljama in 1207.[113] At the same time, the king exercised certain general taxation rights without her collaboration or consent. In a convention between the Templars and Ramon de Montcada from later in 1202, the noble complained that the commander was collecting the *questia* that he had been enlisted to levy on the king's behalf.[114]

New enactments by the king would further confuse the extent of royal rights within the town and complicate the legal record of the transmission of lordship to the seigniorial regime. Perhaps in response to his mother's increasing age and reclusiveness in her Hospitaller monastery of Sigena, Pere confirmed (or possibly reenacted) his father's donation of Tortosa to the Templars in July 1202 albeit without any acknowledgment of his recent compromise with Sancha.[115] He may also have been under pressure from the Order to restore its rights in return for additional credit; that same day, he recognized a debt to the Templars of one thousand morabetins.[116] Although bearing all of the signs of a legal instrument, the charter suspiciously lacked the subscriptions of any of the relevant local potentates (Sancha, Ramon de Montcada, or the bishop) or even a single Catalan magnate; the witnesses were exclusively Aragonese lords. These omissions led A. J. Forey to suspect that the grant was "ineffective."[117] While its confirmation made no mention of the changes in royal or seigniorial rights that the town had undergone since 1182, it did detail the Order's expansive jurisdictional rights in the town, symbolized by the king's donation of "those three persons, namely the Christian, Muslim, and Jew, whom I possess in that same city."[118] Sancha soon contested her son's reversal by appealing for a renewal of apostolic protection for her dower holdings from Innocent III, which she received in 1203.[119] Yet, we have no further evidence of her exercise of lordship in Tortosa before her death in 1208.[120]

In December 1207, another royal enactment added further confusion to Tortosa's jurisdictional situation. Despite confirming all of the Templars' donations from his father and grandfather the previous year, Pere granted lordship over the town and the neighboring village of Benifallet to the noble Guillem (IV) de Cervera. The grant made no reference to earlier exchanges, and the rights to jurisdiction and revenues awarded to Guillem were, in fact, much more expansive than those granted to the Templars in 1182 and 1202. The noble received all levies and judicial fines imposed by the municipal court as well as incomes from local offices. He would also possess, for his lifetime, all revenues from the lordship, including those generated by royal property, "just as at any time Lord King Alfons, our father, and Doña Sancha, our mother, and we had, held, and possessed."[121] In other words, his rights were legally greater than the Templars' had been, according to the 1182 transfer. The crown retained only rights to military service and to collection of fines for breaking the peace and the *questia* on Christian residents. As with the most recent donation to the Templars, Guillem obtained unrestricted jurisdiction over Christians, Jews, and Muslims. Unlike Pere's reconciliation with Sancha in 1200, no provisions were made for prerogatives held by the Templars.

This latest change could indicate that the king no longer had confidence in the Order's ability or willingness to administer the lower Ebro region in the best interests of the crown. He may have been wary of the Order's increasing wealth and autonomy or may have blamed its administration for Tortosa's mounting economic woes and threatened viability as a settlement. In the king's view, a trustworthy baron bound by traditional feudal relationships arguably could have been more amenable to taking direction from the king and collaborating with his objectives. These sentiments would explain why Pere was willing to pay such a high price to assign responsibility over the area to Guillem, who would owe the crown nothing in the future from Tortosa's revenues. The king depicted the noble's protection of the town as a virtuous deed in the king's service, "for the honor of God and the defense of Christendom."[122]

It was therefore fitting that the following year, in November 1208, Pere also invested the noble with the castle of Benifassà, which was on the fringes of Muslim territory to the south and strategically crucial to both Tortosa's defense and the general war effort along that frontier.[123] Yet, unlike Tortosa's donation, this castle was offered by the king as a fief according to the "customs" of Barcelona, with the explicit right to regain "power" over Benifassà upon demand. Guillem would have to assume all of the costs of provisioning and defending the position, but any improvement in its security would ultimately benefit the king, who could recall the fief and regain control over that active front at any time.[124]

Pere was cautiously optimistic about these agreements with Guillem. He seems to have hoped that with such increased incentives and ongoing aid from neighboring centers, Guillem would reverse the region's decline and promote the growth and consolidation necessary to secure the frontier. Only such optimism would have led him to license the noble to assume full jurisdictional rights over "all settlements you are able to establish in all of [Tortosa's district] at any time."[125] Signs are that Guillem de Cervera was willing to represent the king, in collaboration with the Montcada family, but not to forget completely his own interests. In 1209, he and co-lord Ramon de Montcada carried out a sentence, delivered by the leading men of the town, that restored some lands outside the town, which had been entrusted to Christian settlers, to the Muslim community of Benifallet. They broadcast that they were performing this administrative duty "for us and for the lord king."[126] When they ordered the decision overturned the following year, however, they noted that it was "on behalf of Tortosa's seigniorial regime [senioraticum]," without mention of the monarchy.[127]

Cervera and Montcada also appear to have permitted the king momentary heightened access to the resources of their non-Christian communities. As we discussed earlier concerning the royal privileges maintained by the *alfaquim*'s widow and her family, under the past few decades of Templar lordship, the crown had ostensibly only been able to manipulate or extend existing franchises that it had granted before the transfer of authority to the Order. These co-lords, by contrast, on at least one occasion accommodated novel enfranchisement by the crown. In 1208, Pere ruled that a Muslim resident, Ali Almohac, and his extended family would be perennially exempt (*franchus*) from all royal and local (*regale ac vicinale*) "exactions and demands." At the same time, as a pious donation, he permanently removed the family from the lordship of Tortosa's seigniorial regime in order to subject it to the lordship of the monastery of Poblet.[128] In the future, the property and incomes of this family, which included both existing members as well as any future spouses or children, would exclusively benefit the monastery. Guillem de Cervera and Ramon de Montcada signaled their consent by subscribing the charter. We have no evidence of the crown trying to establish similar exemptions for non-office-holding Jews or Muslims for the remainder of the seigniorial period, through the final years of the thirteenth century.

While not explicitly linked to the repayment of any loans, Pere's transfer of lordship to Guillem de Cervera may also have served fiscal objectives. Even though the Templars remained an important creditor, the king may have been aiming to secure additional, desperately needed, short-term support from Guillem. These transactions also stood to solidify the loyalty of a baron who was offering the king vital assistance in his battles against rebellious vassals in western Catalonia at the time.[129] Their dealings would soon increase in magnitude. In November 1209, the king recognized that he owed Guillem 21,500 morabetins that had to be repaid by the following year, before Pentecost in order to avoid a 20 percent interest penalty. Guillem received in pledge, and thereby was to administer, a long list of additional royal domains in both Catalonia and Aragon whose incomes would help pay down the debt.[130]

Although the king continued to maintain close relations with the Templars and borrow extensively from them, no evidence exists of disputes over Guillem de Cervera's administrative rights in Tortosa. It is a possibility that the Order was exerting silent pressure by threatening to deny Pere additional credit. For his part, the king may have grown disappointed by his latest appointee's performance, inspiring him to enact yet another confusing transfer. By September 1210, Pere had reversed his earlier decision and was advocating the restoration of the Order's prerogatives to Tortosa, Ascó, and Riba-roja, as defined in his father's original donation from 1182.[131] He couched the grant as repayment for the Templars' service in the recent successful campaigns into Andalusi territory. A transaction the following month, however, indicated that he was transferring Ascó, in particular, in return for a list of property. He would receive the Order's retained fifth share of these holdings, two captured frontier castles in northern Valencia, rights to certain commerce levies and two hundred morabetins of annual revenues, and a five-thousand-morabetin payment.[132]

Pere's right to reallocate Tortosa was legally dubious, given the nature of the 1208 donation to Guillem de Cervera. The Templars thus had good reason to try to defend the transaction by reaching a satisfactory resolution with the noble. In a meeting between the Order's leaders and Guillem before a panel of arbitrators the following month, the Templars claimed that the king had commanded Guillem to swear homage and fealty to them for Tortosa. The noble, however, denied this responsibility, asserting that he still held these rights from the king's donation. Apparently, once pressed by the Order, Pere backpedaled and professed that he had mistakenly granted rights to Guillem that belonged to the Templars. This admission solved the immediate problem of neutralizing Guillem's claim but, at the same time, set a precedent concerning the king's inability to reverse valid donations such as he had made to the Order. Pere's temporary solution was to recast the donation to Guillem as an infeudation that could then be subjected to the Order's authority as overlord.[133] Even though this reinterpretation ran counter to the language of the charter awarding Guillem his prerogatives, the fact that the king had restored the Templars' lordship as established in 1182 and 1202 may have convinced the judges to rule in the Order's favor. A month later, the Templars donated Tortosa to Guillem and his son, for their lifetimes, "in fief . . . just as you had the city and everything in fief from the donation of [the king]."[134]

The Order must have been willing to recognize Guillem's temporary rights because it understood that its receipt of Tortosa was inevitable. Even though the seigniorial parties had already resolved the disagreement without direct royal intervention, the following day the king nevertheless sought to insert himself in the transaction, possibly in order to maintain a track record of royal involvement in the chain of transmission. Pere mandated that the noble and his son swear homage and fealty to the Order for their possession of Tortosa, which they would hold from the Templars, even though, he carefully noted, "we gave [it] to you."[135]

In spite of these latest efforts by the king, the nature of seigniorial dominium over Tortosa and the crown's involvement in the chain of transmission remained ambiguous. Guillem retained these fiefs for only a short time before transferring them, without any retentions, to the Order in 1215, and Pere did not live to influence that final transaction. He had fallen unexpectedly at the battle of Muret two years earlier. The fact that this latest transfer was exclusively seigniorial and that it took place during the troubled years of Jaume I's minority would make it all the more difficult for the monarchy to regain control over the rights of lordship possessed by the seigniorial regime in Tortosa. The Order made a one-time payment of 2,500 morabetins for quit-claims from Guillem's brother and son to ensure that it would be able to enjoy the fruits of these rights without further conflict for many years to come.[136]

The Templars had been made to wait decades for the reception of the financial prerogatives and administrative rights to Tortosa and Ascó that they had originally been promised in 1182, with no guarantee that they would ever be realized. Yet, the convoluted exchanges during the final years of Sancha's life and following the involvement of Guillem de Cervera, together with the final indirect, nonroyal transmission, ultimately earned the Order a much more autonomous and legally defensible hold over Tortosa than it had ever been offered in direct transactions with the crown. Furthermore, the assumption of Guillem's rights in this fashion provided the Templars with a legal rationale for rejecting as null and void the restrictions stipulated in the Templars' arrangements with the crown established in 1182, renewed in 1202, and then revived in 1210.

Conclusions

Even though both Alfons and Pere took conscious steps to depart from the policies regarding Tortosa and its frontier established by Ramon Berenguer IV and to move toward indirect administration, seigniorial control over Tortosa ended up emerging significantly tighter than either of them had envisioned. Both monarchs had tried to maintain what proved to be an impossible balancing act of safeguarding royal control while continually diverting or reallocating vital resources from these sectors of their patrimony, resulting in limited rights and an unclear chain of transmission. Already the chief beneficiaries of these policies, the Templars also accumulated ceded royal revenues from other parties—for example, their purchase of a right to two hundred morabetins in annual revenue from Ramon de Montcada in 1216.[137]

Signs are that Pere, in particular, was increasingly facing the reality that his monarchy did not have the capacity to assert its authority everywhere and thus had to prioritize its engagement with individual lordships. We lack sufficient evidence, however, to prove that he was fully conscious of the extent of the jurisdictional dislocation that was brewing in Tortosa. Indeed, given that he and Alfons had never formally alienated the holding, Pere might well have been surprised at many of the problems he left his son to face following his sudden death in 1213. As famously recollected in Jaume I's autobiographical *Llibre dels feits*, the difficult years of his minority, when he was ensconced in the fortress of Monzón with "not even enough food for one day, so wasted and pledged was the land," were the direct result of the spendthrift policies of his father and grandfather, who had all but bankrupted the crown's finances and enlarged the extent of seigniorial control of royal demesne lands.[138]

This phase of leveraging and alleged fiscal irresponsibility, combined with the legal ambiguities inherent in Ramon Berenguer IV's foundation of the community immediately following the conquest, generated the conditions that would invest the seigniorial regime with legitimate control over Tortosa's Jews for the bulk of the thirteenth century. The nature of this foundation and withdrawal would eventually provide the lords with a formidable legal defense of their jurisdictional autonomy. Yet, it would be decades before Jaume fleshed out and developed the administrative capacity to implement any royal policy of exclusive possession of the Jews to challenge what was then a considerably ingrained status quo in Tortosa, as well as other nonroyal autonomies throughout the realms of the Crown of Aragon. Before turning to observe how the lords of Tortosa set to work organizing and running their lordship, we first need to scrutinize the evolution of regalian ideology and administration during Jaume's reign and the implications it had for autonomous lords and their Jewish, Muslim, and Christian subjects alike.

2

ROYAL ADMINISTRATIVE CHANGE AND THE EMERGENCE OF A JEWISH POLICY

Before delving into the development of Tortosa's seigniorial regime and management of its Jewish community, we first need to consider how the monarchy managed this problematic situation with Tortosa during the ensuing foundational first decades of Jaume's reign. The jurisdictional dislocation we saw materialize in chapter 1 was emblematic of the widespread disconnect between the crown's emergent regalian ideology and jurisdictional legal limitations on the ground throughout the realms. Jaume's manner of engagement with Tortosa over these years and his eventual decision to try to regain administrative rights there around the mid-thirteenth century were linked to a broader expansion of royal governance. This process of expansion involved, among other elements, the augmentation and application of a policy of exclusive jurisdiction over non-Christian subjects. Far from following a master plan and being seamlessly implemented, this administrative development was piecemeal and disjointed, and was pursued by means of a diversity of strategies and mechanisms.

A good starting point for this discussion is an illuminating source from 1247 that paints a vivid picture of the competition between royal and seigniorial administrative agendas in the town and the strict limitations on royal intervention there at that time. The charter records the resolution of some "frequently argued" disagreements over royal rights in Tortosa between

Jaume and the local Templar commander.[1] The text does not indicate the precise origins or duration of the conflict, but it appears that recent changes in the king's local property holdings had prompted him to revive an existing dispute.

Jaume referred to a recent purchase that allegedly had increased his share of Tortosa to over one-third. He argued that this enlarged stake entitled him to exercise some jurisdictional powers there. This assertion confirms that until that time and probably since Pere's transactions decades earlier, the monarchy had possessed no such authority within the town. Jaume requested from the Templars the right to maintain a resident bailiff in the town who would collect royal rents and certain levies ("incomes and the *pedatge*") and be involved "in all cases, treaties, and conventions."[2] He based his claim exclusively on crown property rights and made no attempt to utilize the principles of regalian control over public authority or jurisdiction over Jews promoted by the *Usatges de Barcelona,* peace constitutions, and other legal instruments.

Rather than reject the king's petition altogether and risk embroiling the dispute further, the Templar commander made the strategic choice to agree to a carefully manipulated version of his demands. In return for valuable concessions in the form of property and exemptions, the commander submitted to admitting a royal bailiff on the condition that his powers be strictly limited to managing royal property. The opening of the charter initially made it seem as if the Templars were conceding to the crown's full demands: "We recognize and concede to you, Lord King, and your successors in perpetuity, that you shall have . . . a bailiff in Tortosa who is able to be involved in all cases, treaties, and compositions that the bailiff of the Templars makes." Yet the commander added a careful qualification to this concession that sought to remove any possibility that this officer could be used as a licit mechanism for restoring royal jurisdiction within the town: "Your bailiff shall not, however, have jurisdiction or coercive power here [*iurisdiccionem vel cohercionem aliquam*] but only receive your incomes from the hand of the bailiff of the Temple."[3]

In order to be perfectly clear about these limitations, the commander proceeded to compare the limited capacity of the royal bailiff with the expansive autonomous authority of the Order's officer: "The bailiff of the Temple can organize and dispense with justice, just as he has been accustomed until now [*possit componere et dimitere de iusticiis sicut consuevit hactenus*], neither expecting nor requiring the consent of your bailiff nor your successors."[4] The agreement did not make specific mention of non-Christian residents. Yet, its administrative stipulations, like those of earlier jurisdictional concords, must have concerned the jurisdictional circumstances of all of the town's inhabitants, irrespective of their ethnoreligious identities. Charter evidence often neglects to single out ethnoreligious groups in general mandates when they are implicitly included as town community members.[5]

The Templars thereby denied the monarchy any broader administrative role in the town while receiving tacit confirmation of their lordship's jurisdictional autonomy. They remained under no obligation to consult the king concerning their governance. For his part, Jaume had garnered a means to oversee his financial interests in the town, which possibly included a share of the taxation on the Jewish community maintained from the days of his father and grandfather, but nothing more. The crown's management of its financial rights within the lordship, without impinging upon the jurisdictional activities of the lords, sat squarely within the precedent established during the monarchy's piecemeal withdrawal over the later twelfth and early thirteenth centuries.

This document and other evidence we will consider in this chapter raise important questions about the pace and circumstances of the decline of royal authority in Tortosa and about the grounds on which the king initiated his efforts to restore some of the former presence of royal administration there. What factors motivated Jaume to want increased involvement, on what legal grounds did royal governmental rights depend, and how did the king try to engineer their increase? The intensification of royal efforts to enunciate and assert the crown's exclusive authority over Jews was clearly a function of administrative and political changes affecting the monarchy's standing within the realms. This resolution with the Templars seems to indicate that substantial property rights alone did not automatically entitle the monarchy to administrative prerogatives, but it does not confirm whether an increased administrative presence hinged exclusively on the amenability of the seigniorial regime. Here we will explore these issues by measuring the actual influence that the crown seems to have been able to exert in Tortosa via royal visitations and the presence and activity of officers leading up to this shift in 1247. We will conduct this analysis with frequent reference to the broader context during these formative years of Jaume's administration when the monarchy was campaigning to promote its regalia with regard to Jews as a facet of its claimed pervasive public authority.

Governmental Activity Through Jaume's Minority

One telling feature of the 1247 agreement is its lack of any reference to regalian rights. We cannot know what arguments were voiced by the king and his advisors during the "frequently argued" negotiations with the Order. However, in the final agreement Jaume made no attempt to justify his prerogatives by drawing on the "conception of territorial sovereignty" promoted by the *Usatges de Barcelona*, the *Liber feudorum maior*, and the tradition of peace legislation that Alfons had inaugurated to govern all of Catalonia.[6] Since the rationale used by the king's appeal was based solely on his property rights in the town, it was available to any common lord and by no means exclusive to the monarchy.

It may have grown apparent to Jaume over the course of these negotiations that reference to controversial regalian claims would not help him gain the prerogatives he sought in this instance. As we have seen, Tortosa already had a particularly complicated jurisdictional history as well as a seigniorial regime with the wherewithal to mount a formidable legal challenge to novel regalian preserves. The king may have been conscious that the development of an administrative presence in the town needed to take place gradually or felt that the priority had to be servicing his holdings in the town. An official with powers limited to attending to local royal property satisfied his present needs. Another possibility is that the seigniorial regime's ill-defined rights of lordship simply dissuaded or prevented the king from demanding more. The agreement, indeed, seemed to confirm a major limitation concerning the development of monarchical authority over the subjects throughout the realms. If the king were not even able to establish a royal bailiff lacking executive privileges without seigniorial consent, general principles of royal authority would have been of little use for securing control over public order.

On the other hand, we might have expected more aggressive promotion of royal prerogatives from Jaume on this occasion. Since the early years of his reign, he had been building on the ideological foundations of royal power inherited from his predecessors and repairing the setbacks to their provisions for public order. He had been particularly diligent about defining a protective policy concerning Jews and Muslims and had begun to issue laws in the spirit of the servi regis provision from the *Fueros de Teruel*.

Jaume had, in fact, orchestrated a pronounced shift in the monarchy's Jewish policy. Earlier peace constitutions had not explicitly transmitted the provisions of the *Usatges de Barcelona* that were meant to extend royal control over Jews and Muslims. Indeed, the royal peace maintained by Alfons and Pere was ambiguous about whether its protections over public order extended to non-Christians as inhabitants or "subjects" of the realm. Constitutions issued by Jaume, however, clearly included Jews and Muslims among the "men" (*homines*) they implicated.[7]

The earliest sign of an explicit protective policy that distinguished Jews and Muslims from the general populace within the peace legislation appeared at the Corts of Vilafranca del Penedès in 1218, during Jaume's minority. In one sense, the measure felt conservative because it almost imperceptibly placed Jews and Muslims and their property under the existing royal peace rather than defining a separate principle of protection. On the other hand, the added stipulation that these non-Christians were inhabitants "who evidently [*videlicet*] live in Catalonia under royal fidelity and protection [*fide et custodia regia*]" did seem to accord them a special degree of royal protection above and beyond the general peace that theoretically applied to all subjects.[8]

We need to consider what changes in the monarchy's dealings with its subjects and finances had permitted it to enlarge the peace so soon after Jaume's predecessors had withdrawn important protections in response to baronial pressure. The concessions Alfons had granted to the nobility during the troubled assemblies of 1188 and 1192 had never repealed the core public-safety provisions initially established at Fondarella in 1173.[9] Later, Pere's desperate need to maintain his realm-wide *bovatge* and *monedatge* levies put even these elements of the Peace and Truce at risk.[10] Barons were utilizing the monarchy's own centralizing peace assemblies to generate laws that increased their autonomy. At Barcelona in 1200, for example, nobles manipulated the applicability of royal peace provisions safeguarding public roads that had been present in the *Usatges* and prominent in the constitutions from Fondarella. They inserted crucial exceptions for magnates engaged in war or pursuing runaway enserfed peasants (*homines proprii*).[11] Similarly, in a compromise between the king and his nobility, the 1202 assembly at Cervera barred peasants enserfed to magnates from lodging complaints about abusive lordship in royal court.[12] While not fully legalizing such seigniorial mistreatment, such a provision, according to Freedman, nevertheless indicated how the "sway of the Peace and Truce, of the *Usatges,* and of legislation governing the protection of persons (as on public thoroughfares) yielded to seigneurial, private jurisdiction."[13]

The resulting Peace and Truce was less expansive but arguably more enforceable since it had earned putative noble support. Increased accommodation of seigniorial jurisdiction inspired magnates to pledge to uphold it. By contrast, Alfons's insistence on maintaining controversial elements of the peace had generated constitutions in 1188 and 1192 that nobles were unwilling to subscribe and were therefore unenforceable.[14] Pere's pragmatism and tremendous financial need generated peace constitutions from 1200 onward that were sworn to by an impressive list of Catalonia's nobles. At the same time, this phenomenon taught the nobles that they could resist distasteful royal policies effectively, which they did in 1205 when the king imposed new taxes in Catalonia contrary to custom and they pressured him to confess his excess and promise to desist.[15] Rather than reiterating specific provisions concerning public order, the brief set of peace constitutions issued at Puigcerdà in 1207 focused on the issue of compliance. The king outlined chiefly feudo-vassalic mechanisms intended to pressure recalcitrant barons to respect royal authority. Men who resisted, or whose men resisted, the royal Peace and Truce or the monarchy's right to collect the *bovatge* would have their castles or other fiefs seized by the king or his vicar.[16]

The enforceability of the peace would be further enhanced by the monarchy's systematization of local administration under its direct control throughout Catalonia. The involvement of bishops and bailiffs prominent in earlier peace legislation had faded by the later twelfth century as the monarchy sought to assert greater responsibility over public order.[17] In their place, vicars were increasingly responsible for upholding the provisions of the peace. Their growing role likely inspired one of the demands imposed upon the king by his Catalan magnates in 1205. All future vicars would be "knights and from this land [i.e., Catalonia]," selected "with the counsel of magnates and wise men of that land." They would, furthermore, be held to "swear that they would treat the land and common justice legally and guard well the *ius* and custom of the land and not make here in the future any new exactions."¹⁸

A capable regency, bolstered by papal support, enhanced the monarchy's ability to strengthen the peace during Jaume's minority. With its engagement in the Albigensian Crusade and status as suzerain over the monarchy, the papacy was positioned to intervene and stabilize the kingdom in the wake of Pere's sudden death in 1213. Cardinal legate Pierre de Douai quickly placed the boy king under the protection of the Templars of Monzón and helped establish a regency under the supervision of Jaume's great uncle, Count Sanç of Provence.¹⁹ Pierre also convoked, on Jaume's behalf, an assembly of the Catalan and Aragonese nobility and representatives from the major towns. The assembly occurred in 1214, and its attendants swore an oath of fidelity to the young king and pledged to help him uphold the royal peace.²⁰ The involvement of the papacy and rapid installation of the regency may explain why the 1214 council restored some of the controversial provisions of the peace that had been silenced in the constitutions ratified during the final years of Pere's reign, such as general protections over roads without any exception for knights engaged in personal wars.²¹ Equally important were the tax concessions Pierre offered to the assembled subjects. He revoked the novel *pedatge* and *lleuda* commerce levies Pere had recently sought to impose and offered all of the cities of Catalonia full exemption from *questias* until Jaume reached puberty. Then he invited them to submit "voluntary" payments to assist the king with his debts, ostensibly hoping to capitalize on the representatives' sense of loyalty to the monarchy and concern for its stability.²²

The records of the Corts of 1214 in Lleida described a more intricate and hierarchical system that prioritized the vicars and did not award the bailiffs a significant role.²³ A "procurator of Catalonia" would be responsible for appointing those royal officials publicly sworn to uphold the peace in most towns, except, of course, for anomalies such as Tortosa where the office remained under seigniorial control.²⁴ Yet, there were subtle drawbacks to this system that unexpectedly increased seigniorial autonomy. This peace implicitly challenged locally developed systems of protection, including the consulates in towns such as Lleida, Vic, and Perpignan. As Daileader has shown, it co-opted preexisting consuls in these towns, recasting them as *paers* answerable to the vicars. In theory, such integration of existing mechanisms in these towns should have helped the monarchy centralize and systematize public safety. In practice, however, this shift would primarily benefit the lords, who may have pressured Pere and the regents of the young Jaume to expand royal justice in anticipation that it would be less effective in challenging their own authority than were the independent consulates.[25]

As Jaume emerged from his minority, there are signs that his monarchy was making progress in rebuilding its finances and regaining control of its pawned domains, which, in turn, would put it in a better position to assert its authority. Peace to the south facilitated these efforts; as he was establishing the regency, Pierre de Douai commissioned a Jewish officer in 1216 to forge a peace with the Muslims of Valencia.[26] The cardinal legate also kept with tradition by entrusting management of the crown's finances to the Templars. The Order was apparently able to maintain operations throughout the regency without significant borrowing while collecting more detailed information about outstanding debts through interviews with Jewish and Muslim creditors.[27]

Added revenues came from diverse sources, some routine and some extraordinary. In keeping with Pierre de Douai's request for "voluntary" contributions at the Corts of 1214, a bull from Innocent III in 1216 mandated that the towns in both Catalonia and Aragon render payments to the monarchy to help it reduce its debts.[28] Furthermore, a reconciliation at the Corts of Monzón in 1217 with Viscount Guerau Ponç IV of Cabrera and Àger earned the monarchy a massive payment of seventy-five thousand solidi.[29] A number of magnates appear to have reduced or remitted huge debts owed to them by the crown.[30] Count Sanç's retirement pension of twenty-five thousand solidi from castral domains in Aragon and revenues from two towns in Catalonia further seem to indicate that the crown had recovered substantial landed rights in Aragon and begun to rebuild its income stream.[31]

Papal intervention, however, suggests that this restoration of the crown's fiscal circumstances still faced significant obstacles. In a series of bulls to bishops, nobles, and townspeople throughout the realms in 1216, Innocent III emphasized the importance of abiding by the directives imposed by Pierre de Douai in 1214 to render payments to the Templar fiscal administrators and otherwise collaborate with them to support their work on the monarchy's behalf.[32]

There may be reason to believe that this effort to restore the crown's finances helped inspire aspects of the royal peace's expansion during Jaume's early reign and, in particular, its initial targeting of religious minorities in 1218. The king's recollection described later in his reign in his *Llibre dels feits*, that his father had pawned the royal patrimony to Jews and Muslims seems to link up with Pierre de Douai's mandate, mentioned earlier, that Jewish and Muslim creditors report to the Templar administrators about outstanding royal debts.[33] The administration's efforts to manage this debt also may have alerted the king and his supporters to the extent of these subjects' resources. The demographic development of Jewish communities, in particular, could have made them a more attractive prize for the imposition of royal authority.[34] Depicting these Jewish and Muslim creditors as members of communities that were invariably "under royal fidelity and protection" and introducing the principle of regalian possession at the Corts of Vilafranca del Penedès thus could have served to make the monarchy's debt seem like less of a liability.[35]

It is possible that the gathering at this meeting of the Corts in 1218 conceded to these changes as part of a conscious transaction. The protections for Jews and Muslims were paired with concessions to the nobility that had been offered by Pere in the early 1200s but were then removed from the constitutions negotiated by the cardinal legate in 1214. Did the much shorter list of provisions passed in 1218 exempt nobles conducting private wars on public roads from the peace in order to extend the peace to apply to Jews and Muslims?[36] The constitutions contain other novelties that could have played a role in such a compromise. As an example, for the first time the assembly stipulated precise territorial limits of the peace that covered Catalonia's full extent, "from the Cinca River through to Tortosa and through to Salses, with its limits."[37] One further possibility is that the ambiguous wording of the statute made it seem less controversial to the assembled barons; it could be read as limiting the application of the peace to only those Jews and Muslims living under royal protection on royal domains.[38] Such ambiguity, if noticed at the time, could have played to the interests of both sides. Whereas the monarchy benefited from the unprecedented ratification of a statute confirming its jurisdiction over some Jews and Muslims, the barons could assert that they had approved a provision that did not apply to their domains.

By the time the king convoked his general court at Tortosa in 1225, there were even clearer signs that the royal administrative agenda was benefiting from the increased fiscal and political stability provided by the Templars' fiscal stewardship. Jaume had continued to borrow from baronial creditors, but, according to Bisson, these transactions had not often come at the price of reduced royal authority.[39] For several years, armed with the offer of indulgences from a supportive papacy, Jaume had been preparing to renew hostilities against Muslim Valencia. This escalation was improving his ability to borrow on credit from projected earnings from future conquests or tribute (*parias*) from the Muslims, rather than from incomes produced by his patrimony.[40] The constitutions ratified at Tortosa were the most expansive and assertive witnessed to date, a solid indicator of the monarchy's improved standing. Without offering any fiscal concessions, the king once again removed exclusions to the protection of public roads while maintaining unchanged the novel provision extending protection over resident Jews and Muslims and their property.[41]

First and foremost, holding the court at Tortosa enabled Jaume to broadcast his intentions to take a leadership role along the frontier and, in particular, coordinate a new campaign against Muslim Penyíscola with the financial support of the local bishop.[42] As a secondary motive, the opportunity for the king to display his capacity to take up temporary residence and assert political influence over this dislocated jurisdiction was likely attractive. The town's co-lord, Ramon de Montcada, was in attendance and even subscribed the *acta* of the general court. In the same way that the Templars were willing to serve as fiscal advisors and creditors to the crown, Ramon may have been content to support the king's ambitious peace initiatives and his campaign against Valencia because, at this point, they did not seem incompatible with the integrity and vitality of his seigniorial prerogatives in Tortosa.

Vicissitudes of Royal Administration

At the time of the Corts of Tortosa, Jaume may have been making gestures regarding his authority, but he was still over two decades away from gaining permission to establish a permanent administrative presence in the town. The 1247 agreement indicates that Pere's ambiguous adjustments forty years earlier had set in motion two potentially interrelated phenomena with significant implications for the crown's contact with local Jews. First, royal property holdings in the town had declined sharply. The one-third share Jaume had acquired before the concord, about which we know nothing specific, was well below the one-half share plus *dominicaturas* established by the transfer of 1182 (and likely renewed in 1202 and 1210).[43] Guillem de Cervera's dealings with the Templars may have dramatically reduced the monarchy's holdings in the town although it remains possible that subsequent contracts from Jaume's minority that have not survived played a role. Second, the monarchy had lost all of the local officers capable of servicing its holdings in the town, likely as a result of its reduced patrimonial rights there. The initial transfer of administrative responsibilities to the Templars appears to have caused the withdrawal of a dedicated royal bailiff around 1186.[44] This removal seems to have been unanticipated; indeed, the memorial over crown regalia in Tortosa from 1184 had indicated that the local royal bailiff should resolve any complaints through reference to the town's customary laws.[45] Aside from the brief appearance of the queen's delegate in 1202, we have no further evidence of fixed royal officers.[46] Further confirmation comes from Pere's 1208 enfranchisement of the Muslim family in Tortosa that we discussed in the previous chapter. In place of a local royal official, Bernat Amelii, who bore the titles of steward (*repositarius*), bailiff, and vicar of Lleida, subscribed the agreement and probably bore much of the responsibility for carrying out its mandate.[47] The disappearance of local officers must have impeded the monarchy's contact with Jews and other residents and hindered its imposition of the statutes of its general peace constitutions, as we will discuss later in this chapter.

It is true that alternate channels of contact were available, however. Present were temporary delegates and nonroyal officers who arguably had the potential to carry out royal business. The most likely candidate would be the vicar based in Tortosa, who, among his administrative duties, oversaw the municipal court (*curia*).[48] Unlike in many other urban centers in the realms, this officeholder had always been an appointee of the Montcada lord, which may have limited the monarchy's ability to utilize the position to its fullest potential, if at all.[49] Nevertheless, regardless of whether the monarchy possessed or lacked administrative rights in the town, kings directed orders at the vicar as if he were their official.[50] Finally, former lord Guillem de Cervera served as a temporary and unofficial royal operative in 1228 when he witnessed a donation by the lords to the Jews of Tortosa as the "lieutenant of the Lord King in Tortosa."[51]

Another measure of royal contact with the wider community was the rate of visitation by the itinerant royal court. Studies have shown that effective governance even in royal towns in the more administratively sophisticated later Middle Ages often depended on the king's physical presence and personal attention.[52] However, attention to the physical presence of the king does not discount the importance of royal transactions concerning the town made in other locations, sometimes involving town delegations and the lords or their representatives. Such dealings arguably had the potential to influence the town and the administrative conditions there more than any mere royal visit.[53] The lack of dedicated royal officials in seigniorial environments such as Tortosa likely made royal visitations all the more potent and vital to the crown's agenda. Such contact stood to advertise the extra-local authority of the royal *curia,* rendering its services more accessible, and implicitly undercut the jurisdictional powers of the lords as the king addressed violations, issued confirmations, and otherwise imposed himself on local affairs.

Over a period of decades, kings' rates of visitation to Tortosa were consistently lower than to other towns that pertained to the crown. Although less exposed than Tortosa as a frontier holding before the definitive conquest of northern Valencia in the 1230s, Lleida, to the northwest, was conquered during the campaigning that captured the lower Ebro Valley and settled with a similar package of customary privileges. Lleida's rise as a royal administrative center attracted increased attention and more frequent visits from the crown—contact that, in turn, apparently encouraged more careful management of the local Jewish community by resident officials.[54] Interaction with Tortosa, by contrast, stagnated during the reigns of Alfons and Pere and through the midpoint of Jaume's rule (table 1).[55]

These royal visitation data indicate that contact with Tortosa grew somewhat as Jaume emerged from his minority in the 1220s and began organizing campaigns into northern Valencia. This trend culminated in the meeting of the Corts in Tortosa and the unsuccessful campaign to take Muslim-held Penyíscola sponsored by the bishop of Tortosa in 1225.[56] These interactions were minimal, however, as compared to those involving Lleida. The king visited Tortosa only fourteen times but came to Lleida on at least fifty-four distinct visits (often for several months at a time) between 1225 and 1265, the year Jaume finally began to enjoy the fruits of having a bailiff to oversee royal interests in Tortosa.[57] After an extended absence of eight years between

TABLE 1: Number of distinct royal visitations (per reign) to Tortosa and Lleida by Alfons I, Pere I, and Jaume I through 1265

King	Tortosa	Lleida
Alfons I (r. 1162–96)[a]	6	23
Pere I (r. 1196–1213)[b]	1	17
Jaume I (r. 1213–76)[c]	14	54

[a] Based on data from Miret y Sans 1904b. Documented royal visits to Tortosa: 1176, 1178, 1180, 1182, 1184, and 1190. Lleida: 1181 (three times), 1182, 1184, 1185 (twice), 1186, 1188 (twice), 1189, 1190, 1191 (twice), 1192 (three times), 1194 (three times), 1195 (twice), and 1196.

[b] Based on data from Miret y Sans 1905–6. Documented royal visits to Tortosa: 1200 (to Tortosa or neighboring Amposta). Lleida: 1196, 1200 (twice), 1203 (three times), 1205, 1209 (four times), 1210 (four times), 1211, and 1212.

[c] Based on data from Miret y Sans 1918. Visits alleged in the *Llibre dels feits* and/or Zurita's *Anales* without corresponding charter evidence have not been counted. Documented royal visits to Tortosa: 1220, 1225, 1231, 1234, 1237, 1245, 1246, 1248, 1257 (twice), 1258 (twice), 1260, 1261. Lleida: 1218 (possibly twice), 1222, 1223, 1225 (twice), 1226, 1227, 1228 (three times), 1228–29 (extended stay), 1230 (possibly twice), 1231, 1232, 1233 (twice), 1234 (twice), 1235, 1236 (twice), 1237 (possibly three times), 1243, 1245, 1246 (extended stay), 1247, 1248, 1250, 1251, 1252, 1253 (twice), 1254, 1255, 1257 (three times, including extended stay), 1259 (twice), 1260 (three times, including extended stay), 1261 (two times, including extended stay), 1262 (extended stay), 1263 (two times, including extended stay), 1264 (three times), 1265 (four times).

1237 and 1245, the king visited the town in the years preceding and following his 1247 agreement with the Templars. That agreement was, in fact, arranged and documented in Huesca, and Jaume did not visit Tortosa that year. Following his visit in 1248, however, the king neglected to return to Tortosa until 1257, during which time he traveled to Lleida at least eight times. In the years leading up to his appointment of a local bailiff in Tortosa in 1263, Jaume visited the town somewhat more regularly (six times between 1257 and 1261), albeit with noticeable absences before and after the installation of this officer. He did not return to Tortosa until 1266.[58]

Leading up to the commencement of the chancery registers in the 1250s, but predating the 1247 agreement, sparse charter evidence reveals how Jaume was negotiating with Tortosa's lords regarding his taxation and property rights within the town. In 1244, returning to his realms briefly during the siege of Xàtiva, the king received confirmation from Guillem de Montcada that his right to retain one-third of the *monedatge* levy from Tortosa was conditional on royal consent.[59] Farming out this tax to the noble lord in this way was a logical strategy given the crown's lack of local administrators. Just weeks after Montcada's pledge, Jaume authorized the town's other lord, Guillem de Cardona, master of the Templars in Catalonia and Aragon, to collect two thousand solidi from the royal rents of Tortosa and its district, in addition to an unspecified amount to repay all of the tithes and rights pertaining to the Templars that the king had collected for himself since the siege of Valencia.[60]

In spite of the decline in its local administrative capacity, the monarchy thus maintained some measure of engagement with the town and its lords. The young king was beginning to involve himself with the town's leadership and gradually make moves to exert a tighter rein on the remaining royal property and express general royal prerogatives there from the early years of his majority in the 1220s. But these novelties did not amount to administrative rights and a capacity to exercise in Tortosa the authority the king was claiming throughout his realms, particularly when compared with centers of heavy royal business such as Lleida.

The Development and Diffusion of Royal Policies

The king must have been well aware, given the patent administrative limitations within Tortosa and other domains beyond direct royal control, that the efficacy of his general mandates would depend heavily on the willingness of local lords to comply. He could not reliably implement them by fiat. Scrutinizing whether and by what means royal regulations concerning the Jews during this period came to be applied in royal and seigniorial domains will help us expose their practical limitations as well as explore the complicated mechanisms of thirteenth-century policy diffusion.

After Tortosa's assembly in 1225, the next session of the Corts, held at Barcelona in 1228, issued a number of novel regulations. These included restrictions on Jews holding public office and having Christian women in their households, a privilege concerning the dowers of Jewish wives, and regulations on moneylending.[61] Some of these provisions must have derived from the directives of the Fourth Lateran Council (1215); it is possible the meeting addressed these issues in anticipation of Cardinal legate Jean d'Abbeville's visit to the Crown of Aragon, during which he would sharply criticize its lack of adherence to that council's dictates.⁶² The inclusion of these measures in the business of the general court nevertheless had great symbolic importance. It conveyed that the king had the authority to dictate these conditions for all of the Jews residing in his realms, regardless of their jurisdictional circumstances.

There are other signs that the king was feeling empowered to revive and expand the royal peace at this meeting. Most significantly, he reintroduced for the first time since the legislation of Alfons and Pere the Roman legal principle that violence committed on the public roads would represent an offense against the crown's authority—the crime of *lèse majesté*.⁶³ Jaume's earlier assemblies had extended protection over the roads by means of a consensus with the nobles and without similar emphasis of the king's pivotal role in maintaining public order.⁶⁴

Although the provision of protection over both Jews and Muslims expressed at the two prior meetings of the general court was not repeated on this occasion, it is arguable that the earlier promulgations had a lingering influence. Other laws that had appeared only once in the peace constitutions ended up exerting strong influence over Catalonia's legal and institutional development. The *ius maletractandi* licensed at the assembly of 1202, for example, was never again formally reissued but nevertheless retained legal force and evolved into an ingrained seigniorial prerogative in parts of Catalonia.⁶⁵ The meeting of 1228 did address an aspect of the same issue by extending "our peace" (*nostra pace*) over Jews and their possessions, as well as over "citizens and burghers, and all of our men."⁶⁶ This statute expressed the same legal principle witnessed at the Corts of 1218—that Jews were protected as subjects under the standard Peace and Truce and not as a separate subset benefiting from a special service relationship with the crown.

This general court of 1228 featured an assortment of lay and religious barons that included Ramon de Montcada (lord of Tortosa), Guillem de Cervera, and Count Hug IV of Empúries (r. 1200–1230), but no named representatives from the Templar Order. The presence of these magnates was not only customary, but also instrumental for the application of the promulgated regulations. The regulations, as stipulated, technically applied to "our kingdom." They ambiguously invoked the royal and collective "we" simultaneously, possibly with the aim of strengthening the sense of responsibility of the assembled men over these *acta*. The assembly's interest cap of 20 percent on all Jewish lending, for example, applied to "Jews of our land" (*iudei terre nostre*), which could logically be construed as referring to only royal domains or, alternatively, both royal and baronial domains.[67]

The implications of such an assembly for the primacy of royal authority were therefore mixed. Although the king had succeeded in garnering support for these measures from among his barons, the necessity of their involvement naturally signaled the incapacity of the monarchy to impose these regulations unilaterally. The monarchy's ability to regulate resident Jews within the realm continued to depend on the willingness of such magnates to subscribe and then adhere to these collective pledges within their own personal domains. Barons were notably not legally obliged to attend these assemblies or support their initiatives.

These limitations of royally led policy-making are attested by the king's own administrative activity following this meeting and subsequent assemblies. Rather than relying on the legal force of these statutes from the 1228 gathering alone, Jaume issued a separate charter several months later reminding his local delegate, the bishop of Girona, that he was obliged to adhere to all of the regulations concerning the Jews on the basis that they pertained to "our jurisdiction."[68] The king once again publicly confirmed these laws over a year later when he ordered residents throughout his realms to observe them "without fail." As added justification, he carefully clarified that these were not novel regulations but instead "those constitutions that we made formerly in the court at Barcelona, just as was contained in charters of Peace and Truce."[69] He similarly sought to apply the new laws on Jewish usury and the oaths Jews were now required to take. To increase compliance, he ordered his officials throughout Catalonia and Aragon to add these provisions to local laws, such as the *Fueros de Teruel* and the *Furs de València* in the 1240s.[70] Such efforts attest to the forces of inertia resisting the application of such regulations even within royal domains. Subsequent sources reveal that the residents in Girona were attempting to resist these rules. Several years later, after first directing their request for changes in Jewish lending policies to the royal court, the petitioners heard from the king that appeals concerning individual loans had to be lodged at the court of the bishop, which would handle them on a case-by-case basis. The general restrictions, however, would stand unchanged.[71] Similar resistance would have been easier to mount within nonroyal domains, so long as the alterations were agreeable to the local lord.

Evidence to confirm whether these regulations on Jewish lending, for example, penetrated nonroyal lordships or to indicate how independent barons handled them is scarce. Sources from the independent barony of Empúries—whose counts had been present at the 1228 assembly and the Corts of 1235 in Tarragona, which produced identical lending guidelines for Jewish creditors—do offer some clues. Count Ponç Hug III of Empúries (r. 1230–69) issued his Jews a charter of privileges in 1238 that licensed them to perform moneylending at or below a 20 percent interest-rate cap. Yet, he indicated clearly that this regulation emanated from "our court" and made no mention of royal mandates or the resolutions of the most recent Corts.[72] This omission must have been deliberate; it certainly served the count's interest in portraying himself as an independent baron. When Ponç Hug did make allusions in the charter to privileges and regulations established by the monarchy, it was to signal that his provisions for the Jews "in my land" were emulative rather than derivative, in order to attract new Jewish residents, among other competitive motives. He was responding to previously issued privileges and regulations held by the Jews of Barcelona and nearby Girona voluntarily and not obligations flowing from royal decree or his dynasty's participation in the recent sessions of the Corts.

We lack similar evidence to show that Ramon de Montcada made any attempt to impose regulations from the Corts in Tortosa in 1225, before his death the following year. Yet, there are indications that Jewish lending in Tortosa was not adhering to these limits during these years—behavior that would prompt Jaume to seek to impose these regulations directly later in his reign.[73] Continued widespread defiance of the royal policy appears to have encouraged Jaume to reissue his mandates with greater intensity on two separate occasions in 1241 when he threatened punishment for Jews and Christians who failed to heed them.[74] The intervention of the king to resolve specific questions concerning the application of his laws in Girona and Barcelona that same year indicates that the new regulations were at least being implemented in those jurisdictions under firm royal control.[75]

Future promulgations by the royal court devoted limited attention to the real-world jurisdictional constraints on the application of these laws. It is possible Jaume and his advisors thought that raising the issue of implementation would be a sign of weakness or an invitation for barons to resist royal statutes, and thus they intentionally left application unaddressed or vague. In 1243, when the king issued a general policy establishing that

Jews and Muslims would not lose their property on account of their baptism, he only obliquely addressed enforcement. He first applied the law to the realms over which he asserted his "universal dominion" as king, without any acknowledgment of jurisdictional limitations: "Aragon and Catalonia, Mallorca, Montpellier, and Valencia." Then he added language to signal that the law would benefit from the expansion of the monarchy's administrative rights; he applied it to "our jurisdiction which we and our successors have elsewhere, now and in posterity and, with God's help, will have."[76]

Royal assemblies would continue to issue similar statutes—some repeated, others new—relating to non-Christians, without any specifics concerning their application. When Jaume convoked an ecclesiastical *parlament* at the archiepiscopal court of Tarragona in February 1235 meant to address Cardinal legate Abbeville's recent critique, he reiterated the interest-rate cap on Jewish moneylending. The provisions also sought to shelter Jewish and Muslim communities from the threat of apostasy. Although the law encouraged non-Christians to convert to Christianity, Jews and Muslims were barred from converting to each other's religions.[77] At an emergency meeting of the general court a month later, convoked to deal with a severe famine afflicting Catalonia along with greater Europe, the king asserted his authority to administer Jews and Muslims as members of the general population of "men of Catalonia." For the space of one year, until food shortages subsided, he mandated that inhabitants of the diocese of Tortosa, in addition to those of Lleida, Urgell, and Tarragona, "both Jew and Muslim," would be obliged to sell all of their wheat at an established price, except for a small amount to pay their expenses and feed their families.[78] A potentially spurious record of the Corts held in Girona in 1251—the next Catalonian assembly for which a record survives—addressed general restrictions on Jewish moneylending and regulations on Jewish oath taking at length, without reflecting any concern about problems with adherence or implementation.[79] In 1258, however, Jaume sought to impose a major disincentive for Jews wanting to relocate from royal lands. He declared that Jews who moved from "our land" (*terra nostra*) to reside "in other lands or under the dominion of another lord or lords" without royal license past Lent of the following year would have their outstanding loans canceled.[80]

In the meantime, the king had continued to develop and broadcast royal policies concerning non-Christians in other forums outside Catalonia. Most significantly, he promulgated a Romanized compilation of the Aragonese fueros known as the *Vidal Mayor* at the Cortes of Huesca in 1247, which declared that any property alienations by Jews and Muslims were subject to royal approval.[81] Recent scholarship has grown more skeptical of the practical influence of these sorts of legal compilations. As with the measures passed in the general court, such regulations could only be reliably implemented within jurisdictions that stood under tight royal administrative control. According to Jesús Morales Arrizabalaga, for instance, far from implementing an effective expansion of royal prerogatives, the *Vidal Mayor* instead represented a largely failed attempt by the king to increase his authority without provoking overt resistance from the Aragonese barons.[82] Jaume's strategy emulated what Ramon Berenguer IV had done with the *Usatges de Barcelona* a century earlier. His jurists presented the new regalian codification as if it largely represented a faithful synthesis of the established fueros throughout Aragon. Executing such a synthesis was innately artificial and objectionable, however, since it dismissed the patent diversity of these local foral traditions across Aragon's intricate jurisdictional landscape and quietly prioritized regalia at the expense of nonroyal prerogatives.

The *Customs of Catalonia* (or *Commemoracions*) developed by the royal jurist Pere Albert in the 1230s and 1240s sought to build on the *Usatges de Barcelona* and employ Roman law to conduct similar work in Catalonia.[83] The corpus was similarly regalian in its central case that any vassal was bound to serve the king as "prince of the land" (*princeps terre*), regardless of other allegiances he might owe his lord. The king's exclusive "right of general jurisdiction" (*ius generalis iurisdictionis*), furthermore, was absolute and nontransferable.[84] These were principles that stood in conflict with the circumstances the monarchy faced in Tortosa and elsewhere.

Alongside such sweeping measures enunciated in royal assemblies and codifications that advertised regalian authority, the crown also led by example through its handling of Jewish communities under its direct administration. Royal privileges awarded on an ad hoc basis were particularly important in ushering in the transition from Jewish communal "autonomy by default" to "autonomy by design" during these early decades of Jaume's reign. Such policy-making by the crown could, in turn, inspire or pressure certain lords to award their Jews similar rights in order to remain competitive in the market for residents.

The earliest extant example is the charter of privileges awarded to the Jewish community of Calatayud in 1229. It gave them the right to elect four "leading citizens" (*probi homines*) as *adelantats*. The mandate that they consult with the rabbi, who was likely appointed by the crown, increased royal influence over the election of these important officials. Furthermore, these men were required to consult with other members of the aljama in governing the community. The king warned lords, various royal officials, "and most of all, the *concejo* of Calatayud" to respect these provisions.[85] Much like the servi regis statute of the *Fueros de Teruel* decades earlier, however, the privilege did not have legal force or direct implications beyond Calatayud's urban district.

The king would nevertheless issue similar privileges to other communities under his direct administration in the coming years, thus broadening the application of this paradigm in a piecemeal fashion throughout the royal domain. These localities included Mallorca in 1231, Valencia in 1239, Barcelona in 1241, and Girona in 1258.[86] The entitlements to communal officials granted to the former two towns, which had been recently established under Christian rule, were part of the package of prerogatives and regulations awarded by the king when he initially licensed their Jewish aljamas. As a result, these grants addressed a wider range of issues, such as the ratio of Jewish to non-Jewish witnesses in court cases, loan procedures, and conversion. Similar to what Ramon Berenguer IV had done when settling Tortosa's first Jews, each license also drew on existing bodies of customs and fueros held by prominent Jewries in neighboring bases of colonization under direct royal control: Barcelona for Mallorca and Zaragoza for Valencia City. Although these settlement licenses were traditional in that they appropriated the existing packages of customs and privileges and emulated the administrative practices of Jaume's distant forebears, each of them bears some faint clues that they were crafted with his emergent Jewish policy in mind. In addition to applying specifically the Jewish customary laws of Barcelona, the grant to Mallorca's community subjected its Jews to all of the relevant provisions of the *Usatges de Barcelona,* including their safeguards regarding Jewish protection and obligations to the king as *postat*. Jews settling throughout Mallorca "in any place of our lordship" would be enfranchised, per these privileges, and enjoy royal protection.[87] The charter to Valencia made it clear that the king was personally guaranteeing its Jews' protection and free mobility throughout his realms and that the prerogative would be enforced by his officers.[88]

Unlike the provisions of the general court and regalian law codes, such ad hoc charters do not seem to have been as part of an overt effort by the crown to challenge seigniorial authority. There is, in fact, no evidence that the king ever attempted to circumvent seigniorial jurisdictional rights by awarding one of these charters to a community over which he did not already possess administrative rights. None of these ad hoc privileges and licenses, furthermore, devoted explicit attention to the question of royal possession of Jews beyond the limits of the monarchy's direct jurisdiction. These omissions may have been the result of the still nascent and unstable elaboration of the crown's Jewish policy and regalian prerogatives, especially in the case of the charters from the 1230s and 1240s. Yet, it is also possible that the king did not see the need to raise these claims within the context of territories over which he exerted uncommon dominion due to either established jurisdictional rights or recent conquest.

The emergence and maturation of the territorial law for the kingdom of Valencia known as the *Furs de València,* which was in circulation and development from the 1240s but not formally promulgated until 1261, further illustrates this avoidance of legal justifications by the king and royal jurists. In the code, Jaume emphatically ruled out the possibility that independent beneficiaries of his post-conquest distribution in Valencia would be able to question his possession of non-Christians and their property in the manner that such beneficiaries had in Catalonia and Aragon following the conquests of his predecessors.[89] The *Furs* advanced a vision of pervasive royal authority that threatened anyone who disturbed public order, aided enemies, plotted rebellion, or otherwise violated the king's regalian rights with the crime of *lèse majesté*. Accordingly, it maintained that all Jews would be subject to royal dominion, even if they resided within noble or ecclesiastical domains.[90] It did so, however, without explanation or justification.

The basis for this assumed claim of universal royal possession and jurisdiction remained neither qualified nor substantiated in either individualized privileges or generalized legal promulgations for years to come. It was not until the king issued an unusual ad hoc privilege reestablishing the terms of the bailiwick of Montpellier in 1258 that he revealed at least one of the intended legal foundations for this policy. In the document, the king justified his claims of an exclusive right to tax the Jews through comparison to the condition of Jews and the prerogatives held by other Christian monarchs elsewhere in European society. In keeping with the long tradition of theological writings on the Jewish presence in Latin Christendom, the king argued that the original source of this servitude was the insult the Jews had committed against "their and our Creator." This offense necessitated their handing over to the *princeps* of the land.[91]

One important novelty outside of Catalonia during these years that supported the monarchy's agenda was the establishment of crown administrators entrusted with the power to judge all Jews in a given locality or principality.[92] The origins of the institution are unclear, but it appears to date from the mid-thirteenth century, when it would have been encouraged by the administrative trends we have been witnessing. Jaume may have introduced such a position in Valencia before 1258, according to a privilege later presented in royal court. It authorized Mosse Alconstantini, grandson of a Jewish magistrate (*alfaqui*) named Salamó, to serve as his grandfather's lieutenant and judge all cases "according to Jewish law between the Jews of Valencia." Verifying whether this privilege was presented and carried out in this fashion is complicated by the fact that Jaume later ruled, in 1271, that it was somehow falsified. He sided with a Jewish rival who alleged that Salamó had never "held the power of judging between Jews in the kingdom of Valencia from [the king]."[93] In this same court case, Mosse furthermore contended that his father, also named Salamó and an *alfaqui,* had obtained similar exclusive judicial privileges over the Jews of Zaragoza and the entire kingdom of Aragon. He claimed that this right had been usurped by rival Jews in the aljama of Zaragoza, where the office was based. Jafuda de la Cavalleria and other elite Jews had allegedly colluded to enact a statute that distributed this judicial authority among a tribunal composed of Salamó, Samuel Almeridi, and Azac Abenbruc. Mosse and his brother, presumably on their father's behalf, denounced this usurpation before the king and demanded that their rivals be forced to dissolve the tribunal as well as pay the king an enormous fine of five hundred gold pieces. Jafuda, however, succeeded in sidetracking the complaint by shifting attention to the privilege Mosse had furnished concerning his family's similar rights in Valencia. Mosse's miscalculation and failure to deliver additional evidence he had promised not only cost him the case but also half of his property—the penalty for filing a false claim. Only an appeal from the king's daughter, Queen Violant of Castile-León, a patron of the prominent Alconstantini family, convinced the king to show Mosse leniency in sentencing.

This record did not stipulate what Jaume intended to do about judicial jurisdiction in Aragon. Royal documentation from 1284, however, indicates that Salamó Abenbruc, a relative of the tribunal member mentioned in 1271, had been serving as "judge" over the Jews of Zaragoza before being murdered in factional strife earlier that year.[94] Salamó's death may have later prompted Pere II (r. 1276–85) to do away with the position of local judge and pursue his agenda of standardizing and monopolizing jurisdiction over all Jews through the designation of another judge for the entire kingdom of Aragon. Pere appointed Salamó Alconstantini as "judge or rabbi over all the Jews of Aragon," a position he managed to retain under Alfons II (r. 1285–91). By 1294, however, Jaume II (r. 1291–1327) noticed that Salamó's use of the office was causing "great damage . . . to all of the said Jews" of Aragon due to the factional strife it had fomented. Violant, then queen mother of Castile-León, again intervened on the family's behalf, but Jaume responded curtly to his aunt, "You ought not to want that, for one Jew, we lose the others."[95] He instituted a dramatically reduced version of the office in 1305 when he invested Içmael de Portella with authority over all appeals concerning cases between "Jews in the aljamas of Aragon" already heard in court by "Jewish judges."[96] The rampant competition between elite Jews, accompanied by the crown's piecemeal and vacillatory elaboration and implementation of these regalian principles and regulations, thus arguably helped ensure that potentially threatening novelties in royal policy ultimately did little to challenge de facto or de jure seigniorial jurisdiction during this period.

In Catalonia, the crown made no concerted effort to systematize its engagement with either royal or seigniorial Jewish communities. In fact, the monarchy would not attempt to standardize the conditions established by these numerous ad hoc privileges and pacts until 1280. In a blanket privilege directed at all of the Jewish aljamas throughout Catalonia, Pere II offered the right to elect a certain number of "leading men" as communal authorities and representatives.[97] This was a major step forward in Jewish communal organization, to say nothing of the general message it broadcast about the crown's relationship with all Jews. It furthered specific royal administrative objectives while responding to the Jews' perceived desire for additional explicit rights of self-governance. Klein was certainly correct to assert that the functions of these offices paralleled the genesis, with royal sponsorship, of a system of peace men (*paers*) and later *consellers* in

Barcelona and other communities. In drawing attention to these similarities, she hypothesized that even though these early charters do not assign the adelantats any financial responsibilities, these Jewish officers may have fulfilled predominantly fiscal functions, similar to those of the *paers*. These duties would have served the interests of the kings as they increasingly satisfied their fiscal needs with taxation rather than demesne exploitation. Later documentation illustrates that these Jewish communal officers would play a vital role in the collection of royal taxes from groups of aljamas known as *collectas*.[98]

This tendency contrasts sharply with what scholars have observed in other kingdoms where monarchies ostensibly exercised greater authority. In northern Castile, for example, Alfonso VII and Alfonso X were able to intervene and establish new fueros in Sahagún that limited the jurisdiction over resident Jews exercised by the local abbot and that adjusted, by fiat, the aljama's customary prerogatives. According to Maya Soifer Irish, Alfonso X's new fuero's "unmistakable intent was to give the Jews of Sahagún a model of governance found in the royal aljamas of Northern Castile," including the right to elect *adelantados* and judge Jewish cases.[99]

Working with the Status Quo

What we have been able to observe thus far in this chapter is a range of circumstantial evidence regarding the evolution of the monarchy's Jewish policy. These efforts consisted of the crown enunciating its capacity to dictate conditions for Jews as members of the general populace and making targeted attempts to manage specific Jewish populations already under royal control. The lack of evidence of direct engagement by the monarchy during these seminal years of its institutional and ideological development suggests that Jaume was not yet seeking to apply this evolving royal Jewish policy to encroach upon the exercise of authority within dislocated jurisdictions. He was committed to elaborating and expressing the principles of royal authority via the provisions promulgated in his general court and perhaps leading by example with the administration of his personal domains, yet remained exceedingly cautious about arbitrarily implementing them within seigniorial domains. This reticence would only begin to disappear toward the final years of Jaume's reign, and the effort to systematically apply a pervasive Jewish policy at the expense of seigniorial authority would only intensify under his successors, as we will see in subsequent chapters.

We can see this delicate balance at work within the context of Tortosa in a series of documents dating from the late 1220s, as Jaume continued to elaborate general provisions intended for all subjects. After a three-decade hiatus following his father's initial ruling on the conflict in 1199, the king intervened to render an opinion on the continuing disputes between Tortosa's lords and the citizens' *universitas* (municipal collective) in April 1228. Jaume's decision was sympathetic to the citizens and delivered the message that the lords could not increase their authority at the expense of privileges received from the crown since the time of Tortosa's initial settlement. For example, an attempt by the lords to impose a new levy—the *tasca,* collected on products that Tortosa's residents derived from mountains and pastures in Tortosa's district—struck the king as illegitimate. The free use of these common lands and resources, Jaume noted, had indeed been guaranteed by the original population charter "for over seventy years." He criticized the lords' attempt to force the citizens to trudge up the hill to plead their cases in the seigniorial castle (*çuda*): "That place . . . is neither safe nor suitable . . . because [it] cannot be attended by the citizens without the inconvenience of the litigants and the utmost damage and danger."[100] By contrast, the town *curia* presided over by the vicar and leading men of the town (*probi homines* or *prohoms*) was, in the king's mind, "trustworthy and honest" and well established by time-honored custom.

Assisted by his clerks and advisors, the king also took the opportunity to expound on his unique qualifications for sorting out such disagreements. If we recall, later this same year Jaume would revive the principle that violations of the peace on public roads represented crimes against the royal dignity (*lèse majesté*).[101] In this charter, he foreshadowed such an escalation by asserting that he alone was the "true king" (*verus princeps*), whose revived Peace and Truce claimed to protect all subjects from certain abuses regardless of their jurisdictional circumstances. As a result, the *sentencia* argued, his "office" bore the duty of imposing a correct interpretation of the law. It was his job to make "what is doubtful, clear and certain," and to place "in the light" "that which is obscured in shadows."[102] The unsacred character of Jaume's position arguably increased his reliance on these Roman legal principles and the idea of his contractual obligations to the governed in order to define and justify his primacy as king.[103]

The behavior of Tortosa's lords had thus enabled Jaume to highlight his comparatively just rulership. He could present himself to the residents as overseer, universal judge, and impartial protector in the face of arbitrary seigniorial novelty. Jaume would employ this same strategy of offering a purportedly superior alternative to encourage collaboration by motivated residents in the future. In the 1260s, as we shall see, he would recommend that they appeal their cases to his court in order to escape seigniorial impartiality and benefit from the protections that royal governance alone could provide.[104]

The same day as his verdict, Jaume added further emphasis to this argument in a general privilege to Tortosa's residents. Citing his desire to "restore the renown [*gloriam*] of the city and citizens," he extended his protection over "all male and female inhabitants of Tortosa" and their property "through all places of lordship [*dominacionis*] and our kingdom and those of all of our allies [*amicorum*] in land and sea and whatever [body of] freshwater." The king also promised to restore double the value of any lost property as well as to fine officials and other men three thousand solidi for noncompliance.[105] The implications of the grant, insofar as it affected seigniorial Tortosa, were left unclear, and perhaps deliberately so. Yet, it was notably more than a standard privilege of safe passage (*guidaticum*) in this context. By applying the guarantee to both his personal lordships (where the king certainly did exercise considerable authority) and lands beyond his realms (where his protections hinged on good relations with other rulers), Jaume dismissed any obstacles to his safeguards presented by the mixed jurisdictional situation inherent in "our kingdom."[106] The ruling ideology embodied in this privilege clearly underscored the notion of the *verus princeps* advertised in Jaume's verdict from that same day. Yet in this case, rather than simply wielding the responsibility to clarify matters of governance as a supreme judge, the king insinuated that he was equipped to pledge sweeping protections to the subjects of the Templar-Montcada regime in Tortosa.

Although neither of these documents mentions non-Christians specifically, Jews and Muslims must have been influenced by the mandates by implication. Tortosa's *universitas* could represent the interests of all residents, and its local law would dictate that its court receive all cases involving Jews.[107]

The king had directed his privilege at all of the town's inhabitants, without restriction, thus reaching out to forge a bond with Christians, Jews, and Muslims alike.

Conclusions

These potent enactments from 1228 promoted within Tortosa's local context an image of royal authority encompassing all subjects. As we have seen in this chapter, this image was drawn from the evolving general principles concerning the crown's qualifications and regalian prerogatives emanating from Jaume's administration since his minority, which would continue to develop over the following years. These documents indicate that Jaume aimed to entice local residents to want, or even clamor for, these purported advantages of royal governance. They also seem to show that, by this time, the king had developed plans to apply these general principles and policies specifically to Tortosa, as he did with other dislocated jurisdictions within his realms.

The extant evidence makes it difficult to know to what extent he succeeded with the former ambition. The fact that the citizens' dispute with the lords over their customary prerogatives continued to fester does not stand as proof that they wanted anything more than respectful governance on the part of the Templar-Montcada regime. We cannot conclude that these citizens viewed royal administrative control as preferable. In the next chapter, we will see faint signs that the Jews understood elements of the king's message, albeit without confirmation that they believed the lords were comparatively unequipped to uphold their end of the social contract. Tortosa's Christians and Jews both seemed to recognize the advantage of maintaining the king as a distant, unentitled, interested party while keeping the legal channels to his court open for checking seigniorial authority and ensuring a smooth transition to royal control, if it ever happened.

For the time being, and for a considerable period to come as the 1247 concord makes clear, the king remained logistically or contractually barred from implementing his regalian policies regarding the Jews or other subjects in Tortosa. The royal bailiff authorized by that agreement would have been indistinguishable from any bailiff representing a petty lord, impotent to intervene in the sorts of administrative affairs that would have preoccupied royal officers in lordships under Jaume's direct control. Over the coming years, however, as royal regnal principles and regulatory policies were strengthened by the crown's increase in legitimacy and resources, this official would, for a time, manage to manipulate the clear legal restrictions stipulated in this agreement and exercise some significant executive powers in Tortosa. We will consider this shift in chapter 4, after examining the administrative activity of the seigniorial regime in the next chapter.

3

SEIGNIORIAL ADMINISTRATION AND MICRO-CONVIVENCIA

In chapter 1, we saw how the crown's successive manipulation of the 1182 indirect administration agreement with the Templars had confused its jurisdictional relationship with Tortosa. Guillem de Cervera's reception of ostensibly unconditional possession of the town led to the reinstallation of the Templar Order as Tortosa's chief jurisdictional lord by 1215, with the Montcada family as the primary minority lord. During the years that followed, as Jaume and the regency were preoccupied with stabilizing the monarchy's political situation after Pere's sudden death, the seigniorial regime in Tortosa began to consolidate its authority over Tortosa's inhabitants in earnest.

This chapter builds on what we covered in chapter 1 by examining the dynamics of the lords' management of the Jewish community from this foundational period during Jaume's minority through the remainder of the thirteenth century. We need to assess whether and by what means those emerging royal initiatives about public safety and Jewish coexistence we explored in chapter 2 influenced Tortosa's lords and residents. The monarchy's dearth of local officers with executive authority and relative absence, as well as the lack of written limits on the dominium possessed by the lords, invested the seigniorial regime with substantial authority to shape Tortosa's administrative conditions as it saw fit. Yet, this insulation did not necessarily signify that this local environment was completely unaffected by royal initiatives.

As we shall see, the lords themselves chose to maintain existing or apply new royal policies. Their takeover did not bring about a complete rewriting of the Jews' social contract. The Templars and Montcadas were instead remarkably respectful of many established prerogatives and customary practices. Such conservatism did not preclude policy innovation, however. As Tortosa's Jewish community and larger urban society grew and developed in complexity, the lords created new institutions and regulations. While some changes were clearly made in response to demands by the community in order to maintain the lordship's attractiveness for residents, the lords also introduced policies that served their own interests. These included initiatives that responded to growing competition from the royal administration as well as the continuing efforts of Tortosa's own citizens to develop a municipal regime.

Such policy-making was rarely neat and tidy, however. The community's own internal development and changing relationship with the wider town and society beyond the lordship conditioned what issues were raised and how they were reconciled. The seigniorial regime also had to consider the competing interests of local constituencies as well as manage its own internal disputes. The Templars and Montcada family, as unequal co-lords, often had incompatible objectives regarding the lordship that embroiled them in conflict over its administration. A number of overlooked seigniorial records will provide rare glimpses of the interactions among the Jews, lords, and broader citizenry of the town, that reveal how the local modes of coexistence in Tortosa were shaped internally by this mixture of complex factors and not simply by external royal initiatives. The collaboration and conflict of these different constituencies within Tortosa's urban environment variegated and adapted the lordship's inherited infrastructure and traditional privileges, thus adding further unique influences to the micro-convivencia developing in the town.

Continuity

The charters of settlement and subsequent privileges had profiled the local governmental institutions of Muslim residents in much greater detail than those of the Jewish community. Signs are that Tortosa's Jews thus persisted in a situation of "autonomy by default."[1] So far as we can determine from the extant sources, their officers and communal institutions, if in existence at this point, had never been officially recognized by the crown or its delegates. This situation would continue under seigniorial administration, which, as we will see later, never intervened to authorize or regulate the officials internal to the Jewish community.

The Muslim community presented a different scenario to the seigniorial regime, however, because its communal officials had been authorized and managed by crown administrators before the transition to nonroyal control. The lords apparently committed to maintaining this established tradition of oversight as soon as they assumed authority over the lordship from Guillem de Cervera. In the middle of 1215, the Templars and Ramon de Montcada collectively invested Abobacher Avinahole as *alcaydus* (community leader and magistrate) of the Muslim aljama.[2] Although it chose to mimic royal administrative practices in the investiture, the seigniorial regime signaled its autonomy by making no mention of royal authorization or confirmation. Since the town was now their domain, the lords had an incentive to establish a reputation of fair governance among the residents by respecting expected privileges and practices. They also had reason to be wary of attracting the attention of the monarchy despite the instability it was experiencing at that time. Memories of what had transpired in 1199 must have still been fresh. The Christian citizens of Tortosa had complained to the crown that the seigniorial administrators were constraining the rights of self-governance guaranteed by their charter of settlement, inviting the king to render an opinion that was unfavorable to seigniorial authority.[3] This reconstituted seigniorial regime now possessed greater justification of its autonomy but must not have wanted to encourage further royal intervention, in any case.

This appointment of the alcaydus upheld established administrative practices in multiple respects. When Queen Sancha's bailiff had installed, with Ramon de Montcada's express consent, a previous alcaydus in 1207, the procedure had similarly invoked the consent of the "entire aljama of Muslims of Tortosa."[4] Both of these investitures established that, in accordance with "local custom [*mos*] in Tortosa," the alcaydus, if accused, would be judged "according to the *sunna* and custom of the Muslims" and that any claim would have to be upheld by at least four legitimate Muslim witnesses. Seigniorial respect for the tradition of seeking the consent of the aljama when filling these offices must have facilitated their monopolization by the same elite families. Abobacher was not only the son of the earlier alcaydus appointed by the queen mother's bailiff, but was a previous *zalmedina* (magistrate). The original surrender treaty had defined only the Muslim community's general right to such officers and had not established policies concerning elections. These regulations likely derived from the adaptation of pre-conquest practices by Ramon Berenguer IV, the lords he had invested with lands from the conquest, and community leaders during the initial years of Christian rule.[5]

Another phenomenon enhancing administrative continuity under the seigniorial regime was that the Montcadas had apparently exerted control over at least one local office, as an element of their minority seigniorial rights since the conquest. Again in 1207, when Queen Sancha still controlled the town, Ramon de Montcada alone, without reference to other authorities, had invested this younger Abobacher with this office of zalmedina.[6] Local custom and the involvement of the community had similarly influenced the defined responsibilities and liabilities of this office. Ramon de Montcada had made the appointment with "the consent and will of the Muslim aljama of Tortosa." The charter had also required the "counsel and cognition of the aljama" in order for the officeholder to be found guilty of crimes. The conditions of the investiture had made it clear that the zalmedina was expected to "judge fairly" and not abuse his authority. Local custom furthermore dictated that Abobacher be exempted from participating in the community's taxation for as long as he held the magistracy.[7]

Effective lordship demanded attention to standing agreements and ingrained practices as well as responsiveness to new problems. The seigniorial regime would have been inclined to maintain existing royal policies that were compatible with its objectives first and foremost because they encompassed valuable entitlements to mitigate the lords' inherited obligations. It is therefore not surprising that the Templar archive for Tortosa contains copies of many important royal instruments predating the Order's assumption of jurisdiction, a number of which concerned the Jewish and Muslim communities.[8]

The lords were not simply mini-kings, however, with identical objectives and a carbon-copy administrative logic informing their handling of their Jewish residents. As Tortosa grew in size and complexity, its lords exercised their right to elaborate new policies tailored to the town's environment.

Some of these measures diverged from what the crown was implementing within communities under its direct administration and thereby gradually shaped the town's distinctive micro-convivencia.

Innovation

Although it shared administrative objectives with the crown, the seigniorial regime could afford to be more directly engaged in Tortosa's everyday management. It is true that the Templars and the Montcada family possessed extensive domains scattered throughout the realms and thus, to varying extents, relied on local delegates, bailiffs, and other officers to administer the town. However, the smaller scale of these seigniorial economies, the relative importance of this holding within them, and their manner of organization encouraged more attentive oversight. The heads of this branch of the Montcadas were frequently resident in the town during the first half of the thirteenth century until the family shifted its primary focus to its lordship of Fraga in eastern Aragon.[9] The Templars designated Tortosa as an administrative command post, known as a *comanda*, that was overseen by a fixed operative.[10] Increased oversight did raise the potential for disruptive policing and micromanagement, as Tortosa's citizens had experienced in their conflicts with the regime beginning in 1199. At the same time, however, it had the potential to render the lords more responsive to shifts in local conditions and inclined to make targeted adjustments in the community's regulations that could serve mutual interests.

The earliest evidence of the seigniorial regime's openness to innovating in order to alter the circumstances of the Jewish community dates from 1228, over a decade after its assumption of full authority over the town. According to extant records, until this year neither the monarchy nor the lords had made any official modification of the provisions concerning infrastructure established by the original settlement charter from 1149. In May 1228, the lords licensed a major modification of the living conditions of local Jews by allocating a previously unoccupied, fortified zone for exclusively Jewish settlement.[11] Scholars have long recognized that kings during this period tended to provide Jews with fortified refuges.[12] This evidence confirms that some lords sought to offer similar amenities if they were requested by the community or recommended by the local environment. The exclusion of non-Jewish groups from this zone, however, seemingly broke from standing local policy. As we saw in chapter 1, the charter of security had not explicitly segregated the Jewish community, and the twelfth-century property market appears to have generated mixed Jewish and Christian land ownership and occupancy throughout Remolins.

Yet, in other respects, this license maintained royal policies. Negotiation over a new zone of Jewish settlement apparently prompted the recipients to request language that would guarantee their entitlement to the corpus of customary privileges enjoyed by residents of the original district—the area that would eventually come to be known as the "old" Jewish call.[13] Previously this quarter had often simply been termed the Jewish call or the Jewish *villa*, similar to other towns in the region.[14] The charter did segment the Jewish community by limiting its provisions to a distinct subset of twenty-five families already residing in Tortosa, who were identified in the document by their heads of household. It distinguished clearly between these recipients of the grant and "those Jews residing in the Jewish call." These implicated families would remain entitled to "all the good customs, which those who live in the Jewish call have"—namely, those privileges contained in the monarchy's "charters of acquisition."[15]

The primary characteristic of "good" lordship stressed by the license was protection. In pledging to defend both the Jews' persons and property, "just as if it were our own," the lords even implied that the Jews themselves were seigniorial possessions: "And whoever would attempt to act contrary to this charter, let it be known that he would incur our anger for trespassing on our property."[16] In extending to the Jews' themselves, this protective language went beyond earlier royal expressions of protection, such as Alfons's privilege to Dona and her family from 1185, which we discussed in chapter 1. The nature of our sources, however, makes it impossible to confirm whether this language was intended to emulate statements concerning the Jews emanating from the monarchy. These Jews, in turn, would be obliged to remain faithful subjects to the lords in the present and future. This was a renewal of the standard bond of fidelity between lord and subject that had initially been established in Ramon Berenguer IV's settlement license. The parties may have deemed it necessary to renew the relationship for the new area of residence given the changes in lordship since then.

The charter unfortunately does not provide direct details of the negotiations that must have brought about these privileges. Although demographic growth was also likely a factor, we do not know whether the allotment of sixty houses by Ramon Berenguer IV in his original charter of security had been filled by this point.[17] There are indirect signs that the Jewish community had grown in size, complexity, and wealth since the demographic crises two decades earlier. Tortosa as a whole was experiencing increased economic activity and an accompanying expansion of the arable land in the surrounding countryside, including the zones to the south that had formerly been unstable due to Muslim raiding and banditry.[18] The growth of the town's overall population had led to an expansion of settlement throughout Tortosa's wider district and more aggressive tithe collection by the local diocese.[19] Although Jewish wills do not survive from this period, Christian wills indicate that Tortosa's Christian urban patriciate had accumulated sufficient landed holdings and wealth to support sizeable distributions.[20] These trends must have benefited the Jewish community due to its participation in the local agrarian economy and its concentration in Remolins, which remained the town's most active locus of artisanal production and commerce, with markets, trade depots (*fonduk*), and workshops.[21] The bishop's sense of Tortosa's unrealized potential to expand economically beyond the frontier and thereby generate increased tithe revenues likely helped motivate him to fund Jaume's unsuccessful campaign to conquer Valencia and restore the putative southern limits of his ancient diocese in 1225.[22]

Local Jewish elites at this time were wealthy enough to provide their children with unrivaled educations. The well-known doctor Shem Tov ben Isaac, for example, was born in Tortosa in 1198. After traveling to further his family's business interests in the eastern Mediterranean, he left the town to study with Rabbi Isaac ben Meshullam in Barcelona and later went to Montpellier before establishing himself as a physician in Marseille. During his tenure in Marseille, using language skills and a knowledge of medicine and literature that he must have improved during his extensive travels, he conducted the translation of numerous Arabic scientific treatises into Hebrew, in what appears to have been an effort to give Jews direct access to the best medical information so that they would not have to rely on Gentile doctors.[23] Joseph Shatzmiller speculates that Shem Tov must have had some family who attracted him to Marseille.[24] Another appealing feature of Marseille during

Shem Tov's residency there was certainly that Charles of Anjou, who took control of the town in 1257, awarded the community privileges that recognized local Jews as citizens and sheltered them from harassment by external judicial institutions such as the Inquisition.[25] In 1280, another Jew from Tortosa named Abraham was at work with Simon of Genoa on translating al-Zahrāwī's medicinal treatise into Latin, possibly using Shem Tov's Hebrew translation.[26] In sum, even though we lack direct evidence to prove that the prosperity of Tortosa's Jewish residents as a whole was on the rise when the lords presented this charter, there is considerable circumstantial evidence that local Jews shared in the socioeconomic upswing experienced by the broader town community.

There are signs in the license, however, that these measures were occasioned by more than simply overcrowding in the call. Although it describes the heads of household receiving these new privileges as "now residing in Tortosa," the charter distinguishes between them and "those who will reside and [currently] reside in the Jewish call." It seems unlikely that these twenty-five families had taken up residence in the new zone prior to the issuance of this license, inasmuch as it grants them rights to the *future* occupation and modification of the site. Indeed, they may have been residing elsewhere in the city due to factional conflict or space constraints when the lords issued the charter. Although the grant refers to the Jews still living in the call in awarding these select families similar prerogatives, it conveys the sense that these were distinctly separate communities. The lords did perpetuate this apparent rift with their license, yet also seemed to exhibit concern over its future dysfunction. They urged the Jews to maintain communal relations albeit without detailing precisely how: "And you and those who will reside in the Jewish call . . . let you always be one [community]."[27]

We do not know enough about the composition of Tortosa's Jewish community to determine whether these families represented a traditional or new elite and were singled out in response to communal conflict, similar to what Klein has noticed within Barcelona during this same period.[28] Nevertheless, it does seem clear that they were elites, given their receipt of special protections and an exclusive privileged level of self-determination in this agreement. Identifying elite families within the community is difficult because the charter of settlement did not name any of the initial residents and because no other extant documents through the early thirteenth century identify the members of leading Jewish families (*nesi'im*). It is evident, however, that several of the men listed in this seigniorial charter had prominent backgrounds. Iossa, son of "the deceased *alfaquim* of Mallorca," for instance, may have been an elite newcomer to Tortosa, which might explain why he numbered among this group isolated from the old call. Abrahim Xixó "the Elder" belonged to the illustrious Sephardic ben-Shushan family.[29] The charter's expectation, as we shall see, that these Jews would be able to manage the fortification's defense autonomously suggests that they came from families of means.

The charter's details reveal that these families desired greater security, self-sufficiency and more defined boundaries that would increase the social distance between their community and the growing Christian-ruled society occupying Tortosa's urban sector.[30] Although we do not have evidence of any specific local incidents that may have prompted these concerns, a wide range of scholarship suggests that communities throughout Iberia and greater Europe over the course of the thirteenth century were featuring more structured segregation reinforced by deliberate material and socio-legal boundaries.[31] Historians also now recognize that some factions within ethnoreligious minority groups such as the Jews maintained an interest in raising social boundaries through a range of techniques in order to preserve the cohesiveness and solidarity of their communities.[32] According to Ray, such communal integrity was often a concern primarily for rabbinic scholars, whereas non-rabbinic elites tended to be more preoccupied with accumulating power over the community even if it came at the price of solidarity.[33]

Until this point, the Jewish quarter appears to have lacked restrictions on non-Jewish traffic and property ownership. This new license, by contrast, described a space that was isolated and sealed off from the rest of the town and entirely under Jewish control. It strictly outlawed the construction or ownership of houses and loitering by Christians (as well as, presumably, Muslims). The Jews received the castle known as Banyeres, which appears to have been situated outside the town walls across the Barranc del Cèlio from the seigniorial fortress, or *çuda*, on the site of the future Bastides fortification constructed centuries later.[34] This positioning must have been ideal for its residents; it was a highly defensible site a short distance from the town walls that retained accessibility to the seigniorial castle.

The charter confirms that this proximity was no accident by addressing in considerable detail the relationship between the Jews' fortified residence and the çuda. It permitted the Jews to close their castle's existing opening at the base of its wall facing the river and create a new portal directed at the çuda, presumably by means of a short path crossing the Barranc del Cèlio. The Jews could take refuge under seigniorial guard or facilitate the entry of seigniorial forces into Banyeres, thus improving the regime's ability to fulfill its pledges of protection in times of extraordinary danger. This accessibility to the çuda also enabled these Jews to circumvent the streets of Tortosa's urban core in their movement of agricultural products and other goods to the Jewish community for consumption or processing. Since wine grapes were particularly vulnerable to pollution by Gentiles, it is fitting that the parties drafting the license identified them as one of the commodities that the Jews would want to traffic via the portals of the çuda. The lords would also permit "all other [products] that you [i.e., the Jews] might want to send."[35]

The charter recognized that the existing fortification would require other modifications to suit the Jews' needs. Its greatest emphasis was on the capacity of these Jews to make Banyeres self-sufficient and subject to their authority alone. In addition to the modification of the portal, these families could adapt the castle's existing fortifications and amenities as they saw fit in order to make it more defensible and suited to their specific socioeconomic needs, ostensibly at their own expense. The licensed alterations included creating new windows and arrow slits in its walls and towers and internal dwellings, opening drainage canals for sewage, and accessing the freshwater source at the base of the canal (presumably in the Barranc del Cèlio).[36] These features seemed to be designed chiefly to enable the Jewish community to seal off the castle and live there viably for a considerable length of time. Authorization to construct a new synagogue and oven within the confines of Banyeres further enhanced the enclosure's defensibility as well as its independence from the existing (old) call. The fact that these provisions stood to increase the self-sufficiency of the new residence must have heightened the lords' concern that these families and the Jews residing within the town walls make an effort to interact as a single community.

In keeping with this concept of absolute segregation, the Jews would exercise exclusive authority over Banyeres. The license strictly forbade the lords from stationing any man in the castle; even potentially vital seigniorial officers, such as a gate guard (*portarium*) to facilitate a castle's defense, were barred from the enclosure unless expressly invited by the Jews. The terms were that the beneficiaries of the grant would retain full control of the castle at all times. They would hold the key to the castle's main door, enabling them to lock or unlock the castle at their discretion, and would not be required to render possession of Banyeres to the lords or any other party under any condition. Ramon de Montcada (or his delegate) would have a duplicate key, but he pledged to use it in the best interests of this Jewish community and by no means to "cause violence." Even though the lords asserted their capacity as the primary jurisdictional authorities to guarantee the safety of these Jews, the extent of the autonomy requested by this community limited the possible extent of direct seigniorial protection.

In conceding the right to construct a new synagogue, the lords were prioritizing local administrative concerns over compliance with existing papal policy. In recent years, Innocent III and Honorius III had each pressured prominent monarchs and prelates in western Europe to halt the construction of new synagogues although these mandates did not prevent the construction of untold numbers of new Jewish temples over the thirteenth century with the approval of lay and religious lords alike.[37] It may have been that the relatively low profile of the seigniorial regime and the lack of oversight permitted it to make these sorts of concessions with impunity. In any case, the license stands as a further indicator of the lords' heightened motivation to cater to these Jewish families at this moment in Tortosa's administrative history. The Templars and Montcadas appear to have understood that the new community of Banyeres would only be viable if it contained its own house of worship, and this need thus overrode any general restrictions emanating from distant authorities.

The lords' primary role in negotiating and enacting these changes in the living conditions of the Jewish aljama did not necessarily signify that the king was completely removed from these affairs. In fact, a royal "lieutenant"—none other than Guillem de Cervera, who had ceded his rights to Tortosa to the Templars around a decade earlier—witnessed and subscribed the license. This presence of a royal representative in otherwise seigniorial Tortosa raises many questions. Was it merely symbolic of putative, overarching royal oversight, or did it signify that the king indeed approved of these measures? Are we to understand from this reference that the monarchy had somehow been involved in these changes or at least been kept apprised as the lords had engaged in negotiation with these Jewish families? Given that the charter itself never invokes royal authority in conferring its prerogatives, it seems unlikely that the king or his delegate had a role in drafting it.

Yet, there is reason to believe that Guillem de Cervera's presence was more than simply symbolic. In concluding the transaction, the lords added, "We promise to you that we will have this charter subscribed by the Lord King."[38] The wording of the pledge implies that the request for royal approval was coming from the Jews, who may have been skeptical that the lords had sufficient independent authority to enact these changes. Or perhaps they wanted assurance from the crown that the provisions would be upheld. It is worth remembering that Jaume had delivered the bold statements we analyzed in the previous chapter during his visit to Tortosa just two weeks earlier.[39] He had broadcast his competent protective abilities and administrative prowess not just to the lords, but also to the entire town's populace. It seems likely that the Jews would have been conscious of these recent decrees and that the king's assertions would have led them to realize or recall that he claimed exclusive authority over all Jews and was, in fact, able to exercise this right within other communities. They also must have understood that the lords' privilege aimed to override the original settlement charter from the monarchy, which had limited the number of homes the Jews could build and delimited where they could construct them. As a result, these Jews may have deemed it prudent to secure royal approval in order to ensure the legal validity of this seigniorial license as well as protect their investment in this fortification in the event of jurisdictional changes in the future. The lords' concluding commitment thus seems to illustrate how pressure to conform to elements of the monarchy's emergent vision of its special relationship with its Jewish subjects could emanate from the Jews themselves, who remained attuned to the initial guidelines for the community's growth and development established by the crown.

Aside from this concluding statement, the agreement was exclusively seigniorial, with no further references to the king or his officials. Instead, the lords played the part of the king by mimicking a clause standard in royal mandates obligating the compliance of their officials ("our bailiffs, vicars, zalmedinas, and all other men") and pledging protection on their authority alone: "We receive you, aforementioned Jews, under our oversight and special protection and finest security." Like royal enactments, the charter first extended this protection to the lands under their direct control: "through all of the places of our lordship and those of our allies."⁴⁰ Yet, the lords also implied that they were guaranteeing more sweeping territorial safety to these Jews, again without stipulating the precise mechanism of enforcement. The language of the charter—especially the lords' appropriation of a variant of the royal privilege of safe passage (*guidaticum*)—is indeed comparable to what the king tended to offer in contemporaneous charters of security or enfranchisement. The general privilege Jaume had issued to Tortosa's citizens two weeks earlier, for instance, had declared, "Let you be safe and secure and protected [*guidati*], in [your] houses or outside of [your] houses, in the town or outside the town, on the road or off the road, in fresh or saltwater."⁴¹ In addition, the lords' threats against anyone who sought to violate these guarantees borrowed from existing formulas of royal anger commonly employed in contemporaneous royal decrees.⁴²

In couching its licenses as a reward for the faithfulness and service of the Jews and their ancestors to the lords, the charter constituted an informal contract for a continued special relationship in the future.⁴³ The document thus shares ground with other baronial provisions from this period. In 1238, for instance, Count Ponç Hug III of Empúries granted the Jews of his own independent domains a privilege in which he similarly collaborated with the Jewish aljama to redesign its material autonomy. Along with awarding customs and privileges, the count's act established a relationship of protection and service between lord and Jewish subject.⁴⁴ Without any prior royal privileges or languishing royal jurisdictional ties afflicting the Jewish communities of the county of Empúries, the recipients of the privilege had little incentive to request confirmation by the king, and no such request appears in the document.

Competitive Initiatives

It is worth reflecting further on the king's intervention in the lordship's affairs two weeks before the appearance of this license for the new call in Banyeres. Jaume had offered sweeping exemptions throughout his domains to Tortosa's inhabitants. Such royal intervention, he implied in his enactments, was necessary to restore the town's proper prosperity, which it had enjoyed before the arrival of the seigniorial regime.⁴⁵ The nostalgia evoked by the privilege, as we have noted, seems to have been calculated to reinforce the connotation of the king's verdict issued that same day concerning allegedly abusive and illegitimate policies perpetrated by the lords: that under isolated seigniorial rule and without the munificence and judiciousness only the king was prepared to offer, the best days of Tortosa's people were behind them.[46] How might the seigniorial regime's willingness to reformulate the Jewish quarter have been conditioned by these political messages and exemptions so recently distributed by the king?

Offering a charter of security to the Jewish community in the immediate aftermath of this episode would have enabled the lords to undermine this characterization by the king obliquely, without a direct challenge or criticism. Their enactment advanced a competing narrative about how their administrative policies would augment the future security and prosperity of this economically vital subset of the urban community that was being targeted by emergent regalian policies. Far from compromising the lords' autonomy, accommodating a royal lieutenant to witness, subscribe, and then deliver the privilege for confirmation by the king arguably served to promote seigniorial administrative independence. By so doing, the lords publicly presented the king with hard evidence of the validity and constructiveness of the very sort of seigniorial policy-making that he had sought to cast in doubt with his recent ruling and privilege. If he opted to refuse the confirmation, Jaume would risk assisting the lords' narrative by impeding reforms that were seen as essential by certain prominent Jews in the community.

Such developments sent the king the message that successful engagement with dislocated communities such as Tortosa needed to be handled strategically, ideally in collaboration with nonroyal authorities or empowered local constituencies. At this point in the monarchy's growth, ill-considered attempts to impress the regalian governmental agenda on rival lords and their tenants stood a good chance of being fruitless or even counterproductive. Valuable opportunities for intervention therefore must have been rare because they hinged chiefly on locals' willingness to involve the crown. Indeed, like this apparent request for confirmation from the Jews, Jaume's role in judging the case between the lords and universitas had only materialized because he had been invited, possibly as a last resort. Indeed, because the parties chose to use ecclesiastical rather than royal mediators to handle the dispute in the future, the crown would have no further involvement.[47]

The belief that the monarchy exercised its claimed exclusive authority over Jews has encouraged scholars to conclude that the crown alone, but possibly in collaboration with its Jewish subjects, determined the nature and pace of its regulations. Here, by contrast, we have witnessed that the crown sought to oversee and even meddle in the administrative affairs of certain autonomous lords. Furthermore, the king was consciously competing with such lords for Jewish residents, who must have been cognizant of the different privileges and amenities offered by distinct jurisdictions. The existence of this competitive market for Jewish residents raises the possibility that the monarchy might have crafted its policies partly in response to seigniorial innovations. Accordingly, the reception of these privileges by Tortosa's Jews—ostensibly the earliest such seigniorial privileges to survive from the Crown of Aragon—could have inspired the king to compete by hastening his elaboration of a concrete Jewish policy for the localities under his administrative control.

We have no evidence of a direct link between these policy enactments, but their timing makes it possible that the lords' privilege stimulated a response from the crown. As we saw in chapter 2, the monarchy granted its first known privilege designing Jewish communal autonomy to Calatayud in Lower Aragon in 1229, just short of a year following the lords' charter modifying the Jews' living conditions in Tortosa.[48] Although Calatayud had long stood under direct royal authority, the monarchy had previously devoted no attention to defining its Jews' rights to self-governance. Rather, Pere's administration had prioritized its own fiscal control at the direct expense of Jewish self-determination. After awarding tithes from Calatayud's Jews and Muslims to the bishop of Tarazona around 1201, Pere had given his mother rights to the persons, property, and incomes of a prominent Jewish family there just months before her death in 1208.[49] In this donation, the king had explicitly undercut the default powers of the aljama by barring its members from speaking out against or otherwise obstructing his measures to reallocate the family. The enactment had removed these family members from the financial and judicial jurisdiction of the community and designated their resources for the use of the queen mother.[50] The aljama was even restricted from imposing religious censure on the family if it would disrupt Sancha's rights. Based on Jaume's license of 1229, his interaction with the community sought to design and authorize its autonomy rather than undercut it to serve ephemeral fiscal or political objectives. In the future, Jaume would generally avoid violating any aljama's right to excommunicate members in accordance with Jewish law, even if it meant reducing the protection of his Jewish officers.[51]

If the king were prompted to move forward with the privilege for Calatayud by the unprecedented initiatives made by Tortosa's lords the previous year, he would have been responding to their decision to offer the license rather than to its content. The prerogatives and competencies he conferred on Calatayud's community were completely distinct. In place of the seigniorial regime's almost exclusive focus on the material conditions of its Jews, the king's privilege to Calatayud addressed the community's right to elect representatives (*adelantats*) invested with judicial and executive powers over internal affairs.

Calatayud's Jews may have had their own local reasons for desiring recognized communal offices reminiscent of those possessed by the local town council (*concejo*) more than, for instance, the changes to the conditions of the Jewish quarter enacted in Tortosa or other conceivable prerogatives. And news of Calatayud's privilege must have led other communities to seek out similar entitlements. The sizeable aljama of Barcelona, for instance, certainly must have known of the license when it negotiated a similar arrangement with the king in 1241.[52] Many other communities under royal control, however, do not appear to have sought, and were not offered, identical privileges. They only came to receive licenses for similar institutions with the crown's later sophistication of its Jewish policy as it inched toward uniform regulations for its Jewish communities.[53] The sporadic nature of these grants suggests that both Jewish agency and the crown's receptiveness to local considerations played a role. The monarchy does not seem to have been following a blueprint for Jewish communal standardization during these early years.

Enactments such as Calatayud's privilege appear as important milestones in retrospect because they remained integral to local customary law and had a profound influence on the broader pattern affecting neighboring communities.[54] Yet, they are not clearly linked to the crown's evolving of a systemic administrative policy for the Jewish communities throughout the realms. The standardization of Jewish communal autonomy and fiscal administration of Jews on royal domains was a long-term, gradually elaborated, and still incomplete product of Jaume's reign that would be picked up and further refined by his successors.

Tracking Changes to the Calls

For reasons that remain unclear, the installation licensed by the 1228 charter was apparently never carried out. Scholars have yet to conduct archaeological investigations of the Bastides site to determine whether any high medieval remains support the existence of a castle fitting Banyeres's description in the charter. No subsequent textual sources, however, appear to refer to Banyeres. Future modifications to the call and administrative activity, furthermore, do not seem to reflect any of the alterations stipulated by the license.

Textual and archaeological evidence instead suggests that Jewish desire or seigniorial support for the division of the community into two isolated, noncontiguous areas had waned by the time of the next verifiable modification, within several decades of the issue of this document. The complicated logistics and considerable expense of maintaining a separate community in Banyeres may also have dissuaded the parties from acting on the privilege. The lords and Jews instead expanded the existing call into the zone across from Remolins's main artery (the Carrer Major de Remolins) to where the Andalusi easternmost and northernmost town walls appear to have sat.[55] Reconstructing the precise characteristics and timing of this alteration is difficult due to deficiencies in the extant documentation, but an abundance of later evidence does demonstrate that it was carried out. Already by 1269, the rental of a house in the "lower Jewish call" (*calle iudaico inferiori*) recognized the existence of a separate district.[56] The fact that Tortosa's customary laws, which were compiled in the 1260s, referred to the call as a single walled entity could indicate that the expansion was a recent development.[57]

Although adjacent, these zones nevertheless existed as distinct districts. The new territory eventually would be referred to as the "new" Jewish quarter (*call nou*).[58] Only by the fourteenth century can we confirm that the calls were walled separately and featured portals communicating them with the rest of the enclosed town.[59] However, the old and new calls must have been separate spaces featuring some of this defensive infrastructure from their inception since the main street of Remolins had always run between them. One of the egresses, identified as the "upper door of the call," had been positioned to face the Porta (Gate) del Ferre in the town walls, which opened onto the Jewish cemetery. Trial records from the 1320s make it clear, however, that this gate was not exclusively for Jewish use. Like the Porta de Vimpeçol, positioned along the Carrer Major de Remolins, the Porta del Ferre was a passage "through which all the people go," suggesting that the calls retained a high degree of openness to the surrounding community despite being enclosed.[60] Similar doors providing access to the Carrer Major de Remolins and the major marketplace zone (Plaça del Assoç) are clearly demarcated in later sources.[61] These portals fit into the basic orientation of the old and new calls that would persist, with only minor adjustments, throughout the medieval period.[62]

The decision to expand the call eastward across Remolins's main street must have been constrained by existing infrastructure. By the second half of the thirteenth century, the old call was hemmed in by the *morería* to the south, the river to the west, and the town walls to the north. Yet, there may have been other advantages to this method of expansion. Positioning the call alongside the northern and western walls over an existing sector of the town could have reduced the need to fabricate new defensive infrastructure. As with the reuse of Banyeres, the Jews would have been obliged to adapt existing dwellings as well as fabricate new ones. The location also increased the community's proximity to the çuda. The Porta del Ferre, if in existence at this point, would have provided access to the çuda similar to what had been envisioned for Banyeres, thus permitting the Jews to receive seigniorial aid in times of need as well as to circumvent the main arteries of the town when transporting vulnerable goods.

The division created by the Carrer Major de Remolins also could have suited the interests of any Jewish families still desiring separation from the old call. The synagogue that certain Jews were seeking to build in 1262 must have been intended for the new call and likely represented an attempt to outfit the new quarter with a degree of internal autonomy similar to what had been planned for Banyeres. Given the dearth of archaeological remains, the location of the existing synagogue remains tentative. The most sophisticated research to date, by Albert Curto, has suggested that it sat along the Carrer Jerusalem near the southern boundary of the old call.[63] The new temple's primary backer, Astruc Xixó, a wealthy resident and creditor to the crown who would soon serve as royal bailiff, was probably related to Abrahim Xixó "the Elder" identified in the 1228 charter. Aspects of the division within the Jewish community mentioned in the Banyeres license may then have persisted into the next generation and similarly motivated the creation of this new call.

In this case, however, for reasons that have not come to light, the lords reversed their position from 1228 and opposed this second synagogue.[64] This decision was in keeping with papal policy and, in turn, paralleled contemporaneous royal efforts to limit the expansion or proliferation of Jewish religious space.[65] Yet, the lords may also have intended to promote the communal cohesion they had encouraged in the earlier license. According to the 1228 plans, the concession of a new synagogue would have been essential to the defensive objectives of the community's enclosure at Banyeres. This new scenario, by contrast, permitted expansion without absolute separation. The two calls could be mutually enclosed yet still permit collaboration as a single community. The calls shared their oven, synagogue, and other internal facilities, as well as common urban amenities such as the meat market in the Plaça del Assoç.[66] This relationship between the two spaces established by the lords would persist until long after the seigniorial period. The community never succeeded in building another synagogue; a record from the year after the late fifteenth-century expulsion of the Jews indicates that the municipality wanted to sell the town's lone synagogue in order to repay a debt.[67] Such codependency appears to have encouraged cooperation among the different factions within the calls. Mid-fourteenth-century records, for instance, indicate that the entire aljama would hold special meetings concerning communal issues in the synagogue.[68]

This dispute over the proposed temple in 1262 is also useful for illustrating how the complex mix of factors responsible for determining local modes of coexistence were not always under the complete, uncontested control of the seigniorial regime. Astruc Xixó managed to challenge the lords' ruling through third-party mediators. An ad hoc judicial panel composed of a petty noble (*miles*) and a cleric heard his case and ultimately ruled that the Jew did indeed have the right to construct a new synagogue on a parcel of land he owned. The Templars, however, were incensed by this intrusion into their administration and appointed a procurator to challenge the validity of the panel's ruling. The judges backpedaled and eventually sided with the lords.[69] Preexisting rivalries between the seigniorial regime and the constituencies represented by the noble and cleric, patronage relationships with the plaintiff, or a wish to encourage the development of the Jewish community and steer local regulations in this direction could have influenced the panel's decision to intervene and overturn the lords' restriction.

Seigniorial and Royal Policy-Making

If we dismiss the unlikely possibility of the loss of a subsequent charter, it appears that Tortosa's lords never saw fit to expand or update their Jews' package of privileges. Instead, they left the community in a state of "autonomy by default." This status would persist until the monarchy took control of the lordship and imposed its then standardized set of prerogatives licensing limited self-governance by Jewish communities in Catalonia under royal jurisdiction.

There are many conceivable causes for this situation. One possibility is that the lords themselves were disinclined to authorize such communal institutions. Indeed, the difficulties the seigniorial regime was still experiencing with the local universitas easily could have dissuaded it from facilitating the creation of a parallel official representative body within the Jewish community. The lords may have wanted to avoid the formal creation of officers whom the monarchy could then seek to utilize to gain administrative influence over the community and access its resources. It is also possible that the Jewish community was content to live without recognized officers. The Jews may not have seen the utility of emulating the institutions of communities under royal administration especially since, as we shall see, there may have been certain tax advantages to remaining a seigniorial aljama. Furthermore, the continued informality of communal institutions may have served to shelter the aljama from intervention by either the lords or the universitas. In any case, the lords and Jews seem to have been mounting at least passive resistance to the licensing of Jewish communal officials in contravention of a growing royal practice of authorizing and regulating Jewish governance.

The monarchy was the only party noticeably seeking to disrupt this policy stasis in Tortosa. It faced an uphill battle. General legislation promulgated by the king or at the Corts, as we witnessed in chapter 2, had little bearing on nonroyal jurisdictions without seigniorial compliance. And despite assertions in these forums of the crown's ability to regulate and protect the general Jewish population, the king never made any known direct attempt during the early decades of his reign to intrude on seigniorial administrative rights by offering privileges to Jewish communities that were not already under royal control. Yet, the crown's apparent impotence did not preclude indirect intervention.

On at least one occasion during these years, the king seems to have tried to publicize among Tortosa's Jews and lords a depiction of Jewish self-governance and the role it ought to play in the fiscal obligations owed to the monarchy. In 1258, he used a visit to Tortosa to confer prominently on other Jewish communities in Catalonia the prerogatives of self-governance that Tortosa's Jews still did not officially possess. He gave the *collecta* of Girona and Besalú the right to elect five Jews who would exercise authority over their aljamas. Rather than reiterating the judicial and executive faculties customarily awarded to elected adelantats in previous royal privileges, the charter focused exclusively on the role of these officials in fulfilling the *collecta*'s fiscal responsibilities. Their authority, first and foremost, was directed at compelling community members to contribute to the taxation and other payments (*peytas* and *questias, expensas* and *messiones*) owed "communally" to the king, in accordance with the proportions determined by the *secretarii* of the *collecta*. Residents who wished to lodge complaints concerning their assigned share would have their petitions heard by these elected officials in proceedings governed by Jewish law. The king explicitly barred his resident officials (the vicar, bailiff, and justice of Girona and Besalú) from intervening in these proceedings in any way.[70] This structuring illustrates how the crown was linking "autonomy by design" to its growing financial impositions. Engaging in the primary business of implementing a more rigid and uniform fiscal system for Jews on the king's own domains in this fashion thus served to broadcast to nonroyal authorities and subjects the expectations and workings of the "normative" conditions that upheld the monarchy's regalian prerogatives.

Given the nature of these objectives and the enactment's timing, it seems unlikely that the king's issue of this charter at Tortosa, of all places, was purely coincidental. His visitations to Tortosa, as we saw in the previous chapter, were rare and had usually featured calculated acts tailored to communicate with the lords or local populace, ostensibly in the service of ulterior motives. Although the itinerant royal court often did conduct administrative business remotely, earlier Jewish privileges of this sort had each been awarded during visitations to the affected local communities: Calatayud (1229) and Barcelona (1241), for example. As far as we know, there was nothing pressing or time-sensitive about Girona's and Besalú's privilege. Furthermore, dictating these highly localized terms in a removed setting such as Tortosa was arguably counterproductive and certainly not conducive to their rapid implementation within the distant *collecta*. Instead, the chosen venue of Tortosa is most intelligible if it was selected to advance the crown's desired normative institutional framework in support of its anticipated fiscal relationship with the entire Jewish populace.

If Jaume's promulgation of the law had this secondary intended purpose, he must have expected it to influence the lords and Jews in distinct ways. He could have wanted to encourage seigniorial emulation of his policies in order to standardize conditions for all Jews in the expectation that this mirroring within nonroyal jurisdictions would later facilitate centralization under the crown. At the same time, he could have aimed to sow the seeds of discontentment among the Jews in the town in order to destabilize the seigniorial regime and perhaps even stimulate some Jewish emigration to royal domains. Another possibility is that Jaume did not intend for the legislation to be enticing for either constituency but instead crafted it as a display of royal power, administrative competency, and institutional precociousness. It could have served as an indication of the normative fiscal and jurisdictional ordering that would inevitably be imposed on dislocated jurisdictions such as Tortosa.

Other business conducted by the king on this visit could have been meant to add to this message about the benefits (and costs) of royal protection and the potential for Jews in Tortosa to profit from it. Jaume mandated the continued protection of Jewish creditors (and accordingly royal revenues) in Girona and Besalú by authorizing his local officials there to seize both real estate and moveable property to repay delinquent loans.[71] At the same time, as a defiant display of his claimed ability to circumvent the seigniorial regime's jurisdiction, the king granted potent and valuable protections to individual Jews in Tortosa that were to be used beyond the town's limits. He awarded Jafias Avinzabarra, "Jew of Tortosa," a license of safe passage (*guidatge*), violation of which was punishable by a five-hundred-morabetin fine.

He also ordered all royal officials to assist Jafias by "compelling and detaining all people owing [him] debts . . . knights and clerics as well as anyone else," and seizing their property if necessary.[72] Jafias had helped prompt this patronage by loaning the king one thousand solidi that were still outstanding when these privileges were issued.[73] Jaume also licensed and safeguarded slave-trading operations by another Tortosan Jew, Abrahim Albarine, who was trafficking Muslims captured along the frontiers of Castile to North Africa, via the port of Dénia in southern Valencia. In return, the king would receive a payment in silver for each slave transported.[74] Jaume's ability to offer realm-wide and overseas protections, which Tortosa's lords were less equipped to provide, thus enabled him to lay claim to, and benefit financially from, certain sectors of the town's burgeoning trading economy.

Tortosa was just one independent lordship of many in the realms, each with its own unique relationship with royal administrative activity during these formative years. Other autonomous lords notably responded in different ways to emergent royal policies as they managed their own Jewish residents. The nature of these reactions tended to reflect these lords' distinctive positions of authority. In contrast to the concerted indifference to royal initiatives and overtures manifested by Tortosa's seigniorial regime, for example, the counts of Empúries explicitly borrowed from the royal privileges received by neighboring Jewish communities. As a result, the interrelation of royal and baronial policy-making dynamics is somewhat easier to deduce for Empúries than for Tortosa. Count Ponç Hug III's privilege of 1238, mentioned earlier, cited the general privileges awarded by Ramon Berenguer IV and his successors as well as the specific prerogatives obtained by the Jews of Barcelona, Girona, and Besalú—locales that had the potential to drain Jewish residents from the count's lands. As Bensch has suggested, such emulation served to advertise boldly the count's autonomy and status as an equal to the House of Barcelona.[75] The fact that none of these competitor Jewish aljamas had yet received royal licenses to elect adelantats may explain why this feature was also absent from this count's privileges.

On the other hand, Ponç Hug and his successors did not subsequently respond to these new royal initiatives by awarding the Jewish community similar rights of self-governance. The motives of these counts to resist copying this trend in policy-making after openly emulating earlier royal initiatives remain enigmatic. The calculus of the counts of Empúries may have been that unless the leading men of its aljama made an appeal for change, these Jews had enough of the privileges enjoyed by the other communities under royal administration to be disinclined to relocate. The lack of licensed officials also reduced the risk that the community would organize against the interests of the count or respond in an officially coordinated fashion to overtures from the monarchy.

The increasing pressure felt by these rulers to submit to royal authority thus could have motivated a shift in strategy, away from emulation and toward differentiation. Or, perhaps similar to what we have hypothesized for Tortosa, the counts believed that implementing Jewish communal structures that were increasingly being utilized by the king to extract revenues would only serve to entice the monarchy to attempt further encroachment into institutionally compatible administrative spaces.

Developments in Seigniorial Administration

Although we possess chiefly circumstantial evidence about royal and local attempts to challenge seigniorial authority over the Jews, we do know a great deal from direct evidence about disagreements between the co-lords over the administration of non-Christians within Tortosa. Given that the royal Jewish policy fluctuated as it evolved under different monarchs with distinct objectives and changing religious, political, and financial pressures, it is not surprising to learn that the lords' administrative handling of Tortosa's aljama was also variable. Tortosa's local dynamics of coexistence, its micro-convivencia, responded to disagreements among the lords themselves and to the town's changing societal context, competitive local authorities and constituencies, and shifts in royal policy. Delving into the mechanics of the seigniorial regime and the disputes they occasioned—along with some glimpses of the interaction and influence of these competing constituencies—will further illuminate the factors influencing the lords' administrative policies.

Most of these conflicts originated in disagreement over the nature and implications of the lordship's hierarchy. Most notably, the Templars sought to make the most of their status as dominant lords in order to subjugate the Montcadas as their feudatories. In the early thirteenth century, for instance, when Ramon de Montcada was arbitrating a case between the Hospitallers and the Templars over rights in the city, the Templar Ponç de Menescal reportedly turned to him and said, "Lord Ramon de Montcada, you hold Tortosa for the brothers of the Temple, and therefore I order you, by means of that donation [i.e., Tortosa] which we have over you [i.e., on account of which you are dependent on us], to force the master and brothers of the Hospital to do us justice concerning the aforementioned [claims]." On this occasion, the noble lord did not dispute the charge and promised to comply with Ponç's wishes.[76] The Order's claims reveal that its leaders chose to believe that it had fully inherited the political associations linked to the crown's former executive powers in Tortosa. From this perspective, the Montcada family had received its share of jurisdictional lordship from Ramon Berenguer IV. Its minority, subordinate status established by that transmission now naturally benefited the Templars.

Judicial experts mediating these disputes tended to uphold this Templar rendition of the local hierarchy. In a round of litigation from 1263, it came to light that Ramon de Montcada had received homage from all of the men in Tortosa, apparently similar to what we saw Alfons accept at the start of his reign in chapter 1.[77] The judges here agreed with the Templars that this action had maligned the Order's prerogatives. They barred Ramon from similar behavior in the future without the prior consent of his "greater lord."[78] The Montcadas, for their part, naturally had an interest in challenging the Templars' interpretation in order to secure greater latitude within the lordship. To that end, they opportunistically continued to defy the Order's mandates and unilaterally enacted self-serving policies.

An earlier round of arbitration in 1261 illustrates how these disagreements could affect Tortosa's ethnoreligious minority communities.[79] The appointed judges agreed with the Templars that when Ramon de Montcada's bailiff seized and tried Jews or Muslims without adequate cause, he violated the Order's prerogatives.[80] In his defense, the noble responded that the Templars had not been sufficiently diligent in punishing malefactors in the town, thereby necessitating his intervention. He referred to a recent incident in which a Christian, Jewish, and Muslim trio of thieves had been unjustly released by a Templar brother. Ramon had moved to impose the appropriate penalty. Such unilateral intervention enabled Montcada to emphasize his autonomy and possibly secure a greater share of the judicial fines. As the only member of the regime with forebears who were installed by the town's conqueror and founder, Montcada may also have been challenging the Order's very theory of his subordination. His behavior in these incidents illustrated how he alone within the seigniorial regime was upholding the standards of law and order established by Ramon Berenguer IV and his successors. Accordingly, he was a more legitimate, and thus rightfully autonomous, delegate for dispensing crown authority within the lordship.

These disagreements made the complex arrangement of dividing revenues from Jews and Muslims a source of conflict. In April 1261, an earlier Montcada bailiff had met with the Templar commander to decide how they would share revenues already collected from Tortosa and its district. They itemized receipts from diverse sources. These included the *lleuda* commerce levy collected from local Jews and nonresident Jewish merchants, the arbitrary *questia* levy taken from the Jews, and *calonias* (fines from justice) that derived from the "court of Christians, Jews, and Muslims." They also recorded levies on Muslim prostitutes, the transport of animals, tanneries, dye works, and ovens in the Muslim quarter.[81] The collection of the *questia* by the lords was especially significant because, by this time, jurists were viewing it as a marker of the personal dependence of tenants to their lords. In recognition of this juridical significance, already at the Corts of Tortosa in 1225 the king had sought to bar officers as well as nobles from demanding the *questia* on wheat from anyone residing outside of their jurisdictions or domains.[82] Ramon de Montcada's annual share from all of these sources, as tallied in the charter, amounted to about three thousand solidi. During the mediation later that same year, however, the Templars sought to control what the noble did with his incomes. The Order complained that, as senior lord, it had the right to approve or deny Ramon's reallocation of any part of his quarter share of taxes on merchandise marketed by Jewish merchants. His failure to seek this approval, it alleged, had harmed its rights of lordship. Montcada's bailiff, the Order claimed, had also collected levies such as the *lleuda* without the collaboration or consent of the Templar's bailiff. The judges ruled that the noble's bailiff could only collect up to ten solidi of the *lleuda* alone, with larger amounts requiring the involvement of the Order's officer.[83]

Around 1265, the Templars drafted two memorials that chiefly documented continuing disputes with the Montcada family over jurisdiction and the management of officials.[84] In both records, the Templars claimed that the Montcada lord was not adhering to the ruling from 1261. For instance, he was continuing to dispense justice illegitimately, thus damaging the Order's prerogatives. His bailiff, furthermore, was still collecting the *lleuda* alone, above and beyond the stipulated maximum. The memorials are also rich in details concerning the administration of Jews and Muslims. We learn, for instance, that the lords were expected to split the fines from justice from non-Christians. Following the subtraction of the Templars' fifth—their original post-conquest share conceded by Ramon Berenguer IV—the Order was supposed to receive two-thirds and Montcada the remainder. The noble, however, allegedly contested the deduction of the Order's one-fifth share before the split.

The Montcada family's hereditary rights over local offices also exacerbated tensions with the Templars. When the commander ordered the zalmedina, who was "responsible for making the arrests [*forcias*] and detentions [*districtas*] of Muslims," to seize a Muslim man accused of beating his wife, Montcada's bailiff reportedly interfered. As recounted by the Templars, the bailiff, Ramon de Guardia, deliberately publicized the seigniorial power struggle to foment dissension among the town's Muslim officials. He instructed the zalmedina "in the presence of the commander, alcaydus, and many others" that "he should do nothing for the commander." Turning to the Templar brother, Ramon de Guardia added, threateningly, that the Order would not find anyone "who would dare to go there for the Temple," presumably referring to the *morería*. In exposing this alleged usurpation of his lord's prerogatives of authority, Ramon de Guardia dramatically disputed the chain of command before the Templar commander and the Muslim officials and questioned the senior lord's ability to administer the lordship in a legitimate fashion. Elsewhere the record states more clearly that Ramon de Montcada exercised authority over the zalmedina and, as a result, claimed an increased share of fines from justice dispensed by the official.[85] This situation had led the Order to seek to limit the kinds of cases heard by the zalmedina, thus reducing the incomes receivable by the Montcadas. For example, the Templars claimed that the zalmedina should not handle cases concerning adultery and extravagant spending (*luxuria*), both of which were punishable under Islamic law (*segons çuna de sarrayns*).[86]

In one extended treatment in the second memorial, the Templars ordered Ramon de Guardia to arrest a certain Jew, Azac Albaney, who was accused of slandering another local Jew named Mosse Avincara. When the bailiff placed Azac in jail, he provoked one of Azac's Christian patrons, an otherwise unknown local potentate called Dona Margalida. Perhaps Azac had served her as a creditor, performed administrative duties, or been a faithful tenant to earn this support. Margalida's intervention was effective, to a degree. Although she had sufficient influence to prompt the Templar commander to send Ramon de Guardia with the town's vicar to meet with her, Margalida failed to attain the Jew's release. Her advocacy could not reverse the case's outcome but may have ameliorated Azac's treatment. She demanded that he be well cared for while incarcerated and threatened the commander that if he "did anything to the said Jew, never in Spain had such great vengeance been undertaken as what she would do for [Azac]."[87] While Tortosa's jurisdictional independence may have temporarily sheltered the Templars from royal micromanagement, it did not isolate them from the local advocates of influential Jews who had the incentives, presence, and means to apply considerable pressure.[88]

On another occasion, Azac escalated this feud by attacking and wounding Mosse. This time, Margalida did not intervene, but Azac nevertheless caught a lucky break. The incident provoked conflict between the lords, who disagreed on how to dispense justice. Ramon de Guardia again took charge, not only arresting Azac, but also judging his case again without authorization from the Templars. The Templar commander intended to put the officer and his lord in their places following this most recent act of insubordination. He protested that the ruling had offended the rights of the Order and therefore had to be nullified. In making this demand, he cited the following principle: "It is in the customs of Barcelona that whoever stabs a Jew be punished according to the judgment of the count of Barcelona; and that right and lordship [*ius et dominium*] that the count had in Tortosa the Temple has. And if Ramon [de Montcada] without the will of the Templars is able to make [this judgment] then the Temple loses this aforementioned lordship and [Ramon] has that lordship [instead]." According to the memorial, "Ramon agreed that the Temple ought to have [this lordship] by law [*de iure*]."[89]

The commander's rationale, notably recorded in a source generated by the Order, provides a rare and illuminating glimpse into these lords' conception of their seigniorial authority over Tortosa. Far from rejecting the principle of royal jurisdiction over Jews, the Templars recognized it insofar as it served to legitimize their authority as the superior lords. By "customs," the

Templars must have been referring to the *Usatges de Barcelona*.[90] As we saw in chapter 1, this code did indeed stipulate that anyone injuring a Jew would be subject to punishment at the "will of the overlord [*postat*]."[91] Within the context of the *Usatges*, it must have been clear to all that *postat* referred to the *potestas* of the prince. Yet, the vague nature of this reference apparently made it possible for other lords to appropriate the *Usatges* to justify and qualify their own authority.

Nevertheless, the ambiguity of this law does not fully explain why the Templar commander was motivated to appeal to it to define his authority to administer local Jews. No royal statement about the donation of lordship to the Templars (or Montcadas) had ever relied upon the *Usatges* to define this seigniorial authority or extend it explicitly over Jews and Muslims.[92] In fact, any pronouncement from the monarchy to this effect would have been designed to limit rather than promote seigniorial authority.[93] Following a period of negligible widespread influence during the later twelfth and early thirteenth centuries, this "regalian" code was coming to serve as a foundation for an expanding, Catalonia-wide "national" law by this point in the mid-thirteenth century.[94]

The regional influence of the *Usatges* was growing, due in part to noble collaboration. In spite of the long-intended role of the code in the promotion of royal authority, many lords perceived it as preferable to other bodies of law. Tellingly, in response to pressure from his nobility to restrain the centralizing novelties of Roman law, Jaume ruled in 1243, confirmed at the Corts of Barcelona in 1251, and conceded again in 1276 that the *Usatges*, alongside local custom and common sense, should be utilized in courts throughout the realms in preference to other available codes.[95] The barons did not indicate specific reasons for their preference, but it was likely due to the familiarity and flexibility of the *Usatges*. If the existence of a pervasive national law was becoming increasingly inevitable, this code stood to interfere with their autonomy much less than the Romanized *ius commune*, which was even more supportive of central royal authority and somewhat less susceptible to reinterpretation in favor of seigniorial objectives.[96]

The application of a statute from the regalian *Usatges* within this Templar memorial illustrates how seemingly collaborative behavior by lords did not necessarily serve royal ends. The ambiguity of the *Usatges*, combined with the uncertain transmission of the lordship, empowered the Templars to depict their exercise of jurisdiction over non-Christians in Tortosa as a legally defensible right rather than one seized illegitimately and furtively following the royal withdrawal. From the lords' vantage point, the concept of pervasive crown authority seeking to repair the fragmentation of royal jurisdiction was the questionable novelty.

Thus, appropriating the *Usatges* in this fashion could have been part of a strategy to make seigniorial authority over these local Jews appear more normative. And although using preexisting royal regulations concerning the Jews to define the seigniorial regime's authority had the potential to limit the lords' ability to innovate with new policies, similar choices by the lords to co-opt inherited customs and traditions did not necessarily stand to impair their authority within the lordship. As with the *Usatges*, these ingrained regulations were often vague and prone to manipulation, investing the lords with considerable interpretive license. When disagreements with rival constituencies did emerge, the lords could contest the interpretation and application rather than the outright validity of customary prerogatives and regulations.

Such opportunistic conservatism concerning local customary legal traditions in support of seigniorial objectives appears elsewhere in the second memorial, most notably regarding Jewish involvement in the customary legal dispute between the lords and citizens. In the years since the bishop of Lleida had ruled on these jurisdictional conflicts in 1241, the citizen's *universitas* had continued to utilize the town's evolving customary law within the municipal *curia* without seigniorial authorization. The memorial reports how the Templar commander complained that the Jews were similarly employing "the bad customs which are used by the Christians . . . against the authority [of the Templars]" instead of the customs of the Jews of Barcelona with which they had been settled by Ramon Berenguer IV.[97] In this case, however, the lords split over the issue, with Montcada's bailiff urging the Jews not to respond to the Templar commander's allegations.[98] Unfortunately, the memorial does not indicate the basis for his bailiff's objection. His point could have been that the Jews were not restricted by their original terms of settlement to using only the customary laws of the Jews of Barcelona, or simply that the Templar campaign against these "bad customs" maintained by the citizens was misguided. Montcada had dropped out of the ongoing dispute with the citizens by this point, leaving the Templars to pursue the costly case alone.[99]

The Order's principal objection was likely Jewish support of the universitas's resistance through the use of its court and unofficial customary laws. The mandate that the Jews utilize the customs their ancestors had received from the original charter of settlement upheld administrative continuity, but not for continuity's sake alone or for the benefit of the Jewish community. The Jews' use of a distinct, originally royal body of customary law would segment the citizenry as well as emphasize the aljama's normative subjugation to the royal authority that had subsequently been transmitted to the Templars.

The Jews may have had their own motives for supporting the Christian citizens in this conflict at the risk of antagonizing their lords. In fact, the ongoing campaign by the universitas to uphold its customary privileges and rights of self-governance had both direct and indirect implications for the ethnoreligious minority communities in Tortosa. Since the Jews were not permitted to handle their own legal disputes, the issue of what judicial forums were available to them in the local environment would have been critical for their community. In this respect, before the approval of customary law clarified the line between municipal and seigniorial jurisdiction over Jewish cases, the municipal *curia* could have served as a useful venue for Jews to seek to escape seigniorial jurisdiction within the confines of the lordship.[100] Certain Jews would have had an interest in utilizing the customary laws in the municipal *curia* and avoiding the seigniorial one in the çuda, which had been deemed such an inhospitable venue by the king in 1228. They also would have wished to secure entitlement to the favorable customary prerogatives that had been awarded to the town's general populace. In fact, in its litigation with the Templars over the authorization of the customary laws around this same time in the 1260s, the universitas argued that the Order had illegitimately barred Jewish and Muslim patrons from using the town baths and that these wronged residents had possessed no legal recourse to defend their entitlements.[101] On other occasions, however, the seigniorial court may have been preferable—in cases against the universitas, for example.

In this contentious, largely unregulated period during which Tortosa's general customary laws remained unofficial, the Jews would have benefited from the availability of multiple judicial forums—municipal, seigniorial, and royal—as well as ad hoc judicial panels. It is not surprising that Tortosa's

Jews were so inclined, given widespread evidence that ethnoreligious communities throughout the Crown of Aragon sought to maintain access to different judicial and legal systems.[102]

Local Customary Conditions

The cumulative impact of situational innovation and manipulation of standing custom shaped the development of Tortosa's micro-convivencia. It is important to recognize, however, that this elaboration was rarely unilateral; rather, it was usually the product of contestation. We can observe this process by scrutinizing the revision of Tortosa's customary laws that ultimately resolved this enduring dispute between the lords and the *universitas*. The unofficial customary laws developed by the citizens over the course of the thirteenth century and codified in preparation for formal review by a tribunal of experts in the early 1270s were entitled the *Consuetudines Dertuse civitatis*. The revised version produced by the tribunal in 1279 that was ultimately certified by the seigniorial regime came to be known as the *Costums de Tortosa*.

Both of these codes maintained a delicate balance between facilitating the interaction of non-Christians as community members and enforcing boundaries in accordance with their secondary social status. Jews, for example, had to respect local statutes, utilize Christian-run courts, and contribute to the local taxes paid by other residents.[103] When present in the town court for a trial, Jews and Muslims had to sit at the feet of Christian *prohoms* assembled there.[104] The codes also share numerous restrictions on social interaction, from sumptuary laws and butchery restrictions to punishments for miscegenation with Christian women and protections for Jews desiring baptism.[105] Some of these provisions are similar to those of other legal compilations within the Crown of Aragon, the Peninsula, and wider European society, raising the likelihood of cross-pollination and common sources, such as canonical material, papal mandates, and influential secular laws. While legal scholars have noticed a close relationship (and mutual dependence on Roman legal principles) between the *Costums* and the royal *Furs de València*, for example, they disagree over which code was dependent on the other and how this sharing might have taken place. Study of this relationship and other important inquiries about Tortosa's laws are hampered by a dearth of evidence about the gradual genesis of the *Consuetudines*.[106]

That a distinct customary legal tradition could be susceptible to adaptation by borrowing from other bodies of customary law or responding to Christendom-wide regulations does not signify that these changes were being made casually, without careful consideration of the local contexts. Seemingly minor alterations in otherwise analogous regulations, such as the number of Christian witnesses required for cases with Jewish and Christian litigants or the participation in municipal taxes demanded of non-Christians, may have reflected different local needs and insecurities at play within each locality. Movement toward and away from this overarching trend of standardization in the management of Jewish communities by customary laws does appear to have been conditioned by complex processes of negotiation between numerous local constituencies. And even when the form of the micro-convivencia in Tortosa came to parallel circumstances in other localities, these commonalities did not necessarily have identical causes but instead likely remained locally conditioned. Furthermore, the significance of these regulations for the constituencies involved, as well as for the populace as a whole, could be radically different from one locality to the next, depending on the comprehensive package of statutes and privileges and underlying structural differences in the organization of each community.

The records of the tribunal responsible for revising the unofficial laws provide glimpses of this process of contestation at work with regard to certain principles crucial to Jewish coexistence. The citizenry and lords, for example, maintained different understandings of the status of Jews in the local community. The *Consuetudines* produced by the universitas held that all "citizens and residents, both Jews and Christians," were entitled to enjoy the town's privileges. However, this clause was flatly rejected as illegitimate by the lords and ultimately stricken by the tribunal during the process of revision. Under the *Costums*, Jews and Christians would not have identical prerogatives as residents.[107]

It would be simplistic to conclude that the universitas had developed this position in the *Consuetudines* simply out of generosity or a feeling of communal camaraderie with the Jews that was not shared by the lords. In fact, there are reasons to believe that each side was equally opportunistic and calculating in its attempts to shape local customary law to its respective advantage.[108] For example, Muslims were conspicuously absent from the citizenship clause in the *Consuetudines*, even though they were commonly included in other statutes concerning the Jews elsewhere in the compilation that did not stand to benefit the universitas financially. The motivation for including only the Jews in this case was probably their relative wealth rather than discriminatory sentiments toward Muslims. A similar intention likely led the citizens to seek immunity for Jewish and Christian (but not Muslim) residents from civil or criminal accusation.[109]

The lords seem to have approached the laws with a similar rationale. With regard to statutes lacking major financial repercussions, the seigniorial regime made few objections, and the tribunal had seen fit to maintain their applicability to all residents. In both the *Consuetudines* and the *Costums*, for example, free use of the town's baths was consigned to "all citizens and inhabitants, Muslims, Jews, and Christians."[110] The citizens had an interest in reserving the Jews' financial resources to contribute to their municipal taxes and other shared financial obligations. Jewish exemption from the *questia*, *cena*, and other levies like Christian citizens would reduce dramatically the incomes receivable by the lords. It is also possible that the lords were again modeling their authority on the general example set by the king as well as other barons, who had not yet devoted such prominent attention to administrative prerogatives over Muslims.

Although this particular revision to the citizenship clause supported seigniorial interests, the tribunal seems to have ruled based on its interpretation of earlier privileges and judgments rather than on any preference for the lords' agenda. Its reasoning, ostensibly, was that since the Jews had received their own customary laws when their community was originally licensed, they could not simultaneously benefit from these customary privileges associated with the general population charter.[111] For the tribunal to uphold the inclusion of Jews in this clause, it arguably would have needed to insert language into the *Costums* to explain the mechanics of this reconciliation of distinct bodies of privileges as well as a rationale for the omission of Muslims.

The tribunal was headed by the bishop-elect of Tortosa, but its other members were from Girona and Lleida. The officials therefore likely had the background to understand that their ruling on this clause was consistent with precedents from other urban settings. In the town of Perpignan to the north, for example, jurisdictional circumstances had led the citizens to adopt an opposite stance. Jews were automatically denied "membership in the community of citizens" and all of the privileges that went with it, which were jealously guarded by the Christian townsfolk.[112] In Daileader's view, this competitive animosity between Christian citizens and members of the Jewish aljama in Perpignan had been generated, first and foremost, by the royal privileges awarded exclusively to Jewish residents and intended to reserve control over their financial resources and administration.[113] In Tortosa, by contrast, jurisdictional conflict with the lords encouraged the Christians to seek to insulate the Jews from seigniorial administration as entitled citizens and residents, thereby increasing the financial resources of the municipal regime.

The inability of the crown to standardize the privileges and obligations of Tortosa's Jews as servi regis made possible this unique, ephemeral alliance of Christian and Jewish residents in Tortosa. Shared conflict with the seigniorial regime and the malleability of unofficial, localized customary laws enabled Christians, and presumably Jews, to embrace a different paradigm of corporate communal coexistence in the *Consuetudines*. The revisions that yielded the *Costums* rejected this local reimagining of citizenship and adopted in its place a more commonplace model of segregated ethnoreligious communities with distinct privileges and obligations. In certain respects, the process of revision was simplified by the citizens' awareness of what legal principles were nonnegotiable for the lords. When they edited their *Consuetudines* for the review, for example, the citizens must have known that the lords would refuse to have their own cases with the Jews heard by the municipal court. Accordingly, they included in the *Consuetudines* the regulation that any lawsuit with Jews concerning seigniorial interests would be handled by the lords' court in the çuda, and the *Costums* retained this clause without alteration.[114] This division of judicial procedure was unique to Tortosa and resulted from its history of jurisdictional disputing. In towns throughout the Peninsula under less diligent and attentive royal lordship, by contrast, customary laws could afford to assign ambiguously the handling of all Jewish cases to both "the king and the municipality" without additional stipulation.[115]

Customary ethnoreligious boundaries, however, were less suited to negotiated manipulation within the local environment. Certain judicial policies were vaguely delimited by the original charters of settlement. The subordinate statuses of Jews and Muslims, moreover, were ingrained in the social fabric of Christian-ruled society. The tribunal's review transcripts indicate that these regulations were not a source of conflict for the lords and citizens and therefore experienced virtually no modification. The mandate that Jews and Muslims sit on the floor of the municipal court, for instance, is present in both the *Consuetudines* and *Costums*. Both codes also condemned the use of Christian servants by Jews and Muslims and imposed sumptuary laws barring excessive luxury by any non-Christian. They each advanced a typically dim view of certain forms of miscegenation. Any Jew or Muslim male caught with a Christian female would be drawn and quartered; the woman would be burned in Jewish or Muslim garb. Anyone could make an accusation about illicit mixing without fear of legal repercussions should the allegation be proven unfounded (the *pena talionis*).[116]

Certain important issues concerning coexistence that were not addressed in the *Consuetudines* had to be negotiated separately between the lords and citizens as the tribunal conducted its work. Most notably, in the *Carta de la Paeria* (1275), these parties made resolutions regarding the functioning of the municipal government (*paeria*) that were then inserted into the codified *Costums*. In profiling the responsibilities of the local *paers* to be carried out in cooperation with the lords and vicar, the agreement sheltered Jews and Muslims from certain judicial proceedings conducted in the municipal court. If capital cases or trials incorporating torture were heard there, they would have to involve Jewish witnesses. Although the *Carta* asserted that Muslims were "not to be judged or punished by the vicar nor by the *paers*," it is evident from the *Costums* that this exclusion concerned only capital cases.[117]

The *Consuetudines* contained related policies that were sharpened but not fundamentally changed in the *Costums*. In both texts, all noncapital cases involving Jews would be handled by the municipal court. Muslims, however, were only obliged to come to the Christian court when involved in a case with a Christian or Jew. These unusual requirements that Jews and Muslims use the municipal court necessitated further attention in each code to the religious identities of witnesses in mixed cases and the presentation of the Jewish oath to help ensure truthful testimony.[118]

This complex process of contestation that helped shape the development and adjustment of Tortosa's micro-convivencia fell under no constituency's absolute control. As a result, it was highly unpredictable, fluid, and locally conditioned. Not every element of Tortosa's unique coexistence was in flux, however. Each side of this debate seems to have been cognizant of which aspects of the customary practices defining Tortosa's micro-convivencia were up for negotiation and which were rigid because of incontrovertible written guarantees, unbending requirements maintained by one group, or consensus. Shifts in group priorities, policy initiatives, and changing community circumstances, however, could transform the mix of possibilities and limitations for development or modification.

Conclusions

The distinctive, localized micro-convivencias materializing in dislocated environments such as Tortosa over the course of the thirteenth century deviated from the popular model of an exclusively monarchy-driven "process of standardization" in the external and internal governance of Jewish communities.[119] While jurisdictional fragmentation not did not preclude the diffusion or parallel development of institutions and practices among royal and nonroyal environments, this chapter has made the case that standardization was not always the direct, predictable result of royal lawmaking. As the crown's Jewish policy became better articulated over the second quarter of the thirteenth century, the lords, in collaboration with the Jewish community, could assess whether they wanted to adopt royal policy selectively, embrace it completely, or forge their own entirely customized regulations.

Groups in Tortosa could not make choices exclusively in response to their town's isolated urban context, however. They also had to respond to the broader circumstances of Jewish settlement and communal development outside of Tortosa as well as to the wider conflict between royal and seigniorial authority. As we shall see in the next chapter, this dynamic between local norms and extra-local policies became more complex and pressing as the king and royal officers sought to develop an administrative foothold in the town and exercise the crown's claimed authority over Jewish and non-Jewish subjects alike.

4

ROYAL ADMINISTRATIVE ADVANCES

During the final two decades of Jaume's reign, in the 1260s and 1270s, Tortosa's seigniorial regime experienced increased intrusion by royal administrators as the king incrementally made use of his new prerogatives from the 1247 agreement with the Templars. This pressure from the monarchy served to complicate the shifting negotiations among the lords, Jews, and the wider citizenry in Tortosa that we discussed in the previous chapter. The crown took its time in augmenting its engagement with the community, however, and witnessed mixed results. Even by the late 1250s, Jaume had not significantly increased his capacity for administration or his engagement with the Jewish community.

In this chapter, we will chart and examine this gradual administrative shift. Of particular interest will be the career of the Tortosan Jew Astruc Xixó, who served as the king's first bailiff in the town during the 1260s. As we will see, for over a decade, rather than simply administering royal property in accordance with the 1247 agreement, Astruc and subsequent royal agents pushed against the contract's restrictions in a sustained effort to advance the monarchy's claimed regalian prerogatives within the town. At the same time, the king himself sought to entice local Jews to collaborate with his initiatives as well as to utilize the royal court for their legal needs. Overall, this activity faced resistance from the lords and subjects alike. For distinct reasons, they opposed efforts to integrate Tortosa into the crown's increasingly elaborate standardized and systematized fiscal and legal framework.

The Return of a Royal Bailiff

Even after Jaume secured permission from the Templars to reestablish limited administrative rights, his negotiations with Tortosa's lords and his policy-making did not entirely support his agenda of asserting regalian prerogatives there. He conducted business that ended up bolstering the security of the seigniorial regime's autonomy, thereby raising additional obstacles to the crown's development of an administrative presence in the town. It seems unlikely that these decisions signified that the king lacked, or was not fully committed to, a coherent plan concerning Tortosa. Rather, it is probable that a shortage of resources, caused foremost by the ongoing military efforts in the kingdom of Valencia, forced him to prioritize consciously other competing objectives.[1]

Desperate to finance the pacification of Valencia in 1258 following continued revolting by the *mudéjares* there, for example, Jaume pledged not to take further action against the Order's habitual collection and retention of all tax income from "Christians, Muslims, and Jews" in Tortosa, including the *questia* of the Jews, in return for a substantial loan. In addition, the king granted the Templars the *questia* of the Jews and incomes from the exemptions of citizens in Lleida. He also permitted that "all bailiffs of the Temple . . . in the city of Tortosa, use fully and freely . . . their jurisdiction [*iurisdiccione sua*] . . . according to that which is contained in instruments between our predecessors and [the Templars]."[2] For their part, the lords had not restrained themselves from creating service relationships with certain elite Jews. A year before this authorization from Jaume, the seigniorial regime had already designated Abraham Maimó as its joint bailiff, possibly in emulation of the crown's continued use of Jews as officers. The king not only made no attempt to halt this arrangement but also cooperated with Abraham in his official capacity as bailiff by granting him a license to export grain from Tortosa on the lords' behalf.[3]

With the turn of the new decade, however, the monarchy's efforts to engage with Tortosa and its Jews underwent a marked shift. A temporary lull in the conflicts in Valencia, combined with Jaume's fateful decision to renounce his dynasty's long-cherished claims north of the Pyrenees with the Treaty of Corbeil in May 1258, helped provide him with the means and resolve to resume imposing his regalian prerogatives on lordships in the heartland of his realms, such as Tortosa.[4] For the first time in the extant sources, Jaume began trying to impose directly on the financial resources of Tortosa's corporate Jewish community. He mandated that the Jews begin paying the tribute that had increasingly become customary for royal communities. In 1260, citing the impoverishment (*paupertatem*) of the aljamas of Besalú and Girona, Jaume exempted their *collecta* from the annual tribute of 2,000 solidi. The Jews of Tortosa, Perpignan, and Lleida would instead assume responsibility for this sum: 800, 700, and 500 solidi, respectively.[5] Royal demands from *collectas* throughout the realms in 1266 assigned Tortosa's Jews the responsibility to pay 2,000 solidi. Tortosa's share was small for a wealthy and sizeable aljama and in comparison to the amounts assigned to other towns: Valencia, Lleida, Zaragoza, and Barcelona owed 3,000, 4,500, 11,000, and 22,500 solidi, respectively.[6] Perhaps the king intended to ease Tortosa's Jews into the practice of paying tribute by assigning them a manageable assessment in the initial years.

Jaume also began to increase his administrative presence in the town. Although initially this activity respected the provisions of the 1247 agreement, it soon began to exceed those limits, as we shall see. The earliest evidence of a royal bailiff based in Tortosa dates from March 1263. The king's decision to give the elite Jew Astruc Jacob Xixó the bailiwick could have been in response to the presence of at least one elite Jew in the seigniorial administration at that time: the aforementioned joint bailiff Abraham Maimó.[7] The use of such Jews as officers served multiple ends for the crown, which helps explain why the practice became widespread in Jaume's administration and that of his son. Jews from prominent families were viewed as useful servants by the king and lords alike because of their prowess in handling fiscal matters and ability to draw upon their own considerable financial resources.[8] Astruc already had a good track record of lending to the monarchy.[9] It may also have been significant that Astruc had already defied and antagonized the seigniorial regime: as we saw earlier, he was the primary plaintiff in the case to construct a new synagogue on his lands in 1262, which had been opposed by the lords.[10]

As the lone royal bailiff in Tortosa, Astruc assumed primary responsibility over the crown's local administrative affairs, the cultivation of its prerogatives there, and its jurisdictional conflict with the seigniorial regime.[11] These duties were intertwined with his continued activity as a creditor to the monarchy. He received the castle and town of Penyíscola from the crown, for instance, to secure a loan to fund the crown's continued legal troubles with Tortosa's seigniorial regime.[12] When he invested Astruc with the office, the king stipulated that it concerned resident "Christians and Jews," an indicator of where the two located the concentration of wealth within the town.[13] This stipulation may also reflect the provisions of the Muslims' surrender treaty, which had guaranteed that no Jew could exercise jurisdiction over them.[14] Nonetheless, its direct mention of Jews supports our earlier hypothesis that Jaume had campaigned for a local bailiff with an eye to building relations with both Jews and Christians. Mark Meyerson has made the case that the "general dependence" of the Jews on the crown further qualified them as bailiffs in royal Morvedre and other similarly governed Valencian towns. In Tortosa's jurisdictional context, however, it seems to have been the lack of straightforward dependence that made an elite Tortosan Jew a most useful royal bailiff for the king.[15]

Astruc's service responsibilities grew as he worked diligently on the monarchy's behalf within Tortosa and its region while continuing to extend further credit to the crown. He dutifully fulfilled royal mandates to collect money and seize property from both Christians and Jews as well as to receive payments destined for royal coffers from other royal officials to the south.[16] In 1263, the king expanded Astruc's jurisdiction to the castle and surrounding districts (*alquerias*) of Penyíscola, assigning him royal rights and incomes there for a space of five years in repayment of an enormous thirty-thousand-solidi loan. Jaume also enlisted him to collect a levy on property (*peyta*) from Penyíscola and neighboring Borriana, Onda, and Morvedre to help repay this debt.[17]

We know that his new role in Tortosa frequently demanded that Astruc put pressure on local constituencies. His willingness to do so earned him additional favors from the crown. Around this same time in 1263, he was hounding Tortosa's Jewish aljama for payment of a subsidy of nine thousand solidi owed to the king.[18] Astruc's success in Tortosa and his continued lending motivated the king to give him the bailiwick for his lifetime in 1265.[19] By

1267, he had earned satellite appointments in northern Valencia as bailiff of Borriana, Morella, and Penyíscola.[20]

Astruc's burgeoning career drew other Jewish residents of Tortosa into royal service. The Jew Muschet Mordofay served as his lieutenant in northern Valencia from the late 1260s.[21] At some point in his career, Astruc also carried out royal business in Teruel, in Lower Aragon. A resolution between his son and heir, Abraham, and the *concejo* of that town in 1285 concerned the sixteen thousand solidi the town still owed the family from Astruc's collection of the *peyta* years earlier.[22]

Burns once made the point that Astruc, as bailiff, was far more than the "rather parochial figure" in Tortosa and northern Valencia traditionally envisioned by historians.[23] Although this observation is certainly true, it is important to recognize that many of the choices that drew Astruc away from his roots in Tortosa and eventually ended his tenure as bailiff there were necessitated not simply by the nature of his work, but also by the rather parochial conflicts it engendered with his coreligionists. Indeed, the bailiff as well as his family paid a hefty social price for his service to the crown. The increased priority Jaume placed on securing fiscal control of the resources in Tortosa all but guaranteed that Astruc's work for the crown would preclude continued harmonious relations with his lords and fellow residents.

It is possible that Astruc was already experiencing negative repercussions from his ascent to prominence as a royal agent when the king awarded him a sweeping exemption during a visit to Tortosa in 1266. As a "charter of safe passage" (*carta guidatici*) valid "through all the land and jurisdiction of the Lord King," it sought to prevent Astruc from being intimidated as he conducted business beyond his hometown. By exempting Astruc and his family from the authority of "any aljama of Jews of the lands or jurisdiction of the Lord King," the charter left it unclear whether Jaume meant for the protection to apply to all aljamas on the basis that they existed within his realms and were innately subject to royal jurisdiction (per the servi regis principle) or acknowledged that nonroyal aljamas would likely be able to ignore the mandate with impunity.[24]

The privilege also barred Jewish associations and anyone else from trying to force the Xixó family to contribute to the payments they owed their lords or the crown—from commercial levies such as the *lleuda*, *pedatge*, and *mesuratge* to arbitrary duties such as the *questia*, *bovatge*, *monedatge*, and *exercitus*. The appointment of elite Jews as officers accordingly served to establish royal control over targeted pools of wealth in localities where jurisdictional conditions limited effective royal control over the larger Jewish community. As an added benefit, the exemption must have freed up more of Astruc's wealth for financing royal debt and tax-farming operations, as was typical with the enfranchisement of ethnoreligious elites. Thus, while such exemptions clearly raised the tax burden for the nonexempt members of the aljama, they did not often spare their wealthy Jewish beneficiaries from taxation entirely. The special relationships with the crown maintained by these elite Jews in fact made their wealth even more vulnerable to seizure through forced loans and other irregular mandatory transactions benefiting the monarchy.[25]

The king did carefully stipulate that the exemption did not completely liberate Astruc from Jewish religious jurisdiction. Although no aljama could "put him or his [family] under a ban or communal ordinance or any other restrictions besides," it could subject them to "excommunication for informers" (*malshinim* or *malsins*).[26] Since the punishment of a *malsin* prioritized the community's rights of complaint over those of a rebellious individual, this exception safeguarded the integrity of the aljama's internal authority. Astruc's person and his property were therefore theoretically immune to nonroyal jurisdiction except when it came to his membership in his broader ethnoreligious community. His special status differentiated him from his fellow Jews, investing him with extraordinary influence over the community, yet at the cost of rendering him an outsider.[27] Jaume thus refused to violate this cornerstone of Jewish juridical autonomy, even if it meant exposing his valued official to retribution. The nature of the sorts of offenses meriting excommunication, however, did substantially reduce the likelihood that this vulnerability would impair Astruc's fiscal duties.[28]

Before and after Astruc Xixó's ascent as a royal creditor and agent, the king was also directly cultivating relationships with other Jews in Tortosa. These tended to be reinforced exclusively by moneylending rather than in combination with office holding. Jaume borrowed smaller sums and bestowed, in return, favors such as the right of safe passage (*guidatge*) and property rights.[29] In 1258, he assisted Jafias Maimó's efforts to collect debts owed to the Jew by the lord of Oteiza.[30] Such intervention displayed the king's efficacy as a patron. It also demonstrates how he took a hand in policing the lending that constituted a major source of the Jewish wealth claimed as part of the royal patrimony.[31]

Whereas Jewish service as tax farmers and administrators was well established throughout Iberia, these particular contacts with individual Jews constituted part of the crown's growing effort to reestablish fiscal access and jurisdictional rights to the Jewish aljama as a whole.[32] From the early 1260s, the king sought for the first time to challenge the seigniorial regime and regulate the business practices of the Jewish community in accordance with norms he had established throughout his realms. In 1263, for example, he acquitted the entire Jewish population of Tortosa, as a collective, of exceeding the maximum rate of interest and authorized the Jews to sell certain merchandise to Christians, Muslims, and other Jews.[33] Echoing the individual transaction he had made with Jafias Maimó in 1258, he sought to establish himself as the chief protector of the aljama's fiscal integrity by demanding the repayment of all debts owed to the Jews of Tortosa.[34]

Early royal chancery records also contain the first evidence of the king intervening in judicial matters. Cases concerning individual Jews and the Jewish aljama could circumvent seigniorial administration and fall under his jurisdiction via appeal. In 1263, in a dispute received by the royal court, Jaume ruled in favor of the Tortosan Jew Mosse Alcohen, who had been accused of wrongdoing by a family member.[35] The next year, in another appeal, he upheld as legitimate the marriage of Jahuda Albala to Mira, daughter of Jucef Almuli, a Jewish resident of Valencia. The Jews of Tortosa had declared it invalid. The king also restricted the judicial role of the community, forbidding Tortosa's aljama to take action against or impose pecuniary penalties on Jahuda relating to this case.[36]

These appeals were exceptional, however, because they were instances of Jewish litigants opportunistically drawing royal justice into local affairs in pursuit of favorable legal outcomes. Historians have recognized this phenomenon elsewhere in medieval society. In an influential article from several decades ago, for example, Frederic Cheyette made the important point that there "is no reason to believe that individuals . . . prefer objective neutrality to partiality in their own favor." William Chester Jordan later noticed a similar scenario in thirteenth-century France: "The very multiplicity of jurisdictions . . . was a positive factor for the politically savvy Jewish leadership, which could sometimes, if not always, play one lord off against another in times of crisis."[37] In short, although these cases are a significant sign of increased local influence by the crown, they do not confirm that the king could assert routine judicial rights in Tortosa by this point.

This evidence reveals how, only a short time after Astruc's appointment as bailiff in Tortosa, the monarchy was already using its new administrative capacity as a channel for imposing regalian prerogatives. Although mandating that Tortosa's Jews contribute to subsidies and receiving case appeals in royal court did not, according to the crown, legally depend on local rights of lordship, the presence of a bailiff clearly facilitated these sorts of interactions. Astruc represented both an instrument of royal power within the local ambit and an omnipresent reminder for residents of the potent reality of royal oversight. In short, this bailiff helped put local weight behind the increasingly bold claims Jaume had been making about his unparalleled governmental powers over the past several decades.

By the time Astruc had been in office just one month, the Templars had grown aware of the considerable threat that he presented to their prerogatives in Tortosa as well as to the independence of the lordship. They seemed to recognize that the 1247 agreement had been a serious miscalculation. In spite of their carefully worded limitations, it had opened the floodgates to royal intervention. These lords thus quickly set to work developing a legal challenge to Astruc's activity. Curiously, they decided not to refer directly to the 1247 concord and argue that the bailiff violated its explicit restrictions on "jurisdiction and coercive power."[38] Perhaps they feared that the crown would try to reinterpret or even overrule those legal barriers. Instead, the Templars opted to base their defense on the traditional jurisdictional rights collectively exercised by the seigniorial regime, which were strengthened by the fact (embraced by each co-lord) that they originally derived from royal donation.[39]

This strategy required that the Templars repair relations with their estranged partners, the Montcadas. The family's well-established jurisdictional prerogatives, dating from the reign of Ramon Berenguer IV, stood to serve as a formidable defense against the novelties introduced by the crown. The local Templar commander drafted a communication to Ramon de Montcada in April 1263 urging him to join them in legal action against Astruc. The appointment of such a bailiff, the commander argued, violated Montcada's "vicariate." The noble lord should not hesitate to defend "the jurisdiction which you have in Tortosa" against the monarchy's encroachment.[40]

We know that the Templars succeeded in organizing this legal offensive but not how far they went with it. In June, the crown allocated resources to fund Astruc's handling of the "inquiry that the master of the Templars,

Ramon de Montcada, and Pere de Montcada [i.e., Tortosa's lords] have made against us" in defense of their seigniorial administrative prerogatives.[41] However, no further records attest to continued litigation. It is possible that the lords withdrew the case upon receiving assurances from the king. They may have been content to warn the crown and its new bailiff about the dangers of asserting undue authority in a legal "shot across the bow," rather than to enter into a pitched battle.

If this was the lords' strategy, these maneuvers appear to have served their purpose albeit only temporarily and partly. The king and his bailiff refrained from making further tribute demands of Tortosa's Jews or imposing other claimed regalian prerogatives until the turn of the next decade. Other impositions by the crown in Tortosa, however, continued to irk the Order. The second Templar internal memorial introduced in the last chapter enables us to observe the major grievances between 1263 and 1264 that the Order apparently did not publicize. Circumstances appear to have worsened when the king made personal visits and expected extraordinary concessions from the residents. "When the lord king is in Tortosa," they complained, "he takes *questias* and *calonias* from the Jews and Muslims."[42] These particular collections ostensibly violated both the Templars' established jurisdictional prerogatives and the king's concession from 1258 discussed earlier. As we have seen, Jaume had signed off on the Order's right to retain tax revenues from all residents and, specifically, the *questia* owed by the Jews.[43] Also at issue in the memorial was the crown's continued failure to pay the Order its one-fifth share of any incomes produced by the lordship, which derived from its participation in the conquest.[44] Furthermore, the lords suffered financially from merchants based in Valencia and Aragon who refused to pay levies due in Tortosa on the grounds that exemptions granted to them by the monarchy should be valid there.[45] Astruc's routine duties as bailiff, however, did appear to respect the guidelines of the 1247 arrangement. He did not interfere with the collection of taxes and levies by the seigniorial bailiffs but simply demanded what he claimed to be the king's rightful share of the proceeds.[46]

Escalation and Conflict

In the 1270s, Jaume appears to have recovered from the legal backlash orchestrated by the lords several years earlier. He adopted a much more aggressive approach to increasing the presence and authority of royal administration and imposing his claimed regalian prerogatives in Tortosa. He resumed requiring its Jewish population to contribute to the tribute paid by Jews under royal jurisdiction. In 1271, he demanded that the aljama pay 4,000 solidi, to be added to the amount owed by other communities in Aragon and Valencia.[47] Yet, the king may have failed to collect at this moment, since Tortosa is not included among the detailed lists of collection receipts for each implicated community.[48] The following year, however, the king apparently did succeed in extracting an even greater sum. The royal register notes that his agent, Joan de Guimerà, received 6,000 solidi from Tortosa's Jews. This sum was large in comparison to what he obtained from some of the other aljamas on this occasion, and it may have been an attempt to compensate for the lack of payment the previous year, when he had demanded 2,000 less, or to penalize the community for the delay. Lleida, by comparison, paid only 5,000 solidi. These levels could also have been a function of perceived ability to pay, based on size, indebtedness, economic vitality, and so forth, since certain other communities paid considerably more. Barcelona, Girona and Besalú, and Perpignan rendered 50,000, 20,000, and 15,000, respectively.[49] The simple fact that the king had been successful in forcing Tortosa's unaccustomed Jews and lords to cooperate with his tribute demands made any collection a significant achievement. Although arguably a powerful precedent for future years, this incident of payment did not, however, inaugurate a pattern of regular participation by Tortosa's Jews or preclude considerable resistance to further attempts to collect tribute by Jaume's successors, as we shall see.

At the time of his unsuccessful tribute request of 1271, Jaume made additional demands that ran directly counter to the 1247 arrangement. He ordered the lords to concede broader jurisdictional powers to his bailiff and called for inquests against the lords' collectors of the *questia* from the Jews and Muslims. This was a levy he had initially agreed to let the lords keep in 1258, as we have seen, and later decided to split with them in 1263–64, according to the Templar memorial. Unspecified prior agreements between the lords and the Jews, Jaume alleged, had limited their share of the *questia* to two hundred solidi, but "corrupt" tax collectors had subsequently allowed the lords to exceed this amount.[50]

The lords were again quick to respond to this shift. In fact, earlier in 1271, before the king had even announced his tribute demands, the Templar commander had already resumed the seigniorial regime's legal defense from almost a decade earlier. He addressed another letter to Ramon de Montcada, informing him of recent demands by the king concerning "questions about jurisdiction, incomes, and other rights in Tortosa that affect you and us." The lords had reason to be concerned. For the first time, the king was behaving as an overlord rather than a silent minority partner or even a co-lord. He was seeking not simply to insert himself into the local environment in order to manage his patrimony, as he had arranged in the 1247 agreement, but instead to monopolize jurisdiction over local non-Christians, tacitly in keeping with the servi regis principle. According to the Templars, Jaume claimed "that he ought to have the *questia* from Jews and Muslims . . . [and] that the master and brothers of the Temple and Ramon de Montcada should not demand any *questia* or service from the Jews of Tortosa [beyond the agreed-upon amount] . . . [and] that all of the Muslims and Jews of his land are his."[51] Whereas the Templars were determined to reassert at least some of the jurisdictional rights they had enjoyed over Tortosa's non-Christians during the long absence of royal administration, Jaume was intent on micromanaging the Jews and Muslims, thus aligning conditions in this locality with those in his increasingly standardized royal domains.

The letter seems to capture the raw indignation of the Templar lord in the face of these royal demands. Yet, as perturbed as the lords must have been about the threatening encroachments, his alarmed tone was likely a product of calculated rhetoric rather than genuine surprise. The itemization of claims that Montcada was doubtlessly aware of, and that the monarchy had been promoting with growing intensity and specificity for decades, served to publicize the confrontation and heighten its relevance to the larger community of lay and religious barons throughout the realms. The most effective weapon in the lords' arsenal was exposing the fact that this royal intrusion concerning jurisdiction over Jews and Muslims represented interpretation rather than fact and theory rather than law; most importantly, it was a novelty defying decades of established custom.

This local conflict was part of the broader struggle between the royal ideology of pervasive jurisdiction and baronial autonomy that influenced the lives of subjects throughout the realms, regardless of their religious identity. Each realm within the Crown of Aragon witnessed resistance by barons against the monarchy's efforts to centralize public order and administration through lawmaking and codification. Starting in 1226, Catalan barons, occasionally in collaboration with the Aragonese nobility, began exchanging oaths of self-defense in an effort to undermine the authority of the resurgent royal Peace and Truce.[52] The regalian legal tools fashioned and honed by Jaume's predecessors equipped him to denounce these noble revolts as treasonous violations of the public peace that he, as *princeps*, was obliged to uphold.[53] Most significantly, the *Princeps namque* clause of the *Usatges de Barcelona* compelled all subjects to help the king defend public order in the realms against both native and foreign enemies.[54] The influential mélange of Roman and canon law known as the *ius commune*—an innately centralizing "natural law" to be applied to all societies—increasingly aided this objective of unifying and standardizing the laws and governmental institutions of the diverse realms.[55] According to royal jurists such as Pere Albert, who reinterpreted Catalonian feudal law in his mid-thirteenth-century *Commemoracions*, the king alone, as the "sovereign lord" (*dominus superior, senyor sobirà*) and "prince of the land" (*princeps terre, príncep de la terra*), was equipped with jurisdiction over all cases (*mixt o mer imperi*) and qualified to defend public safety with his special *protectio*.[56]

Pere Albert's *Commemoracions* would remain, at most, a reference guide containing idealized feudal norms for the crown rather than enforceable law. Similarly, Aragon's nominal legal unification under the Romanized *Fueros de Aragón* in 1247 and the kingdom of Valencia's increasing subjection to the Roman-law influenced *Furs* from the 1240s each met with mixed success in the face of considerable baronial resistance.[57] Catalonia, however, arguably exceeded these realms in its legal fragmentation, and deep-seated foral traditions were especially pronounced in New Catalonia.[58] Catalonia, too, witnessed an aggressive baronial response to the crown's centralizing initiatives. As mentioned earlier, viewing the growing Romanization, standardization, and centralization of judicial law and procedure as a threat to their local privileges and uses, Catalan barons pressured the crown at the Corts held in Barcelona in 1251 to ban the imposition of Roman law and procedure on nonroyal courts.[59] Such resistance checked the advance of centralized royal authority and norms into seigniorial jurisdictions during the reigns of Jaume and his sons.

Jaume's contact with Tortosa's Jewish community through the end of his reign in 1276 aspired to build administrative connections that would further such centralization and standardization under the monarchy. However, royal documentation reveals that he did not pretend to have already achieved this objective. In 1274, the king sent a letter to Tortosa and "the aljamas of all Jews of his land," ordering that each one send two representatives to the royal court to discuss matters beneficial to them and "all Jews of the land." There is no evidence to indicate that Tortosa accepted this invitation to collaborate with the monarchy in this way or that the king succeeded in building tighter relations.[60] Tortosa's inclusion in this missive was unusual, however. In general, royal chancery activity during this period seemed to recognize that Tortosa was different from communities under royal control. It received no copies of the frequent mandates sent to long lists of royal aljamas of the realms.[61] Instead, royal correspondence tended to be directed specifically at Tortosa's aljama or individual Jews and tailored to address the peculiar obstacles that the town's circumstances presented for the enforcement of statutes and levying rights.

The Later Career of Astruc Xixó and New Administrative Techniques

The work of men such as Astruc Xixó illustrates how royal engagement with Tortosa both aggravated and benefited from tensions within its Jewish community. Astruc's relations with his fellow Jews might have been worsened by existing factionalism, but his formidable work to enlarge the crown's administrative presence eventually rendered him unsuitable as a resident bailiff in Tortosa. By 1273, the Jew had given up the bailiwick as well as responsibilities within neighboring centers in northern Valencia.[62] Evidence has not surfaced to determine whether a particular incident motivated this renunciation of his lifetime position in Tortosa or why the king did not immediately entrust the responsibilities to another resident. Per his appointment contract, Astruc had the right to delegate his duties to whomever he chose. Possibly the king decided that local hostility toward the Jew had reduced his efficacy to the point that it was counterproductive to maintain him or a delegate in Tortosa. Within a short time, Astruc's activity as administrator, creditor, tax farmer, and property owner had shifted away from Tortosa and toward opportunities to the south. In 1275, the king arranged repayment of a massive loan of over eighty thousand solidi to Astruc exclusively from incomes from the kingdom of Valencia.⁶³ That same year, he confirmed the Jew's purchase of property in the city and kingdom of Valencia.⁶⁴

Astruc remained directly involved with Tortosa's community only in order to pursue lingering financial interests there or to antagonize it further as an outsider on the monarchy's behalf. After Pere II (r. 1276–85) took the throne, Astruc became embroiled in disputes with Jews in Tortosa over unpaid debts. These may have been personal loans by Astruc or levies advanced to the crown that he had been unable to collect. Intervening on this occasion, probably at Astruc's request, Pere ordered Tortosa's vicar, bailiff, and *prohoms* (identified as *fidelibus suis*) to seize and hold accountable the Jew's debtors residing in the town for their unpaid obligations.⁶⁵ The future assignments Astruc undertook on the monarchy's behalf and prerogatives he received in return seem to have been crafted in direct response to his poor relations with his native community. By 1281, he had been appointed the chief royal officer in the community of Amposta, which neighbored Tortosa to the south, following the king's recent acquisition of the castle and town from the Hospitallers.⁶⁶ With the help of various royal officers from Penyíscola and Morella, Astruc was expected to put this new royal lordship in order as he assumed responsibility of guarding the castle and administering the town, drawing from local revenues as needed.⁶⁷ This reorganization entailed stopping men from Tortosa and other localities from fishing and taking salt or any other natural resources from Amposta's district, as well as collecting customary tolls from Muslim merchants ferrying goods up the Ebro River, which likely reduced what Tortosa's officials could demand. In addition to the revenues Astruc retained from collections, the king rewarded his servant handsomely with houses, mills, and other property in Amposta.⁶⁸ It is hardly surprising that Astruc was not given the assignment of collaborating with Tortosa's Jews. The former bailiff's utility to the crown as an antagonist rendered him an ineffectual liaison.

Astruc's career as a royal officer and creditor was thus a success story and a personal tragedy and serves as a further reminder that the monarchy's objectives, depending on the local environment, were not always best served by Jewish communal solidarity.⁶⁹ On the one hand, Astruc was a Jew who attained an unprecedented level of authority, privilege, and prominence, paving the way for the commissioning of future Jewish officers until the practice was outlawed in the 1280s. On the other hand, he appears as a pawn in the monarchy's attempt to assert greater administrative control over its patrimony, at the expense of jurisdictional competitors. His service to the crown caused his fall from grace as a prominent figure within Tortosa's Jewish community and wider urban populace. It encouraged or forced him to exile himself in pursuit of additional opportunities in the royal employ, some of which served only to antagonize further his former neighbors.

Even though Astruc and his family kept a comfortable distance from the town in the future, Tortosa continued to serve them as an identifier at times. Some royal letters made it seem that Astruc lacked a local community altogether—for instance, Pere II's reference to him simply as "our Jew" in 1277.[70] However, our final notice of him before his death, in 1282, refers to him as a resident of Tortosa,[71] and some years after his death, he remained remembered as "a deceased Jew of Tortosa" in an official record prepared for his son.[72] After their father's death, Astruc's children continued to reside outside of Tortosa. In 1285, they were grouped in a tax demand from Pere II with other residents of the kingdom of Valencia, a comfortable distance from their former neighbors.[73]

Unlike the Jewish bailiffs active in other royal localities, such as Morvedre, Astruc had thus enjoyed a pivotal role in the crown's agenda for seigniorial Tortosa that had rendered him a harmful intruder rather than a valuable advocate for Tortosa's Jewish community.[74] This work for the monarchy had greatly enriched him and entitled him to powerful privileges, but it had also necessitated radical and lasting changes in his family's living situation. If Astruc's poor relations with his fellow Tortosans had motivated his departure and pursuit of other royal assignments, it could explain why Jaume appears to have sought alternatives to appointing a replacement for the remainder of his reign. Indeed, we can observe the king trying to mobilize nonroyal or extra-local officers and personnel to manage royal incomes in Tortosa and advance the crown's administrative objectives during the mid-1270s. In 1276, for example, Ramon de Guardia, the Montcada bailiff, and a Jew named Bonsenyor were appointed to collect the *bovatge* from the diocese of Tortosa.[75] We do not know to what degree the seigniorial bailiff collaborated with the king's demands. Jaume may have been hoping that the notable dysfunction of the seigniorial regime or the Montcada family's long tradition of service to the crown would encourage the noble lord's primary local officer to fulfill these duties. By contrast, there is no evidence of the king ever trying to enlist a Templar official for similar ends.

Further attempts to use alternative administrative mechanisms in subsequent years likely indicate that this first effort to approximate Astruc's local functions failed. At the very end of his reign, in 1275, Jaume employed similar tactics to uphold the regulations adopted at the Corts and confiscate a number of improper loans made by Jews in Tortosa. These loans to Christian borrowers were allegedly invalid since their contracts did not document the performance of the required oaths. The king seized and farmed them out to a former resident, Jafias Maimó. This Jew had been in correspondence with the crown since at least the 1250s but had relocated for unknown reasons from Tortosa to the nearby Jewish aljama of Móra d'Ebre. His departure from the community probably qualified him as a suitable agent for handling locally unpopular royal initiatives. He also would have been familiar with the social and financial particulars of Tortosa's Jewry. Because Jafias was a novice to administration, however, he was expected to work with the king's porter, who was already pursuing other royal interests in and around Tortosa.[76] For instance, the king had directed this porter to recover usurious loans made by certain Jews in Tortosa as well as in other "villages and places" under the jurisdiction of the Templars and Knights of Calatrava.[77] Tellingly, Jafias's exposure to intimidation through this work prompted the king to award him and his family the same special protection and safe passage enjoyed by Astruc Xixó during his tenure as bailiff.[78]

Conclusions

This chapter has surveyed the mixture of achievements and setbacks experienced by Jaume's royal administration in Tortosa in the years following his momentous agreement with the Templars in 1247. As we have seen, in theory, according to its evolving sense of its prerogatives, the monarchy should not have needed a local bailiff to impose its regalian rights within any jurisdiction, either seigniorial or royal. In practice, however, the realization of these claimed and controversial prerogatives demanded not only considerable legitimacy and resources but also a local administrative presence. The crown faced a complicated strategic battle that could only be pursued in this hostile seigniorial climate by securing small administrative victories. This context explains why the crown was at times willing to work hard to establish new precedents even if they did not yield significant incomes. Following Astruc Xixó's departure in 1275, for example, the king made a concerted effort to demonstrate his ability to enforce regulations over moneylending activities. In addition to raising money from the aljama by seizing some of its loans, such punitive measures during a time of administrative disruption served to broadcast the continued potency of royal authority within the community. Within a month, however, after the monarchy had demonstrated its capacity for enforcement via fines and confiscated loans, it awarded these Jews remissions for their infractions.[79]

It is difficult to demonstrate whether the crown had entered into its administrative agreement with the Templars under false pretenses, with the premeditated plan to bend or break the careful rules barring any royal bailiff from intruding upon the seigniorial regime's executive authority. The Templars appear to have realized quickly that it was futile to try to render a royal officer innocuous by means of the restrictions in this agreement. Astruc Xixó's very presence served as a channel for royal influence. For his part, Jaume soon discovered that the greatest advancement in his objectives for Tortosa occurred when he had this capable local operative working on his behalf.

For all of its comparative success, however, Astruc's performance was difficult to sustain and left an unclear legacy. Worsening relations with the community reduced his efficacy and likely forced his departure. As we have witnessed, nonresident Jews and officers moved in to cover some of his roles, as Astruc himself later did from a strategic position outside of the town. Yet, in spite of Astruc's proven efficacy, neither Jaume nor his successors succeeded in appointing a long-term replacement who achieved even a fraction of Astruc's results through the remainder of the seigniorial period. Perhaps the crown believed that the position unnecessarily aggravated residents and the seigniorial regime or had difficulty enticing a suitable local figure to sign on, given the likelihood of following in Astruc's footsteps. In the future, the crown would continue to experiment with a range of alternative administrative strategies, none of which would be nearly as effective.

In the end, Jaume did less than we might have expected to impose on the lords' administration when compared with their worst fears listed in the Templar commander's letters to the Montcadas. The crown did not succeed in building important precedents—such as Tortosa's contributions to the crown's Jewish subsidy demands—into consistent patterns of obligation similar to what it had been able to establish within communities under royal jurisdiction. Its claims that the servi regis principle should apply to Tortosa's Jews and Muslims saw partial application only in the area of taxation. By the end of Jaume's reign, the monarchy had yet to even broach the issue of the lords' exercise of unauthorized executive authority over non-Christians, which violated the claim of exclusive royal possession.

In short, in spite of considerable effort and some significant administrative milestones, the monarchy's ability to exert its claimed regalian prerogatives in Tortosa remained quite limited when compared with communities under its direct administration. Further attempts by Jaume's successors to build on these foundations would also witness only limited success. These outcomes, as we will see in the next chapter, encouraged the monarchy to try to reestablish direct control over the town.

5
ADMINISTRATIVE STRATEGIES AND THE ROYAL TAKEOVER

In this chapter, we turn to analyzing the mechanisms that brought about increased, yet still limited and inconsistent, royal intervention within Tortosa in the wake of the measured achievements by Jaume's administration in the 1260s and 1270s. Over time, this engagement revealed the incompatibility of the indirect administrative model in Tortosa for upholding the crown's claimed regalian prerogatives and culminated in the monarchy's successful recovery of jurisdiction over the lordship in the 1290s. Tortosa's purchase was not an isolated incident but rather part of a broader effort by the monarchy to reestablish direct administrative control of the domains along the lower Ebro Valley that had been alienated since their conquest in the mid-twelfth century. Political, economic, and military conditions in the wider Crown of Aragon and the development and positioning of these territories had helped move the restoration of control over Tortosa and other lordships up on the monarchy's list of priorities. In retrospect, the alienation of these domains to powerful military orders and barons must have looked like miscalculations to these kings and their advisors. At this point they had no legal alternative, however, but to work within the ingrained administrative circumstances in these locales.

We will witness in this chapter that royal activity was not exclusively responsible for this shift toward acquisition. The monarchy certainly had the means to encourage the lords to participate in its reordering of its patrimonial resources and imposition of its administrative designs through both punitive and conciliatory measures. Yet, the lords themselves, in Tortosa as in other seigniorial environments, also seem to have been motivated to collaborate by their own strategic considerations. These dynamics can be reconstructed through creative analytical approaches to the extant documentation. We will read between the lines and against the grain of these texts, paying close attention to silences and scrutinizing general administrative documentation, instead of simply focusing on sources directed at the Jews. As we will see, local constituencies—Jewish, Christian, and Muslim—could possess considerable agency in shaping their jurisdictional circumstances and may have played a role in bringing about this transition to royal control through their conflict with the lords and other means.

Administration Without a Bailiff

Jaume's son, Pere II (r. 1276–85), pursued similar administrative goals, primarily using an expansion of tactics his father had already begun to implement by the final years of his reign. As we saw in the previous chapter, rather than reappointing a new bailiff, Jaume had employed two mechanisms to fill the vacuum created by Astruc Xixó's departure, ostensibly with mixed success: mobilizing extra-local royal agents and commandeering nonroyal local officials. Pere had been heavily involved in royal administration as the Infant during Jaume's final years, and it is quite possible that he himself had helped orchestrate the search for personnel to support increased administrative engagement that continued into his own reign. This tradition of involvement by crown princes encouraged greater consistency in the overarching royal policy and strategy during these years of the monarchy's administrative ascendency and may have accelerated the recovery of dislocated lordships such as Tortosa. The fact that Jaume had not yet discovered a viable alternative to a fixed bailiff meant that Pere, as king, was obliged to continue with this process of experimentation. We can witness the new king employing the former mechanism with his mandates that royal porters travel to Tortosa to collect the *bovatge* levy in 1278, 1280, and 1282.[1] His attempts to use the latter mechanism were arguably more controversial and prone to failure, as we shall see.

Other factors encouraged Pere to continue experimenting. The formal recognition of Tortosa's municipal regime and customary law by the lords, starting in 1272, had ushered in a new juridical climate. This shift would have demanded some degree of recalibration by the monarchy. Furthermore, the banning of Jewish bailiffs from royal administration required the king to pursue different avenues, particularly with regard to his interaction with the Jewish community. During the early years of his reign, Pere had in fact expanded Jewish officialdom. He did this in defiance of both prohibitions from the Corts that had been in place since 1228 and more recent local customary laws emerging in Catalonia and Valencia over the 1260s.[2] However, increasing opposition to these diligent and effective bailiffs was strengthened by the growing aversion to Jews in positions of authority. Pere eventually capitulated and dismissed his bailiffs in 1283.[3] The dearth of evidence of royal bailiffs in Tortosa by that time could be a by-product of Astruc's notoriously bittersweet experience, which may have dissuaded other elite Jews from filling the vacancy. An isolated reference from 1283 indicates that the king still owed a local Jew, Samuel Robi, compensation for his premature return of Tortosa's bailiwick to the crown.[4] It is not clear whether Samuel gave up the position voluntarily or because of this shift in royal policy, but the failure of this appointment may have left an impression on the king. The fact that the crown apparently did not entrust the post to anyone else, Jew or otherwise, until after its acquisition of the town suggests that there were other considerations motivating the king to continue his attempts to utilize unconventional methods to administer seigniorial Tortosa.

There are indeed signs that the king was shaping his administrative approaches to capitalize on changing conditions in Tortosa and thereby nudge the town progressively closer to conforming to his overarching vision of the monarchy's sovereign governance over the realms. With Tortosa's municipal government officially in existence and the codification of its local law under way, Pere may have sensed that he had an opportunity to co-opt its officials within his imagined, centralized bureaucracy. Although appointed by the seigniorial regime, Tortosa's vicar customarily presided over the town court with the prohoms, assisted by *paers* elected from the citizenry.[5] As we observed in chapter 2, the vicar in other localities had traditionally figured prominently in the administrative system designed to uphold the Peace and Truce that had originally been planned in the later twelfth century. In 1277,

Pere commanded Tortosa's vicar, bailiffs, prohoms, and *paers* to seize two Christian citizens of Tortosa and their accomplices, allegedly commissioned by a party of Jews, and restore stolen property to a distinct group of Tortosan Jews.[6] Pere contacted this same group of local officials when he sought to help Astruc Xixó force repayment of delinquent loans later that year. These unpaid debts were old business inherited from Jaume, who reportedly had already sent "many letters and two porters to Tortosa for demanding and receiving the aforementioned debts." After these initial attempts had failed, Jaume enlisted Astruc to intervene, licensing him to seize collateral if necessary. Pere now ordered the local officials to compel the resistant debtors to satisfy their obligations to Astruc and to help him seize the property he was owed.[7] Records do not confirm whether they carried out the king's mandate. Yet, it stands to reason that these officials would have been under pressure from the lords and local populace to ignore it, not least because the chief beneficiary remained persona non grata from his years of service as bailiff.

With other affairs, Pere had no choice but to try to influence and redirect local, nonroyal officials because the regular performance of their duties stood to harm his agenda. In one illuminating example, Romeu de Castellet, a knight who resided in Tortosa, was accused of numerous offenses. Romeu had allegedly refused to repay money he owed to the Barcelonan Jew and crown servant Mosse Escandarani, and the king had taken up Mosse's cause. In 1280, Pere had little choice but to appeal to the vicar, bailiff, and prohoms of Tortosa to collaborate with the crown's prosecution of the knight's case. Other local grievances against Romeu had already led these officials to exile him from the town, presumably to prevent him from causing more mischief. Fearing that this move would encourage Romeu to become a fugitive and delay the resolution of Mosse's claims, Pere pressured the officials to prioritize the crown's business. They were to let the knight return to Tortosa and refrain from proceeding against him in any way until the Jew's grievances could be considered and resolved. In the meantime, Mosse would have to stop trying to wrest compensation from Romeu's men in Tortosa. The king nevertheless foresaw the likelihood that the officials would not submit to his command, especially since, in this case, the monarchy and local governance were at cross-purposes. In a separate letter to Mosse, Pere authorized him to recommence property seizure from Romeu's tenants in Tortosa if the vicar, bailiff, and prohoms disobeyed these royal commands.[8]

The monarchy had a greater chance of success when it sought to commandeer nonroyal officials to conduct the administrative business a royal bailiff would have been entitled to carry out per the 1247 agreement with the Templars. In 1283, for example, the Infant Alfons ordered the subvicar Sebastià Delmas to render a sum to a former Jewish administrator.[9] Pere may have dialed back his expectations for the subvicar on this occasion after failing to enlist him for much more controversial business the previous year. He had asked Sebastià to exercise justice on behalf of the crown by judging a dispute between Astruc Xixó and his son-in-law, Jucef Cohen, over his daughter's dower according to Jewish law.[10] Although we have no evidence regarding the king's justification for establishing jurisdiction over this case, perhaps that the crown was making use of the legal protections Astruc had received when he was initially appointed bailiff. According to those guarantees, which had been conceded for life, Astruc had access to royal justice wherever he went.[11]

Had he wanted to comply, handling the case per the king's instructions would have been a difficult, if not impossible, task for the subvicar. Signs that the order went nowhere are therefore not surprising: the case remained unresolved by the time of Astruc's death around the summer of 1284. The former bailiff's demise made the resolution of the dispute all the more pressing. In November, even though all of the living participants were residents of Tortosa, the king made the wise decision to expedite the case by relocating it to a venue under direct royal control. He ordered Jucef, identified as a "Jew of Tortosa," to travel to Lleida in November to present his claims in the court of the crown's bailiff there, Esteve de Cardona.[12] This relocation must also have been related to Esteve de Cardona's assigned responsibility over Astruc's estate. Pere instructed a witness, Arnau Guardia, a "citizen [*civis*] of Tortosa" who claimed to possess official documents concerning the prior litigation, to appear in the bailiff's court.[13] The king must have been eager to resolve Jucef's grievances in order to proceed with the monarchy's own claims to Astruc's assets. In fact, a month earlier, Pere had ordered his vicar in Barcelona to sequester the former bailiff's property in Barcelona and Granollers, citing outstanding obligations to the crown. Then, on this same day in November, as he was making preparations for the court proceedings in Lleida, the king directed his bailiff in Valencia to seize from Astruc's property what the Jew owed the crown from his collection of the *tercia* levy. He enlisted Esteve de Cardona to calculate the precise figure.[14]

As had been the case with his father, Pere's experimentation with these renewed administrative strategies witnessed only modest success. Whereas Astruc Xixó had been willing to push against the limits imposed by the Templars, nonroyal officials were naturally disinclined to carry out royal mandates that might offend local potentates and encroach upon the jurisdiction of local institutions. We do not know precisely what factors led Pere to delay the reestablishment of a bailiff in Tortosa for so long, considering how much Astruc had been able to achieve in comparison. One possibility is that this king was interested in pursuing his objectives in Tortosa without dedicated royal officials in order to illustrate that his authority stood upon regalian rather than seigniorial underpinnings. Just as each subject Christian, Muslim, or Jew was to look to the king as supreme lawgiver and peacemaker, all officials, regardless of their institutional affiliation, were ultimately subject to royal command. This chain of command was consistent with the legal principles originally stipulated in the *Usatges de Barcelona* and recently revived in the Romanized *Commemoracions* of Pere Albert, which asserted that the king, as *dominus superior*, ultimately controlled all jurisdictions within his realms.[15] Pere's continued marginal success in achieving his administrative goals revealed that his monarchy had a great deal of work to do to bring real-world conditions in line with this evolving vision of regalian power.

Other Crown Initiatives

During his short reign, Pere was also busy continuing his father's efforts to centralize and enhance standardization of governance over the Jews in his realms. This activity was innately threatening to independent, localized jurisdictions such as Tortosa. Once again, gains were hard-fought and, for the most part, relatively limited. Policies that seemed potent in theory could end up influencing nonroyal domains relatively little. At the very least, however, these measures did set important precedents. Some of them would have significant implications for the future as the monarchy gained resources and legitimacy, enabling it to apply firmer pressure on resistant lords to comply.

First, Pere launched a systematic campaign to collect information about past royal privileges directly from all Jewish aljamas, irrespective of their jurisdictional circumstances. He initially issued generic orders that the aljamas send delegates with written general and community-specific privileges to the royal court to have these examined, verified, and documented in 1278. Later, the king targeted individual aljamas that had failed to comply or about which he wished to know more.[16] In 1281, as we observed earlier, he ordered a Jewish officer to bring him all of the royal charters in the possession of the Jews of Tortosa.[17]

Second, the monarchy began trying to impose on the aljama of Tortosa and those of other seigniorial communities existing policies that it had previously only applied to Jewish communities under royal jurisdiction. Starting in 1242, for instance, Jaume had licensed the Dominicans to deliver sermons in synagogues throughout his realms, but many communities with uncooperative lords appear to have been spared the campaigns.[18] Early in his reign, however, Pere expanded the mission to include the Franciscans and began to target specific communities with new licenses, including, for the first time, Tortosa.[19] Several years later, in 1283, the Infant Alfons alerted the "vicar and bailiff of Tortosa," among a long list of other local officials in urban centers throughout Aragon, Valencia, and Catalonia, that he was renewing his father's mandate that they protect local Jews against ritual stoning during Holy Week.[20] It is unlikely that this general order responded to any expressed need or complaint on the part of the Jewish or Christian communities in Tortosa. Instead, it seems that the Infant was grouping Tortosa with other communities expected to adhere to a normative package of royal protections.[21] For other localities, such as the firmly royal town of Girona to the north, the sequestering of the Jews during Holy Week was often framed as a privilege to the Christian citizenry rather than a protective guarantee to the Jewish community.[22] Such an unprecedented systematic effort to commandeer local administrative resources to shelter Jewish aljamas during this period of high volatility may indeed have been intended to display to multiple constituencies how the monarchy was entitled and best equipped to provide the security required by Jews throughout the realms.

Even if their immediate impact was slight, such directives could have influenced, in unpredictable ways, local Jews' impressions of the advantages and disadvantages of royal administration. Royal support of the missionary project, however, represented a significant, incontrovertible threat to Jewish religious autonomy. Such activity stood to antagonize the local population as well as likely to generate tension within the broader urban populace by drawing attention to Jewish nonconformity. Pere seems to have been aware of these potential issues—in particular, the danger that local Christians accompanying the friars might taunt or ridicule the Jews—and sought to limit the potential for escalation by prohibiting any more than a few Christians from attending the sermons and by banning incendiary anti-Jewish remarks.[23] On the other hand, Tortosa's Jews could have coveted the protections offered by the crown during Holy Week and throughout the year, particularly given the signs that their local lords were not prepared to grant similar services.[24]

The monarchy, under Pere, also made the unprecedented decision to offer a package of communal rights for all Catalan Jews, as we have seen. The king clearly had internal motives for refining the "autonomy by design" of communities under royal control, and this had already led him to offer these rights to individual aljamas on an ad hoc basis. Yet, there are reasons to believe that these open-ended measures were also calculated to usurp the policy-making role from independent lords and thereby encourage Jews in nonroyal domains to look to the crown as their chief patron and protector. From the king's perspective, his pervasive authority entitled him not only to tax, but also to enfranchise Jews throughout his realms, even without the explicit sanction of their jurisdictional lords.

The timing of Pere's campaign, in 1280, appears to have been encouraged by the contentious political situation with the nobility. The Viscount of Cardona and the Count of Foix had led a group of Catalan nobles in rebellion against the king since 1277. They were especially upset about his refusal to convoke a general court to confirm their traditional liberties. By the summer of 1280, Pere was locked in a siege of Balaguer against this rebel confederation.[25]

On 31 July, Pere granted a license to "all of the aljamas of Jews of Catalonia" to elect internal officials from among their "leading men" (*probi homines*). These men would have the authority to investigate and judge controversies and complaints arising between Jews as well as between Jews and Christians. They would be expected to "correct, condemn, and punish"—in accordance with Jewish law for criminal and civil crimes—Jews who belonged to their aljama or resided within their wider *collecta*. In keeping with the all-purpose nature of the privilege, the king accounted for size differences between the aljamas within Catalonia by permitting them to decide for themselves how many officials they wanted to elect—between two and seven.[26] This model of standardized Jewish communal institutions throughout Catalonia was by no means completely new. It based itself on the "autonomy-by-design" principle developed by Jaume for individual Jewries under direct royal control over previous decades.

Although Aragonese communities such as Calatayud and Teruel had been the testing grounds for innovative royal administrative techniques regarding the Jews, with this general communal privilege Catalonia's aljamas became the forerunners in the crown's campaign to extend its control over Jewish autonomy. Royal Jewish communities in Aragon continued to receive ad hoc licenses to elect leaders to fulfill these same official functions.[27] Pere did, however, issue realm-wide licenses to Aragon and Valencia, as well as to Catalonia, regarding other important regulatory matters, such as Jewish trading and moneylending.[28]

Another sign that this policy-making was confrontational and meant to advance the crown's regalian agenda is Pere's later effort to force Tortosa's seigniorial regime to abide by these privileges. In December 1280, Pere ordered Ramon de Montcada to stop violating "the privileges conceded to [the Jews] by us and our predecessors . . . by compelling them to be subject to the customs of Tortosa and [its] *paeria*." He was determined to override the localized requirement in the recently authorized *Costums de Tortosa* that the Jews litigate in the town court, in order to uphold his standardized package of Jewish communal privileges.[29] In sharp contrast with the king's recent regulations, the *Costums* had made no provisions whatsoever for the judgment and punishment of civil or criminal cases by Jewish officials.[30] Even though the seigniorial regime had not redacted the town's customary laws, it had approved this local policy and shared responsibility for its enforcement. The king may have viewed Ramon de Montcada as the most suitable agent to enforce his new policies because of the Montcada family's service relationship to the crown and traditional control of Tortosa's vicar, who presided over the *paeria*'s court.

The primary justification in Pere's injunction against Tortosa's procedures may, in fact, be a sign of weakness in the crown's legal position in this case. Rather than basing his opposition to Tortosa's procedural norms on his regalian right to administer all Jews throughout his realms, Pere referred generically to the body of royal privileges granted by him and his predecessors. Since, as we have observed, his predecessors had never before granted the right to elect communal officials to Tortosa's Jews, either directly or as part of a general privilege, it is unclear as to what precise earlier concessions he was appealing. It is possible that the king simply intended for his allusion to make his regulation of Tortosa's Jews seem more traditional and legitimate. The Jewish charter of settlement's indistinct use of the customs of Barcelona, combined with the town's complicated administrative history, arguably left the Jews' prerogatives ambiguous and subject to interpretation. Such a reference helped Pere portray himself as a traditionalist enforcing ingrained royal standards in the face of illicit novelty on the part of the universitas and seigniorial regime.

The seigniorial regime's decision to leave its Jews without explicit rights of self-governance, in a state of "autonomy by default," had provided the crown with an opportunity to intervene and assert its unparalleled capacity to protect. Similar in effect to the argument presented by Jaume when he had intervened in the dispute between the lords and universitas decades earlier, this license advertised among the local community (and the Jewish aljama, in particular) an image of the king's pervasive, preeminent authority as lawgiver and protector. There were already indications that Tortosa's Jews were amenable to collaborating with the monarchy to increase or protect their privileges. We have seen, for example, how they had been inclined to seek the monarchy's confirmation of the security provisions awarded to them by the seigniorial regime in 1228. This recent license for communal officials had the potential to pressure the lords to comply with royal policy, thereby establishing a precedent of royal administrative oversight as a by-product. If they did nothing, the lords risked protest or even an exodus of Jewish residents in search of similar privileges in communities under royal influence or control.

As had been the case with other royal policy-making concerning the Jews, these ostensibly favorable privileges were, in reality, bittersweet. They were paired with theoretically powerful protections as well as with onerous obligations and unwelcome changes in regulation. The license, for instance, contained prominent directives for the newly elected Jewish officials designed to channel resources from the aljama into royal coffers. These officers were not only expected to coordinate the collection of taxes and tribute, but also required to hand over all of the fines from Jewish court cases to the royal bailiff or corresponding official.[31] Pere also dealt a significant blow to

Jewish self-determination in an update to court procedures for "all Jews of Catalonia." Whereas Jaume in an earlier decree had required that convictions of Jews in any kind of trial involve both Jewish and Christian witnesses, Pere's law limited these guarantees to civil trials and cases concerning debts. Criminal cases against Jews could now be conducted using only Christian witnesses if it proved infeasible to involve Jewish witnesses. The only noticeable concession was that "any official of ours" would be barred from imposing corporal punishment in criminal cases utilizing no Jewish witnesses.[32]

Other actions by the monarchy during this vulnerable time in the summer of 1280 sought to facilitate Jewish lending as well as enhance incentives for Jewish creditors in nonroyal jurisdictions to appeal to royal justice. In June, Pere issued a mandate to the vicar and bailiff of Barcelona that renewed the spirit of another earlier order by his father. These officials were to compel debtors of "Jews of our land" to repay their outstanding loans, even if they had been determined to be usurious. The king forwarded copies of the mandate to a mixture of royal (e.g., Zaragoza, Tarazona, and Girona) and seigniorial communities (e.g., Tortosa, Fraga, and Monzón), but left unclear which of their officials would be expected to enforce the regulations. Whereas the local lord or official of each town was listed on the mandate, in the case of Tortosa alone the "Jews" themselves appear as the addressees.[33] This discrepancy could have been the result of the crown's continued lack of a local bailiff and poor relations with the seigniorial regime at that time. In two more enactments the following month, Pere adjusted his father's existing policies on moneylending, again addressing his decree to "all and single Jews of Catalonia." Jewish creditors would be permitted to collect interest at a lower rate, and, if borrowers agreed, it could be added to the principal and refinanced under a new loan.[34] These policy changes stood to increase the profits available for taxation. The king also renewed his father's license for Jews to continue to collect for six months on loans that had doubled due to interest accrual. He offered the services of his officers and courts to handle disputes concerning these sorts of loans.[35]

If Tortosa was representative of other nonroyal communities in Catalonia, it seems unlikely that these enactments could have influenced all Jewish aljamas promptly and uniformly, as their confident wording would suggest. In spite of Pere's efforts to pressure the lords to comply, his blanket license for Jewish officials exerted no measurable influence on Tortosa's community. It remained a pronouncement of the monarchy's ability to elaborate a standardized Jewish policy, rather than to effectively implement it. And if the Jewish community seized upon the opportunity to clamor at all for these rights, this left no noticeable traces in the extant documentation. Although royal pronouncements may have grown more assertive and ideologically potent under Pere, executing the shift to a uniform system of "autonomy by design" arguably remained a piecemeal process limited primarily to royal domains and advanced as much by ad hoc privileges as by sweeping declarations. Indeed, the limited practical implications of this king's communal privilege in nonroyal jurisdictions may explain why it apparently prompted no observable seigniorial complaint or response beyond tacit noncompliance.

Regulation, Subsidies, and Opportunities for Evasion

This range of regulatory maneuvers accompanied even more systematic efforts to force Tortosa's Jews to contribute to the subsidies regularly imposed on other Jewish aljamas under tight royal administrative control. While in the 1260s and 1270s, as we have witnessed, Jaume tried to collect tribute from the Jews of Tortosa on a number of occasions, these requests were sporadic. Tortosa's inclusion with groups of neighboring communities (*collectas*) that were obliged to meet specific taxation demands had been unofficial and irregular. The monarchy's treatment of the community was especially anomalous when compared with Catalonian royal aljamas, such as Barcelona and Lleida, that consistently appear in subsidy lists over these same decades.[36]

Early attempts by Pere to impose new subsidies on Tortosa's aljama were complicated by this lack of a consistent track record. In a revealing case from 1280, the king ordered the Jews of Tortosa to contribute to the payment of 1,600 solidi he had recently demanded from the impoverished aljama of Alcañíz, in Lower Aragon.[37] Even though Tortosa had long been described as lying within the limits of Catalonia, the king felt empowered to dip into this untapped resource past Aragon's fringe to assist the needy community.[38] The *collecta* system theoretically offered the king flexibility in how he assigned tax responsibilities: there was no strict rule that aljamas from different realms could not contribute together. Furthermore, the association was not completely arbitrary. Tortosa sat closer to Alcañíz than to other prominent Catalonian aljamas, and Tortosa's Jews had regular business dealings and even held property there. In fact, tax evasion by the owners of property in Alcañíz who maintained their primary residence in Tortosa was sufficiently common that it prompted Pere to issue a law that even part-time residents would be liable for community taxes.[39]

Tortosa's spotty track record of subsidy payments and this inconsistency in its assignment to a *collecta* soon informed an attempt by its Jews to evade such taxation altogether. In November 1282, the king ordered all Catalonian aljamas, explicitly including Tortosa, to send representatives to Barcelona to coordinate payment of a sizeable subsidy.[40] Tortosa's Jews, however—with the support of Ramon de Montcada and the Templar master, who joined in the complaint—argued on the basis of custom that they should not have to contribute. The collaboration of Tortosa's lords is not surprising especially because it appears that the Jews were also challenging the very notion that their wealth was subject to royal subsidies. The seigniorial regime had every interest in sheltering the financial resources of the Jews under its lordship.

The Jews claimed—falsely, we now know—that unlike the other Catalonian aljamas listed in the subsidy demands, their community had never participated in such payments in the past.[41] Perhaps they intended to assert that they had never contributed *regularly* to such subsidies or *with Barcelona*. In any event, it is odd that the community had not put forth similar objections to evade Jaume's earlier subsidy demands, at least one of which yielded a significant payment from Tortosa, as we have seen.

There were other details that strengthened their position, however. Most importantly, owing to the monarchy's lack of consistency in its collection of subsidies, there was ongoing confusion over whether Tortosa's *collecta* indeed pertained to Catalonia.[42] Pere's recent grouping of Tortosa with Alcañíz's subsidy notably conflicted with recent claims by the *sobrejuntero* of Zaragoza that the limits of his *junta* extended along the course of the Ebro River to the Mediterranean, encompassing the Ulldecona (today Sénia) River and the district of Morella and thus excluding the main town of Tortosa and its municipal district extending northward from the Ebro's left bank.[43] There are other indications from around this time, however, that Tortosa instead pertained to the kingdom of Valencia. In the registered royal tribute demand from 1265, the aljama had been grouped with Morella and Morvedre under the heading "Tribute of the Jews of the Kingdom of Valencia" and clearly distinguished from *collectas* in Aragon and Catalonia.[44]

Surprisingly, the Infant Alfons decided to lend credence to Tortosa's claims. He reasoned that the burden of proof concerning liability to pay lay with the Jews of Barcelona. Barcelona's aljama was to desist from its attempts to litigate against the Jews of Tortosa and instead pay their share of the subsidy unless it could present Alfons with sufficient evidence to uphold its claim.[45] Presumably assuming that no such evidence would be forthcoming, on that same day Alfons ordered two of his officials to make the Jews of Barcelona pay the 2,065 solidi that had been demanded from Tortosa's aljama and not to force the Jews of Tortosa to pay this contribution.[46] Taken together, the Infant's decision to consider Tortosa's claimed exemption and his unwillingness to impose a uniform policy of obligation on the aljamas of his realms suggest that he (and presumably the king as well) still recognized a potential for variegation within the royal administration of non-Christian populations.

The lack of consistency in royal policy concerning the composition of *collectas* continued to cause similar complications in the future. In 1283, for example, Pere had to order his administrator to desist from forcing the *collecta* of Lleida to contribute to the tribute owed by the Jews of Aragon. The debate over whether Lleida indeed belonged to Catalonia had been settled decades earlier. Nevertheless, the allocation of its *collecta* appears to have remained confusing for administrators, not least because it included territory that was technically Aragonese.[47] In the 1283 case, Lleida's Jews were not trying to shirk their obligations but instead requiring the crown to be consistent, presumably so that Lleida would not run the risk of getting double taxed. In turn, the king acknowledged that his administrator's demands ran counter to rulings by his father that Lleida's Jews pay a reduced amount with the aljamas of Catalonia. Such administrative diversity bred infighting and raised the potential for fraud. Pere clearly suspected as much in 1284 when he ordered an investigation into abnormalities in the payment of subsidies. He demanded that the aljama of Barcelona, along with other aljamas in Valencia, Aragon, and Catalonia (including Tortosa's), send representatives bearing all of their communities' records regarding the collections the crown had made over the past fifteen years.[48]

The conflict between Tortosa and Barcelona in 1282 had especially high stakes because its resolution promised to establish a powerful precedent for future subsidy assessments. Barcelona's community risked angering the Infant by continuing to defy his orders. It sought to delay payment of Tortosa's share while it waited for a final ruling from the royal court. Alfons, however, appeared unconcerned about the risk to Barcelona or inclined to rush the royal court's decision; he reiterated his order that its aljama render Tortosa's share.[49] If Barcelona's Jews wanted to continue to challenge this exemption, he asserted, they would have to do so only after first satisfying his demands.

The trail of evidence disappears at this point, and we might surmise from the silence that Barcelona's community proved unable to produce the necessary evidence to involve Tortosa in this subsidy demand. While the Jews of Tortosa thus apparently emerged unscathed among the implicated Catalonian aljamas, the victory was arguably more momentous for the town's lords. In collaboration with its local Jews, the seigniorial regime had averted the loss of a significant sum to the royal coffers by shifting the burden to Jews beyond its jurisdiction. These resources consequently remained available for the lords to profit from. The fact that Tortosa's Jews were able to resist some forms of royal taxation due, in part, to the seigniorial regime and relative weakness of the monarchy may explain why no evidence survives of the community campaigning for a return of royal administration. The Jews of Sahagún in northern Castile, by contrast, reportedly appeared before Alfonso X in 1255 to profess that they belonged to the king rather than to the oppressive local abbot, thus prompting the king to issue them new fueros that aimed to reduce the abbot's authority. Soifer Irish speculates that the Jews had been motivated to mount this challenge and seek out crown lordship because "they were already paying most of their taxes to the king."[50]

Such alliances in these local environments could be ephemeral, however. Only a few years earlier, Tortosa's aljama appears to have been playing on royal-seigniorial conflict to repel attempts by the lords to collect what were purportedly royal levies. In 1280, the king had ordered Ramon de Montcada and the master of the Templars to stop forcing the Jews to pay them the *cena* (originally a royal hospitality tax), which he argued belonged exclusively to Queen Constança of Sicily.[51] Defiant, Ramon de Montcada got caught commanding his porter to collect *cenas* illegitimately from both Jews and

Muslims in Tortosa in 1284. Yet, on this occasion, the Infant Alfons made no mention of the queen's prerogative.[52] It seems possible that the Jews of the town had taken the initiative to alert the monarchy about these infractions in hopes that it would bolster the rights of the less administratively capable collector. At the very least, the incident would prevent the Jews from having to pay these levies twice. Tortosa's checkered administrative history and the growing tension between royal and seigniorial authority invested its Jews with an increased ability to evade demands from either side.

Renegotiation

The taxation dispute between Tortosa and Barcelona in 1282 took place shortly before the monarchy became embroiled in a major crisis that threatened to reverse many of its gains in administrative prerogatives over the past few decades. The following year, the Aragonese capture of Sicily culminated in a papacy-supported French invasion of the Crown of Aragon. Desperate for additional financial and military support, Pere was forced to convoke a general court at Barcelona in late December. Here the assembled lay and religious lords and townspeople pressured him to make considerable concessions in return for their assistance with his war effort.[53]

The dynamics of the negotiations at this session of the general court are difficult to reconstruct from the extant *acta*. Source deficiencies make it challenging, in particular, to assess the agendas and strategies of each constituency present at the meeting. We know that the king was able to preserve standing crown policies concerning ethnoreligious minorities better than other prerogatives, but it is not clear whether this added success was the result of him prioritizing these rights or the lords valuing them less. Many of the provisions sought to increase the monarchy's accountability while further insulating seigniorial domains from royal intervention. The *acta* stipulate that Pere and his successors would be required to convoke the Corts every year and solicit the estates' approval for the passage of new laws. Furthermore, the kings' imposition of numerous royal levies would be more tightly restricted, and royal officials would be barred from entering seigniorial domains even when discharging their duties of upholding the royal peace.[54]

Rather than setting fixed procedural norms for all of Catalonia, a number of the crown's most important concessions adopted a flexible approach. When the *Usatges de Barcelona* could not serve as a reliable guide, the new policies based limits for royal prerogatives on established local customary laws.[55] Deference to custom was, of course, an established tradition that remained a crucial basis of law for influential contemporary jurists such as Pere Albert.[56] It also served as a pragmatic device for achieving compromise: in theory, it promised to restore established prerogatives and strip away unwelcome novelties, potentially to the detriment of either side, depending on the circumstances. Thus, the famous provision that permitted lords to demand redemption from their tenants—now viewed as a crucial step in the development of a legally recognized system of peasant servitude in Catalonia—limited its applicability to "lands and places where men are accustomed to being redeemed . . . just as it is customary to be done from ancient times [*antiquitus*] in whichever place." The territory designated by these customary legal characteristics happened to be predominantly the more heavily populated countryside of Old Catalonia in the northeast.[57] Similarly, lords would be entitled to exercise "civil justice [*mixtum imperium*] and jurisdiction" only in cases where they or their predecessors had done so "since ancient times [*ab antiquo*]." And royal officials would be barred from entering seigniorial domains wherever those restrictions had been customary during Jaume's reign.[58]

When it came to jurisdictional rights over Jews and Muslims, the nobility proposed new regulations that threatened to erase the principle of universal royal possession altogether. Jews and Muslims, they contended, should belong to the one exercising lordship over the castle or town in which they reside. If upheld, these changes would have brought an end to the monarchy's campaign to tax, judge, and protect Jews living beyond royal demesne lands. Given the nature of the other compromises, however, Pere was in a strong position when he insisted on utilizing customary guidelines. The parties agreed to base jurisdictional guidelines on traditional practice. At the same time, the king secured a significant legal victory by inserting a significant loophole into the language of the law that would permit the future expansion of royal jurisdiction. Customary norms regarding Jews and Muslims, the compromise stipulated, could be modified or overruled by "privileges and special agreements."[59] Unlike in many other provisions established at this momentous meeting of the general court, the king thus appears to have succeeded in preserving a narrow pathway forward to continue elaborating and expanding the servi regis policy. Customary exemption from royal jurisdiction over non-Christians would not just be difficult for many lords to demonstrate; the monarchy had preserved the legal means to undo ingrained customary limits on its intervention through negotiations with individual lords.

The Corts of 1283 had the effect of increasing the monarchy's reliance on subsidies from the non-Christian "royal treasure" within the patrimony by reducing its access to extraordinary levies from Christian subjects. At the same time, the session had exposed the risk to the crown's Jewish policy posed by Catalonia's barons, who clearly manifested their shared desire to retain full possession of their non-Christian tenants. The outcome of the Corts encouraged the monarchy to continue its pursuit of taxation from seigniorial aljamas in order to maintain contact and possibly develop a new sense of customary standing.

Accordingly, just months after the meeting of the general court concluded, the king ordered the aljama of Tortosa, among others, to send delegates to the royal court to make arrangements for the payment of tribute and various levies for 1284.[60] Another notice sent the following year suggests that this latest appeal had also failed, prompting the king to try yet another strategy to encourage compliance. In October 1285, Pere contacted the seigniorial aljamas of Monzón, Fraga, and Tortosa to urge them to satisfy their obligations to the crown. Without citing the principle directly, his letter nonetheless seems to have employed the legal spirit of the *Princeps namque* provision of the *Usatges de Barcelona*. As we discussed in chapter 4, this controversial and usually unheeded law obligated all men who were fit to fight to come to the prince's aid during a time of attack or risk losing all of the property they held from him. Those derelict subjects who did not hold fiefs from the prince would, in theory, be required to make satisfaction with their property.[61] This obligation undergirded the image of the king, promoted elsewhere in the *Usatges*, and amplified in the *Commemoracions*, as the "sovereign" defender of the public peace, who was supplemented by the armed, financial, and moral support and counsel of his faithful subjects.[62]

The interpretation advanced in the king's appeal seems to have been that the members of these aljamas, as subjects, were beneficiaries of the king's protection and consequently beholden to do their expected part, regardless of their personal jurisdictional conditions. Accordingly, in his letter, Pere emphasized that the shared danger facing the realm, with the war emerging from the Sicilian Vespers, affected these Jews and that his subsidy demand would contribute directly to the common good: "You [Jews] know well about the great affairs that have preoccupied us and continue to do so in defending the land for us and for you from enemies." He noted that he was not singling out these seigniorial aljamas and had also sent this plea for assistance to "all of the said aljamas of the Jews of our land."

Pere did not rely exclusively, however, on evoking a sense of the realms' urgent need and these Jews' undeniable shared duty to motivate compliance. Pere asserted that the Jews were also held to respect the royal "right" (*ius*) established "by the accounts, charters, and privileges held from us and from our predecessors." "Accounts" presumably signified records of previous attempts by him and his father to collect subsidies or other taxation from these communities. It is not clear to what specific written privileges the king was referring that would have bound these Jews to contribute in this fashion. He could have been employing a formula or compiled the list in an effort to sound more authoritative and entitled. He also threatened the aljamas with severe penalties if they defied his mandate and ordered them to send two prohoms as procurators to satisfy these claims within six days. Possibly in keeping with the *Princeps namque* provision, the king warned that he would move against their persons and property if they did not comply with his directives.[63] It is not clear how these communities responded or whether royal administrators continued to pursue these alleged obligations following Pere's premature death less than a month later, in November 1285.

Possibly borrowing from this incorporative strategy, the new king, Alfons, sought to ease Tortosa's Jews into the tradition of paying tribute by involving them in the process. He assigned them shared responsibility with other communities while deferring or reducing their assigned obligations. Thus, in 1287, a year in which the king granted many communities fractional remissions, he offered the Jews of Tortosa an unusual full reprieve from their entire ten-thousand-solidi share, pending a revised mandate.[64]

Other evidence, while depicting the monarchy's continued effort to exercise authority over Jews in Tortosa, also emphasizes the distinction between the seigniorial nature of Tortosa's aljama and Jews under direct royal administration elsewhere. In 1288, for example, Alfons acted on a complaint from his "royal Jew," David Alaçar, that a Jewish resident of Tortosa, Azac Avinachura, had caused him damages. Rather than relying on local seigniorial or municipal officials to try the case, he ordered Azac to appear in the royal court within ten days to answer to these charges.[65]

Transfer to Royal Control and Continuing Challenges

By the early years of his reign in the 1290s, Alfons's successor, Jaume II (r. 1291–1327), had already abandoned further attempts to share power with the seigniorial regime. He had good reasons to doubt that his administration would succeed, where his predecessors had failed, in imposing the monarchy's claimed prerogatives in Tortosa without unadulterated rights of jurisdictional lordship. He orchestrated an outright purchase of the town from the seigniorial regime using other crown possessions in 1294.

In September of that year, Templar representatives officially exchanged the Order's majority share of jurisdiction in Tortosa for the northern Valencian castles and towns of Penyíscola, Ares, and Coves de Vinromà.[66] In order to secure these rights to Tortosa, the monarchy had to invest the Templars with a high degree of administrative autonomy over their new possessions, similar to what they had formerly held within Tortosa. These lordships came with "all men and women, Christian, Jewish, and Muslim, who are living or will be living here, and with full lordship [*dominium*] and with criminal and civil justice [*merum et mixtum imperium*] . . . and the *pena*, judicial fines, the *lleuda*," and a long list of additional levies.[67] Recuperation of this holding thus came at the price of the dislocation of other royal jurisdictions. Only days after the Templars enacted the exchange, Guillem de Montcada transferred his share of Tortosa and its *çuda* to the monarchy in return for similar rights to the Aragonese castles and towns of Ballobar and Zaidín.[68]

It is difficult to know from the extant documentation to what extent the monarchy's long history of troubles in maintaining its claimed prerogatives within Tortosa motivated this exchange. As we have witnessed, over the past decades a range of strategies had yielded only limited administrative gains in advancing regalian rights there. Given that he had served as king of Sicily since 1285, Jaume II was relatively experienced at ruling and prepared to act by the time he assumed the titles for the rest of the Crown of Aragon in 1291. Preparations for the complicated transfer must have been time-consuming and thus initiated shortly after his assumption of power in Catalonia. The king was clearly aware of the long track record of seigniorial opposition to the crown's Jewish policy. He must have understood that his acquisition of rights of jurisdiction was instrumental for realizing the full extent of royal claims to the treasure represented by the Jews of Tortosa. At the same time, it is highly likely that Jaume's decision to acquire full jurisdiction over the town had been motivated by other concerns and strategic interests. In addition to Tortosa's positioning within the territories of the Crown of Aragon, which had motivated his predecessors' administrative overtures, its status as a vibrant port city at the mouth of the Ebro trade corridor may have fit into the king's plans to increase his kingdom's Mediterranean presence.[69] The seigniorial regime manifested no signs of reluctance to engage in the transaction. Indeed, it seems probable that, after years of conflict with the citizens' universitas, the lords had grown eager to exchange this troublesome lordship for other, more easily exploitable holdings that were less encumbered by customary privileges.

Following the transfer, for the first time in generations, the monarchy suddenly found itself empowered to enact policies in Tortosa without seigniorial opposition. Jaume did, however, recognize the potential for continued resistance from residents and set out to smooth the transition to Christian rule and begin building relationships with the different constituencies in the town. Within a month of the transfer, he confirmed to the Jewish aljama all of the privileges granted by his predecessors and added some new ones. His granting of pardons, favors, and privileges could have supported an effort to reiterate to the aljama that royal lordship came with its advantages.[70] In 1299, in return for a payment of four thousand solidi, he agreed to stop prosecuting the Jews for past usury abuses, a concession only the king was equipped to offer.[71] Although Jaume was soon collecting a wide range of royal levies from the aljama,[72] he was also building relationships with the town's Jewish elites by issuing franchises from routine taxation in repayment for loyal service.[73] With Tortosa's decades-long jurisdictional dislocation now resolved, such engagement with the upper strata of local Jewish society could be aligned with the normative patterns already firmly in place in other localities under royal lordship and redirected toward serving royal fiscal objectives. Such efforts were bolstered by the king's transformation of Tortosa into the hub of an administrative network extending throughout southern New Catalonia. By 1303, less than a decade after his acquisition of the town, Jaume had established a *supravicaria* based in Tortosa that exercised jurisdiction over the Catalonian vicariates of Tortosa, Ribera d'Ebre, Tarragona and its *camp*, the mountains of Prades, and Montblanc.⁷⁴

Beyond Tortosa, Jaume was demonstrably more systematic about administration building and proactive about defending his interests as "prince of the land" than any of his predecessors.⁷⁵ When he confronted lords throughout his realms who defied his Jewish policy, he tenaciously challenged their alleged encroachments with sophisticated and consistent legal argumentation. In 1299, for instance, the king heard reports that the archbishop of Tarragona, who exercised lordship over his archiepiscopal town, was obstructing royal tax collectors from taking payments from the local Jews. Jaume used the opportunity to reject the notion of seigniorial possession and establish more boldly than ever before that all Jews in Catalonia pertained to the royal patrimony. He employed the formula "property of our private chamber" (*res proprie camere nostre*), which was gaining currency elsewhere in medieval Europe, most notably in the Holy Roman Empire, and would have long and widespread influence in the Crown of Aragon:⁷⁶ "In Catalonia it is manifest to all that all Jews of this city and of other cities and places in Catalonia, and their goods, are property of our private chamber, and we and our predecessors have been able and accustomed to impose *questias, subsidia, collectas*, and other [levies] and to demand and have petitions from them, just as is pleasing to our will."⁷⁷ From Jaume's perspective, not only did the monarchy enjoy unfettered possession of Jews in Tarragona and throughout the land, but also this right was customary. This assertion may well have been calculated to invoke the customary legal underpinnings of the provision enacted at the Corts of 1283 and upheld in subsequent assemblies.

Such bold rhetoric notwithstanding, the king continued to encounter difficulties with noncompliance similar to what his predecessors had faced in Tortosa and other locales. Five years later, the same archbishop once again resisted royal officials' efforts to tax the local aljama. In response, Jaume stressed that "it cannot come in doubt, indeed it is apparent and obvious to all," that "the Jews of our land" are "property of our chamber and subjugated as our *regalia*."⁷⁸

By blocking the crown's access to Jewish revenues in defense of their exercise of private territorial jurisdiction, independent lords inadvertently goaded the monarchy into developing a bolder and more self-justified Jewish policy. Although Jaume and his successors in the fourteenth century would face obstructionism similar to what his thirteenth-century predecessors had confronted, their progressive strengthening of central and local royal administration increased their ability to identify abuses, hold resistant lords accountable, and to access isolated Jewish communities. These moments served as opportunities to develop and broadcast these royal claims, thus cultivating a popular conception that they were normative and justified. They also made examples of lords who sought to disregard these prerogatives. Nevertheless, so long as the crown had to share jurisdiction or delegate it to nonroyal authorities, thus perpetuating the familiar jurisdictional zero-sum game we have witnessed throughout this book, its ability to exert its claim of full possession of all Jews would remain elusive.

6

SEIGNIORIAL JURISDICTION AND THE TRANSITION TO ROYAL GOVERNANCE

Complete royal withdrawal paired with the development of an independent seigniorial regime, followed by increasing royal engagement and finally the full assumption of jurisdictional rights—these administrative rhythms affected Jews and non-Jews alike in Tortosa over the later twelfth and thirteenth centuries. They could also describe a large subset of urban and rural localities throughout the Crown of Aragon as well as wider medieval Europe. Running counter to the traditional teleology of supreme royal power, we have found in Tortosa a capable, self-confident, and legally defensible independent seigniorial regime.

The administrative picture we have pieced together thus far in this book aligns neatly with the vision of high medieval governance evoked in Thomas Bisson's most recent monograph, *The Crisis of the Twelfth Century*. According to Bisson, the scene witnessed in Tortosa was common throughout Europe as a whole during the long twelfth century; it endured longest in Catalonia, where "the narrative of progressive change [in royal governance] is offset by those of responsive shifts of direction, setbacks, and complacency."[1] Despite the monarchy's development of new administrative tools and techniques designed to promote centralization and standardization, cases such as Tortosa and others we will consider in the remaining pages of this book should lead us to question to what extent these limitations completely faded away over the course of the high and late Middle Ages.

The seigniorial autonomies that materialized and the customary traditions these regimes helped establish or harden during the High Middle Ages proved highly resilient and resistant to elimination or alteration. Their powerful inertia impeded the development of pervasive and uniform royal authority as well as the crown's efforts to standardize governance and regulation. The Crown of Aragon indeed remained, as Bisson has argued elsewhere, "federative rather than integrative."[2] Local heterogeneity, enhanced rather than diminished by centuries of expansionism, remained the norm rather than the exception. As a means of bringing this study to a close, this chapter will reflect on Tortosa's jurisdictional transitions and persistent customary legal traditions within the context of the greater Crown of Aragon. We will consider in what ways they represent expressions of these administrative counternarratives as well as review the methodological approaches we have employed to observe them.

The Implications of Seigniorial Governance

Throughout the foregoing chapters, we have employed a methodology that has prioritized localization by questioning the assumption that general mandates emanating from the crown were felt equally throughout the diversely governed communities of the realms. Rather than automatically viewing any king's claim or pronouncement as a fait accompli, we have sought to condition our estimate of its influence on evidence of its local application. Appreciating the importance of localization encourages a rereading of many royal policies that can all too easily be viewed as neatly descriptive of normative conditions. Given what we know were formidable barriers to direct royal influence in many quarters, the rights that the crown was able to assert over Jews within its own domains should not be extrapolated casually to other, nonroyal jurisdictions. Jaume I, for example, felt empowered to require relatives of his deceased Jewish bailiff of Barcelona to remit all of the crown's debts held by the Jew in return for the right to inherit his estate in 1227. Yet, evidence that this enactment emanated from the king's court should not lead us to conclude that the crown's "borrowing from the Jews remained a form of tallage" invariably throughout the Crown of Aragon.³

A chronic shortage of resources prevented the monarchy from pursuing its objectives in the same manner or to the same degree in every locality. Unless the monarchy were able to invest new, nonlanded resources to fund acquisitions or somehow strip away seigniorial prerogatives within freshly allocated holdings, shrewd kings and their advisors had little choice but to prioritize. Transactions that strengthened the crown's administrative standing in some localities were often funded by reductions in its holdings elsewhere. We observed this process at work in the previous chapter with the crown's purchase of lordship over Tortosa. The king compensated the Templars and Montcada for their rights there by assigning them equally unfettered jurisdictional prerogatives to other holdings.

Similarly, earlier in the thirteenth century, as the monarchy was finalizing its withdrawal from Tortosa thus facilitating the ascendancy of the seigniorial regime, it was simultaneously investing resources to extend its control over non-Christians living in seigniorial domains elsewhere. In 1210, Pere I sought to secure possession of all of the Jews and a select few Muslims residing in the Hospitaller domains between the Segre and Ariza Rivers and across the rest of Aragon in exchange for the castle of Cabañas and water rights to irrigate the Order's local estates. The transaction, however, specifically excluded the family of Rabbi Aser Abinbentalcan, who, the king acknowledged, had already elected to have the Hospitallers as his patron. The rabbi and his family renewed their fidelity to the Order and pledged the service owed as part of their "common *societas*" at the general chapter meeting in Zaragoza the following year, in return for further personal guarantees. The parties made clear their shared awareness that the rabbi had a choice of patrons. If the Hospitallers violated their obligations, the rabbi would have the right to seek damages not only via the king, but also using the Order's "other lords and associates."⁴ The contract, in other words, did not prioritize royal over seigniorial oversight.

The Hospitaller domains in Catalonia and Aragon represent yet another parallel case of increasing seigniorial independent authority. Already in 1208, Pere had issued the Order a sweeping exemption from royal taxation and levying and any forcible imposition by the crown throughout the Hospitaller domains. The privilege, Pere stressed twice in the document, would apply to all of its property, brethren, and subjects, male and female, "Christians, Jews, and Muslims."[5]

In seeking out evidence of more complicated, locally variegated applications of general royal mandates, this study has also questioned the assumption that documentation that does not explicitly mention ethnoreligious minorities is consequently of little or no relevance to their history. As we have noticed, several of the more critical documents to our understanding of Jews' administrative situation in Tortosa were not directed specifically at that subset of the population. Throughout much of the time frame observed by this book, the Jews were subject to administrative conditions similar to those of the rest of Tortosa's populace. Even though the Jews were recognized as a community apart from the time of their initial settlement charter, they were not immune to the forces of lordship that shaped Tortosa's broader urban history. Documentation relating to the wider administrative context of Tortosa and the surrounding realms has enabled us to see the interconnections between the history of the Jewish community and that of the broader town, with significant implications for the study of each.

Such an approach has enabled us to capitalize on the assets of the extant evidence from Tortosa. Although it borrows from the methodology employed by Klein in her study of the Jews of Barcelona, which sought to identify parallels between Jewish and Christian communal development, our study has been better equipped to show how Jews participated in and were implicated by the major developments in the jurisdictional history of the town. This orientation responds to a gap in the literature and conforms to the assets and deficiencies of the local evidence, which tells us so much about jurisdictional conflict yet yields so little information about the social composition of Tortosa's Jewish aljama.

Our methodology has been influenced by an important observation regarding both traditional and more recent scholarship. Although scholars have assiduously explored the complexities of both convivencia and governance in relative isolation, they have done comparatively little to scrutinize the potential interrelation of these subfields. As a result, scholarship on ethnoreligious minorities has tended to overestimate the crown's ability to enact its administrative policies, and work on governance has not appreciated the role that ethnoreligious relations played in the dynamics of royal-seigniorial administrative competition. Yet, as we have perceived, Jews were not simply bystanders or passive subjects when it came to these engagements. Rather, they played an integral role in the administrative history of the town.

Part of the Jews' importance had to do with the strategies elaborated by the crown that we have explored over the past several chapters. The monarchy's quest to establish jurisdictional control over Tortosa's Jewish aljama in conformity with its emerging Jewish policy was not simply an end in its own right. It was also part of, and helped facilitate in crucial ways, the monarchy's wider effort to develop its administrative capacity and secure control over public order in keeping with the regalian principles that had been under development for generations. Recognizing the ties between these sorts of general policies and specific moves to regulate non-Christian residents as special subjects has helped us reconstruct and reinterpret the patterns of royal engagement with the situation in Tortosa. This approach has also enabled us to de-provincialize the history of Jews in the Crown of Aragon by observing, from the perspective of an unusually rich case study, how their communities and community members were directly involved, implicated, and shaped by competition and cooperation between royal and seigniorial authority.

We have seen how complex dynamics of conflict, negotiation, and collaboration involving the lords, Christian, Muslim, and Jewish townspeople, other local potentates, and only sporadically the king or royal delegates forged the localized coexistence—the unique micro-convivencia—in seigniorial Tortosa. With the fragmentation of jurisdiction, the development of norms of self-determination for Jewish (and Muslim) aljamas became a complicated, decentralized process that did not always respond to royal direction. Accordingly, this shift by the thirteenth century from "autonomy by default" (experienced by the Jews because of royal impotence or indifference) and to "autonomy by design" (in which the king managed the shape of the community, its powers, and its operation) that has been proposed by Klein should be expanded to include equally viable nonroyal forms of lordship.[6] For many local environments, seigniorial privileges and other internal documents illustrate what Bensch has observed for Empúries—that "within their territories, barons were just as interested as the king in intervening to create durable structures for Jews."[7]

In this respect, our primary local case of Tortosa has been particularly illuminating. It has allowed us to appreciate, with unusual detail, how jurisdictional isolation could permit some level of variegation in these policies.

At the same time, it has empowered us to recognize that this town's microconvivencia was not fashioned out of whole cloth. Rather, Tortosa's unique coexistence was constrained by a number of factors: these included customary legal traditions, the activity of local constituencies, competition for Jewish residents, and the broader socioreligious context mandating certain administrative norms for Jewish residents. The same forces that encouraged the independent counts of Empúries to emulate features of the Jewish policies of the count-kings, not surprisingly, came to influence the seigniorial regime in Tortosa albeit in markedly different ways. Tortosa's lords and emergent municipal regime could be inclined to respect the principle of autonomy alongside other royal provisions, yet did so out of their own respective self-interest to maintain and utilize the Jewish residents rather than out of blind obedience to royal dictates. Ultimately, these local actors possessed considerable power to reject, adopt, or modify aspects of these initiatives emanating from the royal court or move in a different direction altogether.

Over time, the jurisdictional regulations of both royal and nonroyal authorities thereby interacted with existing local policies and customary laws. This contact, particularly when there were moments of synergy between royal policies and nonroyal agendas, served to generate or adjust the modes of coexistence in force in a given locality. This dynamic process helped differentiate a given town's conditions considerably from those of other communities with distinct jurisdictional circumstances and legal norms. We have observed, for instance, how the customary legal traditions in Tortosa that came to be officially codified as the *Costums de Tortosa* in the early 1270s would continue to regulate many of the important aspects of the coexistence of Christians, Jews, and Muslims in the local environment. According to these laws, only the Jews lacked their own autonomous judicial forum for cases with coreligionists—a stipulation that notably ran counter to the crown's emerging Jewish policy. The Muslim aljama, by contrast, appears to have possessed jurisdiction over internal cases throughout the period of Christian rule. This distinction may have originated in the initial Jewish and Muslim settlement privileges. While the charter of security for the Muslims awarded them judicial privileges, the stipulations of the Jewish charter were unclear, since they applied the prerogatives enjoyed by the Jews of Barcelona, which do not survive.[8] The *Costums* were clear, however, that both Jews and Muslims would have to appear in either the municipal or seigniorial courts for any case involving Christians and did not make any allowance for the participation of Muslim or Jewish judges.[9]

Nearby Lleida, by comparison, possessed a different judicial framework that supported distinct patterns of interaction between its resident ethnoreligious groups. It is difficult to measure the extent to which these differences were established at the time of the post-conquest distribution since no settlement charters survive for either the Muslim or Jewish communities in Lleida. Scholars commonly assume that they would have been similar to those from Tortosa because the towns were both conquered and settled by Ramon Berenguer IV at roughly the same time. Yet, it is impossible to know whether the judicial system had been ushered in by these constitutional enactments or was elaborated later in response to the development of the urban communities.

Lleida's most notable jurisdictional distinction was that the crown maintained it as part of its patrimony. As a result, in contrast to the situation with Tortosa, kings experienced no decrease in their means to intervene to manipulate or create institutions and policies within the town. In the early thirteenth century, at a time when Pere I involved himself very rarely with the administrative affairs in Tortosa, he intervened to authorize a consular regime in Lleida as well as to defend the judicial autonomy of ethnoreligious minorities in the town.[10] In 1202, he issued a decree indicating that Muslim residents in Lleida possessed their own court governed by the *zalmedina* or *alcaydus*, which exercised jurisdiction over any cases involving local Muslims. Resident Muslims engaged in cases involving Jews or Christians could not be tried by any other court unless the *zalmedina* or *alcaydus* were involved in handling and judging them.[11] The king did not mandate that local Jews should have identical prerogatives on this occasion. Yet, his charter did indicate that the Jews possessed a local court with jurisdiction over internal cases as well as cases with Muslims, so long as those same Muslim officials were involved. We possess clear confirmation of this scenario much later, in 1270, with the appointment of Naci Açday as Lleida's crown rabbi.[12] Jaume I indicated that Naci would not only serve the Jews of his aljama as rabbi in accordance with "the commandments of the Old Laws" but also have the capacity to judge all cases between Jews with the counsel of two reputable local Jews of his choosing.[13] This precise arrangement must have been short-lived, however, since it ran counter to Pere II's mandate from 1280, discussed in chapter 2, which standardized the system of adelantats throughout the royal domains in Catalonia.[14]

Such privileges received by the residents proceeded to define elements of Lleida's micro-convivencia, differentiating them from the localized legal norms of other communities for generations to come. Indeed, the regulations instituted by this particular royal charter from 1202 survive only because the document was cited repeatedly by later kings until the fourteenth century. Each upheld and confirmed the increasingly time-honored privilege.[15] Such profound respect for custom in medieval law frequently led the monarchy and lords to preserve local distinctions in rules regarding coexistence that were not of their own making or that had arguably outlived their raison d'être. Irrespective of what ruler, faction, or historical circumstance initially prompted them, privileges and regulations thus had enormous staying power. Like Darwin's finches, after generations of accumulated responses to local stimuli, micro-convivencias within these environments evolved with significant, persistent characteristics.

Accordingly, enactments by nonroyal authorities had the potential to cast a shadow over the period of royal governance, just as early comital and royal privileges initiated customary traditions that had informed or constrained seigniorial rule. Indeed, the agreements, customary laws, and documents generated under the lords retained force of law in Tortosa after the royal transfer. For example, legal victories secured or losses suffered by the seigniorial regime during its jurisdictional battles against the universitas of Tortosa were inherited by the crown and shaped its administrative authority over the Jews. Jaume II had clearly been conscious of the importance of these precedents in the years after he assumed administrative control of the town. In addition to his enactments mandating that local royal officials comply with the *Costums de Tortosa* when discharging their duties, he also guaranteed, in 1295, that under royal lordship the municipal regime would suffer no reduction in status or privileges that it had possessed during the seigniorial period. The leaders of the universitas had apparently taken advantage of an opportune moment to request such assurances regarding their customary rights when the king demanded that the citizens perform homage to him as their lord.[16] Limitations based on enactments or privileges made or nurtured during the seigniorial period continued to influence the exercise of royal governance. Within a year of the royal takeover, the universitas objected to the king's mandate that its Christian citizens respond to the call to arms on the grounds that they were exempt. The town would continue to wage a stern defense of this alleged exemption against similar requests by the monarchy until at least the sixteenth century.[17]

Similar complications marked the crown's administration of the Jewish community. In a case from 1394, for example, town officials challenged the privilege of "safe passage and protection" that King Joan I (r. 1387–96) had conceded to the Jewish aljama at its request. He had ordered municipal officials to announce it within Tortosa. The Jews likely had been interested in securing further guarantees of royal protection after having their persons and property attacked during the summer and fall of 1391 in the wave of anti-Jewish aggression that had swept across the Peninsula. The king had moved to try to halt further violence and restore normalcy to Tortosa at that time.[18] The community nevertheless suffered significant damage from the attack, leading Joan to issue it special licenses and dispensations to assist with the dire financial situation that had emerged "when the Jews here were forcefully persecuted, destroyed, and robbed."[19]

In opposition, the citizens' procurators asserted that the king was not authorized to grant such a privilege or force the municipal officials to uphold it since it ran counter to the "customs, privileges and liberties of the city." They sent a petition to the royal court and the governor of Catalonia demanding that the privilege be rescinded.[20] The petition cited a law from the *Costums de Tortosa* that upheld most of the *Carta de la Paeria*. That agreement from 1275, as we have seen, had defined the jurisdiction of the town court and mandated specific procedures and punishments for certain kinds of cases. Most importantly, whereas capital punishment was mandatory for any Christian, Jew, or Muslim found guilty of murdering a Christian, Christians could exonerate themselves for homicides of Jews or Muslims by paying a fine. These procedures had allegedly been customary for untold years.[21] The *Carta* had assigned jurisdiction over these sorts of crimes involving Jews to the municipal court, so long as they did not directly involve the lords, and had entitled the seigniorial regime to only part of the one-fifth share of the fines owed to the court. Thus, the king, the citizens' procurators alleged, was not equipped to award the entire aljama such a sweeping privilege of protection.

The petition's argument hinged implicitly on the alleged primacy of Tortosa's customary laws. The *Costums* therefore overruled both standing royal Jewish policy and the jurisdictional provisions of the *Usatges de Barcelona* that sought to award the king full authority over cases concerning the injury or death of Jews.[22] In response, Joan did not try to challenge the standing of the *Costums* or even the validity of this particular law in order to uphold the crown's idealized standard of exclusive royal protection over the Jews. Instead, he appears to have embraced the fact that royal policy would have to adapt to coexist with Tortosa's ingrained legal traditions. He deferred to the citizens' privileges and rescinded his privilege of protection. The king, furthermore, made it clear that he, in keeping with the monarchy's established practice, stood in full support of Tortosa's customary privileges. He did so by sending the procurators confirmations by him and his predecessor, Pere III (r. 1336–87), along with an order to all royal officials to desist from any activity that might prejudice these privileges.[23] Although the town court would continue to exercise independent jurisdiction over many cases involving the Jews, Joan may already have realized that the liabilities he had inherited from the seigniorial regime were offset by other beneficial elements of the local customary laws. Most importantly, as town lord, he could reserve jurisdiction over any case implicating the crown or its interests.[24]

The Implications of the Transition to Royal Authority

Despite all that we know about the changing jurisdictional situation in Tortosa, we are left with some lingering queries about the persistence of royal rights and the extent to which these were necessary for the engagement attempted by Jaume I and his successors over the second half of the thirteenth century. It remains unclear under what circumstances and for what specific motives Jaume increased his stake in Tortosa prior to the 1247 agreement with the lords. Could the crown have justifiably sought to build up an administrative presence in Tortosa had it not preserved any financial stake in the town by the early years of Jaume's reign? Could the lords have flatly denied the king's request for an official in the town? The king's willingness to motivate them with considerable concessions and make do with the limited position they permitted him suggests that the lords possessed some degree of agency in the lengthy negotiations.

It is difficult to ascertain whether the monarchy was fully conscious of or bothered by these limitations on its general policies in places such as

Tortosa throughout the thirteenth century. If the crown was, we should consider to what extent the administrative techniques we have observed were deliberately calculated to erode seigniorial independence. Another possibility is that the monarchy pursued these measures in accordance with its interpretation of its regalian prerogatives with no ulterior motives. Royal administrators must have been aware that instruments originally intended to increase the pervasiveness and potency of royal authority, such as the regalian principles of the *Usatges de Barcelona,* were being marshaled by lords to bolster their own local authority. As we have witnessed, the lords' conception that they were fully entitled to the powers of the *postat* defined by the *Usatges de Barcelona* arguably served to reinforce the monarchy's emerging precept that the policies applying to non-Christians and jurisdictional rights emanated from the crown. Yet, the fact that some lords were asserting these rights without clear royal sanction tarnished these same royal claims. Indeed, the unexpected utility of these time-honored laws for the seigniorial agenda helps explain why barons in Catalonia and Aragon expended precious political capital to force the monarchy to prioritize the *Usatges* and bar the application of much more threatening Roman legal principles from the mid-thirteenth century.[25]

What is clear from Jaume's dealings with the seigniorial regime beginning in 1247 is that the leveraging and administrative changes enacted by Alfons I and Pere I produced an administrative withdrawal that the crown struggled to reverse. This vision of royal impotence is unfamiliar among scholarship on the administration of ethnoreligious minorities. Most work has found that monarchies in the Peninsula tended to alienate primarily fiscal rights over non-Christians and that delegation was controlled and purposeful. Lords acquired jurisdictional capacity over non-Christians only when it was deliberately assigned by the crown—grants that the monarchs, accordingly, possessed full capacity to revoke at will.[26] Tortosa, however, presents the opposite situation and should lead us to speculate how many other empowered nonroyal jurisdictions emerged in a similar fashion. Moreover, the monarchy's engagement with Tortosa leading up to its purchase was empowered more by its possession of property than by the record of seigniorial investiture or by regalian claims. The monarchy's pronouncements and lawmaking did not always dictate normative conditions and should be carefully scrutinized rather than accepted at face value.

As individuals bonded together into a corporate community, Tortosa's Jews appear to have understood the jurisdictional situation and to have taken advantage of it to the extent that they could. Seigniorial jurisdiction, for example, had provided the aljama with an effective means to mitigate or shirk altogether the monarchy's tribute obligations suffered by other Jewish communities under direct royal control. Ray's observation that the "persistence of royal concern regarding jurisdiction over the Jews reflects both the limits of monarchical authority and the practical necessity for Jews to develop social, economic, and political ties to a variety of lay and ecclesiastical lords" certainly rings true for Tortosa.[27] The tension between the lords and the king encouraged local Jews to select the most beneficial patrons and serve as officers and creditors for both seigniorial and royal administrations. These roles may have worked to these Jews' individual benefit. Yet, as we saw with Astruc Xixó and other Jewish royal officers, these responsibilities also appear to have damaged the financial well-being and solidarity of the local Jewish community in certain cases.

Tortosa's reception by the monarchy—part of the "narrative of progressive change" described earlier by Bisson—may have made its Jews more vulnerable to exploitation in some respects. Yet, it also arguably improved their standing in others. Some significant improvements in Jewish autonomy first surface in the sources following the monarchy's purchase, but they cannot be directly tied, using available documentation, to the return of royal administration. A charter from 1295, for instance, appears to indicate that, by this point, the community had acquired adelantats as well as the right to judge cases between its members.[28] We lack sources to document the establishment of these changes, and it is possible that they were implemented during the seigniorial period even though they are not reflected in the extant sources from that time. There can be no question that the Jews were aware of the advantages of the tension between the king and lords when it came to the royal subsidy demands as well as judicial matters. Their ambiguous jurisdictional situation, as we have seen, provided them with a means to evade or appeal to either seigniorial or royal authority as they saw fit. In the future, without the assistance of motivated seigniorial advocates, it would be more difficult for the aljama to delay, renegotiate, or avoid altogether its imputed responsibility to contribute to royal subsidies on the basis that it stood under distinct jurisdictional conditions that carried special traditions and exemptions. Furthermore, the king may have been less motivated to cater to the community as a whole than when the Templars and Montcadas had been present to compete with his authority. He now had the unadulterated legal and administrative means to assert his claimed regalian possession of these Jews.

The most important basis for the special status of Tortosa's Jews were now gone even if distinctive elements of the town's customary laws still necessitated some modifications to royal policies. The community now had to compete on a level playing field with other aljamas similarly administered by the crown. Of course, Jews could still attempt to shirk their tax responsibilities using other techniques and rationales. One popular maneuver throughout the realms was for Jews to maintain residences in multiple communities and use them as a pretext for strategic exemption when certain communities were hit hard by tax demands. Tortosa's Jews were, in fact, already familiar with this technique, having employed it to try to escape taxation in Alcañíz, as we saw in chapter 5. The crown, however, generally moved quickly to close such loopholes. In 1314, for example, it mandated that any Jew with real estate in Tortosa would have to contribute to the aljama's taxes.[29] The monarchy did maintain its practice of issuing grants of tax exemption and other privileges to elite Jews, which were often responsible for escalating tension within the aljama. Possibly with an eye to reducing such communal conflict, in 1323 the king extended the benefits of temporary immunity from certain fines (*penas*) requested by one constituency to Tortosa's entire aljama.[30] Nevertheless, by Jaume II's own admission in 1326, heavy and frequent royal subsidy demands had reduced the aljama to a degree of poverty it apparently had not experienced under seigniorial rule.[31]

Already by the turn of the fourteenth century, Jaume II had set to work integrating Tortosa's aljama into the monarchy's increasingly standardized system of taxation and regulation. In 1299, he indicated that Tortosa would represent the head of a new *collecta* consisting of communities from southeastern Catalonia. On this first occasion, the *collecta* had to pay the *monedatge* levy together with a number of unaffiliated Aragonese communities.[32] The enforcement of royal regulations limited the activity of the remaining lords in Tortosa's district. In 1300, for example, this same king ordered the bishop of Tortosa to recall his officials from investigating charges that local Jews had violated the royal usury regulations dating from the reign of Jaume I, which had capped the maximum allowable interest for loans to Christians at 20 percent. If this report of the bishop's actions were true, the king confessed, he would be "greatly astonished, since it is known that [this matter] pertains to us and not to you."[33] This encroachment by the bishop may have been even more offensive to the king because it directly contradicted a recent royal enactment. Jaume had just sold the Jews an exemption from litigation over past usury offenses, making the handling of these sorts of investigations especially delicate.[34] On the other hand, the king was content to leave other traditionally unregulated aspects of Jewish lending alone. In 1321, for example, he assured his bailiff in Tortosa that Jews could charge resident and extra-local Muslims whatever interest rate, for however long a term, they could negotiate, as was the case with the rest of the "Jews of Our land and realms."[35]

With the direct lordship secured, the king faced the problem of ensuring that his own officials would execute his commands faithfully and not exploit the Jews for personal profit.[36] His track record for this enterprise was mixed. Tortosa's jailer failed to abide by the king's mandate from 1301 that he desist from demanding maintenance payments (the *carcellagium*) from Jews that he did not also collect from Christians. The king had to repeat this order in 1303.[37] The jailer's opportunistic exploitation of the Jews was particularly offensive since, as the king explained in his first mandate, his collections ran "against the use and observance of the aforementioned privileges," which had been "accustomed . . . since ancient times [*ab antiquo*]." In 1314, the king responded to complaints that his bailiff was impeding a local custom that granted the Jewish aljama the authority to bar delinquent debtors from attending rabbinical orations in the synagogue. Upholding the general principle of "autonomy by design," he deemed it unreasonable and unproductive for the bailiff to disturb the community by intervening in its internal affairs.[38]

The relative newness of royal administration could have inspired heightened caution regarding the defense of customary laws in Tortosa. By contrast, the monarchy was less wary of moving against both time-honored and recent customs in other royal jurisdictions. After Jaume I confirmed the "good and useful customs" of Perpignan in 1243, for example, he abrogated nine of them in 1250 on the grounds that they conflicted with the standard he wished to see applied throughout Catalonia.[39] The fact that Tortosa's customary laws had developed chiefly under seigniorial rule may have dissuaded Jaume II and his successors from so overtly challenging the status quo in order to satisfy their objectives for the town or to bring it in line with royal policies in other jurisdictions. The infamous litigiousness of Tortosa's constituencies also could have functioned as a deterrent.

Coexistence and Customary Laws in Royal Tortosa

The influence of the seigniorial regime had been tempered by the foundations established during the first decades of comital-royal administration. Similarly, institutional inertia and the continued involvement of other local constituencies—most importantly, the universitas of citizens, the Muslim aljama, and the Jewish community—limited the potential impact of the monarchy's reestablishment of its administrative authority. Indeed, longstanding disagreements among these groups over their respective customary privileges and liabilities continued to shape local modes of coexistence under royal jurisdiction. Although the monarchy often intervened and helped decide these disputes, it did not prompt them, generate the agendas at play, or exercise full control over the factors (customary laws, privileges, regulations, etc.) that largely determined their outcomes. Some of the most important conflicts over Jewish coexistence in the city were initiated by and resolved in accordance with early royal privileges that had been amplified during the decades of seigniorial rule.

Before we bring this study to a close, it is worthwhile to explore how some of the complexities of the departure from and return to royal administration colored coexistence in later medieval Tortosa. Two case studies will illustrate how different constituencies contested the implications of customary legal guidelines regarding the presence of the Jewish community. As we shall observe, these customary laws contained both privileges and liabilities that were distinct from those of other communities that had long stood under direct royal control. As a result, the legal circumstances of Tortosa's Jewish aljama could not simply be standardized by fiat. The situation there was clearly more constrained than in Cervera and Tàrrega, for example, when Jaume II ordered their vicar to accord them the privileges already possessed by the Jews of Lleida in 1325.[40]

Our first case study emerged in the sources as an existing dispute over Jewish oath-taking rituals between the Jewish aljama and the Christian universitas. With its requirement that Jews utilize Christian courts, the *Costums de Tortosa* had adopted the widespread practice of obligating Jews to swear an elaborate oath when testifying in cases against non-Jews in the municipal court. For civil cases, the nature of the oath varied with the amount in dispute. Jews could simply swear on the "law of Moses" in cases worth less than five solidi. In disagreements over larger sums, they would also have to perform the so-called "oath of maledictions."[41] The review tribunal for the *Costums* had stripped away some incidental ritual requirements of the oath taking mandated in the *Consuetudines Dertuse civitatis*—most notably the lighting and snuffing out of a candle during the oath—but let the main regulations stand.[42]

Christian litigants and authorities in the town apparently believed that having the Jewish witness threaten himself with bodily harm, misfortunes, and earthly and infernal torments appearing in his own sacred scriptures reduced the risk of perjury. According to Joseph Ziegler, "The oath had to neutralize the fear of Christians, who were giving the right of justification by oath to an outsider who was not a member of the Christian community, who belonged to a group long reputed for its perfidy, and who could not be threatened by the punishment of excommunication."[43] These were not isolated sentiments. The monarchy had been elaborating a similar policy of Jewish oath taking since the mid-thirteenth century and pressuring conformity throughout royal and nonroyal domains. In 1241, Jaume sent his chief official in Valencia the text of the Jewish oath so that he could ensure compliance with the regulations in the *Furs de València*. At the Corts of Girona later that same year, he sought not only to standardize the use of the oath throughout Catalonia based on customary practice in Barcelona, but also to simplify its application. Jews were to swear on the Decalogue and make whatever curses were required as part of the Jewish oath in "courts or wherever judges adjudicate" rather than in their synagogues.[44] The king then tried to impose a standard oath formula and regulations throughout Aragon at the Cortes of Huesca in 1247.[45]

Subsequent monarchs, by contrast, promoted some diversity in the application of the Jewish oath, ostensibly in response to complications within certain localities under royal jurisdiction. In 1284, for example, Pere II ordered his officials in Huesca and Calatayud to change their use of the Jewish oath in hopes of streamlining mixed cases and avoiding conflicts with the Jewish communities there. He noted that the oath-taking procedure had grown unnecessarily long and had antagonized Jewish litigants by forcing them to bring their own "scrolls" containing much superfluous material to court. These officials were to coordinate the Jewish aljamas' preparation of texts, specifically for use in court, that would contain only the necessary oaths and maledictions. The Jews were to read the maledictions and swear on the "laws of Moses" but nothing more.[46]

Even though the precise formula and regulations included in the *Costums de Tortosa* were unique, the existence of an established royal policy from at least the 1240s makes it possible that the oath-taking policy developed by the universitas in seigniorial Tortosa derived from royal example. Since the function of the oath in place in Tortosa was similar to that of the oaths mandated by crown laws and enforced on royal domains, the monarchy had little reason to seek to alter or disrupt these local policies when it assumed administrative control of the town in the mid-1290s. Nevertheless, ongoing disputes between local constituencies brought about the subtle adjustment of ill-defined local policies so that they would align more closely with standing royal regulations. With each successful clarification, however, these local customary policies grew progressively more difficult to manipulate.

A resolution established in 1297 known as the *Carta del sagrament* noted that the universitas and Jewish aljama had been at odds "for a long time" over the "oath of calumny" required in any case between a Jew and a Christian.[47] Without crediting royal policy or giving any signs that the monarchy had influenced the negotiations, the adelantats and the universitas agreed to adopt a policy similar to what the monarchy had implemented a decade earlier. Rather than requiring the Jews to carry the "laws of Moses" from their synagogue to the municipal court, officials would oversee the recopying of the Decalogue in a special tome that would be kept at the municipal house (*paeria*) solely for the purpose of taking the Jewish oath and maledictions. Most Jews would be allowed to hold this text while they performed these rituals in the house of the court notary and in the presence of their opponent in the case, as stipulated by the *Costums*. Some members of the Jewish community, however, would have to take oaths at their personal residences in the presence of the vicar, judges or court notary, and case opponent. This requirement applied to residents who were not well known or did not enjoy confirmed good repute in the town because, the *Carta* stipulated, they did not frequent common places such as the mills, ovens, or wells.

The extant evidence makes it impossible to verify which side suggested this compromise or whether it had indeed been informed by royal policy or pressured by crown officials charged with the running of the town court, chiefly the vicar and bailiff. The enactment could reveal how oppositional constituencies might have nudged homegrown regulations in the direction of standardized royal norms on their own accord, not simply out of respect for crown authority but because these policies were vetted, legitimate, and thus well suited to end an arbitrational impasse. In most other respects, however, Tortosa's policies regarding the oath remained remarkably faithful to the stipulations of the *Costums*. For instance, questions arose in 1302 about whether Jews should have to perform the additional ritual elements of the oath that had been purged during the revision of the *Consuetudines Dertuse civitatis*, in the 1270s, in order to render the procedure more efficacious. The assigned judges ruled that the established requirements of the *Costums* had to be followed to the letter, without exception.[48]

The king did intervene, after a considerable delay, to confirm and defend these locally negotiated policies from attempts by both sides to manipulate them. In 1314, Jaume II issued a statement approving of the concord, and in 1317 he rejected an appeal by the Jewish aljama to have the policy altered.[49] The following year, however, the king responded to complaints by the adelantats that the vicar was not adhering to the provisions of the *Carta del sagrament*, to the detriment of Jewish litigants, and firmly ordered him to observe them without fail.[50] Continued problems reportedly experienced by the Jews prompted them to request from the king, in 1320, new copies of the confirmations and rulings he had issued in 1314 and 1317.[51]

Conflict over the oath requirements flared up during litigation between the universitas and aljama in the 1320s. Representatives for the universitas sought to override Tortosa's customary oath-taking procedures in favor of the royal formula dating from 1242 that was contained in an authoritative compilation of royal legislation called the *Constitucions de Catalunya*.[52] Their ambition seems to have been to impose more onerous and thus (to them) preferable requirements using the argument that Tortosa should be governed by (in their view) normative and more efficacious royal policies used in other districts administered by the monarchy.[53]

The request may have been partly motivated by strategic interests concerning not simply this important case but also future Jewish-Christian litigation. The universitas and its members arguably stood to gain, in the short term at least, if certain Jews found procedures for mixed litigation sufficiently distasteful so as to dissuade them from defending their claims in court. And the fact that neighboring towns, as well as Catalonia's general law, had similarly strict oath-taking requirements reduced the risk of Jewish migration.

The prospects for success in this effort to alter the town's customary oath were admittedly slim. Early on in the proceedings, the justices handling the case indicated that neither Tortosa's current jurisdictional circumstances nor the standing of these royal regulations was grounds for the overruling of local customs and legal agreements. They explained that even the king lacked the authority to override the procedures stipulated by the *Carta del sagrament* without the consent of the universitas and the Jewish aljama, the parties which had formulated that concord.[54] So long as the court maintained this position, subsequent attempts by the universitas to have the king intervene to impose the provisions of the *Constitucions de Catalunya* and override local custom were unlikely to succeed due to the Jewish community's opposition.

The universitas nevertheless pressed on with its campaign. Its representatives submitted ten written articles that reaffirmed the validity of the guidelines contained in the *Constitucions de Catalunya* and detailed the distinctive elements that made them more humiliating to the Jewish oath taker and thus preferable to current practice in Tortosa. Among these were the controversial provisions that the oath should be performed publicly rather than in the private chambers of the court scribe, as stipulated by the *Costums de Tortosa*, and that the oath taker would have to raise the scroll of maledictions in an insulting manner.[55] The articles also reversed the justices' stance on which procedures should take precedence: the *Constitucions de Catalunya*, they alleged, naturally superseded local practices and even barred royal privileges or letters from mitigating or overriding their legal authority.[56] Although this argument served the universitas's objectives regarding the oath, it was dangerous because it potentially opened the door to the displacement of other, favorable local customary laws by regional norms.

The Jewish adelantats, for their part, continued to reject the proposition that they or the members of their community should perform any oath publicly while holding the scroll in the manner desired by the universitas.[57] The court continued to uphold received custom in support of the Jews' position. The judges criticized the attempt by "part of the universitas" to solicit royal intervention as "frivolous and inane," since any such intervention, in its view, would naturally be illicit. They mandated that the adelantats swear their oath of maledictions for the current case just as they had in the past. The Jewish leaders soon complied, in the face of continuing protest by the universitas, allowing the case to proceed.[58]

This dispute over the Jewish oath shows how, even with the willing assistance of a powerful subset of the community such as the universitas, the monarchy at this time still would have faced significant obstacles had it wanted to manipulate local customary traditions. The staying power of local legal traditions inhibited their alignment with standardized bodies of law such as the *Constitucions de Catalunya*. It is arguable that the resilience of such local laws detrimentally reduced the malleability of regulations on which the sustainability of coexistence depended. The universitas's desire for changes to the oath-taking policies reflected a growing Christian distrust of Jewish litigants that parallels broader trends historians have noticed throughout the Crown of Aragon and wider Europe. Such a decline in intracommunal solidarity necessitated an updating of these sorts of regulations in order to preserve the court's ability to resolve mixed disputes to the satisfaction of both parties. Yet, such alterations remained difficult to implement due to the rigidity of ingrained traditions that had originated when jurisdictional conditions and ethnoreligious relations had ostensibly been quite different. This innate inflexibility of local regulations may ultimately have been detrimental to the overarching, shared objective of sustaining workable Jewish-Christian coexistence.

The contrast between Tortosa's traditional oath-taking policies and the stricter, revised ones advocated by Catalonia's general laws and used by numerous other localities may have caused certain Christian residents to feel less confident that their cases against Jews could be resolved fairly without being compromised by perjurious testimony. This subset of the universitas clearly felt this concern in this present trial. Following the adelantats' performance of the oath of maledictions outlined in the *Costums* of Tortosa, the citizens' representatives complained that it was insufficient for just these communal leaders to perform it. They demanded that every individual in the aljama be made to swear similarly, since the case involved the entire community.[59] Members of the universitas may well have been genuinely concerned about adequate safeguards against Jewish perjury. With the door to more onerous oath-taking procedures now closed, however, this demand also could have represented the renewed pursuit of the strategy of increasing the distastefulness for Jews of participating in mixed cases.

The litigation that ushered in such an extended dispute over Jewish oath taking had been prompted by devastating flooding affecting the northern quadrant of the town in 1324—our second case study. Heavy spring rains had caused the Ebro River to crest, and its waters eroded the street, plaça, town walls, and other urban infrastructure along its banks. The downpour had apparently also created a torrent that flowed down the Barranc del Cèlio, damaging the northern town walls as well as much of the housing and property within the neighboring Jewish quarter, particularly the old call, which stood on lower ground.[60] It is hard to determine to what extent the walls and towers were repaired or rebuilt following the disaster yet before the town's external fortifications were greatly improved starting in the mid-1360s.[61] The incident led these same local constituencies to litigate over their respective responsibilities for repairing the damage to public property according to local customary laws and privileges. Due in part to the intervening dispute over the oath regulations, the case took over two years to resolve.

The length of the case also owed to the tenacity of the parties. Each of them was suffering in the wake of the disaster and understood that the outcome would assuredly establish a powerful precedent for future liability. A letter to the king from a local officer, Guillem de Ceret, written on behalf of the Jewish aljama in mid-October 1325, over a year after the disaster, reveals the substantial extent of the devastation. This was Ceret's fourth letter to the king about the situation but the only one to have survived. Apparently, the monarch had kept apprised of the situation remotely but not seen the damage firsthand. Many Jewish residents, Ceret wrote, had lost their houses and moveable property, including the fruits from the recent harvest, when the town walls bordering the call had given way to the floodwaters. Moneylenders were on the brink of ruin because their Christian clients' loss of homes and other property was preventing them from repaying their debts on time. The letter thus requested that the king allow them to extend the term of loan repayment beyond the legal limit of two years.[62] Unfortunately, no response from the king has come to light.

This case is especially worthy of examination because it further illuminates how the monarchy, court officials, and ethnoreligious communities in Tortosa each sought to strengthen their respective agendas through direct reference to the town's complicated customary legal traditions. These parties marshaled their justifications in distinctly different ways from what we have observed with regard to the intervening litigation over the oath of maledictions.

The universitas, joined by the Muslim aljama, opposed the Jewish community in municipal court. They claimed that the Jews bore sole liability for repairing the damage.[63] The basis for their argument shifted over the duration of the case. Initially, the universitas alleged that the Jewish community had at one time received a royal privilege granting it title to the destroyed land along the riverbank. The adelantats' denial that they possessed such a privilege prompted the universitas to demand that they swear concerning the truth of this claim using the enhanced oath of maledictions we have already discussed. This motion eventually led to the aforementioned digression over the legitimate oath-taking procedures.[64]

The universitas did not rely solely on the supposed legal implications of this alleged donation, however. As that petition was pending, the universitas proceeded to defend its position through reference to living custom: the Jewish community's habitual use of the damaged area. In a set of sixteen accusations delivered to the court, the citizens' representatives argued that the positioning of the Jewish call and its primary entrance was such that its residents got the greatest utility from the damaged area. They also added that the use of the zone by the Jews for their fish market and cement works had aggravated the destruction caused by the flooding.[65] The universitas was walking a fine line with this argument; it wanted to assign the Jewish community exclusive responsibility for the repairs of the plaça, walls, and towers without simultaneously reclassifying the zone as falling exclusively under Jewish control. Both the Christian and Muslim communities required continued access to the open space and thoroughfare along the riverbank.

This paradoxical attempt to extend private liability over a public space prompted the universitas to present some complicated, legally dubious distinctions. Jewish stewardship over the area, it argued, was the product of much greater proximity as well as extraordinary use. In the morning light, the walls and towers enclosing the call cast shadows covering the entire damaged area and reaching to the river. Furthermore, the Jewish community alone had a sewer for "its personal use and service" that passed under this land to drain into the river.[66] As a result, according to the universitas, in its damaged state the plaça pertained solely to the Jews and by extension to the king due to his ownership of their community. Once repaired, however, the plaça had to be restored as a public place for the benefit of all of Tortosa's residents.[67]

The universitas's loss of its procedural objection over the oath months later permitted the adelantats to uphold their assertions about the nonexistence of the alleged charter of donation. Subsequently, the universitas sought to support the most important elements of its list of accusations by means of a royal privilege that it already had in its possession. It cited text from the Jews' twelfth-century settlement charter, which had enlisted the Jews to build and maintain the dwellings licensed by Ramon Berenguer IV and, by extension, other infrastructure pertaining to the old call. The universitas sought to use the charter to argue that the boundary (*fronteria*) of the call extended to the riverbank despite the fact that the extramural land was designated for public use as a thoroughfare. "According to custom and law," the Jews were responsible to pay for routine maintenance and extraordinary repair in order to preserve public safety.[68] This interpretation of local law was not a double standard, the universitas maintained, because in the past Christians had been forced to pay for repairs to public spaces that bordered their neighborhoods. At the very least, the aljama should be held to the same expectations, since "Jews ought not to be in a better condition than Christians."[69] Like autonomy itself, the community's original settlement license thus represented a double-edged sword for the Jews. It contained powerful privileges that offered some protection for the aljama's immunities and self-determination but also ambiguities that rendered it vulnerable to costly liabilities, advanced by competing local constituencies.

Nevertheless, throughout the proceedings, the Jewish adelantats steadfastly denied that they should bear full responsibility. They utilized a range of legal defenses based on their community's special jurisdictional circumstances as well as on the town's general customary traditions. The Jews countered in court that the damaged areas pertained to the public domain. In support, they cited the *Costums de Tortosa*, which list this affected plaça as one of seven public spaces in the town limits. The Muslims, they maintained, whose *morería* neighbored the call and whose meat market was serviced by this street, should arguably bear at least equal responsibility to contribute to the repairs, a claim representatives from the Muslim community, of course, flatly denied.[70]

This local crisis inspired the Jewish aljama's officers to embrace fully the crown's unquestionable ownership of the entire Jewish call. Presumably in hopes of intimidating their opponents and possibly with an eye to invoking royal intervention, the Jews warned the bailiff and other officials involved in the case that they lacked the authority to perform the actions demanded by the universitas. Any such attempt to assign liabilities over a neighboring public space to the Jewish quarter and "coerce or compel" the Jews to pay constituted an affront to the royal patrimony and thus posed "the greatest danger" to the universitas.[71]

Sporadic intervention by the crown to push for a specific outcome did exert considerable influence over the course of the case. When Jaume II initially received a petition regarding the dispute from the universitas in June 1324, he counseled his bailiff in Tortosa that the Christian, Muslim, and Jewish communities should share the costs of repair equally.[72] Over a year later, this time in response to a request from the Jewish community for assistance with the seemingly endless litigation, the king wrote letters reiterating this recommendation to the vicar, who was handling the case. The Infant Alfons sent a similar missive to the adelantats.[73] Such involvement by the monarchy did not necessarily contradict its respect for local precedent, which we have witnessed with regard to oath-taking procedures and other practices, because the customary legal guidelines for this case were so unclear. The king may have been inclined to spare the Jews the full expense of the repairs because these costs would theoretically be borne by the royal treasury. It is more likely, however, that he was acknowledging that the legal basis for exclusive Jewish liability was weak and that the precedent of cost sharing by the entire populace in times of extraordinary crisis would increase solidarity within the town, making governance an easier task for him and his officials. In any event, the king, as the town's chief authority, was clearly interested in expediting the case so that this dangerous situation could be remedied. He must have been eager for the resumption of local economic growth, which relied heavily on commercial activity along the riverbank. A compromise, he assuredly understood, was the most likely means to achieve a quick resolution. Accordingly, in September 1325 another letter from the king sought, albeit unsuccessfully, to have the royal bailiff mandate a settlement between the universitas and adelantats within four days.[74]

Each side tried to utilize this royal intervention to its respective advantage. In the earlier stages of the trial, the Jews referred numerous times to the monarchy's letters demanding that the costs be borne by all of the town's residents. They let it be known to the pressured bailiff that they were prepared to pay their share so long as the universitas and Muslim aljama first agreed to contribute.[75] Signs of royal involvement decrease in the later phases of the proceedings, however. For reasons that remain unclear, the adelantats stopped referring to the earlier royal letters mandating that the costs be split among the three communities. It is possible that the king had tired of the case as it dragged on, leading him to revoke tacitly his formerly active support of the Jewish community's claim. The universitas tended to refer to royal letters selectively and somewhat duplicitously. Later in the trial, for instance, its representatives appealed to the king's letter mandating a quick resolution as further reason that the stubborn Jews should desist in their attempts to safeguard their own financial well-being. The adelantats should instead, the universitas maintained, prioritize public safety and the greater good of the entire town by capitulating, assuming responsibility over the damaged common area, and commencing with the urgent repairs.[76]

The verdict for the case has not been preserved, but the proceedings appear to have been moving in favor of the universitas in the final extant folios, when attention shifted to the Jews' settlement charter. There are also indications that the Jews suspected that they would lose or were otherwise dissatisfied with the court's handling of the case. The Jewish community certainly had reason to be frustrated with the length and course of the trial thus far. In an undated letter to Tortosa's bishop, Berenguer de Prat, the adelantats explained that they would have difficulty demonstrating their rights in the case they were litigating before the bailiff and vicar regarding the damaged plaça. They "humbly" requested that the bishop assume jurisdiction over the case and definitively resolve it. He was entitled to preside over the dispute, they asserted, "according to law, custom, and the power God gives you." They added that they were prepared to give and explain to him any of the documentation he might require to uphold their side.[77]

This illuminating turn in the case serves to remind us how well versed the Jews were about the complex legal foundations of their coexistence in Christian-ruled society. Earlier in the proceedings, the Jewish leaders had found value in emphasizing the principle of royal possession and exclusive jurisdiction. At this point, however, with the court seemingly leaning toward upholding the claims of their opponents, the adelantats saw strategic value in utilizing an alternate interpretation of Jewish accommodation. As we saw in the opening pages of this book, the idea that supreme jurisdiction over the Jews ultimately belonged to the Church had first been expressed by the church fathers and was later evoked by high medieval theologians and embraced by papal policy. Without the multiplicity of judicial forums that had once been afforded by seigniorial-royal jurisdictional competition, Jewish leaders had an incentive to seize upon other means to access alternative patrons when the crown and its associated judicial forums failed to defend their community's safety, financial stability, and autonomy. As we shall see in the epilogue, Jews in other communities made similar opportunistic overtures to prelates in an effort to evade what they viewed as unjust rulings, preferring a potentially more favorable ecclesiastical court.[78]

Conclusions

These two cases, taken together with the other episodes surveyed by this concluding chapter, are useful for tempering this study's focus on the significance of jurisdictional transitions while at the same time underscoring its insistence on the importance of localization. The successive assumptions of local authority in Tortosa (by Ramon Berenguer IV and his successors following the conquest, the seigniorial regime in the early thirteenth century, and the crown, once again, in the final decade of the fourteenth century) were reflective of the waxing and waning of royal and seigniorial power and the mutability of their respective administrative priorities. Yet, while these transfers of authority had profound implications for both the local residents and the town's institutional development, incoming lords found that their options could be severely limited by existing, highly localized customary laws and practices that were highly resistant to unilateral alteration. Lords and their subjects could, at times, fruitfully collaborate to make modest alterations that in some cases brought local policies more into line with regional standards. As we have seen, however, these changes were often difficult or impossible to implement due to resistance by an unwilling constituency. Even privileges that pertained to a specific group, such as the Jews' settlement charter, did not stand under that group's exclusive control and could even subject it to significant, unforeseen liabilities.

New lords and kings with differing objectives thus had to contend with the tremendous and ever-growing staying power of local custom, which, in turn, undergirded the unique micro-convivencia of each town or domain. These powerful forces of localization did not make regime change irrelevant but arguably did complicate the innovation often ushered in by administrative transition, particularly if any proposed modification interfered with an existing policy or entitlement. Consequently, the resistance of Tortosa's micro-convivencia to standardization was sufficiently strong that even the most powerful late medieval monarchs could not fully undo it. This resiliency of local legal traditions regarding the Jews and other sectors of Tortosa's populace ensured that most of the novelties and adjustments witnessed during the seigniorial period would not be completely effaced during the subsequent long rule of the monarchy.

EPILOGUE: CONTESTED TREASURE IN BROADER CONTEXT

Before this study ends, in order to capitalize fully on the value of our primary case study, we must demonstrate further that the phenomena we have examined within Tortosa's local setting connect to broader trends and more widely evidenced situations throughout the Crown of Aragon and medieval Europe. Throughout this book, we have already observed on a number of occasions how the jurisdictional situation in our case shared features with other lordships. Here we will consider more specific examples. Some were strikingly analogous to Tortosa in the degree to which their lords resisted royal control. Others, by contrast, were significantly more constrained by the monarchy's efforts to defend its regalian rights over Jews. Further afield, we will observe that the struggle to secure royal possession of the Jews in the Crown of Aragon, although advanced using a similar rationale, did manifest important differences from contemporaneous conflicts in other kingdoms, most notably in the involvement of the papacy and ecclesiastical institutions.

In spite of this diversity, most of these domains were subject to lords who similarly viewed their autonomy as legitimate. They uniformly rejected the claim that royal control over ethnoreligious minorities and Christian subjects was normative even if they did not always respond to the monarchy's overtures in identical ways. The attitudes and expectations of Tortosa's lords regarding their jurisdictional rights over their subjects in general, and Jews in particular, were therefore unexceptional.

Accordingly, the primary objective of this epilogue is to overturn, once and for all, the notion, manifested in some prominent scholarship surveyed in the introduction and referenced in the ensuing chapters, that Tortosa should be disregarded as an exceptional and thus largely irrelevant case. Our acknowledgment that aspects of the experiences of Tortosa's Jews were felt by a significant subset of the non-Christian population necessitates that we abandon this received model in favor of one that is more accepting of jurisdictional diversity. Here we will try to tie together the different threads of this main argument from throughout the study in order to assemble a new, more nuanced paradigm of the expression of royal authority that leaves room for the lasting role played by assorted nonroyal authorities in the shaping of distinctive micro-convivencias.

Ecclesiastical Jurisdiction

We should begin with a patent point of difference between the scenario in Tortosa and other conflicts regarding jurisdiction over the Jews beyond the limits of the Crown of Aragon. Conflict between religious institutions and rulers over such rights was common throughout European society and often came to involve the papacy and ecclesiastical courts.[1] Similar engagement, however, did not occur within Tortosa, or the rest of the Crown of Aragon for that matter, for reasons that remain somewhat unclear. Given that the dominant lord within the seigniorial regime was an influential and wealthy religious order, why did the possession of the Jews in Tortosa never come to be expressed as an ecclesiastical issue?

Theologians and canon lawyers seem to have been conscious that emerging papal claims of authority over the Jews could, in the vast majority of Christendom, only be meaningfully applied in domains subject to ecclesiastical jurisdiction.[2] Accordingly, within the lands under the jurisdiction of the German emperors during the thirteenth and fourteenth centuries, popes were confirming (and pressuring emperors to respect) the "ownership" of Jews already enjoyed by bishops and monasteries alike. As we will see, however, they rarely pressed rulers to amplify these existing prerogatives.

In the mid-twelfth century, for example, Frederick I Barbarossa conceded that the archbishop of Arles and his suffragan bishop of Marseilles had traditionally exercised jurisdiction over their local Jewish populations.[3] The cathedral's possession of these Jews had already earned papal support in a privilege of general property protection granted by Anastasius IV in 1153 and would continue to be confirmed by both popes and emperors in the thirteenth century.[4] This was a considerable concession given that the emperor was claiming lordship over the Jews throughout Germany. In his confirmation of a charter concerning the Jews of Worms in 1157, for example, he asserted that "they belong to the treasury."[5] In 1220, the pope responded to a complaint from the bishop of Béziers that Count Raymond VI of Toulouse was violating his see's prerogatives, including taxation and jurisdictional rights over Jews in his diocese.[6] Similar attempts by Frederick II to reclaim revenues from certain Jewish populations in southern Italy that had allegedly stood under monastic or episcopal control "since antiquity" prompted bold resistance from Gregory IX, who forbade the emperor from depriving the churches of their property. The emperor defended his actions analogously to what we have witnessed with the monarchy of the Crown of Aragon. He claimed that the Jews were subject to imperial jurisdiction as a result of common law and their special status of belonging to the "imperial chamber" (*camera imperiali*).[7] In this case, the papacy firmly rejected Frederick II's justification and eventually succeeded in forcing the reluctant emperor to restore the Jews to those southern Italian ecclesiastical jurisdictions.[8]

Subsequent rulers likewise proved unable to deprive religious institutions in this region of their established rights over Jews. Indeed, in 1285, Charles II of Anjou conceded to papal claims without resistance. He agreed to exempt all Jewish tenants living on ecclesiastical domains from royal impositions (both offices and taxation) throughout his kingdom of Naples.[9] Although the papacy did issue bulls of general protection to the Jews, similar apostolic privileges awarded to individual Jews within the Crown of Aragon were exceptional and seem to have been executed only with the king's blessing.[10]

In 1305, the *concejo* of Palencia, which had been fighting jurisdictional battles with the local bishop and town lord for years, suggested to Fernando IV during a visitation that he should "take" some of Palencia's Jews and Muslims who rightfully belonged to the crown. When the king moved to follow this advice, however, the bishop quickly lodged a protest, and Fernando had no choice but to retreat and recognize the see's jurisdictional privileges. Somewhat reminiscent of the case with Valldigna, most hurtful to the king's cause was the fact that he had recently confirmed his predecessor Alfonso VIII's donation establishing that Palencia's Jews and Muslims had to answer to the bishop "as their own lord."[11]

The ostensibly passive role played by the papacy and most of the local bishops concerning jurisdiction over Jews within the Crown of Aragon cannot simply be explained by the relatively low incidence of episcopal lordship over Jews compared with other regions in Europe. Many of the recorded conflicts elsewhere, in fact, were the result of prelates deciding to defend ecclesiastical standards or interests on lands over which they did not exercise direct jurisdiction. Over the early decades of the thirteenth century, for instance, Countess Blanche of Champagne lodged numerous grievances with the papacy concerning just this sort of interference by the archbishop of Sens and his suffragan bishops. When she complained that these prelates were forcing her Jews to return interest made on loans to crusaders, Honorius III ruled in her favor. After the comital court handled an altercation between a cleric and a local Jew, however, the bishop of Soissons expressed dissatisfaction with the countess's failure to punish the Jew and placed her lands under interdict, thus necessitating papal intervention.[12]

One possible explanation for a lack of episcopal action in the Crown of Aragon is that many of its bishops, including those of Tortosa, tended to be lackluster administrators and were frequently distracted by conflicts with their cathedral canons and parish clergy. The see of Tortosa's generally low interest in implementing canonical reforms over the course of the thirteenth century, combined with the fact that the dominant local lords were an exempt religious order, may help account for why it failed to engage in similar ways with many of the issues relating to Jewish coexistence in the diocese.[13]

Popes and local prelates did pressure rulers and magnates in the Crown of Aragon on canonical matters, such as adherence to the mandates of the Fourth Lateran Council concerning Jews or their support of missionary efforts. Yet, even though Honorius III sent numerous letters to rulers ordering compliance during his pontificate, he was open to reasonable modifications. For instance, he granted Jaume I's request that Jews in his realms not be required to wear identifying badges since they were already distinguishable on account of their customary clothing.[14] Intervention in routine jurisdictional issues concerning non-ecclesiastical lands, however, was unusual.[15]

This pattern of engagement fit with the emerging papal stance that ecclesiastical courts should exercise jurisdiction over the Jews with regard to offenses relating to moral issues. This attitude had already appeared in the conservative rulings of Honorius III and soon came to be expressed by the canon lawyer and pope Innocent IV in his apparatus to the *Decretals*.[16] Bishops and the papacy, however, tended to ignore general jurisdictional issues and fixate instead on revenues owed in accordance with canon law. The issue raised most commonly by the see of Tortosa and others was the need for Jewish and Muslim residents to render ecclesiastical tithes from lands that had at some point fallen under Christian ownership.[17]

On rare occasions when bishops were invited by local constituencies to intervene in non-ecclesiastical domains, they experienced stiff opposition from the crown or other authorities, especially with the increase of royal jurisdictional control over the urban aljamas in the fourteenth century. The attempt by Tortosa's Jewish community to invoke the aid of the local bishop in its dispute over the flood damage discussed in the previous chapter, for example, faced equally inauspicious odds of success. A parallel case from 1381 illustrates the crown's response to such ecclesiastical intrusions. In this instance, similarly, opportunists within the Jewish community tried to appeal to the local bishop in an unsuccessful bid to circumvent royal jurisdiction. Opponents of the prominent Valencian Jewish physician Omar Tahuell publicly accused him of breaking Jewish law. Realizing perhaps that Omar's faithful service to the king would likely prevent them from receiving the outcome they desired from royal justices, they instead took their petition to the episcopal court. Presumably their justification was similar to what the Jews of Tortosa had articulated in their letter of appeal to the local bishop: that the Church was entitled to intervene in non-ecclesiastical jurisdictions to regulate Jewish moral affairs. The bishop of Valencia apparently convinced himself that the case did indeed fall under his court's purview. By the time Pere III learned of the incident, the bishop had already sent his vicar and commissary to deliver a letter to the royal bailiff requesting that Omar be arrested. The king denounced this intervention as illegitimate and scolded the bishop for treating royal prerogatives as if they were his own. Pere claimed that these actions would result "in great damage to our aljamas and their residents, all of which belong to our patrimony through our laws and regalian rights and are subjugated to our justice and law."[18]

Without any reference to papal claims, Pere thus dismissed the notion that this prelate could exercise judicial authority over Jews under royal jurisdiction on any grounds. He quickly assumed control over the case by delegating investigation of Omar's alleged crimes to his own officials. The king also seems to have been concerned that other bishops would be inclined to make similar transgressions. Several months later, he circulated a memorandum to all of his officials throughout his realms notifying them of this violation. He ordered them to be vigilant in defending royal rights over Jews and Muslims against similar incursions in the future.[19]

Parallel Examples

Although unusually conflictive, extended, and well documented, the case of Tortosa is not unique. Numerous other examples illustrate how the monarchy continued to face opposition to its policy of supremacy over resident non-Christians from different quarters into the fourteenth century and beyond.[20]

The crown notably experienced similar limitations in other urban localities lying within its realms. In these centers, lords exercised considerable authority over their Jewish residents, negotiating the legal obstacles to such autonomy presented by the monarchy. In certain respects, the circumstances in these localities paralleled what we have already noticed within independent principalities addressed throughout the previous chapters, such as the county of Empúries; such principalities appear to have been designing their own Jewish policies in competition with that of the monarchy.

Vic

In contrast to the shared jurisdiction over the entire town by the lords of Tortosa, lordship over the town of Vic, northwest of Barcelona, was split between two sectors. By the twelfth century, the lower sector, containing the bulk of the Jewish population, had fallen under the authority of part of the Montcada family. The local bishop held jurisdiction over the upper part of the town.[21] This spatial jurisdictional division led to the development of two separate calls, one for each lord. Unlike the situation in Tortosa, however, these peculiar material provisions appear to have already been in a state of de facto obsolescence by the end of the seigniorial period. In 1315, only two Jewish families were reportedly living in the bishop's sector.[22]

Although the bishops and Montcada family quarreled throughout the thirteenth century over their respective seigniorial rights within the town, these disagreements apparently did not specifically concern the Jewish community. One reason for this disposition may be that their management of the Jewish community was underdeveloped compared with that of other lordships.[23] There is no evidence that the lords, at this point, recognized the Jews as a corporate aljama or offered them guarantees of protection or other privileges.[24] Instead, the lords tended to negotiate directly with individual Jews residing in their respective domains.[25]

The monarchy had limited contact with the Jews of Vic until Jaume II negotiated an exchange with the bishop for rights to the upper portion of the lordship in 1315. This transaction earned him control over the vicarial administration but not over the more significant Jewish sector under the Montcadas' lordship.[26] Similar to what we have seen in Tortosa with the crown's license to install a bailiff, upon receipt of these limited administrative rights, the king soon sought to establish relations with the Jewish community in 1318. Yet, this shift in the monarchy's administrative presence did not prevent the Montcada family from continuing to administer its own Jewish subjects in Vic without significant royal oversight throughout the fourteenth century.[27]

Solsona

The jurisdictional situation in Vic had a number of parallels in Catalonia. The nearby town of Solsona stood under the joint lordship of the Viscounts of Cardona and the head (*prepositus*) of the collegiate church based there. This line of viscounts, like others in Catalonia, had long asserted its independence from royal authority.[28] The jurisdictional disputes over the Jews resident in Solsona beginning in the mid-thirteenth century solely concerned the lords of the town and featured no apparent royal, episcopal, or papal involvement. In 1252, Viscount Ramon Folch asserted that since he possessed the same exclusive jurisdiction over the Jews that he did over the Christians in the town, his court alone should judge their cases. The church's provost responded that "the earliest Jews in Solsona had fallen under the lordship of his Church and were theirs." He did acknowledge, however, that any Jew who wanted to move to escape his church's lordship could do so, just like any other townsperson. Witnesses from both sides attested that the lords' jurisdictional rights were, in fact, shared.[29]

By the 1280s, the two lords seem to have adopted a compromise similar to what had been engineered earlier in Vic. They divided Solsona into two distinct seigniorial districts in which subsets of the Jewish and Christian populations would fall under the authority of each respective lord.[30] A confirmation of privileges from 1332 demonstrates that the Folch family continued to exercise seemingly unmitigated control over the juridical rights and liabilities of its Jewish subjects.[31]

The monarchy appears to have paid, at most, scant attention to the local Jews here throughout the later thirteenth and into the fourteenth century. During the period of crisis in the summer of 1280 discussed in chapter 5, when he was facing his rebellious Catalan barons at the siege of Balaguer, Pere II did order his officials to compel the Jews of Solsona, along with the aljamas of Cardona, Borja, Vic, Manresa, and Granollers, to contribute to the same extraordinary subsidy he had demanded from Barcelona's call. Advancing the community of Barcelona as the normative case, he stressed that these Jews were expected to pay whatever those residents owed "in *questias*, tribute [*tributis*], and other payments [*collectis*]."[32] It is not known whether Solsona's Jews responded to the king's request. No subsequent tax demands suggestive of any further attempt by the crown to extend its authority over the aljama appear in the remaining royal chancery registers from this period.

The only other recorded instance of royal interaction took place in 1281, when Pere instructed his officials not to detain or seize the property of a certain Vidal Astruc until the Jew's claims had been evaluated and his case resolved. Although Vidal was a resident of Solsona, he belonged to a prominent family based in royally administered Manresa. He appears to have become embroiled in a financial dispute with the crown concerning estate issues following the recent death of his father, Maimó, who had resided in Manresa.[33] As had been the case in Tortosa, the complicated financial and family connections of such elite Jews rendered them more susceptible to royal oversight. Some may, however, have valued access to both royal and seigniorial judicial forums. Although Vidal continued to reside in Solsona, he remained active within Manresa as a creditor, property owner, businessman, witness, and family member until at least the early 1300s.[34]

Fraga

The exercise of lordship by the Montcadas in Fraga, on the Cinca River in Aragon, was distinct from what we have seen with these other cases because the family received its prerogatives through clear and deliberate action by the crown. The monarchy's role here served to map out the extent of independent seigniorial governance over local Jews with much greater precision than in other localities, such as Tortosa, where the transition to seigniorial power was haphazard and ambiguous.

The most vivid glimpse of seigniorial authority in Fraga comes from the first quarter of the fourteenth century. At some point between 1322 and 1328, Guillem de Montcada granted Fraga's Jewish community a charter detailing its privileges and immunities along with its guarantees of protection. These included the authorization of self-governance (the election of six adelantats), use of their law (with detailed provisions concerning their judicial rights and the presentation of witness testimony, as well as the right to punish informers, or *malsins*), and free religious practice (with the explicit right to celebrate "Jewish rites" with a "loud voice").[35] Many of these provisions, like the fueros used by the Christian residents of Fraga, were modeled on the customary laws of nearby Huesca. This relationship with Huesca's foral laws had been established by the king as early as 1242, years before he transferred lordship over Fraga to the Montcadas. It thus serves as another example of the staying power of customary legal foundations.[36] Rather than emphasizing protection of the Jews' persons and property, which he may have viewed as implicit, Guillem stressed his licensing of Jewish self-defense: "And if by chance any Christian, Jew, or Muslim, approaching your Jewish call with reckless daring, invades, robs, forces or makes violence against you or your possessions, we give you full license that you can defend yourselves from them by your own authority."[37] During a period when Jews were increasingly expected to maintain a passive and subservient presence in Christian-ruled society, it is likely that the Jewish community valued and had requested this prerogative. The delegation of administrative rights by the crown would have endowed Guillem with the role of supreme Jewish protector within his lordship, which he then had the sanction to carry out as he pleased.

The Montcada family's jurisdictional lordship over Fraga had been deliberately increased under the reign of Jaume I in order to fund his pursuit of other priorities. In 1255, the king exchanged royal rights to Fraga's castle, town, and district for the Montcadas' minority share of lordship over Lleida.[38] Lleida had developed into arguably the most important administrative center for the crown in Catalonia, outside of Barcelona. Its status justified the assumption of full royal administrative control and the relocation of the noble family's holdings to comparatively peripheral and minor Fraga.

It appears that both parties acknowledged that Fraga was an inferior holding. The Montcada family's minority rights in Lleida had to be compensated not only with full possession of Fraga but also with a sizeable monetary payment of 4,500 morabetins. Ramon de Montcada and his son received the town "in fief according to the *Usatges de Barcelona*" with full jurisdictional rights over all of the male and female inhabitants of the town—Christians, Muslims, and Jews—along with all other royal prerogatives enjoyed there. Residents demanded a certain degree of institutional continuity that must have helped smooth the transition between royal and seigniorial rule. Indeed, the new lords went to some lengths to assure the local populace that their assumption of lordship would not disrupt the status quo. A month before the infeudation, Ramon de Montcada and his son promised to respect all privileges, franchises, fueros, and customs as they had been conceded by Jaume and his predecessors to the universitas of Fraga.[39]

In 1265, Jaume ceded what remained of the crown's holdings in Fraga (chiefly, *potestas* over the town's castle) in return for a sizeable loan from Ramon de Montcada in support of the monarchy's campaign against Muslim Granada.[40] This action violated the king's pledge to the local residents at the time of the Montcada family's reception of Fraga not to alienate or infeudate further royal possessions there.[41] No formal complaint from the populace has come to light, however. The king's promise itself was likely a sign that an influential subset of the local populace was wary of seigniorial administration or at least disliked the threat that shifts in jurisdiction could pose to its existing privileges. The fact that the king was inclined to break this commitment is probably an indication that his continued shortage of resources necessitated further asset liquidation.

Even with Fraga's relatively unambiguous infeudation to the Montcadas, difficult questions nonetheless remained concerning the extent of royal control over residents. There was particular confusion over the crown's remaining ability to regulate and tax the populace, irrespective of the Montcada family's administrative prerogatives. In the summer of 1280, for instance,

Pere II sent the Jews of Fraga a copy of the mandate he had also directed at Tortosa's aljama, which instructed local officials to uphold the royal statute requiring debtors to repay even usurious loans.[42] The order did not prompt a response from the lord, and there is no subsequent evidence to indicate that it was enforced. When Pere demanded taxes from Fraga's aljama a week later, however, Ramon de Montcada protested by lodging a petition at royal court. According to the record generated by the royal court, the noble lord did not mount his defense by referring to his authority over the town afforded by the king's infeudation. Instead, he presented a specific privilege of immunity he had allegedly received from Jaume I, in which the king had stipulated that "the Jews of Fraga should not be compelled to render any monetary payments that the Jews of our land have to give us for the demand that we have made against them."[43] Pere's subsequent instructions to his Jewish bailiff at-large, Jucef Ravaya, indicate that he was suspicious of the noble's claim and wanted to ascertain its validity quickly so that he could proceed with the tax demand. The king appears to have ruled against the noble's petition on the grounds that the privilege had awarded immunity solely from payments owed to the crown for loans and contracts. Instead of appealing his case in order to present new argumentation, Ramon de Montcada apparently opted to ignore the mandate, at least temporarily. A month after the king's ruling, the noble had still failed to satisfy the tax demand; Pere then issued him and Fraga's Jews another demand for these payments.[44]

As conflict with his nobility in Catalonia and Aragon continued to escalate and he mounted his campaigns to capture Sicily from the French, Pere revealed that he was willing to accommodate targeted deviations from the taxation framework that he and his father had sought to establish for the entire Jewish population of his realms. An independent-minded noble such as Ramon de Montcada seems to have preferred to render the king extraordinary aid in order to avoid a precedent of routine tax liability. Because the king was in desperate need of support from his aristocracy, he was apparently prepared to accommodate Ramon's preference. Thus, a month after Pere ordered his officer Pere de Trilles to collect further subsidy payments from the Jews of Fraga in the summer of 1282, he rescinded the mandate on account of the noble's "prayers and goodwill." Unlike Jews on royal domains, the Jews of Fraga would not have to contribute to the subsidy intended to pay for sending horses and foodstuffs to Sicily. For the time being,

Pere de Trilles was not to try to seize their goods or force them to render payments.⁴⁵

The king's calculated reprieve, however, was destined to be short-lived, given how his military expenditures were escalating in proportion to the mounting complications in Sicily. Thus, as we witnessed earlier in chapter 5, Pere sought to reaffirm his right to tax the aljama as well as to collect back taxes in the summer of 1284. He ordered Fraga, along with Tortosa and a number of other aljamas, to send representatives to the royal court with documentation concerning the taxes they had rendered over the past fifteen years, commencing around the point when Pere had first involved himself in his father's administration as the Infant.⁴⁶ This engagement was followed, as we have seen, by his demand the next year that Fraga, Tortosa, and Monzón pay their taxes in order to assist his defense of the state, threatening action against their persons and property if they continued to refuse.⁴⁷

Possibly in reaction to his predecessor Pere's frustrated attempts to subjugate the lordship and integrate its Jews neatly into the taxation system of Jewish aljamas on royal domains, Alfons II sought to recuperate direct jurisdiction over Fraga and assign responsibility for its administration to the vicar of Lleida in 1289–90.⁴⁸ In search of legal support for this usurpation, the crown attempted to question the Montcadas' suitability as feudatories. Its lawyers argued that Guillem's father, Ramon de Montcada, had abused his authority by illegitimately and unjustly detaining townspeople and seizing their property.⁴⁹ This maneuver had a slim chance of success, and ultimately failed, since both Ramon and Guillem had already collectively admitted to and atoned for these abuses in a resolution with the universitas in 1287.⁵⁰

Alfons subsequently abandoned attempts to regain control over Fraga and instead set out to collaborate with the Montcadas. With the king's blessing, Guillem de Montcada reestablished full potestas over the castle, town, and district of Fraga in 1290. The noble used the occasion to formulate a series of concords with the universitas of citizens and the king, fixing levies and seigniorial dues, making further amends for his father's regretful behavior and pledging to respect prior royal privileges.⁵¹ Alfons's participation in these enactments was extraordinary, however. In future years, when the lords and universitas adjusted the tax levels and regulations, the crown played no role.⁵²

In the wake of this failed attempt by the monarchy to regain Fraga and the ensuing détente, the Montcada family enlarged its domains in the area. It accomplished this, first and foremost, through the acquisition of additional lands from the crown. Jaume II purchased Guillem de Montcada's shares of jurisdiction in Tortosa, in part, by consigning to him the castle and territory of Zaidín in Fraga's vicinity.[53] Furthermore, during these same years, the Templars also sold some of their holdings in Fraga to the family.[54]

Several months before exchanging Zaidín, Jaume II had made it clear that he intended to deviate from the policies of his predecessors by supporting Guillem de Montcada's rights to Fraga. He did so by confirming the concords that had stabilized the fief.[55] Although this king made no further attempts to micromanage the town's internal affairs using royal officers, he may have intended for these confirmations to reinforce the principle that the noble's rights stemmed from royal dispensation. In subsequent years, Jaume maintained sporadic oversight of Guillem's administration there, intervening opportunistically to ratify important seigniorial pronouncements and to guarantee royal privileges. In 1294, for example, he confirmed the town's right to the *Fueros de Huesca* as well as its other privileges already authorized by Jaume I at the time of Fraga's infeudation in 1255.[56] Such shrewd, nonconfrontational engagement would serve to safeguard royal overlordship much more surely than would the sort of aggressive maneuvers perpetrated earlier by Alfons II. Indeed, Jaume II's patience paved the way for the crown's definitive recuperation of the fief following Guillem's death.

In spite of Jaume II's apparent amenability, Guillem de Montcada nevertheless remained defensive about his authority to regulate the Jews residing within his domains. His father's mismanagement had demonstrated the lordship's vulnerability to dissolution by the crown. Furthermore, Guillem's eventual reception of his family's traditional office of *seneschal* likely placed additional pressure on him to act in accordance with royal prerogatives and objectives.[57] Concerning judicial matters pertaining to the Jews, for example, he made it clear that his considerable authority within Fraga ceased at the boundaries of his domains: "We concede to you that for any case or demand that we or anyone else should move against you, we are not able to summon, move, or hold you outside the town of Fraga, nor on account of this make any violence against you; but in truth all of your cases are handled and finish in Fraga."[58] Just as many of the provisions of the charter were consciously borrowed from Huesca, cases taken outside of his local jurisdiction, Montcada explained, would be handled according to that town's fueros and Jewish customs.

The noble thus made it clear that he was fully cognizant of the capacities and limits of his authority. He could restrict residency to the Jewish quarter, authorize the construction of a new synagogue and the manner of religious practice, and manage the maintenance of a meat market and the importation and sale of kosher wine within the call. Within his lordship, he claimed the full right to award Jews privileges, such as free transit, rights to fishing, hunting, and firewood, and exemptions from various levies without any royal intervention or oversight. However, he and his Jews did have to respect royal interest caps in their moneylending as well as accede to the monarchy's tribute demands.[59] Beyond those enumerated royal prerogatives, however, Guillem asserted his Jews in Fraga could not be obligated by the king or any other authority to pay any levy or tax.[60]

In spite of Guillem de Montcada's respect for these limitations, he still sought to compete for Jewish revenue from other jurisdictions within the provisions of the law. He encouraged nonresident Jews, for example, to come to Fraga from elsewhere to celebrate weddings, funerals, and other festivities with his Jewish subjects. He pledged that they would be immune from various transport levies within his domains in order to dispel any fears that he might be trying to lure them there in order to exploit them for taxes. In fact, he promised to defend the Jews against anyone who tried to detain them on account of these levies. Guillem indicated that Fraga had offered these amenities to nonlocal Jews for some time; indeed, his father had issued a similar privilege when he was lord.[61]

Guillem de Montcada asserted his powers within his lordship openly, with the understanding that they were legal. We have no evidence that he ever knowingly tried to encroach illicitly or furtively on royal entitlements. Although both the monarchy and the residents of Fraga mostly appear to have accepted this power-sharing relationship as normative and legal, we can recognize faint signs of insecurity among residents about the true extent of the Montcada family's autonomy. In 1322, for example, leading men representing Fraga's universitas asked Jaume to confirm a privilege from Guillem de Montcada earlier that year that conferred commercial rights on the Jews.[62] The king confirmed the provisions of the charter without modification; he does not seem to have used the occasion to undercut the Montcada family's authority in Fraga. In contrast to the royal confirmation requested by Tortosa's Jews in the license to found a new call in 1228, no party voiced or conceded to the request for royal confirmation in the grant itself. Instead, in this case certification by the crown appears to have been an afterthought or perhaps a unilateral enterprise made without Guillem's sanction. In either case, the willingness of the town's universitas to act on the Jewish aljama's behalf to protect its financial interests attests to the potential for conditional, mutually beneficial communal solidarity that approximates what we have observed in Tortosa and certain other localities throughout this study.

The monarchy was unable to realize administrative control of Fraga's Jews through its claimed regalian rights alone. Similar to what we have seen with Tortosa, possession of the Jews ultimately required the reestablishment of direct royal control. By the 1320s, late in Jaume's reign, the monarchy had begun to challenge the independence of the lordship, reviving the policy pursued under Alfons II three decades earlier. In 1322, Jaume complained that Guillem de Montcada was refusing to confirm the monarchy's right to assume control over the castle and town (the feudal right of potestas).[63] In making these demands, the king himself was unwilling to acknowledge that his predecessors had both granted and confirmed the Montcada lords full potestas over Fraga and its castle, as we have witnessed. It may be that this pressure from the monarchy helped inspire the noble to issue his extensive charter of privileges to the Jews discussed earlier and defiantly publicize his independent jurisdictional authority as lord. In 1326, however, Jaume escalated his assault on Fraga's autonomy. Asserting his exclusive preserve over public order, he took advantage of the ongoing discussions about whether Fraga pertained to Aragon or Catalonia in order to declare to "all men of Fraga" that, out of the necessity of "public utility," the lordship would never be separated from crown. Using language that implied a royal takeover was inevitable and imminent, he proclaimed that he, as king and rightful overlord, would respect their customary privileges just as the Montcadas had done in the past.[64]

The timing of Guillem de Montcada's death shortly thereafter played perfectly into the monarchy's renewed ambitions to restore its control over Fraga. Jaume also passed away around this same time, but his heir, Alfons III (r. 1327–36), assumed his father's objective regarding the town. In 1327 he confirmed Jaume's provisions, with the consent of the noble lord's heir and the town's universitas, listing among the crown's inalienable prerogatives taxation rights to "Jews and Muslims" in Fraga.[65] The new king arranged the purchase of the remaining seigniorial rights of lordship with the executors of Guillem's estate, confirming the town's right to use the *Fueros de Huesca* and its general royal privileges later in 1327, as well as the extensive charter of privileges to the Jewish aljama without modification the following year.⁶⁶ Alfons thus signaled that he intended to retain Fraga under direct royal administration rather than infeudate it once again and that, similar to his father's assumption of Tortosa thirty years earlier, for the time being he did not intend to disrupt the traditions developed by the residents, Christian and non-Christian, during decades of noble lordship.

Other Transitions to Royal Control

We can witness similar patterns within other lordships throughout Aragon whereby seigniorial regimes succumbed to the monarchy's efforts to restore its patrimonial rights at moments of dynastic or strategic instability. For instance, the Jewish aljama of the town of Pedrola, near Zaragoza, stood under the lordship of the noble Lope Ferrench de Luna, who had originally received the domain by means of a privilege from Pere II. Luna, however, was forced to submit to Jaume II following his participation in an unsuccessful rebellion in 1302. The king authorized the return of Luna's Jewish "vassals," who had taken refuge with the aljama of Alagón and Zaragoza during the destructive campaigns, with the understanding that their presence was now conditional on continued royal consent. Even though these Jews would no longer be contributing to taxes with these royal aljamas, their susceptibility to royal jurisdiction had increased considerably due to Luna's military defeat.⁶⁷

Independent, nonroyal regimes experienced analogous difficulties in Catalonia, where the monarchy was able to expand its administrative prerogatives painstakingly yet decisively by means of a range of opportunistic strategies. In 1290, Alfons II argued that Count Ponç Hug IV of Empúries had illegitimately ordered an inquest into interest-limit violations by certain Jews in Empúries as well as in Bas and Cabrera, counties that Ponç held in fief from the crown. Until this point, the count had experienced dramatically less interference from the monarchy compared with other lords, such as Tortosa's seigniorial regime. Ponç's possession of royal fiefs, however, rendered his autonomous county susceptible to royal designs in a drawn-out royal campaign to eliminate the counts' autonomy. With Empúries, as with other lordships, Bensch has suggested, "jurisdiction over Jews increasingly became a touchstone for questions of sovereignty" between the king and lords.⁶⁸

In many of these conflicts, the monarchy continued to define and defend its prerogatives with selective reference to laws from the *Usatges de Barcelona* and later twelfth-century peace constitutions that had informed the development of Catalonia's general territorial law in the thirteenth century. In 1383, for example, the Infant Joan used *Usatge* 11 to seek possession of a Jew from Figueres who, while returning from the fair in Girona, had been seized by the bailiff of the Viscount of Rocabertí, based in the castle of Vilademuls. The king noted that captured Jews had to be subjected to the judgment of the potestas, especially if their detention harmed the potestas's rights. In a second royal letter sent the same day, Joan stressed more strongly his public powers and the protections afforded by the royal peace constitutions and other instruments contained in the *Constitucions de Catalunya*. He noted that the bailiff's action had violated the "Peace and Truce and special privilege of safe passage" required by the "general constitutions of Peace and Truce of Catalonia."[69]

Continuing Conflict

The limitations on the exercise of royal authority within well-connected urban spaces were more pervasive and enduring for the minority of Jews and majority of Muslims in rural spaces. Throughout the vast, isolated territories of the Crown of Aragon, lords witnessed far greater success in maintaining their jurisdictional independence.[70] Many of these lordships likewise preserved rights to autonomy that had been granted during earlier periods when the monarchy had been less disciplined in its distribution of administrative powers or had lacked the resources to retain what it understood were irrevocable prerogatives.

For example, the heavily Muslim-populated Templar *comandas* of the Ebro Valley and many lay lordships, such as the Montcada barony of Aitona, near Lleida all possessed full criminal and civil jurisdiction (*merum et mixtum imperium*) legally from royal donation even though these prerogatives eventually came to conflict with royal policy.[71] Growing pressure from kings and royal officials from the later thirteenth century proved unable to revoke these rights.[72] When Jaume II, for instance, appealed to Boniface VIII in both 1297 and 1300 to grant him the exclusive right to exercise criminal jurisdiction (*merum imperium*) within ecclesiastical lordships, specifically including those held by the military orders, the pope flatly rejected his request.[73]

Further impeding the crown's mounting efforts to standardize governance throughout its realms, laws that had been created to promote royal governmental centralization could unpredictably end up empowering nonroyal authorities. The lords of Albarracín, located to the west of the kingdom of Valencia, maintained ties to both Castile and the Crown of Aragon. In the thirteenth century, they borrowed material from the *Fueros de Teruel* to fashion their own customary laws. In revising Teruel's fueros to suit their purposes, they cleverly altered the famous servi regis statute to recast local Jews as *servi domini*, who thereby pertained to their seigniorial fisc (*fisco dominico*) rather than to the king's.[74]

As we saw earlier, the Aragonese foral compilation known as the *Vidal Mayor*, promulgated by the king at the Cortes of 1247, had sought to assert royal control over any and all property alienations by Jews and Muslims.[75] Nevertheless, the compilation also manifested consciousness of the importance of direct jurisdiction. It sought to restrict nobles from accepting Muslim tenants from royal domains while also facilitating the migration of Muslims to crown lands.[76] As later rendered in the Latin *Fueros de Aragón*, the emphasis of these provisions had shifted away from property to the persons themselves: "If a Muslim on crown land . . . moves to the domain of a noble or is converted . . . , the Muslim can take all that he has on his lands, but let the body of this Muslim belong to the Lord King, unless the noble has taken him outside the realm."[77] Although he did not strike this law from the code, Jaume II did supplement it with stricter regulations: "Let all Jews and Muslims living in cities, towns, and any other place under royal lordship be and remain with all of their goods in the protection and special care of the Lord King. And if it happens that any one of them places himself in the care of any noble or he exists in any other condition, let him immediately lose his head, and let all of his goods belong to the Lord King wherever they might be."[78] In practice, however, the king continued to permit these sorts of migrations on the condition that they were licensed. So long as they were officially approved, such relocations did not abrogate the principle that the monarchy exercised inviolable jurisdictional control over these subjects.

In 1326, for instance, Jaume licensed the migration of Jews from Lleida to the Montcada family's rural barony of Aitona. At that time, he instructed the administrators of the aljama of Lleida not to pursue taxes and other payments from these Jews, signifying that they had officially exited their community.[79] Lords such as the monks of Valldigna were able to establish parallel controls in the 1330s. They forbade resident Muslims from establishing vassalage in other parts of the kingdom without the abbot's prior consent. The monks must have been trying to preclude double residency, which, as we have seen, was a common tax-evasion technique.[80] The monastery's laws also entitled the monks to seize the inheritances of their Muslim residents who had died without children. The enforcement of this particular regulation by Valldigna only faced decisive opposition from royal officials in 1442, when the monks targeted the goods of two Muslims who had been simultaneously "vassals of the king in the Moorish quarter of Corbera and landowners in [Valldigna's] Alfàndec valley." The king obstructed the seizure on the grounds that "his own royal prerogative" necessarily took precedence over any seigniorial claim.[81]

The question remained whether the monarchy would have been able to enforce compliance among rival authorities with rural domains had it sought to do so. Many lords continued to resist royal attempts to monopolize jurisdiction and control migration. As we saw in the introduction with the case of the Jewish moneylender from Alzira in 1377, the fact that the monarchy had gradually secured control over many urban Jewish aljamas did not eliminate the potential for jurisdictional conflict. Even if increased royal rights did help crown administrators secure more courtroom victories, much of the activity of the Jews essential to their economic prosperity necessitated their entry into rural seigniorial lands.[82] Creditors had long encountered greater difficulty in securing repayment of their loans from clients living on such lordships due to noncooperative or outwardly hostile lords and seigniorial officials.[83] Jaume's frustration was palpable, for instance, in his mandate to the baron of Entença's bailiff of Falset in 1322. He ordered the officer to force recalcitrant debtors in his town and neighboring Tivissa to repay Isaac Cap, a Jewish resident of the royal town of Montblanc. The loans had been transacted by "public charter," the king argued. The jurisdictional isolation of these towns under the authority of the baron of Entença could not excuse what Jaume viewed as the "failure of justice" that had taken place at the hands of the noble and his officer.[84] The presence of assertive lords situated within or along the peripheries of royal domains continued to create problems for the crown. Meyerson has observed how some Jews in royal towns sought out patronage relationships with nearby lords, sometimes in order to evade or distance themselves from royal authority.[85] Such Jewish initiative naturally imposed additional obstacles for the crown's defense of its claimed regalian prerogatives.

The monarchy was also suffering setbacks to its legal positions in the courts. In the case against Valldigna, the narrowness of the final verdict delivered by the Infant Martí in 1379 and the concessions offered to the abbot and monastery attest to the weak legal footing on which the crown found itself. According to the court and its presiding legal experts, even though Jaume II's privilege had awarded the monastery unconditional jurisdictional rights over the Alfàndec Valley, where the incident had transpired, the fact that this concession, in its "generality" (*generalitat*), had not explicitly made "special mention" of Valldigna's alleged power over nonresident royal Jews restricted it from overriding the provisions of the *Furs de València* and unraveling certain Jews' status as "special regalia . . . [who] continue to belong to the said lord king and fall under his jurisdiction wherever they go . . . as servants and personal property of the said lord king." Yet, rather than proceeding to extend this relationship to all Jews, the verdict emphasized that Abraham Açavella was universally known as a long-term resident of royal Alzira and, in accordance with the *Furs*, could not fall under Valldigna's jurisdiction unless he first established himself as a permanent resident on the monastery's domains. Indeed, it explained, it would be illegitimate for such a general donation to award a lord power over "Jews through all of the king's lands and realms since they are from places, royal cities and towns, that have pertained and still pertain to the lord king for all time." The verdict was therefore arguably a mixed victory for the crown, for in preserving royal jurisdiction over mobile crown Jews, it also hardened the legal underpinnings of seigniorial autonomy and their independent control over their non-Christian residents. Moreover, as a further sign that the case had been chiefly about protecting regalian prerogatives, the court summarily exonerated the abbot and his officials for their usurpation of crown prerogatives and awarded nothing to Abraham for his unlawful incarceration and loss of property. Even though the verdict was thus more favorable to seigniorial rights than it might have been, any gains by the crown with its campaign to establish a doctrine of regalian possession were illegitimate and unwelcome for such lords. Indeed, in response to the verdict, Valldigna's procurator begrudgingly retorted that "he did not consent to the ruling insofar as it ran counter to his side."[86]

Years earlier, the crown's exclusive authority over Muslims was threatened in other respects in a mid-fourteenth-century case regarding an incident in the town of Sestrica, near Calatayud. The dispute concerned the local lord's alleged incarceration of his Muslim tenant for trying to relocate from the seigniorial town to royal lands. Sestrica's aljama mobilized to defend this resident and wisely avoided the seigniorial court by appealing the matter to the crown. At the royal court, however, the jurisconsults split in their rulings and exposed a serious loophole in the crown's policy of exclusive possession. One reasoned that "according to the fuero [the lord] could not seize this Muslim's person, since his person or body belong to the Lord King." Despite the jurist's conclusion, the *justicia* of Aragon sided with the noble because he apparently insisted on viewing the Muslim, rather than the king, as the primary litigant. As a result, the noble's prerogatives took precedence. The *justicia* concluded that "it was absurd to say that the Muslim was more privileged than the Christian" with respect to their vassalage and theorized that the seizure was, in fact, licit.[87]

Even in the fifteenth century, the monarchy continued to have to engage with other lords in the open market for Muslim residents. *Mudéjares* on rural seigniorial domains in Valencia were being enticed by lower rents offered in underpopulated urban *morerías* administered by the monarchy. Other nonfinancial considerations, however, also came into play and worked to the crown's disfavor. Many Muslims chose to remain in the countryside under seigniorial governance because they preferred greater social distance and religious autonomy, even at the price of higher rents.[88]

Scholars have done much to reconstruct the pragmatic attitude of these lords. Many were unwilling to regulate the religious practices of their tenants in accordance with papal, episcopal, or royal mandates because they feared disrupting the economy of their lordships, which was largely driven by Muslim labor. In the early fourteenth century, for example, Guillem and Ot de Montcada famously ignored repeated orders by the king and pope to ban the call to prayer and impose other regulations on the Muslim communities living within their barony of Aitona.[89] In her study of the administration of Muslims in this barony, Marta Monjo suggests that "the lack of royal authority in the face of the ascendant Moncada family . . . permitted this action."[90] The royal bailiff of Tortosa, by contrast, strictly implemented these same orders. He applied the ban to all forms of Muslim religious practice, intervening in the schools, mosques, and readings.[91]

Similar to what we have seen with Fraga, the crown's treatment of Aitona reveals that it was not seeking to expand the limits of its administration's authority in every place to an identical extent or at the same pace. Instead, it continued to conserve its resources cautiously so that it would have the means to target lordships of particular strategic interest. In 1326, Jaume II conceded to Ot de Montcada's request that the secretaries of Lleida not seek to collect levies or other incomes from the Jews in Aitona and its castle. The king agreed that these Jews belonged to the noble and thus should pay tribute only to him.[92] Indeed, even when the monarchy secured direct control over formerly seigniorial Muslim communities through warfare with neighboring kingdoms, it refrained from retaining these jurisdictional rights indefinitely. During the Crown of Aragon's brutal war with Castile in the mid-fourteenth century, Pere III recaptured vast territories along Valencia's western frontier, populated chiefly by Muslims, that had temporarily fallen under Castilian control. In 1365, however, he submitted to pressure from his faithful Valencian lords at the Corts to restore seigniorial control over these areas to what it had been before the war. Not even when playing the part of sovereign conqueror did the king move to wipe the jurisdictional slate clean and erase ingrained seigniorial exemptions and entitlements that compromised royal regalian claims.[93]

The endemic impairment of crown oversight, whether perpetuated by seigniorial resistance or explicit royal concession, would endure until the expulsion of the Jews. Regarding Muslims and crypto-Muslims, it would persist through the seventeenth century, beyond the dissolution of *mudejarism*. One outspoken sixteenth-century Valencian lord's justification to the Inquisition of his tolerance of crypto-Islam among his domains' Moriscos illustrates the magnitude of the challenge faced by the monarchy in its effort to normalize conditions throughout its realms. "In my lands," he claimed, "I am king and pope."[94]

These persistent obstructions in rural settings, which outlived the more ephemeral obstacles in comparatively accessible urban settings such as Tortosa, should encourage us to question the extent to which the crown was universally successful, even by the turn of the fourteenth century, in invariably establishing Jews and Muslims as "special and direct subjects, their 'royal treasure.'" Accordingly, we need to reevaluate the extent to which this relationship "drove a wedge into local seigniorial power, and maintained a monopoly of control over the tax revenues of a significant portion of the population."[95] Viewing the evolution of this policy within the context of broader administration building by the monarchy reveals how royal authority was usually furthered not simply by any generic "special and direct" relationship with non-Christians. It arguably benefited as much from the crown's acquisition of jurisdictional rights to formerly independent lordships as well as from the service relationships the monarchy developed with certain Jewish elites who did not depend on the servi regis principle. All of the crown's tactics and techniques could not change the fact that establishing the primacy of royal jurisdiction over non-Christians as normative was a painstaking and elusive process. Kings could not simply enact these regalian rights everywhere by fiat so that they could be used to further royal control over tax revenues and public order. In spite of the growing influence of Roman legal principles, these monarchs remained undeniably bound by the laws and customs of their realms.[96]

Throughout the premodern period in the Crown of Aragon and beyond, as in other principalities throughout medieval European society, many Jews and Muslims thus continued to live under considerably heterogeneous conditions. According to the late fifteenth-century Edict of Expulsion, more than a dozen baronial Jewries in Aragon alone were formally recognized by the monarchy. Even though the monarchy possessed the means to licitly and successfully execute the order, the daily administration of these communities remained largely under seigniorial control until the exodus.[97]

This persistent state of affairs hindered, or at least complicated, any broad "process of standardization" in both external management and communal organization. When standardization did take place, it often depended on the lords' voluntary emulation of royal policies and Jewish participation as much as on the efficacy of royal mandates or the monarchy's successful infiltration of seigniorial jurisdictions.[98] Such collaboration by Jews could take a variety of forms, as we have witnessed throughout this study. Jews within seigniorial localities could become incentivized to work with the crown to further its administrative growth. We have observed how Jews in Tortosa sometimes appealed cases to royal court, for example. Seigniorial Jews could experience pressure from royal Jews to conform with them to satisfy the crown's demands, as we have noticed in numerous examples, including Tortosa's conflict with Barcelona in 1282.

In the future, royal Jewish communities that were paying an ever-greater price for the detachment of seigniorial Jewries would feel mounting self-interest to assist the monarchy's campaigns to subject these Jews to royal taxation. Around the middle of the fourteenth century, some of these royal Jews imagined that their future would be brighter if all of their coreligionists in the Crown of Aragon could redefine themselves legally as a single community, irrespective of their diverse jurisdictional circumstances. In 1354, the impoverished Jewish community of Barcelona issued an ordinance (*takkanah*) during the instability following the Black Death. These Jews sought to assemble together in their call a council of representatives from throughout the realms to design a new administrative framework for intercommunal collaboration with the monarchy and other governing institutions. The campaign ended up having no lasting impact on the organization it sought to change. Nevertheless, the document generated by the meeting reveals how certain Jewish leaders dreamed of reformulating Jewish coexistence through the emulation of Christian representative institutions in order to build a cohesive, officially networked Jewish community association pervading the Crown of Aragon.[99]

The assembled representatives used the ordinance to list specific benefits they expected from this new relationship as well as to detail the workings of this pan-Jewish communal system. They argued that the Crown of Aragon's Jewish populace, so organized, would be in an improved position to inspire or pressure the king to offer the Jews better protections "for their common safety" as well as valuable prerogatives, on his own accord and by liaising with the pope. Transforming themselves into "a single union with a common treasury" would earn the Jews increased financial stability.[100] In the system envisioned by the attendees, each realm would have the right to appoint commissioners who would work together to represent the interests of the collective Jewish community. As a legally recognized community, the Jews deserved to have representatives at the Cort(e)s in order to safeguard their collective interests. They should also be taxed in common, uniformly and directly, by the king as their one proper lord.[101]

Indeed, the assembled Jewish representatives construed their bond with the king as essential to their security and thus sought to eliminate customs that weakened it. The ordinance, accordingly, was premised upon the argument that the monarchy's ingrained practice of assigning the right to collect future revenues from a Jewish community to repay creditors harmed those Jews' relationship with their recognized sovereign: "For when the communities bring their money to the coffers of the king they find grace in his eyes ... [and] if they are in poor condition our lord, the king, may be generous to them in accordance with his proper custom."[102]

In most of its provisions, the assembly placed the needs of the greater populace over those of single communities or individuals. A major goal of this prioritization appears to have been to reduce the social stratification and community competition prevalent throughout the Crown of Aragon. Anyone acting against the provisions of the ordinance and against the greater good of the wider Jewish community was to be excommunicated as a *malsin* (informer). Individual Jews, furthermore, were not to be targeted by separate taxation but assessed along with the rest of their community.[103] In an effort to prevent certain aljamas from shirking their responsibility to contribute to royal taxation demands, the ordinance tried to encourage the king to compel "each community taking part in this synod to pay the share which is assigned to it in accordance with the division which is made between us." It also sought to preempt any attempt by these communities to alter the nature of their agreements and associations unilaterally by appealing directly to the king.[104] Recognizing that "it is not fit[ting] that we should spend money and that [other communities] should get their share of the benefit sitting comfortably in their homes and not giving their share of the expenditure," the attendees agreed to exhort the king to compel "unrepresented communities to pay their share of the expenses."[105] While clear in its view about the benefits of further standardizing and institutionalizing the administration of separate Jewish communities and the inviolability and pervasiveness of royal lordship, the ordinance nevertheless appreciated that binding noncollaborative Jewish aljamas represented a significant obstacle.

These representatives were thus acutely aware of the continued reality of nonroyal jurisdictions, and yet they did not pursue an entirely consistent policy in their strategy to deal with them. On the one hand, the assembled group urged the king to pursue anyone guilty of killing or inciting violence against Jews into seigniorial domains and to require that the lords render them over to royal justice. On the other hand, the representatives could not agree to support the present royal policy restricting Jewish relocation to seigniorial lands. The king, the ordinance stipulated, should "permit the Jews who live under his government to remove from the places belonging to the King to those under the knights or wherever they may choose, just as this right was given them of yore and that he should set at naught the decree which is in existence at the present day."[106] Even for these royal Jews, the freedom of their coreligionists to choose their places of residency and opt for nonroyal lordship remained an important facet of their personal self-determination, as it had been since the earliest charters of settlement. Such personal autonomy needed to be maintained, in accordance with traditional laws, even if it had the potential to harm the well-being of the greater Jewish community.

The challenge for the monarchy and its theory of exclusive protection, even when promoted by a significant portion of the Jewish populace, was not only that Jews and Jewish communities were divided over what aspects of their autonomy were fit to be limited or sacrificed for more effective collective action, but also that all seigniorial regimes were not, in fact, founded upon insincere promises of temporary liberal conditions to "blind [Jews'] eyes . . . to the dangers of exploitation and repression to which they were exposed later on in the 'lords' domains,'" as Baer once supposed.[107] Royal Jews could condemn their seigniorial coreligionists for their unwillingness to collaborate with these grand designs, but they could not deny that some in this subset of their wider Jewish community viewed nonroyal lordship as a viable, even favorable, alternative. No less than the king, certain lords strove to implement policies to guarantee the security, autonomy, and stability of their non-Christian subjects. As a result, this unrelenting jurisdictional fragmentation would continue to complicate royal efforts to streamline and standardize the administration and coexistence of non-Christians in Christian-ruled society for generations to come.

Notes

Generally only the most reliable version is cited in the case of duplicate archival sources or multiple editions. In addition to the acronyms specified in the bibliography, the following abbreviations are used throughout the notes: c. (carpeta, calaix, capítol), perg. (pergamí/pergamino), Reg. (Registro), and Arm. (Armario).

Introduction

1. Such patterns of lending remained common in the future. See Garcia-Oliver 2011, 112–13.
2. ACA, CR, Procesos en folio, legajo no. 126/2 (1377), fol. 6r–v. See Nirenberg 1996, 177–78, and Garcia-Oliver 2011, 109. On Valldigna's jurisdictional autonomy, see Garcia-Oliver 2011, 1–6.
3. Dualde Serrano 1950–67, c. 8.3. ACA, CR, Procesos en folio, legajo no. 126/2, fol. 6r: "Item dien ut supra quels dits juheus son propries regalies del dit senyor Rey en tal via e manera que de si no les pot partir e son coffre seus on se vulla que vayen vinguen o estiguen los dits juheus dins la sua senyoria e aquells lo dit senyor Rey."
4. Garcia-Oliver 2011, 14.
5. ACA, CR, Procesos en folio, legajo no. 126/2, fol. 7v.
6. ACA, CR, Procesos en folio, legajo no. 126/2, fol. 5v.
7. The abbot presented the full text with subsequent confirmation (22 April 1354) at court: ACA, CR, Procesos en folio, legajo no. 126/2, fols. 17v–22v (4 November 1300). Years earlier, Jaume I had granted the valley to Adán de Paterna on similar terms to repay a loan. ACA, CR, Reg. 17, fol. 43r–v (24 January 1264) [Burns 2001, doc. 523].
8. ACA, CR, Procesos en folio, legajo no. 126/2, fol. 17r.
9. See Ray 2006, 11–35.
10. Jordan 1998, 4. On Roman legal precedents, see Linder 2008.
11. In Latin, Caruana Gómez de Barreda 1974, c. 425: "Nam iudei servi regis sunt et semper fisco regio deputati." In Romance, Gorosch 1950, c. 568: "Qual los jodios sieruos son del sennor Rey et sienpre a la real bolsa son co[n]tados." See Motis Dolader 2005.

12. See Shoval 2004.
13. Abulafia 2004, 111–14.
14. Stow 2007a, 10. See Stow 1992, 63, and Blumenkranz 1960, 296.
15. For example, the *Fuero de Calatayud*: Muñoz y Romero 1847, 457–68.
16. Simonsohn 1991, 4–12. Sapir Abulafia 2011, 3–31, provides an overview. See also Abulafia 2004, 105–8, and Abulafia 2000, 694.
17. Simonsohn 1991, 4–6; Rowe 2011, 16–19. These theological views underscored the personifications of *ecclesia*, which *synagoga* that celebrated Christian triumph and denigrated Jewish error, stubbornness, and blindness. See Rowe 2011, 40–78.
18. Augustine 2009, 16.35, p. 504; see also 16.42, p. 511.
19. Simonsohn 1988, doc. 37.
20. Although Calixtus's original bull has not survived, we can reconstruct its contents based on reissues with minor modifications by subsequent popes. See Simonsohn 1991, 42–45.
21. Ibid., 98.
22. For examples of this work on other regions, see Jordan 1989, Kisch 1970, Mundill 2010, and Soifer Irish 2013a. Similarly, Fancy (2013, 54–57, 72–73) has argued that the monarchy's principle of exclusive possession also recommended its recruitment of Muslim mercenaries, who thus "appeared wholly dependent on the sovereign's will, slaves before the law" (72).
23. Klein 2006, 72–78.
24. Bisson 1989a, 165.
25. For a study of these surveys and accounting innovations, see Bisson 1984, vol. 1, esp. 28–41. On the dating of the *Usatges*, see Bastardas i Parera 1977.
26. Bisson 1989a, 164–65; Bisson 1989e, 244–45; Kosto 2001c, 278–81.
27. Bisson 1989d, 215–36.
28. See Kosto 2001c, 281–85; Kosto 2001a; Bisson 1989a, 170; and Bisson 1989f.
29. Aurell 2012, 122, 125.
30. Bisson 2009, 399. For the case of France, for example, see Baldwin 1986 and Strayer 1971.
31. See Bisson 1989e, 243, Bonnassie 1975–76, 2:705–11, and Salrach 1987, esp. 357. Bisson 1986, chaps. 1 and 2, provides a general overview of this ascendancy.
32. For the case of Urgell, see Gonzalvo i Bou 1990 and Bisson 2009, 506–11.
33. Bensch 1996 and 2005.
34. Bonnassie 1975–76, 2:685–711; Kosto 2001c, chaps. 4 and 5.
35. These examples come from the Second General Capitulary of the *missi* of Thionville from 805, but the objectives appear throughout a wide range of Carolingian capitularies. Boretius and Krause 1883, 123–25, doc. 44, nos. 5 (feuding), 13 (tolls and roads), 18 (coinage), and 9 (oaths). See Nelson 1994, 65–66.
36. For an overview of the eleventh- and twelfth-century uprisings, see Freedman 1991, 65–69, 110–18. Bonnassie (1975–76, 2:625–46, and 1980) conducted the most fundamental work on the eleventh-century crisis, which remains a subject of debate. See Bisson 1994, Barthélemy and White 1996, and Reuther, Wickham, and Bisson 1997.
37. Kosto 2001b.
38. Bisson 2009, 499–515, provides an overview.
39. Gonzalvo i Bou 1994, doc. 21, c. 2 (September 1202).
40. See Freedman 1991, chaps. 3 and 4.
41. See Bisson 1984, vol. 1, chaps. 3 and 4, and Bisson 1989b. For New Catalonia, see Barton 2010, 209–16.
42. See Kagay 2003 and 2007a. Compare, generally, Kantorowicz 1957, chap. 4, and Pennington 1993, chap. 2–3.

43. Sabaté 1995, 619. See Vanlandingham 2002, 83–100, and Sabaté 1997, 226ff.
44. Sabaté 2011, 80.
45. Freedman 2010, 200. See Sabaté 2011, 123–29.
46. Freedman 2010, 200. See Ferrer i Mallol 1970–71, 359–61 and 436–38. I do not mean to imply here that scholars of governance have held static views on the history of sovereignty and its relationship to feudal law. See Davis 2008, chap. 1, for perceptive analysis of this complex historiography.
47. Assis 1997b, 9.
48. See Barton 2011, 310–13.
49. For example, O'Connor 2005.
50. Klein 2006. See also Abulafia 1994, esp. 76–99.
51. See, for example, Ray 2006 and Catlos 2004, respectively.
52. See Barrero García 1979, 74–77. The related Castilian *Fueros de Cuenca* (ca. 1190) feature a similar provision and also witnessed slow diffusion. Barrero García 1976, 722. Compare Abulafia 2004, 99, who cites Barrero García to argue for the rapid transmission of the Teruel model.
53. Roth 1995, 141.
54. Lalinde Abadía 1963a, doc. 5 (1286).
55. Colon, Arcadi, and García Edo 1980–2007, vol. 1, c. 65, followed by laws regulating civil and criminal procedure for cases involving Jews and Muslims under the bailiff's jurisdiction (c. 66 and 67).
56. Assis 1997b, 9; Abulafia 2004, 97–98 and 114–17.
57. Assis 1997b, 9–12. See Bensch 2008, 20.
58. Baer 1961–66, 1:51 (my emphasis). Baer also pointed to royal possession of the Jews as further evidence of their degradation.
59. Baer 1913, 47–50. See Abulafia 2000, 706.
60. This assumption is problematic since the date of 1176 borne by the fuero only indicates the "initial moment of the formation of the law of Teruel." Barrero García 1979, 61.
61. O'Brien 1999, 184. I thank Maya Soifer Irish of Rice University for the reference.
62. Muñoz y Romero 1847, 533: "Maurus vero, et Iudaeus si ibi haereditatem fecerit, sit de palatio."
63. See, for example, Sabaté 1996.
64. On territorial lordship in Germany, see Arnold 1991, 11–60.
65. Jordan 1998, 1–2. Earlier Anglo-Norman kings appear to have exercised less capable control. See Stacey 2001.
66. See Mundill 1998, 45–71, 249–85, and Huscroft 2006.
67. See Jordan 1989 and Langmuir 1990b, 191–92.
68. Teulet et al. 1863–1909, vol. 2, no. 2083 (December 1230).
69. See Jordan 1989, 131–33, and Langmuir 1990a.
70. Jordan 1998, 7–8, 12–13. See Jordan 1989, 200–213.
71. Jordan 1997, 28–31.
72. Compare Abulafia 2004, 122–23. See Willoweit 1988 and Watt 1991.
73. Jordan 1998, 3.
74. Ray 2006, 83.
75. See, for example, Baron 1952–83, 8:83, 233, 341, and Simonsohn 1991, 102–10. Compare Soifer Irish 2013b on the high index of ecclesiastical leadership over Jews in Castile.
76. Simonsohn 1991, 103–4. See the epilogue below.
77. See Nirenberg 1996, 28–29, and the epilogue below.
78. Boswell 1978, 31: "A welter of conflicting claims and jurisdictions resulted . . . which [was] ultimately resolved by the development of absolute monarchical power." Compare Fancy 2013, 43: "the fiction of absolute authority not only grew out of a specific medieval legal

and theological tradition but was also inherently unstable and unattainable."
79. Motis Dolader 1990, 39 (my emphasis).
80. Blasco Martínez 1991, 25, 62. This perspective on the *Fueros de Teruel* is typical among studies of the later Middle Ages. See, for example, Pérez 2007, 18. See also Planas and Forcano 2009, 40–41.
81. Riera i Sans 2009, 141. Riera i Sans 2006, 26–45, presents an overview of these engagements.
82. Riera i Sans 2006, 29.
83. For example, Sapir Abulafia 2011, 109–28.
84. Assis 1988, 22.
85. Segura y Valls 1879, 59–60, publishes the evidence.
86. On Santa Coloma de Queralt, see Milton 2012.
87. See, for example, Goitein 1967–93, esp. vol. 2.
88. Burns 1984, 127.
89. Neuman 1942, 1:6–7.
90. Ray 2006, 80.
91. Consider, for example, Alanyà i Roig 1996, 15–21, on the community of Besalú.
92. Ray 2010, 266.
93. Daileader 2000, 118–32. See also Emery 1959, 89–100.
94. Klein 2006, 70–95.
95. Ibid., 143–61.
96. Bensch 2008. Assis 1997b, 167–69, devotes some attention to baronial Jews.
97. *Convivencia* is assigned diverse meanings but commonly translated as "coexistence." See Glick 1992 and Tolan 1999. This present study tends to construe the term as "a very narrow, technical definition of mundane social interaction between members of different religious groups," as proposed by Soifer 2009, 21.
98. Catlos 2004, 407.
99. Catlos 2001–2, 266–67. See Catlos 2014, which appeared when this book was already in an advanced stage of production.
100. See Brown 2003, 355–82.
101. Casanova Querol 1991, 395, notes the dearth of work on the "government and internal life of the aljama." See also Curto 1999, 9–10. Carreras y Candi 1928 remains the only comprehensive study. Miravall 1973 and 2000, Serrano Daura 2006, Secall i Güell 1983, 38–56, and Bayerri 1933–60, 7:49–51, 323–31, and 8:291–95, remain significant. Serrano Daura 2000b, 1:276–86, reviews the juridical conditions but not royal-seigniorial jurisdictional conflict.
102. See, for example, Maya 1999, 20. Compare Assis 1997b, 188–89, and Celdrán Gomáriz and Martínez 2005, 293. Carreras y Candi 1928, 27–30, did not underscore the seigniorial role in determining local conditions.
103. See Bensch 1995, 135–41.
104. Ray 2006, 5–6.
105. Ibid., 178.
106. See Nirenberg 1996, 27–29, Baer 1961–66, 1:85, and Klein 2006, 35–45. See Chazan 2006 for wider Europe.
107. See Klein 2006, 193–95.
108. Such use of Christian courts in fact permitted the survival of a small number of Hebrew deeds (*shetarot*) although not, unfortunately, from the Jews resident in Tortosa during our period. See Klein 2004, 13–20.
109. Historians have noticed a similar phenomenon elsewhere in Europe; see, for example, Berend 2001, 81–82. While there is limited evidence of Muslim inclusion in general town councils (*universitates, concejos*) in the Crown of Aragon (Catlos 2004, 273–75), similar examples of Jewish participation have not surfaced that parallel what we can witness elsewhere in Europe—for example, the Jews of Rome receiving the status of citizens from the papacy. Simonsohn 1991, doc. 499 (15 April

1402). To Simonsohn (1991, 95, 101), this was a form of limited residential citizenship. See also Roth 1995, 149.
110. ACA, CR, perg. A I, no. 326 (March 1182) [Sánchez Casabón 1995, doc. 339]; ACA, CR, perg. P I, no. 308 (26 November 1208) [Pagarolas 1999, vol. 2, doc. 213; Alvira Cabrer 2010, vol. 2, doc. 833].
111. See Klein 2006, 19–23, and Klein 2005, 60.
112. See, for example, Elukin 2007, 66–67.
113. Bensch 2008, 26–27.

Chapter 1

1. Roth 1994, 11. A sixth-century tombstone with Hebrew inscriptions demonstrates that Jews were resident in the town during Visigothic times. See Celdrán Gomáriz and Martínez 2005, 292.
2. Singer et al. 1908, 8:470–71, and Roth 2003, 31.
3. On persecution of tolerated religious minorities (*dhimmī*) by these groups, see García-Arenal 1997 and Fierro 1997.
4. ACA, AGP, *Cartulari de Tortosa*, fol. 83r, doc. 269; ACTE, perg. no. 195, Comú II, no. 38 (23 December 1149) [Serrano Daura 2000a, doc. 3]. For the sake of simplicity, this study conflates comital and royal rights and refers to them as royal.
5. See Kosto 2001c, 279. Ramon adopted this title even before Tortosa had been captured. See, for example, AHN, Clero: Poblet, c. 2000, no. 6 (22 August 1148) [Altisent 1993, doc. 115].
6. ACA, CR, perg. RB IV, no. 209 ([30] December 1148) [Serrano Daura 2000a, doc. 1].
7. ACTE, perg. no. 463, Privilegis III, no. 6 (30 November 1149) [Font Rius 1969–83, 1:i, doc. 75].
8. Consider Nirenberg 1996, 190–98.
9. Klein 2006, 35–45.
10. See ibid., 43.
11. ACA, AGP, *Cartulari de Tortosa*, fol. 83r.
12. Zimmermann 1988 and 1993. See also Sabaté 1997, 30–33.
13. See Virgili 2001b, 75–81, with a map of the town's division on 77.
14. For example, the Jew Jafia, served as a bailiff for the crown and for the bishop of Tortosa. Baer 1929, vol. 1, doc. 37 (21 April 1176). See Neuman 1942, 2:229–30, and Bisson 1984, 1:68–71.
15. Bisson 1984, 1:25–29.
16. Kosto 2001c, 279.
17. Kosto 2001b.
18. Bastardas i Parera 1984, us. 11, 51, 64, 75. See also Rovira i Ermengol 1933, us. 164 and 171.
19. Bastardas i Parera 1984, us. 64; Rovira i Ermengol 1933, us. 164 and 171.
20. Gonzalvo i Bou 1996, 118.
21. Riera i Sans 2006, 27.
22. See chapter 3 below.
23. Riera i Sans 2006, 27n24.
24. Bastardas i Parera 1984, us. 62, 64, 75.
25. Compare Assis 1997a, 9.
26. Hence the zone bears the name of Drassana ("shipyard") in the charter. See García Biosca et al. 1998, 140, and Miret y Sans 1904a, 202n2, for the shipyards' dedicatory inscription from Abd al-Raḥman III. New building may have been necessitated by the destruction of existing infrastructure during the Christians' siege, as attested by the Genoese chronicler Caffaro (1890, 86): "domos et turres omnes usque ad muschetam destruxerit."
27. See Baer 1961–66, 1:56–57, and Miravall 2000. Curto 1999, 10 and 24 (map), supersedes Casanova Querol 1991, 393–98. See also Curto 2002, 108–17, and Celdrán Gomáriz and Martínez 2005, 286–303. Although it was not indicated in the surrender treaty, the positioning of the *morería* in Remolins is attested in early documentation; see, for example,

Delaville le Roulx 1897, vol. 1, doc. 195. See also Virgili 2001b, 128–29.

28. Land-transfer documentation suggests that Remolins constituted a separate settlement. Virgili 1997a, docs. 395 (3 April 1186) and 402 (26 July 1186). On the remains of Roman and Andalusi walls, see *Catalunya Romànica* 1984–98, 26:111–14, García Biosca et al. 1998 and Vidal Franquet 2008, 124–31.

29. Vidal Franquet 2008, 130. See also Curto 1999, 20, and Bayerri 1933–60, 8:242.

30. See, generally, Haverkamp 1995, 13–15.

31. Sabaté 2003, 286; Catlos 2004, 261–79; Virgili 2001b, 110–12, 128–30, 226–28. Sénac 2000, 449–74, identifies similar patterns in Lower Aragon.

32. The urban geography of Andalusi Tortosa is identified most clearly by al-Ḥimyari; see Lévi-Provençal 1938, no. 115. See García Biosca et al. 1998, 140–42, Virgili 2001b, 104–10, and Miravall 1999, 198–204. Ferrer i Mallol 1998–99, 144–45, provides an overview of the *morería*'s siting.

33. See, for example, ACA, CR, perg. A I, no. 362 (January 1184) [Sánchez Casabón 1995, doc. 382; Miquel Rosell 1945–47, vol. 1, doc. 467], and Massip 1996, c. 4.24.2.

34. ACA, AGP, *Cartulari de Tortosa*, fol. 83r, doc. 269.

35. See Barton 2010, 216–26.

36. Compare Sénac 2000, 449–56, and Catlos 2004, 112–18, on charter clauses referring to former Muslim owners. Several of the parcels also derived from the royal patrimony.

37. On the retention of Muslim rural tenants in this region, see Barton 2011.

38. For example, the Jew Maimo Regine exchanged a house for another that was co-owned by the Templars and Ramon de Montcada. The house he received was bordered by homes also pertaining to Jews. Both of the houses formerly had Andalusi owners. ACA, AGP, *Cartulari de Tortosa*, fols. 6v–7r, doc. 21 (27 September 1193).

39. See, for example, Toda 1938, doc. 181 (6 December 1188).

40. Baer 1961–66, 194.

41. See, for example, Salrach et al. 1999, doc. 530 (26 November 1058). See also Virgili 2001b, 31–42. For archaeological evidence, see Curto 1993, 268–78, and Esco, Giralt, and Sénac 1988, 14–16.

42. Constable 1996, 188 and 196.

43. Adler 1983, 59.

44. Virgili 1997a, doc. 230 (17 July 1172).

45. ACTE, perg. no. 549, Privilegis II, no. 39 (July 1181).

46. ACTE, perg. no. 699, Diversorum II, no. 63/2 (24 September 1189).

47. Compare Catlos 2004, 198–201.

48. ACA, CR, perg. RB IV, no. 209.

49. AML, Fons Municipals, perg. no. 31 [Gual Camarena 1967, 169–73]. Tolls were to be paid at Tudela, Gallur, Alagón, El Castellar, Zaragoza, Pina, Velilla, Mequinenza, Ascó, and Tortosa. See Glick 2005, 135–43.

50. Compare Catlos 2004, 104.

51. AML, Fons Municipals, perg. no. 31.

52. Virgili 1997a, doc. 30, and Virgili 2001a, doc. 577 (31 December 1198). Compare Pagarolas 1984, doc. 87 (27 May 1185). For a systematic survey, see Virgili 2001b, 212–14.

53. See Constable 1996, 138–39.

54. ACTE, perg. no. 657, Diversorum II, no. 21 (20 April 1198). Niermeyer 1997, 1014, s.v. *tasca*. On the *tascha*, see Freedman 1991, 73, and Bisson 1984, 1:38–39.

55. Virgili 2001a, doc. 577 (31 December 1198).

56. Virgili 1997a, docs. 13 ([13 December] 1148) and 28 (5 August 1151). For the papal stance, see ACL, *Llibre vert*, fols. 23v–24r (1159–81), Mansi et al. 1901–27, vol. 22, col. 1054, and Simonsohn 1991, 182–83.

57. Virgili 1997a, docs. 583 and 584 (12 April 1199), 588 ([1199–1213]).
58. Ibid., doc. 697 (28 November 1207).
59. Toda 1938, doc. 211 (10 May 1156).
60. Virgili 1997a, doc. 98 (9 February 1159).
61. Ibid., doc. 160 (19 April 1166), with Hebrew and Arabic subscriptions. See Virgili 2009.
62. Toda 1938, doc. 207 (18 February 1166).
63. See Barton 2010, 215–16, for numerous examples.
64. Virgili 1997a, doc. 103 (14 August 1159).
65. Virgili 2001a, doc. 503 (13 December 1193).
66. Ibid., doc. 676 (27 September 1206).
67. ACA, CR, perg. P I, no. 308 (24 November 1208) [Alvira Cabrer 2010, vol. 2, doc. 833].
68. See Benito i Monclús 2011, 65–66.
69. See Bisson 1984, 1:83, and Barton 2010, 212–15.
70. Bisson 1989g, 151–52. See Kosto 2001a, 8–9, 246, 283; Bisson 2009, 372; and McCrank 1993, 280–83.
71. ACA, CR, perg. A I, no. 67 (20 May 1169) [Bisson 1984, vol. 2, doc. 22].
72. The Order was the most important creditor in Catalonia, advancing at least 8,500 morabetins to Alfons (some 13 percent of his total indebtedness) through 1177. Bisson 1984, 1:82.
73. ACA, CR, perg. A I, no. 200 (25–31 March 1175) [Bisson 1984, vol. 2, doc. 26; Sánchez Casabón 1995, doc. 192].
74. Bisson 1984, vol. 2, doc. 27 ([March ca. 1174–75]). See Orti Gost 2001.
75. AHN, OM, c. 607, no. 10 (26 November 1180) [Sánchez Casabón 1995, doc. 316].
76. Udina Martorell 1947, doc. 235, and Sánchez Casabón 1995, doc. 310 (8 September 1180).
77. Udina Martorell 1947, doc. 246; Sánchez Casabón 1995, doc. 330 (30 October 1181).
78. ACA, CR, perg. A I, no. 326 (March 1182) [Sánchez Casabón 1995, doc. 339;

Miquel Rosell 1945–47, vol. 1, doc. 466; Virgili 1997a, doc. 335]. Forey 1973, 27–28, and Pagarolas 1999, 1:157–58, summarize the agreement.
79. See Bisson 1989e, 242–45, Bonnassie 1975–76, 2:696–701, and Kosto 2001c, 92–93.
80. ACA, CR, perg. A I, no. 326.
81. Ibid.
82. ACA, CR, perg. A I, no. 328 (1 May 1182) [Pagarolas 1999, vol. 2, doc. 206; Sánchez Casabón 1995, doc. 347]; ACA, CR, perg. A I, no. 362 (January 1184).
83. Virgili 2001a, doc. 517 (22 November 1194).
84. Virgili 1997a, doc. 381; Pagarolas 1984, doc. 87 (27 May 1185).
85. ACA, CR, perg. A I, no. 6 (25 April 1163).
86. Compare Sánchez Casabón 1995, docs. 1 and 2 (August 1162 and 1 September 1162), and Font Rius 1969–83, 1:i, doc. 120 (7 February 1163). See Caruana Gómez 1962, 75ff.
87. ACT, Cartulari 4, fol. 111r–v (September 1185) [Virgili 1997a, doc. 389; Baer 1929, vol. 1, doc. 48a], subscribed by the king in Tortosa. See Ray 2006, 14, Assis 1997b, 240–41 and 252–53, and Assis 1997a, 218–23.
88. See Kosto 2001c, 265.
89. ACT, Cartulari 4, fol. 111r–v.
90. ACT, Cartulari 4, fol. 110r (23 March 1156) [Virgili 1997a, doc. 67].
91. Compare Ray 2006, 17–22.
92. ACA, CR, perg. RB IV, no. 16 [Bisson 1984, vol. 2, doc. 4, p. 37].
93. ACT, Cartulari 4, fol. 111v.
94. ACT, Privilegis i Donacions Reials, no. 50 (December 1196) [Virgili 2001a, doc. 552].
95. A similar competitive dynamic between residents with or without heritable *franquitas* can be observed in Muslim and Jewish aljamas elsewhere in the Crown of Aragon, regardless of

jurisdictional conditions. See Catlos 2004, 130–38, Barton 2011, 299–305, and Assis 1997b, 220–23.

96. ACA, AGP, *Cartulari de Tortosa*, fol. 86v, doc. 275 (February 1181) [Sánchez Casabón 1995, doc. 324; Baer 1929, vol. 1, doc. 48]. See Carreras y Candi 1928, 27.

97. Ray 2006, 83.

98. Ubieto Arteta 1951, doc. 57, p. 291 (24 October 1098); Baer 1929, vol. 1, no. 11.

99. Ureña y Smenjaud et al. 1935, c. 29.33, p. 632.

100. Canellas López 1989, 1:47, doc. 79 (26 December 1134); Baer 1929, vol. 1, no. 20. For context, see Zurita 1967–77, vol. 1, I.54–55, pp. 176–84.

101. Fernández Flórez et al. 1976–99, vol. 4, doc. 1312 (5 March 1152). Soifer Irish (2013b, 543–44) hypothesizes that "the gift of jurisdiction over the town's Jews was intended to mitigate the abbot's loss of other privileges" regarding his authority over the town on this same occasion.

102. Abajo Martín 1986, doc. 80 (15 July 1177). See Soifer Irish 2013b, 551.

103. Simonsohn 1991, 105–6, and see the epilogue below.

104. ACA, CR, perg. A I, no. 146 (18 January 1174) [Sánchez Casabón 1995, doc. 161]. On dower rights, see Bensch 1995, 264–65, Lalinde Abadía 1963b, Smith 2004, 21–23, and Johnson 2007, 221–23. One of the problems was that the king continued to exercise control over these holdings after they were assigned to the dower. Bisson 1984, 1:98n75.

105. Compare Pagarolas 1999, 1:157. Alfons's allocation of other holdings in 1187 to compensate for this leveraging was a temporary and ineffectual fix that did not replace the original dower. ACA, CR, perg. A I, no. 454 (May 1187)

[Sánchez Casabón 1995, doc. 442]. Compare Aurell 1995, 470.

106. ACA, CR, A I, Extrainventario nos. 2613 and 2616 [Bisson 1984, vol. 2, docs. 78 and 79 ([November 1189–February 1190])].

107. Pagarolas 1984, doc. 116, and Virgili 2001a, doc. 578 (1 January 1199): "Controversia aliqua fuerit inter Dominos Dertose et habitatores Dertose." Compare Forey 1973, 29.

108. Bisson 1984, 1:224, 230.

109. ACA, CR, perg. A I, no. 700 (December 1194) [Sánchez Casabón 1995, doc. 628]. Compare Pagarolas 1999, 1:159.

110. ACA, CR, perg. P I, no. 98 (26 September 1200) [Alvira Cabrer 2010, vol. 1, doc. 261]. The crown also confirmed that the Order's original one-fifth share would remain unaffected by this transfer. ACA, AGP, Arm. 4 (Tortosa), perg. no. 85 (15 March 1200) [Pagarolas 1984, doc. 57]. See Pano y Ruata 1943, 67–68. Enigmatically, no mention was made of the seigniorial rights still possessed by the Montcada family. While papal intervention by Celestine III and Innocent III at Sancha's request in previous years and months may have helped motivate her son, this agreement was orchestrated by her relative Alfonso VIII of Castile. Alvira Cabrer 2010, vol. 1, docs. 56 and 57; Kehr 1926, docs. 268 and 269 (both 7 August 1196). Alvira Cabrer 2010, vol. 1, doc. 201 (13 May 1199); Smith 2004, doc. 1. Alvira Cabrer 2010, vol. 1, doc. 245; Mansilla 1954, doc. 228; Smith 2004, doc. 3 (5 May 1200).

111. ACA, CR, perg. P I, no. 98.

112. ACA, AGP, *Cartulari de Tortosa*, fols. 46v–47r, doc. 144 (15 January 1202) [Pagarolas 1984, doc. 121].

113. ACA, CR, perg. P I, no. 257 [Alvira Cabrer 2010, vol. 2, doc. 678 (5 April

1207)]. See Virgili 2001a, doc. 667 (5 January 1206).
114. ACA, *Cartulari de Tortosa*, fol. 9, doc. 28 (13 June 1202) [Pagarolas 1984, doc. 122].
115. ACA, CR, perg. P I, no. 139 (3 July 1202) [Pagarolas 1984, doc. 121; Alvira Cabrer 2010, vol. 1, doc. 337].
116. Forey 1973, 30.
117. Ibid.
118. ACA, CR, perg. P I, no. 139: "Addo etiam eidem donationi illas. III. personas illum scilicet Christianum, Iudeum et Sarracenum, quos ego in eadem civitate specialiter possidebam."
119. Alvira Cabrer 2010, vol. 2, doc. 395bis (7 August 1203).
120. Ibid., vol. 2, doc. 824 (9 November 1208).
121. ACA, CR, perg. P I, no. 308 (26 November 1208) [Pagarolas 1999, vol. 2, doc. 213]. The donation must have mystified the Templars, who had recently received confirmation from Pere of all of the privileges and donations granted by Alfons and Ramon Berenguer IV. AHN, OM, c. 583, no. 58 (20 December 1207) [Alvira Cabrer 2010, vol. 2, doc. 732].
122. ACA, CR, perg. P I, no. 308.
123. Font Rius 1969–83, 1:i, doc. 227 (22 November 1208). Alfons's earlier attempt to have the see of Tortosa populate, cultivate, defend, and otherwise improve the castle had apparently yielded few results and was defunct at this time. Font Rius 1969–83, 1:i, doc. 202 (April 1195).
124. See Bisson 1984, 1:124.
125. ACA, CR, perg. P I, no. 308. The grant of Benifassà featured a similar provision. Font Rius 1969–83, 1:i, doc. 227.
126. ACA, AGP, *Cartulari de Tortosa*, fol. 70r, doc. 227 (8 June 1209) [Pagarolas 1984, doc. 130].
127. ACA, AGP, *Cartulari de Tortosa*, fol. 75r–v, doc. 246 (1 June 1210) [Alvira Cabrer 2010, vol. 3, doc. 1050].
128. AHN, Clero: Poblet, c. 2096, no. 10 (9 December 1208) [Alvira Cabrer 2010, vol. 2, doc. 837].
129. Compare Forey 1973, 30, and Pagarolas 1999, 1:162–64. See Aurell 1995, 357.
130. AHN, Clero: Poblet, c. 2099, no. 7 (3 November 1209) [Bisson 1984, vol. 2, doc. 128; Alvira Cabrer 2010, vol. 3, doc. 964].
131. ACA, CR, perg. P I, no. 370 (19 September 1210) [Pagarolas 1999, doc. 134; Alvira Cabrer 2010, vol. 3, doc. 1082].
132. See AHN, OM, c. 636, no. 5 (23 October 1210) [Alvira Cabrer 2010, vol. 3, doc. 1087], concerning El Cuervo and Serrella.
133. Compare Forey 1973, 30.
134. ACA, CR, Reg. 310, fol. 35r–v (3 November 1210) [Pagarolas 1999, vol. 2, doc. 215]. They excluded from the donation "our fifth" and *dominicaturas*.
135. ACA, CR, perg. P I, no. 373 (4 November 1210) [Alvira Cabrer 2010, vol. 3, doc. 1091].
136. ACA, CR, perg. J I, no. 39 (and other copies) (23 March 1215) [Pagarolas 1999, vol. 2, doc. 1]. Compare Shideler 1983, 200–201. ACA, AGP, *Cartulari de Tortosa*, fol. 50v, doc. 154 (23 March 1215) [Pagarolas 1999, vol. 2, doc. 2].
137. ACA, AGP, *Cartulari de Tortosa*, fol. 90r, no. 284 (16 November 1216) [Pagarolas 1999, vol. 2, doc. 6].
138. Soldevila 1971, c. II, p. 7: "E encara les honors, que eren set-centes cavalleries en aquell temps, e nostre pare lo rei don Pere havia-les totes donades e venudes de cent trenta enfora. E no havíem a un dia, quan nós entram en Montsó, què menjar, ¡si era la tera destroïda e empenyorada!" On the use of this text as a historical source, see Kagay 2007b,

165–76. Compare Jenkins 2012, esp. 159–74, who views many of the trends set in motion by the two monarchs as more deliberate and ultimately profitable for the monarchy than what we have witnessed here.

Chapter 2

1. ACA, CR, perg. J I, no. 1083 (28 July 1247) [Huici Miranda and Desamparados Cabanes Pecourt 1976–88, vol. 2, doc. 467].
2. ACA, CR, perg. J I, no. 1083.
3. Ibid.
4. Ibid.
5. On the inconsistency of ethnoreligious classification in sources, see, for example, Catlos 2004, 395–96, and Romano 1991a, 479–82.
6. Bisson 1989g, 152, 163. See also Kosto 2001c, 279, 283.
7. See, for example, Gonzalvo i Bou 1994, doc. 28, c. 16 (17 March 1235): "omnes homines Catalonie, tam nobiles quam laici, quam iudei sive sarraceni."
8. Gonzalvo i Bou 1994, doc. 24, c. 7 (23 July 1218). Earlier peace constitutions had mentioned Jews but not in reference to protection. The assembly at Lleida in 1214 sought to make subinfeudation conditional on the lord's prior consent and presumably singled out Christians and Jews because they were the likeliest groups to be affected by the statute. Ibid., doc. 23, c. 24.
9. Ibid., docs. 15 (1173), 17 (13 August 1188), and 18 (November 1192). See Bisson 2009, 504–8.
10. Bisson 2009, 510–15, provides a summary of these developments.
11. Gonzalvo i Bou 1994, doc. 20, c. 11 (9 June 1200).
12. Ibid., doc. 21 (September 1202), c. 11.
13. Freedman 1991, 116.
14. See Bisson 2009, 505, 507–8.
15. Bisson 1989i; Bisson 2009, 513–14.
16. Gonzalvo i Bou 1994, doc. 22 (1207).
17. Compare ibid., doc. 15, c. 2, 14, and 16, with subsequent assemblies.
18. Bisson 1989i, 212.
19. Bisson 1986, 58–59; Barrau Dihigo and Massó Torrents 1925, c. XXVII.1, p. 57; Sanpere y Miquel 1910, 12–17; Soldevila 1968, 58–60, 70–71. Jaume would later accuse Sanç, along with his uncle Ferran, of plotting to seize his title. Soldevila 1971, c. 11–12, pp. 7–8. Compare Soldevila 1968, 60–65.
20. Soldevila 1968, 83–84.
21. Gonzalvo i Bou 1994, doc. 23 (1214).
22. Ibid., doc. 23, c. 27 and 30.
23. When mentioned in the records, bailiffs are given a minor accessory role at most. See ibid., doc. 23, c. 21.
24. Ibid., doc. 23, c. 13 and 16. See Bisson 1996, 151–52 and below in this chapter.
25. Daileader 1999, 72–79.
26. Mansilla 1954, doc. 537 (23 January 1216).
27. Bisson 1989b, 355. See generally Bisson 1984, vol. 1.
28. Mansilla 1954, doc. 537.
29. Huici Miranda and Desamparados Cabanes Pecourt 1976–88, vol. 1, doc. 2 (19 July 1217). The viscount had waged war against Pere after illegitimately seizing most of the county of Urgell following the death of Ermengol VIII. Innocent III's expansion of the regency the year before to include a council of six nobles with close ties to the royal court likely helped the monarchy come to terms with this rebellious viscount. This was a reconciliation that had even eluded Pere during the final years of his reign. Mansilla 1954, doc. 537. See Bisson 1989b, 354–55, and Domingo 2007, 45–57 and 65–69.
30. Most notably, Guillem Durfort forgave a large portion of the crown's debt to him in his will. See Bisson 1989b, 355 and doc. 2 (12 May 1218).

31. Huici Miranda and Desamparados Cabanes Pecourt 1976–88, vol. 1, doc. 14 (8 September 1218).
32. Mansilla 1954, docs. 538 (to the citizens of Catalonia and Aragon), 539 (to the men of Montpellier), 540 (to Guillem Ramon de Montcada, who was in charge of administrative functions in Catalonia), and 541 (to the archbishop of Tarragona and bishop of Barcelona). See Bisson 1989b, 359–60.
33. Soldevila 1971, c. 11, p. 7. Compare Bisson 1989b, 354. The crown had certainly borrowed from its Jewish officers in the past but probably never to the extent remembered by the king. See chapter 1 above and Bisson 1989b, 354n14.
34. Riera i Sans (2009, 136–40) himself admits that estimating the dates of origin of Catalonian Jewish communities is highly problematic: "No podemos objetar que están condicionados por el azar de la conservación documental." It is highly likely that small Jewish communities long predated the earliest documentary references in charters and the chancery registers.
35. Gonzalvo i Bou 1994, doc. 24, c. 8 (23 June 1218).
36. Ibid., doc. 24, c. 7.
37. Ibid., doc. 24, preamble. Compare, for example, the Corts of 1173 (ibid., doc. 15, preamble), which had extended the peace only to Lleida.
38. Ibid., doc. 24, c. 7: "Item, sub hac pace sint iudei et sarraceni, qui videlicet sub fide et custodia regia in Cathalonia habitant, et omnes res et possessiones eorum."
39. Bisson 1989b, 364–65.
40. Ibid., 370–72. See Soldevila 1968, 166–69, and Mansilla 1954, doc. 404 (15 June 1222).
41. Gonzalvo i Bou 1994, doc. 25, c. 10–11 (28 April 1225).
42. María 1943. The day before the meeting, Jaume had confirmed his father's anticipatory donation of the northern Valencian castles of Mirabet and Zúfera to the see. ACT, Cartulari 8, fols. 28r–30r, and Cartulari 9A, pp. 131–34; ACA, CR, Cartas Reales Diplomáticas, J I, c. 1, no. 86 (27 April 1225) [Huici Miranda and Desamparados Cabanes Pecourt 1976–88, vol. 1, docs. 65 and 66].
43. Jaume's confirmation earlier in his reign that he still owed the Genoese over fourteen thousand pounds for Ramon Berenguer IV's purchase of the republic's share of the town is not proof that the crown still retained those specific holdings. Huici Miranda and Desamparados Cabanes Pecourt 1976–88, vol. 1, doc. 132 (June 1230).
44. Toda 1938, doc. 38 (November 1186). See Aragó Cabañas 1962 and Bisson 1984, 1:68–71.
45. ACA, CR, perg. A I, no. 362 (January 1184) [Sánchez Casabón 1995, doc. 382; Miquel Rosell 1945–47, vol. 1, doc. 467].
46. ACA, AGP, *Cartulari de Tortosa*, fols. 46v–47r, doc. 144 (15 January 1202). See chapter 1 above.
47. ACA, CR, perg. P I, no. 308 (9 December 1208) [Alvira Cabrer 2010, vol. 2, doc. 837].
48. See Pagarolas 1999, 1:189.
49. See Shideler 1983, 11ff. Compare Font Rius 1953, 119, and Virgili 2001b, 187–88. On the norms of the office, see Lalinde Abadía 1967, 174–75, and Lalinde Abadía 1966, 240–44. Bisson 1984, 1:66–68, describes how, throughout the medieval period, the vicariate (with its *curia*) was a saleable office held in fief from the king that could be inherited and alienated like any other fief or money fief.
50. For example, Udina Martorell 1947, doc. 235 (8 September 1180): "meus vicarius." ACA, CR, Reg. 10, fol. 7v

(10 August [1257]) [Pagarolas 1999, vol. 2, doc. 83]: "fidelibus meis." Compare Pagarolas 1999, 1:187.
51. ACA, CR, perg. J I, no. 349 (15 May 1228) [Pagarolas 1999, vol. 2, doc. 32]. Compare Shideler 1983, 200–201. See chapter 3 below.
52. See, for example, Gampel 2012.
53. For example, a delegation from the municipality of Tortosa attended the king's confirmation of the coinage of Jaca in Monzón. ACA, CR, Reg. 22, fol. 105r–v (13 October 1236).
54. See Romano 1991b, 113.
55. See also Bayerri 1933–60, 7:107–9 and 128–38, concerning visits by Alfons and Jaume, respectively.
56. See María 1943, Ubieto Arteta 1975, 1:95, and Ferrer Navarro 1999, 25–27.
57. Miret y Sans 1918, 386. See below. Throughout the later twelfth and thirteenth centuries, Lleida's rate of visitation by the royal court compared favorably with other important towns in the realms. Under Alfons and Pere, it received roughly the same percentage (10–11 percent) of visitations as did Zaragoza and Huesca and more than Barcelona. Under Jaume, 13 percent of royal visits targeted Lleida—roughly the same as Barcelona, Zaragoza, and Valencia, and considerably more than Huesca (at 2 percent). Under Alfons II, however, Lleida fell to 6 percent, while Barcelona climbed to 21 percent. See Bensch 1995, table 1.1 and 42–43.
58. Miret y Sans 1918, 386.
59. ACA, CR, perg. J I, no. 942 (10 March 1244).
60. Miret y Sans 1918, 168.
61. *Cortes de los antiguos reinos 1896–1922*, vol. 1, pt. 1, doc. 17, c. 1–6, pp. 120–21 (21 December 1228). The constitutions in this version (the "Escorial Z" codex) deviate from those of other records, which do not mention the Jews. Compare Gonzalvo i Bou 1994, doc. 26.
62. The Fourth Lateran Council, in keeping with earlier papal pronouncements, had prohibited excessive Jewish usury (i.e., loans that exceeded a 20 percent interest rate). See Chazan 2006, 144–45, and Linehan 1971, 20–34.
63. Gonzalvo i Bou 1994, doc. 26, c. 14. Compare ibid., doc. 15, c. 11 (1173), and doc. 20, c. 11 (1200).
64. Compare ibid., doc. 23, c. 5 (1214), doc. 24, c. 8 (1218), and doc. 25, c. 10 (1225).
65. Freedman 1991, 116–17, 120–21, 172–73.
66. Gonzalvo i Bou 1994, doc. 26, c. 8 (21 December 1228).
67. *Cortes de los antiguos reinos 1896–1922*, vol. 1, pt. 1, doc. 17, c. 1 and 4, pp. 120–21 ("Escorial Z" codex). This regulation was in conformity with canon law. See Simonsohn 1991, 188–95.
68. Villanueva et al. 1803–52, vol. 13, doc. 51 (31 March 1229).
69. Huici Miranda and Desamparados Cabanes Pecourt 1976–88, vol. 1, doc. 143 (30 November 1230).
70. For the *Fueros de Teruel*, see Huici Miranda and Desamparados Cabanes Pecourt 1976–88, vol. 2, doc. 325 ([February] 1241), and Caruana Gómez 1955. For the *Furs de València*, see López Elum 1998, c. 68.
71. Arxiu Històric de la Ciutat de Girona, *Manual d'Acords*, no. 1 (1345–47), fol. 53r (12 April 1232), catalogued in Escribà i Bonastre and Frago i Pérez 1992, no. 11.
72. Bensch 2008, 44: "quod curia nostra distringat." For the 1235 statute, see Gonzalvo i Bou 1994, doc. 28, c. 17 (17 March 1235).
73. See chapter 4.
74. Huici Miranda and Desamparados Cabanes Pecourt 1976–88, vol. 2, docs. 323 and 337 (25 February and

11 November 1241). See Assis 1997b, 15–27, and, generally, Stow 2007b.
75. Huici Miranda and Desamparados Cabanes Pecourt 1976–88, vol. 2, docs. 328 and 331 (23 May and 13 September 1241).
76. Huici Miranda and Desamparados Cabanes Pecourt 1976–88, vol. 2, doc. 369 (12 March 1243).
77. Gonzalvo i Bou 1994, doc. 27, c. 16 and 21 (7 February 1235). Bishop Ponç of Tortosa was present, along with the provincial masters of the Templars and Hospitallers.
78. Ibid., doc. 28, c. 14 (fixing prices) and 16 (17 March 1235). See Benito i Monclús 2011, 72–73.
79. *Cortes de los antiguos reinos* 1896–1922, vol. 1, pt. 1, doc. 20 (26 February 1251).
80. ACA, CR, Reg. 10, fol. 37r (18 February 1258) [Régné 1978, no. 94].
81. Tilander 1956, vol. 2, VIII.14; Tilander 1937, c. 274.
82. Morales Arrizabalaga 2007, esp. 32–48.
83. Pere Albert's activity as a royal judge between the 1230s and 1260s is reflected in the documentation compiled by Ferran i Planas 2006, 318–73 (docs. 1–36).
84. *Commemoració* 39 in Rovira i Ermengol 1933, 186–88. Ferran i Planas 2006, esp. 240–41. See Kagay 2002, xxv–xliv.
85. ACA, CR, Reg. 202, fol. 210r–v (22 April 1229) [Régné 1978, no. 6; Baer 1929, vol. 1, doc. 88]. This particular license does not confirm that the rabbi was appointed by the king at this point. Later instruments reveal that Calatayud's rabbis were under royal influence but not necessarily invested by the king. See, for example, ACA, Reg. 81, fol. 67v (12 March 1290) [Régné 1978, no. 2084].
86. Pérez Martínez 1977, doc. 74 (11 July 1231). ACA, CR, Reg. 941, fols. 176v–177v (6 March 1239), Reg. 16, fol. 158r (9 December 1241), Reg. 10, fol. 54v (31 March 1258) [Baer 1929, vol. 1, docs. 91, 93, 97]. See Klein 2006, 128–29, 147.
87. Pérez Martínez 1977, doc. 74, pp. 84–85. See Maíz Chacón 2010, 28–30.
88. ACA, CR, Reg. 941, fols. 176v–177v.
89. See López Elum 1998, 35–57.
90. Dualde Serrano 1950–67, c. 121 ("De crimine lese maiestatis") and c. 8.3: "Iudei, licet ad alium dominium ecclesiasticum vel secularem confugerint, vel in alterius dominio domicilium fecerint vel morentur, non sint a nostro dominio ideo aliquatenus absoluti quin imperpetuum sint nostri, nisi dominus loci a nobis vel nostris haberet super hiis definitionem vel donationem." This second law was mentioned in the introduction above.
91. Huici Miranda and Desamparados Cabanes Pecourt 1976–88, vol. 4, doc. 1066 (12 October 1258). See Simonsohn 1991, 4–12.
92. For what follows, compare Ray 2004, esp. 321–22.
93. ACA, CR, Reg. 16, fols. 261v–262r (24 April 1271) [Régné 1978, no. 461]. The charter bore the royal seal and its dating was consistent with the king's itinerary, but it does not appear in the chancery registers for 1258. See Miret y Sans 1918, 267–83. Jaume based his ruling on the fact that Mosse failed to appear in court with two additional royal privileges he claimed to possess that would substantiate the one in question.
94. ACA, CR, Reg. 46, fol. 184r (19 April 1284) [Régné 1978, no. 1119]: "qui constitueramus iudicem inter alyamam iudeorum Cesaraugustane."
95. ACA, CR, Reg. 252, fol. 50r (27 October 1294) [Baer 1929, vol. 1, doc. 136].
96. ACA, CR, Reg. 231, fol. 13r–v (12 March 1305) [Baer 1929, vol. 1, doc. 153, no. 5].

97. ACA, CR, Reg. 44, fols. 187v–188r (31 July 1280) [Régné 1978, no. 823]. See chapter 5 below.
98. Klein 2006, 144–46. See Bensch 1995, 317–19, on the *paers* in Barcelona.
99. Soifer Irish 2013b, 543–44, 553–55.
100. ACTE, perg. no. 466, Privilegis III, no. 9 (30 April 1228) [Massip 1984b, doc. 5]. For Pere's earlier opinion, see ACTE, perg. no. 495, Privilegis III, no. 42 (1 January 1199) [Massip 1984b, doc. 4].
101. Gonzalvo i Bou 1994, doc. 26, c. 16.
102. ACTE, perg. no. 466, Privilegis III, no. 9.
103. See Cawsey 2002, 1–22. For a comparison with Castile, see Ruiz 1985 and 2004, 134–49.
104. See chapter 4 below.
105. ACTE, perg. no. 544, Privilegis V, no. 13 (30 April 1228).
106. See Burns 1995.
107. Massip 1996, c. 1.3.1 and 3.6.4. See Carreras y Candi 1928, 21–22. For further details, see chapter 3 below.

Chapter 3

1. We introduced this model of Jewish autonomy, derived from Klein 2006, in the introduction above.
2. ACA, CR, perg. J I, no. 43 (1 June 1215) [Pagarolas 1999, vol. 2, doc. 4, with incorrect date].
3. Pagarolas 1984, doc. 116, and Virgili 2001a, doc. 578 (1 January 1199). Jaume I would later revisit this dispute and verdict, as we witnessed at the end of the previous chapter.
4. ACA, CR, perg. P I, no. 257 (5 April 1207) [Alvira Cabrer 2010, vol. 2, doc. 678]. Compare Catlos 2004, 157. See chapter 1 above.
5. ACA, CR, perg. RB IV, no. 209 ([30] December 1148) [Serrano Daura 2000a, doc. 1].
6. The Montcadas' involvement with Muslim officials could help explain why Guillem Ramon de Montcada and his men carried out a capital sentence against the local alcaydus and were accused of killing the zalmedina (a charge they denied) in the 1150s. Miquel Rosell 1945–47, vol. 1, doc. 465. See below in this chapter for more on the family's subsequent influence over the office of zalmedina.
7. ACA, CR, perg. P I, no. 258 (28 April 1207). The charter bears a number of Arabic subscriptions, including that of the appointee.
8. For example, ACA, AGP, *Cartulari de Tortosa*, fol. 5r, no. 13 (10 March 1285) [Pagarolas 1999, vol. 2, doc. 75].
9. See Salleras and Espinosa 1986 and the epilogue below.
10. See Pagarolas 1984, 115–28, Pagarolas 1999, 1:116–23, and Forey 1973, 90–93.
11. ACA, CR, perg. J I, no. 349 (15 May 1228) [Pagarolas 1999, vol. 2, doc. 32]. See Shideler 1983, 201, 205–6 and Maya 1997, 135–37. Celdrán Gomáriz and Martínez (2005, 291) claim, without evidence, that Pere I licensed the expansion of the call toward the "Bassa del Castell" in the early thirteenth century.
12. See Ray 2006, 146–47, Baer 1961–66, 1:79–81, and León Tello 1989. Compare Soifer 2007, 24–26, 170–71, regarding the practice in Castile-León.
13. For example, ACT, Subtesoreria, c. 3, no. 41 (2 June 1280), in which a Jew transferred property neighboring the "old call" and the bank of the Ebro River ("apud posita callis iudayci veteris ripa flumen").
14. For example, AHN, Clero: Poblet, c. 2082, no. 17 (17 August 1204): "in villa iudeorum."
15. ACA, CR, perg. J I, no. 349.
16. Ibid.
17. ACA, AGP, *Cartulari de Tortosa*, fols. 83–84r, doc. 269; ACTE, perg. no. 195, Comú II, no. 38 (23 December 1149).

18. Numerous contracts obliging tenants to cultivate new lands in Tortosa's vicinity date from the 1220s. For example, ACA, AGP, *Cartulari de Tortosa*, fol. 55r, no. 170, and fol. 4r, no. 9 (2 August 1220 and 6 September 1222) and ACT, Cartulari 6, fol. 96r (27 May 1223).
19. ACA, AGP, *Cartulari de Tortosa*, fols. 4r and 55r, docs. 9 and 170 (6 September 1222 and 2 August 1220); ACA, AGP, Arm. 4 (Tortosa), perg. no. 41 (20 January 1223); ACT, Cartulari 6, fol. 96r (27 May 1223). See Barton 2009, 22–31.
20. For example, ACT, Cartulari 4, fols. 119v–121r (27 September 1219), and Cartulari 2, fols. 135v–137r (1 December 1229). On Jewish wills, see Burns 1996, 22–31.
21. Land sales commonly document the existence of workshops in the area; for example, Virgili 2001a, doc. 657 (11 September 1205). Remolins at this time maintained at least two *fonduk* that would have been accessible to Jewish merchants; see ACT, Cartulari 2, fols. 61v–62r (24 September 1213), and Cartulari 4, fols. 6v–74 (13 April 1225). The *Costums de Tortosa* [(Massip 1996, c. 4.24.2)] indicate that the local market was later held in this area, between the town walls and the Muslim meat market.
22. Acknowledging the see's need for more tithe-paying lands, the king confirmed these limits twice during the preparations for the expedition. ACT, Cartulari 9, fol. 37r–v (27 April 1224), and Cartulari 8, fols. 24v–27v (5 September 1225). See Barton 2009, 22–31. The town would contribute militarily to the future successful conquests of Mallorca and Valencia in the 1230s. See, for example, O'Callaghan 2003, 90–91.
23. Bos et al. 2010, 10–12. To this end, his translation of al-Zahrāwī's *Kitāb at-taṣrīf*, for example, in Bos's view, "represents an attempt to create a new Hebrew medical terminology based on the terminology of the Bible, Mishnah and Talmud, as well as on medieval commentaries and translations." See also Muntner 1957.
24. Shatzmiller 1994, 44–45.
25. Bos et al. 2010, 10. See also Crémieux 1903, 3–4.
26. Shatzmiller 1994, 45.
27. ACA, CR, perg. J I, no. 349.
28. See Klein 2006, chaps. 5 and 6.
29. Celdrán Gomáriz and Martínez 2005, 294. Although the family was Sephardic, Catalonia proper is generally not considered part of Sepharad. See Feliu 2002.
30. See Glick 1992 for more on "social distance."
31. See Ray 2006, chap. 7, and Simonsohn 1991, chap. 3.
32. See Septimus 1979 and Nirenberg 1996, chap. 5.
33. Personal communication, July 2013. See Ray 2013, 16–18, for more on the complex relations between scholars and communal officials.
34. Banyeres was an established rural locality in Tortosa's outskirts that was associated with the Jewish call early on. Virgili 2001a, doc. 679 (1205/1206).
35. ACA, CR, perg. J I, no. 349: "mitere vindemiam per portas Çute et omnia alia que inde mitere volueritis." See García Marsilla 1993, Meyerson 2004a, 110–19, and Roth 2003, 11–14.
36. ACA, CR, perg. J I, no. 349: "Et aperiatis portam a muro Baneres usque ad portam Kastri nostri, ubicumque volueritis versus Remolins, et aperiatis fenestras et balesterias in muris et turribus et besturribus in quocumque locco volueritis, et infra muros predictos domos habeatis et extra muros, et in muros cloachas et vestra necessaria faciatis."
37. See Simonsohn 1991, 122–23.

38. ACA, CR, perg. J I, no. 349: "Promitimus eciam vobis quod hanc cartam a domino rege firmari faciemus."
39. ACTE, perg. no. 544, Privilegis V, no. 13 (30 April 1228).
40. ACA, CR, perg. J I, no. 349.
41. ACTE, perg. no. 544, Privilegis V, no. 13.
42. For example, ACA, CR, perg. J I no. 322 (31 March 1227): "omnem indignationem et iram."
43. ACA, CR, perg. J I, no. 349: "attendentes quantam devocionem et fidelitatem iudei . . . quia qui nostri sunt nostra semper debent proteccione gaudere."
44. Bensch 2008, 44: "Et insuper uos et omnia bona ipsa tanquam nostra propria manuteneamus protegamus atque deffendamus ubique pro uiribus et posse nostro."
45. ACTE, perg. no. 544, Privilegis V, no. 13.
46. ACTE, perg. no. 466, Privilegis III, no. 9.
47. ACTE, perg. no. 507, Privilegis II, no. 47 (8 May 1241) [Massip 1996, doc. 6]. See Barton 2012, 240–44.
48. ACA, CR, Reg. 202, fol. 210r–v (22 April 1229) [Régné 1978, no. 6; Baer 1929, vol. 1, doc. 88].
49. Alvira Cabrer 2010, vol. 1, doc. 269 ([ca. 1201]), and vol. 2, doc. 742 (13 January 1208).
50. In chapter 1, we observed this same king enacting an identical transfer of jurisdiction over a Tortosan Muslim to benefit Poblet later the same year: AHN, Clero: Poblet, c. 2096, no. 10 (9 December 1208) [Alvira Cabrer 2010, vol. 2, doc. 837].
51. See chapter 4 below.
52. Baer 1929, vol. 1, doc. 93 (9 December 1241). See Klein 2006, 128–37.
53. See, for example, Sánchez Real 1951, 340–41.
54. For example, Jaume II renewed Calatayud's privilege verbatim in 1305: ACA, Reg. 202, fol. 210r–v (27 January 1305) [Régné 1978, no. 2836].
55. While some of the goals of these initiatives may have been similar, there is no justification for reading the 1228 charter as establishing the new call. Compare Celdrán Gomáriz and Martínez 2005, 294.
56. ACT, Cartulari 4, fol. 33r–v (15 July 1269). This reference is probably to the original call, which, although positioned to the northwest, sat on lower ground closer to the river.
57. Massip 1996, c. 1.1.3.
58. Curto 1999, 11, surveys thirteenth-century references to the positioning of the new call. Clear usage of this old/new dichotomy is abundant in the fourteenth century, as Curto documents. Such division and nomenclature was unusual but not unique in medieval Catalonia. The town of Agramuntell reportedly also had an old and a new call in the mid-fourteenth century. Carreras y Candi 1928, 15.
59. For example, ACTE, Sèries Històriques, Comú, Manuals Notarials, vol. 62 (1387), fol. 38r: "mur gros vell del call nou." See Curto 1999, 18.
60. Carreras y Candi 1928, 120: "com lo cami veyl et antich per lo qual totes les jens van, es per la *porta del ferre*, passan dauant la porta subirana del cayl" (my emphasis). See his related discussion at 25–26. This trial record makes direct reference to the streets, places, and other infrastructure surveyed by the *Costums* but does not distinguish between the old and new calls. As discussed in chapter 6 below, Carreras y Candi misdated this transcript to the 1270s. See Curto 1991.
61. For an assortment of fourteenth-century references, see Curto 1999, 17–19.

62. See ibid.
63. Curto 1988–89, 30–31.
64. ACA, AGP, Arm. 4 (Tortosa), perg. no. 33 (20 November 1262) [Pagarolas 1999, vol. 2, doc. 97].
65. See Baer 1929, 125, and Assis 1997a, 211.
66. The Jews would not possess their own meat market until they purchased this prerogative from the town in the mid-fourteenth century. Curto 1999, 15–16.
67. ACTE, Paper, Provisions no. 65 (1493–97), fol. 12r. See Curto 1988–89, 30, and Curto 1999, 14.
68. ACTE, perg. no. 205, Comú II no. 48 (4 July 1347): "aljamam convocari congregatique specialiter pro presenti negocio in signagogua callis judayci veteris eiusdem civitatis." See Curto 1999, 14.
69. ACA, AGP, Arm. 4 (Tortosa), perg. no. 33 (20 November 1262) [Pagarolas 1999, vol. 2, doc. 97]. Compare Riera i Sans 2006, 84–85.
70. ACA, CR, Reg. 10, fol. 54v (31 March 1258) [Régné 1978, no. 97; Baer 1929, no. 97].
71. ACA, CR, Reg. 10, fols. 53r and 54v (28 and 31 March 1258) [Régné 1978, nos. 96 and 98].
72. ACA, CR, Reg. 10, fol. 61v (28 April 1258) [Régné 1978, nos. 99 and 100].
73. ACA, CR, Reg. 10, fol. 65r (28 April 1258) [Régné 1978, no. 102]. Jaume authorized the Jew to collect revenues from the bailiwick of Lleida for repayment.
74. ACA, CR, Reg. 10, fol. 62v (1 May 1258) [Régné 1978, no. 101].
75. Bensch 2008, 43–44: "Et confitemur has omnes libertates et consuetudines . . . quas dominus Raymundus bone memorie quondam comes Barchinone et sui successors comites et reges in instrumentis et priuilegiis et consuetudines scriptis et non scriptis in suis usaticis pro iudeis posuerunt constituerunt." See Bensch's further analysis of the charter at 24 and 27–30.
76. ACA, AGP, *Cartulari de Tortosa*, fol. 47, doc. 145. See Shideler 1983, 202, and Pagarolas 1999, 1:166. On Ponç de Menescal's career, see Pagarolas 1984, 122, 124, and 144.
77. See chapter 1 above.
78. ACTE, perg. no. 136, Castellania i Templers II, no. 21 (14 May 1263) [Massip 1984b, doc. 9; Pagarolas 1999, doc. 102]: "La qual cosa es gran destruiment de la senyoria del Temple quan no deu pendre homenatge de nuyl hom de Tortosa ni de sos termes sens voluntat del Temple."
79. See ACA, CR, perg. J I, no. 1657 (4 June 1261) [Pagarolas 1999, vol. 2, doc. 92], which established guidelines for the mediation.
80. ACA, CR, perg. J I, no. 1660 (7 June 1261) [Pagarolas 1999, vol. 2, doc. 93]: "Minva's lo dret del Temple."
81. ACA, AGP, Arm 4 (Tortosa), perg. no. 52 (21 April 1261) [Pagarolas 1999, doc. 91].
82. Gonzalvo i Bou 1994, doc. 25, c. 21. See Benito i Monclús 2003, 421–26.
83. ACA, AGP, Arm. 4 (Tortosa), perg. no. 52.
84. The terminus post quem for the first memorial (ACA, AGP, Arm. 4 (Tortosa), perg. no. 85) is June 1261, as it refers to the mediated case between the lords discussed above. The terminus ante quem is December 1264, when Dalmai de Fonollar, the Templar commander of Tortosa named by the source, left office. See Forey 1973, 442, and Pagarolas 1999, 1:121. The terminus post quem for the second memorial (ACA, AGP, Arm. 4 (Tortosa), perg. no. 81) is March 1263, when Astruc Jacob Xixó, who serves as royal bailiff in the source, received his appointment (see chapter 4

below). It has the same terminus ante quem as the first memorial.
85. ACA, AGP, Arm. 4 (Tortosa), perg. no. 81. As noted earlier, this prerogative had been in force as early as 1207 when Ramon de Montcada's forebear had filled the office without invoking other authorities. ACA, CR, perg. P I, no. 258 (28 April 1207).
86. ACA, AGP, Arm. 4 (Tortosa), perg. no. 81.
87. Ibid.: "Et ipsa misit ad dicendum comendatori per eundem Guardiam quod si comendator aliquid facere de dicto iudeo nunquam in ispanya ita magna vindicta de aliquo fuit accepta quam illa faceret de iudeo."
88. See Meyerson 2004b, 214–16, who describes how elite Jews promoted patronage relationships with the rural aristocracy to the detriment of royal and municipal taxation revenues. This mysterious Margalida seems to have played a similar role in Tortosa. Compare Catlos 2004, 166.
89. ACA, AGP, Arm. 4 (Tortosa), perg. no. 81: "Verum cum cautum sit in usatico Barchinone quod quicum quod percuserit iudeum quod puniatur arbitrio comitis Barchinone. E illud ius et dominium quod abuerit comes in Dertuse abet templum et si hoc posset facere. Raymundus sine voluntate templi perderet templum predictum dominum et abet illud dominium. Raymundus quod de iure templum abet debet."
90. That "usatico Barchinone" is referring to the *Usatges* is supported by the fact that the same source elsewhere refers to the customs practiced by the Jews of Barcelona, the other possibility, as "consuetudinem iudeorum Barchinone." From the later twelfth century, the *Usatges* could be referenced in diverse ways, including variants of "ad usaticum Barchinone" (e.g., ACA, CR, perg. A I, no. 255 [1178]), as illustrated in the evidence collected by Kosto 2001b, 67.
91. Bastardas i Parera 1984, us. 11.
92. Other lords in the area, such as Guillem de Cervera, did hold fiefs according to the *Usatges*. Font Rius 1969–83, 1:i, doc. 227 (22 November 1208): "secundum consuetudinem Barchinone." As we noticed in chapter 1, Pere had applied the *Usatges* when he invested Guillem with Benifassà but made no such reference when he granted him Tortosa and Benifallet.
93. See Bisson 1989e, 467, and Klein 2006, 43.
94. Kosto 2001b. On the influence of the *Usatges* on the thirteenth-century conceptions of royal authority, see Ferran i Planas 2006, 145–54.
95. Gonzalvo i Bou 1994, doc. 29, c. 3 (1251). See Font Rius 1962, 310–18, Montagut Estragués 1993, and Turull i Rubinat and Oleart 2000, 33.
96. For a recent overview of the growing influence of the *ius commune* within the Crown of Aragon, see Kelleher 2010, esp. 19–24. See also chapter 4 below.
97. ACA, AGP, Arm. 4 (Tortosa), perg. no. 81 [Baer 1929, doc. 112, p. 124 (partial)]: "Item cum comendator haberet causas contra aliquos iudeos dixit aliame quod illi qui ad consuetudinem iudeorum Barchinone populati erant secundum quod comes populavit eos si utebantur contra dominacionem illius pravis consuetudinibus quibus utebantur christiani et quod responderet ei secundum quo videbatur eisdem." Representatives for the Order characterized this customary law in a similar way in their contemporaneous case against the universitas. ACA, CR, perg. RB IV, no. 224 [Bofarull y Mascaró et al. 1847–1973, vol. 4, doc. 61, p. 166]. See Barton 2012.

98. ACA, AGP, Arm. 4 (Tortosa), perg. no. 81: "Dictus Guardia mandavit iudeis quod non responderent eidem et hoc mandavit in presencia comendatoris et G. de Sancto Minato fratris A. G. et aliorum."

99. The parchment roll containing the litigation records from the 1260s lists only the Templars [ACA, CR, perg. J I, no. 1796]. Montcada would eventually sign the resolution in which the parties agreed on a process of reviewing and codifying the customary law. See Massip 1984b, 99–101, and Barton 2012, 233.

100. See below for a discussion of these regulations in the *Consuetudines Dertuse civitatis* and *Costums de Tortosa*.

101. ACA, CR, perg. J I, no. 1796: "inhibendo sarracenis et iudeis Dertusensis ut ad ipsum balneum non venirent." The right of all citizens, including Jews and Muslims, to use the baths in Tortosa was eventually included in the *Costums*. Massip 1996, c. 1.1.15: "inclosos jueus i sarraïns (banys de Tortosa)."

102. See O'Connor 2005 and Ray 2005. Envisioning subject ethnoreligious groups as invested with agency to shape their own existence rather than as helpless victims has been a prominent theme in recent historiography, paralleling work within the broader field of subaltern studies. See, for example, O'Hanlon 2000.

103. Massip 1996, c. 1.3.1 (jurisdiction of the vicar over Christians, Jews, and Muslims), 1.1.20 (tax contributions), 3.6.4 (use of the town *curia*). Meyerson 2004b, 257, shows how such a shared tax burden could be stabilizing for Jewish-Christian relations.

104. Massip 1996, c. 1.9.5. Although Jews were in some respects juridically indistinguishable from other residents, there are no indications that they were permitted any direct role in the governance similar to what was possible for Christians. Compare Ray 2006, 90.

105. Massip 1996, c. 1.9.3 (clothing), 9.16.4 (butchery), 9.2.7 (women), 1.10.1 (baptism).

106. See Iglesia Ferreirós 1979 and García i Sanz 1979.

107. Massip 1996, c. 1.1.5: "Són encara los ciutadans e los habitadors de la ciutat e del termen de Tortosa, axí jueus com xrestians, franchs, quitis e deliures d'ost, de cavalgada, d'encalz, de cenes, de questa, de toltes, de forces." Citizen (*ciutadà*) and resident (*habitador*) were not being conflated here or used to assign the Jews a debased citizenship but, in fact, were clearly defined as legal categories for all inhabitants of the town elsewhere in the code. Massip 1996, c. 1.4.14–15. Compare Roth 1995, 151, and Lourie 1990a, 1. On this process of revision, see Font Rius 1985b, 152–59. Daileader 2006, 377–85, is one of the few studies to consider differences in ethnoreligious mandates between the codes.

108. The calculus of Tortosa's universitas reflected the town's micro-convivencia and political realities and thus diverged sharply from what is evident in other cases. Unlike the northern Castilian *concejos* of Sahagún and Palencia studied by Soifer Irish (2013b, 552–65), for example, Tortosa's universitas never openly sought jurisdiction over Jews at the expense of the seigniorial regime or allied with the crown for the restoration of royal governance.

109. Massip 1996, c. 1.1.13: "Encara, seynós ne lur lochtenent, per si ne per altre, no poden acusar civil ni criminal nul hom jueu ni xrestian en Tortosa ne en sos térmens."

110. This issue had been prominent in the litigation of the 1260s, as we noted earlier. Massip 1996, c. 1.1.15: "E tots

los ciutadans e habitadors axí sarrayns, jueus, com crestians, se deuen en aquels baynar." Administration of the baths (and town walls) by the citizens, without mention of their use by Muslims or Jews, had initially been upheld by the *Sentència de Flix* in 1241. Massip 1996, doc. 6.

111. Font Rius 1969–83, 1:i, doc. 75 (30 November 1149). The charter had, on the other hand, been granted without limitation to "all inhabitants of Tortosa." The tribunal did not provide a justification for this deletion. The still definitive ruling delivered by the bishop of Lleida in 1241 may have supported this view, although its terminology is rather ambiguous. The bishop had ordered the lords to confirm to the "men of Tortosa" only the "privileges, customs, and donations" received from the count and by other means. ACTE, perg. no. 507, Privilegis II, no. 47 (8 May 1241) [Massip 1996, doc. 6].

112. Daileader 2000, 115.

113. See ibid., 122–26.

114. Massip 1996, c. 3.6.4: "Jueus de demandes que faça la un contra l'altre, o contra crestià, fan e deuen fer dret en la cort de Tortosa. Levats los pleyts que la seynoria mou contra eyls."

115. For example, Castro and Onís 1916, §399 (Ledesma): "Todos elos iudios feyan en poder del rey e del conceyo."

116. Massip 1996, c. 1.9.1–5, 9.2.7. Iberian Christian laws did condone some types of interreligious mixing. For example, most areas permitted Christian men to have sex with Jewish and Muslim women. See Ray 2006, chap. 7, and Catlos 2004, 305–12.

117. ACTE, perg. no. 430, Privilegis II, no. 19 (12 May 1275) [Massip 1996, doc. 8 (Catalan version)]. See Massip 1996, c. 1.1.14. These stipulations of the *Carta de la Paeria*, as transmitted in the *Costums*, continued to have legal force. For later fourteenth-century case evidence, see chapter 6 below.

118. Massip 1996, c. 3.6.4, 4.11.27–28 (witness testimony), 4.11.38 (Jewish oath). Only the *Costums* (9.30.1) appended the full text of the *sacramentum judeorum* that would subsequently become a source of controversy with the Jewish community. See Carreras y Candi 1928, 39–40. There were no analogous statutes concerning Muslim oath taking in either text.

119. Ray 2006, 178.

Chapter 4

1. See Torró 1999, esp. 68–79.
2. ACA, CR, Reg. 10, fols. 82v–83r (1 July 1258) [Burns 1991, doc. 165].
3. ACA, CR, Reg. 9, fol. 37r (16 September 1257) [Régné 1978, no. 61].
4. Bisson 1986, 68–69, and Guichard 1990–91, 2:421–33.
5. ACA, CR, Reg. 11, fol. 177v (11 June 1260) [Régné 1978, no. 127].
6. ACA, CR, Reg. 17, fols. 20v–22r (27 February 1266).
7. ACA, CR, Reg. 12, fol. 15r (1 March 1263) [Régné 1978, no. 186, and Bofarull 1908, doc. 27, p. 869]: "Astruch Jacob Xixon iudeum Dertuse baiulum nostrum in civitate Dertuse." On Astruc's career, see Baer 1961–66, 1:146, Burns 1975, 285–86, and Carreras y Candi 1928, 44–45, Maya 1997, 139–41, and Romano 1983, 130–33.
8. See Bensch 1995, 323–25.
9. See Burns 1984, 154.
10. ACA, AGP, Arm. 4 (Tortosa), perg. no. 33 (20 November 1262) [Pagarolas 1999, vol. 2, doc. 97]. See chapter 3 above.
11. Astruc thus received the explicit right to give the office to whomever he chose.

ACA, CR, Reg. 12, fol. 15r. Compare this with a more detail-rich description of the office in Morvedre a decade later: ACA, CR, Reg. 19, fol. 66v (31 August 1273) [Burns 1984, 275]. See Ray 2006, 178.

12. ACA, CR, Reg. 14, fol. 25r–v (15 June 1263).
13. ACA, CR, Reg. 12, fol. 15r.
14. ACA, CR, perg. RB IV, no. 209 (30 December 1148) [Serrano Daura 2000a, doc. 1].
15. See Meyerson 2004b, 18. Other work on Tortosa's Jews has tended not to perceive or emphasize the confrontational essence of the office. Compare, for example, Celdrán Gomáriz and Martínez 2005, 293.
16. See ACA, CR, Reg. 12, fol. 119v (30 and 26 September 1263), in which Astruc, as "baiulo nostro Dertuse," was ordered to collect from the "men of the *honor* of Calatrava" and receive payments from the bailiff of the kingdom of Valencia for the coming five years.
17. ACA, CR, Reg. 14, fol. 25r (9,000 solidi) and fol. 25r–v (20,000 solidi) (both 15 June 1263) [Régné 1978, nos. 197 and 198; Bofarull 1908, docs. 31 and 30].
18. ACA, CR, Reg. 12, fol. 119r (30 September 1263) [Régné 1978, no. 222].
19. ACA, CR, Reg. 13, fol. 269v (6 May 1265) [Régné 1978, no. 326]. In 1264, Astruc submitted his accounts from his work as bailiff since receiving the office in 1263. In addition to noting the reception of this submission, the chancery register includes a substantial itemized list of outstanding debts owed to the bailiff. On this occasion, Jaume also assigned Astruc 1,200 solidi in compensation for his office. ACA, CR, Reg. 14, fol. 67r–v (9 November 1264) [Régné 1978, no. 301]. ACA, CR, Reg. 14, fol. 90r (10 June 1267), acknowledges a debt owed to Astruc for commissioning the production of a piece of artillery at Tortosa. The town was a known producer of the lead ore used to make such military hardware. See Burns 2001, 282–83, doc. 729.

20. ACA, CR, Reg. 17, fol. 107v (18 February, 5 March, and 12 March 1267/68) [18 February: Régné 1978, no. 375]. In receiving the castle and town of Penyíscola as a pawn from the king, Astruc had to collect all of the town's revenues as well as maintain the castle guard. ACA, CR, Reg. 14, fol. 25r (14 June 1263).
21. ACA, CR, Reg. 17, fol. 107v (18 February 1267/68). Despite his family's apparent financial interests to the south—for example, Açim Mordofay, "Jew of Tortosa," rented an oven in Penyíscola from the king in 1266—Muschet continued to reside in Tortosa and thus remained identified as a "Jew of Tortosa." ACA, CR, perg. 1840, and Reg. 15, fol. 13v (27 April 1266). On his later career, see Romano 1983, 169–70.
22. ACA, CR, perg. P II, no. 477 (18 May 1285) [Cingolani 2011, doc. 438].
23. Burns 1984, 155.
24. ACA, CR, Reg. 15, fol. 13v (27 April 1266) [Régné 1978, no. 346; Bofarull 1908, doc. 59]: "nulla aljama iudeorum terre vel iurisdictionis domini regis." See Catlos 2004, 215–16.
25. For a relevant discussion of enfranchisement within the context of Muslim aljamas, see Catlos 2004, 136–37.
26. ACA, CR, Reg. 15, fol. 13v. See Burns 1984, 155–56 and 317 n. 14. On the concept and punishment of *malsins*, see Díaz Esteban 1985, 111, Lourie 1990b, 69–72, and Garcia-Oliver 1994, 247–61. For comparative examples, see Garcia-Oliver 2009, 719–22, and Riera i Sans 2000, 103.

27. See the reflections of Klein (2005, esp. 123–29) concerning the communal influence of a contemporaneous bailiff in Zaragoza, Judah de la Cavelleria. We have less information concerning Astruc's (and thus the king's) involvement in internal struggles within the aljama in Tortosa than has been uncovered for this Aragonese case. But, as we shall see below, it would appear that Astruc's standing in the community decreased rather than increased as a result of his activity as bailiff, in contrast to Judah's experience as bailiff. These moves by the king thus did not directly target the autonomous institutions of the aljama (about which we know exceedingly little). The reformulation of the communal structure and leadership of the Barcelona aljama around two decades earlier, in comparison, had been much more intrusive—the product of royal involvement in internal conflict between the established hereditary elites and the "rebels" emerging from traditionally impotent lineages or newcomers seeking greater authority. See Klein 2006, 123–29.
28. See Assis 1997b, 230.
29. The king acknowledged a debt of one thousand solidi to Jafias Avinzabarra, a Jew living in Tortosa, and assigned repayment from rents in Lleida. ACA, CR, Reg. 10, fol. 65 (1 May 1258) [Régné 1978, no. 102]. Several days earlier, he had awarded this same Jafias *guidaticum*. ACA, CR, Reg. 10, fol. 61v (28 April 1258) [Régné 1978, no. 100]. In 1263, he granted *guidaticum* to Alazar Abecimfa, who also appears to have been a resident of, or at least raised in, Tortosa. ACA, CR, Reg. 14, fol. 25r–v (15 June 1263) [Régné 1978, no. 202]. In 1266, Jaume granted another Jew from Tortosa rights to an oven in Penyíscola, which appear to be distinct from those awarded earlier to Astruc Xixó. ACA, CR, Reg. 15, fol. 13v (27 April 1266) [Régné 1978, no. 345].
30. ACA, CR, Reg. 10, fol. 66v (15 May 1258) [Régné 1978, no. 103].
31. ACA, CR, Reg. 15, fol. 13v (27 April 1266) [Régné 1978, no. 345].
32. See, for example, Ray 2004, which describes how the post of crown rabbi often overlapped with the position of tax farmer throughout Iberia.
33. ACA, CR, Reg. 12, fol. 13v (22 February 1263) [Régné 1978, no. 183].
34. ACA, CR, Reg. 14. fol. 11v (22 February 1263) [Régné 1978, no. 184]. This was a general order directed at all officials (including the municipal *paers*) rather than at a particular local operative such as Astruc Xixó.
35. ACA, CR, Reg. 12, fol. 27v (2 May 1263) [Régné 1978, no. 191].
36. ACA, CR, Reg. 13, fol. 157r (27 March 1264) [Régné 1978, no. 250].
37. Cheyette 1970, 290, and Jordan 1998, 3. See also O'Connor 2005.
38. ACA, CR, perg. J I, no. 1083 (28 July 1247) [Huici Miranda and Desamparados Cabanes Pecourt 1976–88, vol. 2, doc. 467].
39. ACA, AGP, Arm. 4 (Tortosa), perg. no. 52 (21 April 1261) [Pagarolas 1999, doc. 91]: "ratione donationis domini regis."
40. ACA, AGP, Arm. 4 (Tortosa), perg. no. 42 (26 April 1263) [Pagarolas 1999, doc. 99]. This was ostensibly a reference to the Montcada family's traditional control of the local vicar's appointment. See chapter 2 above.
41. ACA, CR, Reg. 14, fols. 25r and 25r–v (both 15 June 1263).
42. ACA, AGP, Arm. 4 (Tortosa), perg. no. 81: "Item quan lo senyor R. es en Tortossa pren senes del jueus i dels sarrayns. El davant dit R. de Muncada pren aitant com fa el Rey." These collections by the lords were documented in chapter 3 above.

43. ACA, CR, Reg. 10, fols. 82v–83r (1 July 1258) [Burns 1991, doc. 165].
44. ACA, AGP, Arm. 4 (Tortosa), perg. no. 81: "Item habuit a iudeis racione servicii .CCC. solidos et deberet dare parte[m] suam templo et non fecit. . . . Item habuit .CC. solidos ab eisdem iudeis racione servicii quod fecerit infanti. P. et deberet dare quintam templo et non facit." Ramon Berenguer IV had promised the Order this share of territory it helped capture. ACA, CR, perg. RB IV, n. 159 (27 November 1143) [Sarobe 1998, vol. 1, doc. 9].
45. ACA, AGP, Arm. 4 (Tortosa), perg. no. 81: "Item ha afranquit lo Rey homens de Cataliu e de Terol. E de Peniscola. E de Xativa. E de Malorques. E de Marella. El temple no'a afranquit negun daquests locs."
46. ACA, AGP, Arm. 4 (Tortosa), perg. no. 81. Such as the tribute paid by Jews at Easter: "Item fan los jueus de sens a Pasqua. Al Temple .X. sol. e an R. de Muncada .X. sol. al Rey demana al Temple part dels dits .X. sol. El Temple demana an R. de Muncada part dels .X. sol. que'l pren."
47. ACA, CR, Reg. 18, fol. 63v (1 September 1271) [Régné 1978, no. 482]. The king ordered that Tortosa's aljama send four delegates to Zaragoza within fifteen days to discuss and make arrangements concerning demands the king had made from its group of Jewish communities. Valencia, Xàtiva, and Morvedre, by comparison, were assessed at 4,000, 2,000, and 2,000 solidi, respectively.
48. ACA, CR, Reg. 18, fol. 64r–v; ACA, CR, Reg. 18, fols. 31v–32r (25 April 1272) [Régné 1978, no. 484]. A subsequent undated record notes payments from Lleida, Barcelona, and Valencia and features the ambiguous category "jueus d'Arago e de Catalunya," which could include Tortosa. ACA, CR, Reg. 18, fol. 96r [Régné 1978, no. 485].
49. ACA, CR, Reg. 18, fol. 82r [1272]. This was a much larger tribute demand than the previous year, overall. By comparison, in 1271 the Jews of Barcelona, Girona and Besalú, and Perpignan had paid only 10,625, 7,625, and 2,600 solidi, respectively. ACA, CR, Reg. 18, fol. 64v.
50. ACA, CR, Reg. 18, fol. 63v.
51. ACA, AGP, Arm. 4 (Tortosa), perg. no. 43 (27 August 1271) [Pagarolas 1999, vol. 2, doc. 116].
52. Soldevila 1971, c. 28–33, pp. 18–21.
53. For example, ACA, CR, perg. J I, no. 308 (13 November 1226), and Huici Miranda and Desamparados Cabanes Pecourt 1976–88, vol. 1, doc. 91 (1 April 1227).
54. See, in particular, Bastardas i Parera 1984, us. 68, and Rovira i Ermengol 1933, c. 58. See also Kagay 1988, esp. 66, and Kagay 1999, 57–58, 67–68.
55. See Stein 1999, 52, 72–73.
56. Rovira i Ermengol 1933, c. 10, 11, 12, 25, 40, 43. At c. 43, we read, "No és, emperò, a entendre que per açò aquell senyor haja en aquell seu hom soliu mixt o mer imperi, axí com lo Príncep de la terra, jatsie que haja en ell jurisdictió, e en las suas cosas, axí com dit és." See Ferran i Planas 2006, 238–43.
57. However, Kagay (2002, xxxvi) points out that, like the *Usatges*, the *Commemoracions* "was not a code written to be immediately enacted into law." At xxxvi–xlix, he surveys the genesis and gradual implementation of the *Commemoracions*. Successful juridical unification in these realms did not preclude royal-baronial conflict over jurisdiction, prerogatives, and shared governance. Such opposition was particularly prevalent in Aragon. See González Antón 1975, 1:392–433,

and Kagay 1997. For Valencia, see, for example, Guinot Rodríguez 1995, 43–78, and Guinot Rodríguez 1986, 141–66.
58. Font Rius 1962, 307–11; García i Sanz 1987.
59. Gonzalvo i Bou 1994, doc. 29, c. 3. See chapter 3 above as well as the overview in Vanlandingham 2002, 96–100. These measures did not prevent the *ius commune* from introducing Roman legal material and procedures into customary collections in Catalonia, such as the *Consuetudines Ilerdenses* and the *Costums de Tortosa,* that were evolving away from seigniorial oversight—modifications that were in keeping with the prescriptions of many prominent canonists of the day. Of course, some Roman legal principles were compatible with seigniorial objectives. See Oliver 1876–81, 1:253–304 and 305–38. See generally Font Rius 1962, 297–98, and García 1987, 58–60. Stein (1999, 72–73) notes that certain canonists allowed for the existence of local legal traditions (*ius proprium*) alongside the *ius commune* but advanced the notion that such traditions should be held up against the *ius commune* and encouraged to conform to it as much as possible. On this distinction, see also Bellomo 1989, 153–57. Furthermore, certain later legal projects promoted by the monarchy, such as the *Constitucions de Catalunya,* were obliged to conform to the *ius commune*. See Pons i Guri 1989, 67–70.
60. ACA, CR, Reg. 18, fol. 105r (20 February 1274).
61. For example, ACA, CR, Reg. 14, fol. 127v (7 December 1271) [Régné 1978, no. 496], sent to Barcelona, Cervera, Montblanc, Tarragona, and Villafranca del Penedès.
62. Muschet Mordofay, Astruc's lieutenant, also ceases to be mentioned in regard to northern Valencian cities from 1273. See Doñate Sebastiá and Magdalena Nom de Déu 1990, 171, and Piles Ros 1990, 131–32.
63. ACA, CR, Reg. 20, fol. 247r–v (2 May 1275) [Régné 1978, no. 622].
64. ACA, CR, Reg. 20, fol. 252r–v (6 May 1275) [Régné 1978, no. 623; Burns 1984, appendix 3, doc. 24].
65. ACA, CR, Reg. 40, fol. 18v (16 September 1277) [Régné 1978, no. 688].
66. ACTE, perg. no. 139, Castellania i Templers II, no. 32 (7 December 1280). This was part of a series of transactions—culminating in the purchase of Tortosa in 1294—intended to reestablish direct royal administration over the lower Ebro Valley. ACA, CR, Reg. 49, fol. 93v (13 May 1281). Extant records do not explicitly identify Astruc as bailiff.
67. The justices, bailiffs, and *universitates* of Penyíscola and Morella were ordered to assist Astruc "concerning the business of bailiwicks of Tortosa and Amposta." ACA, CR, Reg. 49, fol. 93v.
68. ACA, CR, Reg. 49, fol. 94r (three documents, all dated 13 May 1281).
69. Compare Klein 2006, 96–115.
70. ACA, CR, Reg. 40, fol. 18v (16 September 1277) [Régné 1978, no. 688].
71. ACA, CR, Reg. 59, fol. 108r (29 September 1282) [Régné 1978, no. 973]: "iudeo habitatori Dertuse."
72. ACA, CR, perg. P II, no. 477 (18 May 1285). He is described as deceased in ACA, CR, Reg. 43, fol. 36v (28 September 1284) [Régné 1978, no. 1212].
73. ACA, CR, Reg. 57, fol. 181r (8 August 1285) [Régné 1978, no. 1422]. The document exempts these heirs, along with residents from Morella, Sant Mateu, Alzira, and Llíria, from the king's tax demand levied on the kingdom of Valencia. It is not clear

from the text that his heirs were necessarily resident in Morella. Compare Burns 1984, 154.
74. Compare Meyerson 2004b, chap. 2.
75. Romano 1983, 154. This may be the same Jew, referred to as Vidal de Bonsenyor, ordered to deliver the privileges of the Jews of Tortosa to the king in 1278. ACA, CR, Reg. 40, fol. 111v (3 June 1278) [Régné 1978, no. 700].
76. ACA, CR, Reg. 20, fols. 272v–273r (21 July 1275) [Régné 1978, no. 637].
77. ACA, CR, Reg. 20, fol. 273r (21 July 1275) [Régné 1978, no. 638].
78. ACA, CR, Reg. 20, fol. 272v (19 July 1275).
79. ACA, CR, Reg. 20, fol. 281r (24 August 1275) [Régné 1978, no. 639]. The remission was directed at the aljama as a whole and concerned violations of the legal rate of interest and oath-taking requirements. The document fails to mention any sums changing hands, but it is likely that the Jewish community paid for this favor.

Chapter 5

1. The collection was performed by Guillem Julià in October 1278, and by Arnau Goeva and Pere de Amsi i Rotlan in August 1280, as noted by Romano 1983, 154.
2. The most comprehensive study on this topic remains Romano 1983, which explores the history and activity of each prominent Jewish bailiff during Pere's reign. Pere's use (while still the Infant) of the credit offered by Jews such as Astruc Xixó further encouraged this continuity of administrative practice. For example, Astruc, identified as royal bailiff, issued a loan of 2,767 solidi to Pere, who assigned repayment from his incomes in Valencia. ACA, CR, Reg. 17, fol. 34v (5 November 1265) [Régné 1978, no. 341]. The *Costums de Tortosa* and *Furs de València* outlawed the appointment of Jews, as well as Muslims and Christians of ill repute, to the office of bailiff. The *Costums* additionally banned Jews from holding the office of vicar. See Massip 1996, c. 9.8, and López Elum 1998, c. CXXXI.3.
3. See Meyerson 2004b, 57–94.
4. ACA, CR, Reg. 60, fol. 3r (18 January 1283) [Régné 1978, no. 1006] See Romano 1983, 134.
5. See Massip 1996, c. 1.3.1–7, which do not mention the role of the *paers*. The peace men were established by the *Carta de la paeria* when Tortosa's customs were under review: ACTE, perg. no. 430, Privilegis II, no. 19 (12 May 1275) [Massip 1996, doc. 8]. On the appearance of the *paers* in other localities in Catalonia, see Daileader 1999, 76–83.
6. ACA, CR, Reg. 39, fol. 169v (27 February 1277) [Régné 1978, no. 679].
7. ACA, CR, Reg. 40, fol. 18v (16 September 1277) [Régné 1978, no. 688].
8. ACA, CR, Reg. 48, fol. 23v (17 May 1280) [Régné 1978, no. 785].
9. ACA, CR, Reg. 60, fol. 3r (18 January 1283) [Régné 1978, no. 1006]. The subvicar was ostensibly also a seigniorial official, since he fell under the command of the vicar. See Bayerri 1933–60, 8:164.
10. ACA, CR, Reg. 44, fol. 226r (17 April 1282) [Régné 1978, no. 906].
11. See chapter 4 above.
12. ACA, CR, Reg. 43, fol. 50r (11 November 1284).
13. Ibid.: "per suas litteras sigillo super sigillatas veritatem super quod exivit ex compositionem de causa que vertebatur inter Astrugum Sexon et Iucefo Coffen Stephano de Cardona."
14. ACA, CR, Reg. 59, fol. 108r (29 September 1282) [Régné 1978, no. 973]. ACA, CR, Reg. 43, fol. 50r: "ad eam quantitatem quam vobis eidem

significabit Stephanus de Cardona cum dictus Astrugus nobis teneatur racione cuiusdam tercii." The six-month reprieve offered to Astruc by Infant Alfons two years earlier was likely related to these outstanding obligations. ACA, CR, Reg. 43, fol. 36v (28 September 1284) [Régné 1978, no. 1212].
15. See chapter 4 above.
16. ACA, CR, Reg. 40, fol. 111v (3 June 1278) [Régné 1978, no. 700]: "Omnia privilegia vestra tam ea que habetis tota aljama tam ea que aliqui ipsius aljame habeant singulariter." Many other aljamas received this same mandate. See Carreras y Candi 1928, 22.
17. ACA, CR, Reg. 49, fol. 94r (13 May 1281) [Régné 1978, no. 865].
18. See Vose 2009, 135–39, and Riera i Sans 1987.
19. ACA, CR, Reg. 42, fols. 148v–149r, 149r–v (both 8 October 1279) [Régné 1978, nos. 747 and 748]. We have no evidence to confirm that the friars acted upon this license during these years. The Dominicans did not maintain a convent in the town. In fact, Tortosa would remain without a convent in spite of its growing prominence as an urban center and venue for prominent missionary events, such as the disputation orchestrated by Vincent Ferrer in the early fifteenth century. See Vose 2009, 76, and Vargas 2011, 104.
20. ACA, Reg. 60, fol. 68v (24 March 1283) [Régné 1978, nos. 1034 and 1035, with the incorrect folio]. It is not known who this bailiff was or whether he was a royal appointee. It remains possible that he had filled the position after the departure of Samuel Robi, discussed earlier. If so, the lack of subsequent notices would seem to indicate a low level of activity, especially when compared with that of Astruc Xixó.

21. See Nirenberg 1996, 200–230.
22. Arxiu Històric de la Ciutat de Girona, *Llibre verd*, fol. 9r (25 January 1284); catalogued in Escribà i Bonastre and Frago i Pérez 1992, no. 38.
23. See Assis 1997a, 212–13.
24. See chapter 3 above.
25. For background, see Carreras y Candi 1905, 70–79.
26. ACA, CR, Reg. 44, fols. 187v–188r (31 July 1280) [Régné 1978, no. 823].
27. For example, the aljama of Zaragoza shortly after the crown issued Catalonia's general license. ACA, CR, Reg. 48, fol. 117r (12 August 1280) [Régné 1978, no. 829].
28. See, for example, ACA, CR, Reg. 44, fol. 187v (24 July 1280) [Régné 1978, no. 819], regarding the sale of food products to Muslims and Christians by the Jews of Aragon, Catalonia, and Valencia.
29. ACA, CR, Reg. 44, fol. 194v (18 December 1280) [Régné 1978, no. 856]. See chapter 3 above.
30. Massip 1996, c. 1.3.1 and 3.6.4.
31. ACA, CR, Reg. 44, fols. 187v–188r.
32. ACA, CR, Reg. 44, fol. 188r (31 July 1280) [Régné 1978, no. 824]. Pere included only a summary of his father's law and not its original date.
33. ACA, CR, Reg. 48, fol. 48r (21 June 1280) [Régné 1978, no. 787]: "Fecimus de hiis unam [cartam]: iudeis Dertuse."
34. ACA, CR, Reg. 44, fol. 188v (both 31 July 1280) [Régné 1978, nos. 826 and 827]. The rate stipulated for the new loan was 3 denarii for each pound (libra) per month. One pound was equivalent to 240 denarii, making this an effective maximum rate of 12.5 percent per annum. As we have seen, the standard annual rate cap maintained by the monarchy had traditionally been 20 percent.
35. ACA, CR, Reg. 44, fol. 188v.

36. For example, ACA, CR, Reg. 23, fols. 3v–9r (1274) [Régné 1978, no. 615].
37. ACA, CR, Reg. 48, fol. 143v (8 September 1280) [Régné 1978, no. 845].
38. Starting with Alfons's earliest peace constitution at Fondarella in 1173, Catalonia had been defined as inclusive of Tortosa. Gonzalvo i Bou 1994, doc. 15, preamble.
39. This ruling was later reversed, however, when Alfons II ordered the Templar commander of Alcañíz to stop trying to force Isach Abencara and two other Jews living in Tortosa to contribute to Alcañíz for properties they owned in its district. ACA, Reg. 81, fol. 176v (3 September 1290) [Régné 1978, no. 2192].
40. ACA, CR, Reg. 59, fol. 147v (3 November 1282) [Régné 1978, no. 982].
41. ACA, CR, Reg. 61, fol. 125r (7 May 1283).
42. This is the explanation offered by Assis 1997a, 173, albeit without the justification added here.
43. ACA, CR, Reg. 44, fol. 146r (25 March 1279). Zaragoza was one of four Aragonese *sobrejunterías* defined in 1279. See Romano 1977, 334–36 and 342–44.
44. ACA, CR, Reg. 17, fol. 20v (27 February 1265): "Tributum Iudeorum Regni Valencie." This association could have been based on the extensive diocesan lands in the kingdom of Valencia administered by the see of Tortosa. For a discussion and map of these limits, see Barton 2009, 8 and 28–31. A royal mandate from 1299 indicates that Tortosa's *collecta*, like its diocese, included some Jewish communities situated within Aragon's boundaries and was expected, at times, to coordinate its tax obligations with other Aragonese Jewish communities that did not pertain to it. ACA, CR, Cartas Reales Diplomáticas, J II, c. 4, no. 578 (28 December 1299) [Escribà i Bonastre and Cinta Mañé 1993, no. 40]: "ad solvendum et contribuendum cum iudeis Aragonie pro mutuis s<uis> et aliquibus locis Aragonum que non sunt de collectia Dertuse." See *Catalunya Romànica* 1984–98, 26:49–50.
45. ACA, CR, Reg. 61, fol. 125r (7 May 1283) [Régné 1978, nos. 1058].
46. ACA, CR, Reg. 61, fol. 125r (7 May 1283) [Régné 1978, nos. 1059 and 1060].
47. ACA, CR, Reg. 46, fol. 173v (18 March 1284) [Régné 1978, no. 1115]. Similarly ambiguous circumstances were impeding the activity of Lleida's vicariate during these years. For example, Pere limited the vicar of Lleida's jurisdiction to the eastern bank of the Cinca River in 1281, establishing Fraga as Aragonese and thus under the governance of the Aragonese *sobrejuntero*. Claims that Fraga was a Catalonian city nevertheless continued to surface through the fifteenth century. See Masiá de Ros 1949 and Salarrullana de Dios 1989b.
48. ACA, CR, Reg. 46, fol. 216r (27 June 1284) [Régné 1978, no. 1163].
49. ACA, CR, Reg. 61, fol. 162v (15 June 1283) [Régné 1978, no. 1075].
50. Soifer Irish 2013b, 553–54.
51. ACA, CR, Reg. 48, fol. 80v (15 July 1280) [Régné 1978, no. 809].
52. ACA, CR, Reg. 62, fol. 104r (8 December 1284) [Régné 1978, no. 1241].
53. See Soldevila 1962, 356–76.
54. *Cortes de los antiguos reinos* 1896–1922, vol. 1, doc. 22, c. 18 (annual requirement), 3, 5–7, 23, 30 (levies), 32 (royal officials). For context, see Vanlandingham 2002, 99–100.
55. Many provisions did rely on the *Usatges*, however: for example, *Cortes de los antiguos reinos* 1896–1922, vol. 1, doc. 22, c. 16, 26, 33, 35, and 40.

56. See Ferran i Planas 2006, 222–31.
57. *Cortes de los antiguos reinos 1896–1922*, vol. I, doc. 22, c. 17. See Freedman 1991, 119–21.
58. *Cortes de los antiguos reinos 1896–1922*, vol. I, doc. 22, c. 2–3.
59. Ibid., vol. I, doc. 22, c. 42. See Riera i Sans 2006, 30.
60. ACA, CR, Reg. 46, fols. 221v–222r (6 July 1284) [Régné 1978, no. 1172].
61. Bastardas i Parera 1984, us. 68; Rovira i Ermengol 1933, c. 58. See Kagay 1999. The general applicability of the *Princeps namque* is further indicated by its transformation into a redemption tax in the fourteenth century. Sánchez Martínez 2005.
62. For example, Bastardas i Parera 1984, us. 64. We also discussed the *Usatges'* rendering of princely sovereignty earlier, in chapter 4.
63. ACA, CR, Reg. 57, fols. 226v–227r (18 October 1285) [Régné 1978, no. 1455].
64. ACA, CR, Reg. 68, fol. 55v (25 October 1287) [Régné 1978, no. 1797].
65. ACA, CR, Reg. 74, fol. 62r (28 January 1288) [Régné 1978, no. 1859].
66. ACTE, perg. no. 138, Castellania i Templers II, no. 31 (15 September 1294) [Pagarolas 1999, vol. 2, doc. 172]; ACTE, paper nos. 1933 and 292, Privilegis, III, nos. 23 and 27 (21 September 1294).
67. ACT, Templers, no. 11 (16 September 1294).
68. ACTE, perg. no. 474, Privilegis III, no. 17; ACA, CR, Reg. 194, fols. 79r–82r; ADM, Montcada, L. 16, no. 21; ADM, Montcada, L. 10, no. 21 (7 October 1294).
69. See Pagarolas 1999, 1:243–45. Oliver (1876–81, II:65) once contended that Tortosa "constituted one of the most rich and powerful aljamas of the Crown of Aragon" in the thirteenth century.
70. ACA, CR, Reg. 194, fol. 95r–v (17 October 1294) [Régné 1978, no. 2546]. The king was doing the same for the Christians in the community, presumably also in hopes of stimulating the local economy. He confirmed previous royal privileges [ACTE, perg. no. 551, Privilegis V, no. 67 (5 January 1295)], licensed a new market [ACTE, perg. no. 275, Consolat i Fira, nos. 4 and 36 (29 January 1295)], expanded the privileges held by the fishermen based in the town [ACTE, perg. no. 528, Privilegis IV, no. 24 (25 February 1295)], and offered merchants valuable trading exemptions within the kingdom of Sicily [ACTE, perg. no. 528, Privilegis IV, no. 24 (25 February 1295)]. See Pagarolas 1999, 1:244.
71. ACA, CR, perg. J II, no. 720 (5 November 1296).
72. See ACA, CR, Cartas Reales Diplomáticas, J II, c. 4, no. 578 (28 December 1299) [Escribà i Bonastre and Cinta Mañé 1993, no. 40], mandating that all Jews whose primary residences were in Tortosa render to the crown "omnibus exaccionibus," including the *monedatge*.
73. See, for example, ACA, CR, Reg. 194, fol. 249r–v (29 August 1296) [Régné 1978, no. 2618], which enfranchised Jucef Chofe from all royal levies except for the *monedatge* for a period of five years.
74. See ACA, CR, Reg. 231, fol. 104r (before 30 October 1307), in which Jaume II defined the limits of the office of the *supravicarium* of Tortosa. See Serrano Daura 1997, 66–67.
75. See González Antón 1993. González Hurtebise 1920 and Udina Martorell 1986 survey the changes to the organization of the chancery archives overseen by Jaume II.
76. See Abulafia 2004.
77. ACA, CR, Reg. 257, fol. 44v (19 March 1300). Riera i Sans 2006, 30–31, directed me to these examples.

78. ACA, CR, Reg. 136, fol. 228r (24 September 1305). See Secall i Güell 1983, 79–101.

Chapter 6

1. Bisson 2009, 580; see his argument for the exceptionalism of Catalonia at 578.
2. Bisson 1996, 144.
3. ACA, CR, perg. J I, no. 326 (21 May 1227) [Bofarull 1908, doc. 2]. Bisson 1989b, 357. Compare ibid, 359: "certain territories and domains were effectively beyond [royal administrators'] control."
4. Canellas López 1961, docs. 26 (6 September 1210) and 29 (31 May 1211).
5. AHN, OM, c. 583, no. 6 (9 September 1208) [Alvira Cabrer 2010, vol. 2, doc. 805]. He issued the privilege in accordance with the wishes of his deceased mother.
6. Klein 2006, 24.
7. Bensch 2008, 42.
8. ACA, AGP, *Cartulari de Tortosa*, fol. 83, doc. 269 (23 December 1149) [Serrano Daura 2000a, appendix: doc. 3]; ACA, CR, perg. RB IV, no. 209 ([30] December 1148) [Serrano Daura 2000a, appendix: doc. 1].
9. Massip 1996, c. 1.3.1 and 3.6.4.
10. AML, Reg. 1372, *Llibre vert petit*, fols. 112r–114r (19 September 1202) [Alvira Cabrer 2010, vol. 1, doc. 348].
11. Alvira Cabrer 2010, vol. 1, doc. 347 (3 September 1202).
12. For more on this case and on the position in general, see Ray 2004, 311–30.
13. ACA, CR, Reg. 16, fol. 202r (28 July 1270) [Régné 1978, no. 446].
14. ACA, CR, Reg. 44, fols. 187v–188r (31 July 1280) [Régné 1978, no. 823].
15. ACA, CR, Reg. 186, fol. 130r–v (26 June 1325), Reg. 903, fols. 203v–205r (1 December 1359), Reg. 721, fol. 142r–v (26 January 1365) [Mutgé i Vives 1992, docs. 77, 152, 159]. See Mutgé i Vives 1992, 101–4 and 159, and Boswell 1978, 140–41.
16. ACTE, Perelló, perg. no. 1 (24 May 1298) [now lost but catalogued in Massip 1995, 1:427]; ACTE, perg. no. 435, Privilegis II, no. 27 (29 January 1295).
17. ACTE, perg. no. 320, Host i Cavalcada II, no. 10 (27 December 1295). The royal bailiff was again pressing the townspeople for compliance by 1298. ACTE, perg. no. 327, Host i Cavalcada II, no. 90 (7 September 1298). For later disputes, see, for example, ACTE, paper nos. 1120 (1378), 1078 (5 December 1431), 1135 (11 November 1521).
18. In August, the king had intervened to restore order and prosecute some of the attackers, initiating a lengthy local inquest conducted by his bailiff, the vicar, and municipal officials. ACTE, paper no. 720, Comú III, no. 197, fols. 2r–4r (26 August 1391). Writing in response to reports that part of the town was still seeking to eliminate the Jewish community, Joan had appealed to the bailiff, vicar, and town procurators to protect the Jews. ACTE, paper no. 441, Comú III, no. 107 (22 October 1391).
19. Using his bailiff and the town's *prohoms*, Joan had offered extensions for the repayment of debts, reduced taxes on meat and wine, and renewed the aljama's license to sell wine. ACTE, paper no. 439, Comú III, no. 105 (20 June 1392); ACTE, paper no. 440, Comú III, no. 106 (2 August 1392).
20. ACTE, paper no. 108, Batlía III, no. 52, fols. 1v–3r (30 October 1394).
21. ACTE, paper no. 108, Batlía III, no. 52, fols. 6v–8v. According to the *Costums de Tortosa* [Massip 1996, c. 1.1.14], "D'aquest ordenament e d'aquesta costuma, sien exceptats jueus e sarayns, los quals sien emenats si hom los ociu, segons que és estat acostumat tro al dia d'uy en Tortosa." This provision is

discussed in Oliver 1876–81, 1:130–31, and Baer 1913, 71.
22. Bastardas i Parera 1984, us. II. See chapter 1 above.
23. ACTE, paper no. 108, Batllía III, no. 52, fols. 9v–12v.
24. Massip 1996, c. 3.6.4.
25. The legislation banned the *ius commune* as well as Visigothic law, as we saw in chapters 3 and 4 above.
26. See, for example, Ray 2006, 178, and Soifer 2007, 41 and 117–18.
27. Ray 2006, 82.
28. ACTE, perg. no. 233, Comú III, no. 19 (13 February 1297) [Pastor y Lluis 1917]: "Açach Avinancara, en Sento Ayincanes e en Maymo Bonsenyor, adelantats de la dita aljama"; "segons que es usat a la sinagoga dels dits juheus a reebre daquels qual que sagrament fer deguessen per lurs pleyts si aquels dits pleyts menassen els contra alguu o alguns o ffosen menats contra els com no sia cosa convinen." Other implications of this agreement are discussed at length below.
29. ACA, CR, Cartas Reales Diplomáticas, J II, c. 41, no. 5052 (7 October 1314) [Escribà i Bonastre and Cinta Mañé 1993, no. 172]. As Meyerson (2004a, 78) has noted, such inter-aljama disputes over a family's tax liabilities were "timed in accordance with the Crown's frequent though irregular fiscal demands." In later centuries, "the particular economic and political strategies of Jewish families determined the timing of conflict between aljamas." Tighter regulation of Jewish migration by the crown increasingly precluded such infighting. Jewish families were required to receive royal licenses to relocate from one *collecta* to another, and these were conditional on their having first satisfied all of their obligations to their original aljama. See, for example, ACA, CR, Cartas Reales Diplomáticas, J II, c. 61, no. 7483 (26 August 1323) [Escribà i Bonastre and Cinta Mañé 1993, no. 276], containing royal authorization of the relocation of a Jewish family from Montblanc to the *collectas* of either Barcelona or Lleida, pending confirmation by the aljama's secretaries that the family had paid the taxes it owed.
30. ACA, CR, Cartas Reales Diplomáticas, J II, c. 61, no. 7558 (9 October 1323) [Escribà i Bonastre and Cinta Mañé 1993, no. 287]. As an example of these other sorts of privileges, Jaume II allowed Tortosa's vicar to violate lending regulations by permitting two Jews to extend the terms of loans (up to six pounds) to various Christians by two years beyond the usual limit of six years. ACA, CR, Cartas Reales Diplomáticas, J II, c. 133, no. 8 (5 December 1321) [Escribà i Bonastre and Cinta Mañé 1993, no. 235]. For a similar incident, see ACA, CR, Cartas Reales Diplomáticas, J II, c. 134, no. 161 (15 May 1326) [Escribà i Bonastre and Cinta Mañé 1993, no. 375].
31. ACA, CR, Cartas Reales Diplomáticas, J II, c. 138, no. 188 (1326) [Escribà i Bonastre and Cinta Mañé 1993, no. 397]: "Quia dicti iudei sunt valde oppressi pluribus subsidiis serviciis et aliis exaccionibus que nobis et inclito infanti alfonso karissimo primogenito et generali procuratori nosto comiti Urgellensi sepe [lacuna]."
32. ACA, CR, Cartas Reales Diplomáticas, J II, c. 4, no. 578 (28 December 1299) [Escribà i Bonastre and Cinta Mañé 1993, no. 40].
33. ACA, CR, Cartas Reales Diplomáticas, J II, c. 7, no. 999 (19 April 1300) [Escribà i Bonastre and Cinta Mañé 1993, no. 53]: "de quo si verum est quam plurimum admiramur, cum hoc ad nos et non ad vos pertinere noscatur." See Assis 1997b, 55.

34. ACA, CR, perg. J II, no. 720 (5 November 1296).
35. ACA, CR, Cartas Reales Diplomáticas, J II, c. 133, no. 4 (18 August 1321) [Escribà i Bonastre and Cinta Mañé 1993, no. 230]. See Catlos 2004, 206–9.
36. See Catlos 2004, 176 and 376.
37. ACA, CR, Cartas Reales Diplomáticas, J II, c. 13, no. 1711 (23 June 1301) [Escribà i Bonastre and Cinta Mañé 1993, no. 79]; ACA, CR, Reg. 200, fol. 196r (9 April 1303) [Régné 1978, no. 2812].
38. ACA, CR, Cartas Reales Diplomáticas, J II, c. 40, no. 5015 (7 October 1314) [Escribà i Bonastre and Cinta Mañé 1993, no. 171].
39. See Daileader 2000, 53.
40. ACA, CR, Cartas Reales Diplomáticas, J II, c. 133, no. 92 (7 October 1314) [Escribà i Bonastre and Cinta Mañé 1993, no. 314].
41. Massip 1996, c. 4.II.38. Oaths elsewhere in European society also varied in accordance with the amounts under dispute. See Kisch 1979, 87, and Kisch 1978, 147–48.
42. Massip 1996, c. 4.II.38.
43. Ziegler 1992, 213. See, generally, Chazan 2006, 213–16.
44. Huici Miranda and Desamparados Cabanes Pecourt 1976–88, vol. 2, doc. 324 (26 February 1241). *Cortes de los antiguos reinos* 1896–1922, vol. 1, pt. 1, doc. 20, p. 136.
45. Tilander 1956, vol. 2, c. II.24, III.31, IX.60. This oath included all of the curses contained in Deuteronomy 28:15ff. See Ziegler 2003, 485. Aspects of this formulation were transmitted to the *Fueros de Aragón*. Tilander 1937, c. II.138–39.
46. ACA, CR, Reg. 43, fol. 24r (5 August 1284) [Régné 1978, no. 1185].
47. ACTE, perg. no. 233, Comú III, no. 19.
48. ACTE, paper no. 67, Batllía III, no. 8, fols. 27v–29v (copy dated 15 March 1302).
49. ACTE, paper no. 67, Batllía III, no. 8, fols. 25v–26v (copies of documents dated 27 February 1314 and 9 July 1317). The Jews' complaint prompting the 1317 ruling has not surfaced, making it impossible to identify how they sought to change the policy.
50. ACTE, paper no. 67, Batllía III, no. 8, fols. 30r–31v (copy dated 26 May 1318).
51. ACTE, paper no. 67, Batllía III, no. 8, fols. 50r–51r (29 January 1320).
52. ACTE, paper no. 67, Batllía III, no. 8, fols. 20v–21r and 40v–41r. This idea that the oath should conform with the general Catalonian use surfaced early in the trial (in late August 1326): ACTE, paper no. 394, Comú II, no. 73, fol. 27r: "per delantatos aliame predicte super maledictionibus iuxta formam constitucionum celebrium catalonie." ACTE possesses later recensions of the *Constitucions de Catalunya* that contain a version of this formula. See Massip 1984a, 126.
53. ACTE, paper no. 67, Batllía III, no. 8, fol. 41r: "Prout in dictam constitucionem continentur et ipsum iuramentum tenentur facere publice videlicet in locis ubi Christiani consueverunt in causis iuramentum prestare ne condicio dictorum Christianorum sit peior dictorum iudeorum."
54. ACTE, paper no. 67, Batllía III, no. 8, fol. 41v: "Illustrissimi domini Regis cum per constitucionem provideatur quod dominus Rex in generali vel speciali non possit concedere aliquod privilegium vel cartam que sit contra formam predicte constitucionis."
55. ACTE, paper no. 67, Batllía III, no. 8, fols. 48v, 55v–56r.
56. ACTE, paper no. 67, Batllía III, no. 8, fols. 48r–49v, at 48v–49r: "Item quod secundum constituciones catalonie si dominus Rex concedat alicui litteram vel privilegium contra . . . formam

dictorum constitucionum . . . quod talis littera vel privilegium non valet."
57. ACTE, paper no. 67, Batllía III, no. 8, fol. 57r.
58. ACTE, paper no. 67, Batllía III, no. 8, fols. 63v–64r: "Ideo antequam dicti adenantati faciant dictum iuramentum debet determinari qualiter dictum iuramentum facere teneantur. Et cum pars dicte universitate ad dominum Regem apellaverit a dicta pronunciatione. Et dicta apellatio sit frivola et inanis tam ob reverentiam excellentissime Regie magestatis deferunt dicte apellationi concedendo dictis sindicis apellatos affirmativos." The performance of the oath of maledictions "written in the customs of Tortosa" by three adelantats appears in the transcript at fol. 65r.
59. ACTE, paper no. 67, Batllía III, no. 8, fol. 65r.
60. Such seasonal flooding is characteristic of a number of communities bordering the Ebro River and continues to afflict Tortosa today, most recently in 2011. The damage is described in detail in ACA, CR, Cartas Reales Diplomáticas, J II, c. 133, no. 386 (16 October [1325]) [Escribà i Bonastre and Cinta Mañé 1993, no. 529].
61. Vidal Franquet 2008, 135–45.
62. ACA, CR, Cartas Reales Diplomáticas, J II, c. 133, no. 386.
63. Carreras y Candi (1928) misdated to the 1270s the now lost partial case transcript he published as doc. 1 of his source appendix. The mention of officials (such as the lieutenant bailiff Pere de Mas) who also appear in the two extant records at the ACTE that carry dates from the 1320s helps confirm that this record summarizes part of this ongoing litigation. The three records appear to sequentially document phases of the litigation between 1325 and 1327. ACTE, paper no. 394, Comú II, no. 73, contains the beginnings of the case and covers late June through late October 1325. ACTE, paper no. 67, Batllía III, no. 8, picks up in November 1325 and continues through early May 1327. Carreras y Candi's case transcript appears to derive from some of the folios that have been lost from the end of this latter manuscript and, accordingly, represents the latest extant transcript, spanning from early May until mid-June 1327. Not only do the same procurator of the Muslim aljama, Avinill Aqyati, and other named officials appear in both transcripts, but Carreras y Candi's text follows precisely, in terms of its dating and content, from where the second ACTE transcript breaks off.
64. ACTE, paper no. 394, Comú II, no. 73, fols. 6v–7r.
65. ACTE, paper no. 394, Comú II, no. 73, fols. 27v–29v (no. 1): "Quod locus ille de cuius reparacione conditur et contenditur fuit dirutius et destructus culpa et opera aliame iudeorum Dertuse." Nos. 2 and 3 stipulate that these *opera* were the fish market and cement works. Nos. 6 and 10–12 make the case that because the main gate (to the old call) was positioned before the plaça, the Jews used the area more than members of the universitas (or Muslim community).
66. ACTE, paper no. 394, Comú II, no. 73, fols. 27v–28r (nos. 4 and 5).
67. ACTE, paper no. 394, Comú II, no. 73, fol. 28v (no. 10): "Quod locus ille qui reparatione indiget sit platea quod illustrissimus dominus Rex haberet partem suam ponere. In reparationem dicti loci cum omnes platee civitate Dertuse sint dicti illustrissimi domini Regis et dicte universitatis Dertuse."
68. Carreras y Candi 1928, doc. 1: "Quels anants et vinens puxen passar aquen

sens reguart et perill de si et de lurs bens."
69. Ibid.: "Nec dicti iudei debent esse melioris condicionis quam cristiani; cum quilibet cristianus de Civitate compelleretur ad reparacionem vie, in quantum fronteria sui ospicii se extendent, si contigeret ipsam vie reparacione indigeret. Et sic factum fuit pluries in Civitatem in simili casu."
70. ACTE, paper no. 394, Comú II, no. 73, fols. 2v–3r. The Muslims' response, voiced by the lieutenant bailiff, appears at fol. 5v. The Jews made a similar argument much later in the case proceedings. Carreras y Candi 1928, doc. 1: "Et comunament en aquell loch ha aytants Sarrayns com altres jens, et fan allen maior passatge que altres jens."
71. ACTE, paper no. 394, Comú II, no. 73, fols. 3v–4r: "Sint alodia francha et libera dicti domini regis . . . compellere non potestis salvo vestro honore cum maximum periculum expectet ad vos si dictam conhercionem seu compulsionem faceretis postquam."
72. ACA, CR, Reg. 182, fol. 182r (18 June 1324).
73. ACA, CR, Cartas Reales Diplomáticas, J II, c. 133, no. 124 (11 October 1325): "Et mandamus quot omnes illos tam Christianos quam iudeos et sarracenos quos inveneritis utilitatem assequi ex opere antedicto compellatis fortiter ad contribuendum in expensis propterea faciendis." ACTE, paper no. 394, Comú II, no. 73, fols. 33v–34v (5 October 1325). The king already must have issued a letter over a month earlier, since the trial transcripts from 29 August 1325 state that the king had mandated that the three communities split the repair expenses. ACTE, paper no. 394, Comú II, no. 73, fols. 22v–23r.
74. ACTE, paper no. 394, Comú II, no. 73, fol. 19r (presented in court on 20 August 1325). On the same day, the bailiff sent the king a letter in which he tried to shirk responsibility for the delay. Under mounting pressure, the bailiff threatened the universitas with the cost of the repairs if it did not expedite its counterclaims (f. 20r–21/22r).
75. ACTE, paper no. 394, Comú II, no. 73, fol. 34v. The last presentation of this royal mandate in court in the extant proceedings occurred on 25 November 1325: ACTE, paper no. 67, Batllía III, no. 8, fols. 5v–6r.
76. Carreras y Candi 1928, doc. 1.
77. ACTE, paper no. 394, Comú II, no. 73, loose, unnumbered folio: "L'aljama aia mostratz en la major partida totz sos dretz e alleuacions en los ditz dos processes e seria dificil e de gran messio a la dita aljama noveylament de mostrar sos dretz. En per aço supliquen los ditz jueus a vos honrat seynor pare bisbe damunt dit quels ditz dos processes vos fassatz venir davant e ab aquells segons dret e costum e el poder a vos senyor donat se degua determenar la dita questio rerense en pero la dita aljama que si volra altres documens donar e ensenyar de son dret que pusca fer en son loc e en son temps." This same bishop, Berenguer de Prats, would perform other services for local Jews. In 1325, for instance, he drafted a letter to the royal scribe, Bernat d'Averçó, on behalf of Vidal Bonsenyor, seeking to expedite some unspecified matters that the Jew was hoping to have addressed at royal court. Two years later, this same bishop sent Bernat a second letter in an effort to secure authorization for Vidal to transfer his household from Tortosa to Barcelona. ACA, CR, Cartas Reales

Diplomáticas, J II, c. 133, no. 127, and c. 134, no. 143 (11 November 1325 and 27 February 1327) [Escribà i Bonastre and Cinta Mañé 1993, nos. 349 and 356]. The bishop does not stipulate Vidal's reasons for leaving, but the Jew may have wanted to escape the collective obligations of Tortosa's impoverished community, which would have fallen unduly on the shoulders of his comparatively well-endowed family. Now that Tortosa was under royal control, the crown naturally would have been reluctant to permit wealthy Jews to flee the town for a less troubled aljama, even families like the Bonsenyors with a track record of royal service. We discussed some of the tasks performed for the crown by two of Vidal's likely ancestors in chapter 4 above.

78. The dysfunction in the handling of disputes involving local ethnoreligious communities by the municipal court and its officials was not limited to the Jewish aljama. As the case over the riverbank repairs ensued, the bailiff and aljama of the Muslims were locked in a dispute with the vicar and *paers* that eventually necessitated intervention by the crown. ACA, CR, Reg. 184, fol. 15v (23 August 1324).

Epilogue

1. Soifer Irish (2013b, 537–42) provides a useful overview of ecclesiastical lordship over Jews throughout western Europe.
2. See Simonsohn 1991, 103–4.
3. Hyacinthe Albanés et al. 1899, col. 81–83, no. 164 (17 April 1164).
4. This source is catalogued in Hyacinthe Albanés et al. 1899, col. 73, no. 154 (26 December 1153), and published in Simonsohn 1988, doc. 47. Ibid., docs. 363 and 364 (both 24 January 1344).
5. Chazan 1980, 63–66 (6 April 1157). See Bönnen 2004 for context and further details about the case.
6. Simonsohn 1988, doc. 104 (21 August 1220).
7. Ibid., doc. 131 (17 September 1232). See Aronius 1902, no. 498, p. 217 (20 September 1236).
8. Simonsohn 1988, docs. 131 and 153 (17 August 1236).
9. Ibid., doc. 254 (17 September 1285). See Simonsohn 1991, 106.
10. For example, the pope awarded protection to Jaume I's Jewish physician, Azac Benveniste, at the king's personal request. Simonsohn 1988, docs. 105 (26 August 1220), 106 (27 August 1220), and 107 (3 September 1220). See doc. 98 (7 November 1217) for a bull of general protection.
11. Soifer Irish 2013b, 563–64.
12. Simonsohn 1991, 106–7, describes these episodes.
13. See Linehan 1971, chaps. 1–3.
14. Simonsohn 1988, doc. 108 (3 September 1220).
15. See Vose 2009, 165–91 and 250–56, for a reinterpretation of Dominican activity in the Crown of Aragon.
16. Simonsohn 1991, 103–4. See Jordan 1986.
17. For a fresh overview, see Ray 2006, 45–52. See also Barton 2010, 260–70. Tortosa continued to face opposition from lords, as its bishop complained in a synod in 1359. Villanueva et al. 1803–52, 5:352–53. That episode is discussed in Boswell 1978, 200–201.
18. ACA, CR, Reg. 1101, fols. 121v–122r (29 May 1381): "Tornen in gran dampnatge de nostres aliames e dels singulars daquelles les quals son propri e singular patrimoni nostre per nostres drets e regalies e son sotmeses a juhi e fur nostre." See Ferragud Domingo 2005, 236, for other similar examples.

19. ACA, CR, Reg. 1101, fols. 169v–170r (8 August 1381).
20. See Riera i Sans 2006, 31–45.
21. Freedman 1983, 71–75, recounts the early history of the shared lordship.
22. Carreras y Candi 1928, 15.
23. For more on these conflicts, see Shideler 1981 and Gudiol y Cunill 1913.
24. This behavior might not be surprising, given this particular seigniorial regime's hostility toward the organization of a communal confederation from the later twelfth century. See Freedman 1979 and 2000.
25. Corbella i Llobet 1984, 94. See also Llop Jordana 2006.
26. Corbella i Llobet 1984, 55.
27. Ibid., 56, 58–78.
28. See Serra Vilaró 1962–68, vol. 1, and Rodríguez-Bernal 2010.
29. Riu y Cabanas 1892, 21.
30. Ibid., 22.
31. Ibid., 22–23.
32. ACA, CR, Reg. 48, fol. 67r–v (2 July 1280) [Régné 1978, no. 803].
33. ACA, CR, Reg. 50, fol. 190r (18 October 1281) [Régné 1978, no. 879].
34. These interactions are documented in local notarial records known as the *Libri Iudeorum*, held at Manresa. Selected documents involving Vidal Astruc in these functions have been published in Támaro 1894, 155–58.
35. ACA, CR, Reg. 476, fols. 136r–140v (15 July 1328) [Salarrullana de Dios 1989a, 21–29]. Only Alfons III's confirmation, which does not conserve the date of the original charter, survives. Guillem de Montcada does refer to an earlier, apparently lost privilege by his father: ACA, CR, Reg. 476, fol. 138v. The terminus post quem must be 1322, since the privilege contains provisions concerning the transport and sale of kosher wine conferred in a confirmation by Jaume II in that year: ACA, CR, Reg. 222, fols. 87v–89v (30 September 1322), discussed further below. The terminus ante quem is Alfons III's assumption of lordship in 1328. The charter also detailed certain obligations and restrictions for which the Jews were responsible. Religious noise by Jews and Muslims had grown as a major concern for Christian authorities. The findings of Constable 2010 regarding the role played by the Council of Vienne in the development of Christian sentiments toward Muslim religious noise are largely applicable to such Jewish cases as well.
36. See ACA, CR, perg. J I, no. 903 (15 February 1242) [Huici Miranda and Desamparados Cabanes Pecourt 1976–88, vol. 2, doc. 348].
37. ACA, CR, Reg. 476, fol. 136v [Salarrullana de Dios 1989b, 158–59].
38. ACA, CR, perg. J I, no. 1423 (26 September 1255). See Zurita 1967–77, vol. 1, III.52, p. 584. For what follows, see Lapeña Paúl 1999, 18–35.
39. Redondo Veintemillas and Sarasa Sánchez 1999, vol. 1, fols. 14v–15r (19 August 1255).
40. ACA, CR, Reg. 14, fol. 69v (7 February 1265) [Salarrullana de Dios 1989b, 161].
41. Redondo Veintemillas and Sarasa Sánchez 1999, vol. 1, fol. 14r–v (10 October 1255).
42. ACA, CR, Reg. 48, fol. 48r (21 June 1280) [Régné 1978, no. 787].
43. ACA, CR, Reg. 48, fol. 63v (29 June 1280) [Régné 1978, no. 799].
44. ACA, CR, Reg. 48, fol. 95v (8 July 1280) [Régné 1978, no. 814].
45. ACA, CR, Reg. 59, fol. 46v (26 July 1282) [Régné 1978, no. 932]; ACA, CR, Reg. 59, fol. 76v (31 August 1282).
46. ACA, CR, Reg. 46, fol. 216r (27 June 1284) [Régné 1978, no. 1163].
47. ACA, CR, Reg. 57, fols. 226v–227r (18 October 1285) [Régné 1978, no. 1455].

48. For example, Pere II had extended the royalist *Fueros de Aragón* to apply to all non-noble citizens in Fraga. Redondo Veintemillas and Sarasa Sánchez 1999, vol. 1, fol. 10v (13 August 1281). On the other hand, he did restrain his officials from seizing the property of Ramon de Montcada's justiciar in Fraga to pay the debts owed by his lord, unless the officer had served as a guarantor (*fideiussor*) for the transactions. ACA, CR, Reg. 44, fol. 171v (24 February 1280).
49. ACA, CR, Reg. 81, fols. 78v–79r (5 April 1289). ACA, CR, Reg. 81, fol. 126r–v (8 June 1289): "propter fallamentum dicti servitii."
50. Redondo Veintemillas and Sarasa Sánchez 1999, vol. 1, fols. 31v–32r (29 August 1287).
51. Ibid., vol. 1, fols. 30v–31r (19 August 1290), 28v–30v (20 August 1290), 31r–v (21 August 1289), 2r–6r (26 August 1290), 27r–28v (25 November 1290).
52. See ibid., vol. 1, fols. 15v–18r (17 July 1293), during the reign of Jaume II.
53. See chapter 5 above.
54. See Salleras and Espinosa 1986, 115–22.
55. Redondo Veintemillas and Sarasa Sánchez 1999, vol. 1, fols. 12v–13v (25 August 1294).
56. Ibid., vol. 1, fols. 11r–v, 11v–12v (both 25 August 1294). The king also confirmed Guillem's statute concerning wine fifteen years after it was enacted. Ibid., vol. 1, fols. 32v–34r (27 June 1309), 39r–40r (31 March 1324).
57. For example, Guillem bore the title in Redondo Veintemillas and Sarasa Sánchez 1999, vol. 1, fols. 35r–38v (23 March 1324).
58. ACA, CR, Reg. 476, fol. 137v.
59. ACA, CR, Reg. 476, fol. 138v. Fraga's Jews contributed as part of the *collecta* of Lleida. Assis 1997b, 199.
60. ACA, CR, Reg. 476, fols. 138v–139r.
61. ACA, CR, Reg. 476, fol. 139v.
62. ACA, CR, Reg. 222, fols. 87v–89v (30 September 1322).
63. The king indicated that the Infant Alfons, acting as general procurator, had lodged the initial request. ACA, CR, Reg. 247, fol. 117r (22 July 1322). See Salarrullana de Dios 1989c, 363–64, and Salleras and Espinosa 1986, 137.
64. ACA, CR, Cartas Reales Diplomáticas, J II, c. 16, no. 3296 (April 1326) [Masiá de Ros 1949, doc. 8].
65. ACA, CR, Reg. 476, fol. 233 (16 January 1327).
66. Archivo Municipal de Fraga, perg. 49, no. 12 (now lost), as cited by Salarrullana de Dios 1989c, 374. The confirmed royal privileges were from Jaume I in 1242 and Jaume II in 1294. The king donated his rights to Fraga to his queen in 1331. ACA, CR, Reg. 485, fol. 154v (26 March 1331). The executors of Guillem's estate later confirmed the monarchy's possession [ACA, CR, Reg. 484, fol. 52v (26 October 1331)]. See Salarrullana de Dios 1989a, 37–48.
67. ACA, CR, Reg. 199, fol. 85r–v (20 May 1302) [Régné 1978, no. 2780].
68. Bensch 2008, 41.
69. ACA, CR, Reg. 1643, fol. 42r–v (12 August 1383); ACA, CR, Reg. 1643, fols. 42v–43r. We discussed the implications of this law in chapter 1 above.
70. See, for example, Lacarra 1981 and Burns 1973, 267–70. See also Domingo Grabiel 1996. These varying rates of success further differentiated the societal conditions of Jewish and Muslim aljamas and the stereotypes associated with these groups. See Nirenberg 1996, 28, and Lourie 1990a, 151.
71. Monjo 2004, 41–42. See Serrano Daura 2000b, 1:412–13. Jaume I had claimed

his exclusive right to *merum imperium* in the kingdoms of Valencia and Aragon in the mid-thirteenth century. See Forey 1973, 130–31.
72. For documentation concerning royal engagement with the Templar domains of the Ribera d'Ebre, see Serrano Daura 1997, docs. 2–17.
73. Finke 1908–22, vol. 1, docs. 30 (15 September 1297) and 59 (13 June and 7 July 1300).
74. González Palencia and González Palencia 1932, 72. But consider the critique of Tilander 1933. For background on this lordship, see Almagro Basch 1959–64, vol. 3.
75. Tilander 1956, vol. 2, VIII.14; Tilander 1937, §274. The prohibition was later generalized in the Latin version of the fueros. Cabarte 1624, fol. 8v.
76. Tilander 1956, VIII.19; Tilander 1937, §277. Promulgation naturally does not necessarily signify enforcement. The Aragonese nobility resisted the *Vidal Mayor* and its Romanist legal principles for generations to come. See Degado Echeverría 1989.
77. Cabarte 1624, fol. 8v.
78. Ibid., fol. 10v.
79. ACA, CR, Reg. 228, fol. 26v (14 February 1326). Confirmation: ACA, CR, Reg. 230, fol. 110r–v (5 September 1327).
80. Garcia-Oliver 2011, 189–90.
81. Ibid., 147.
82. ACA, CR, Procesos en folio, legajo no. 126/2.
83. See Garcia-Oliver 2011, 105–13.
84. ACA, CR, Cartas Reales Diplomáticas, J II, c. 133, no. 15 (28 April 1322). The king noted that he was writing at Isaac's behest.
85. See, for example, Meyerson 2004a, 28–30.
86. ACA, CR, Reg. 2101, fols. 38v–40r (23 May 1379).
87. Jaime Hospital, *Observantiae regni Aragonum*, as cited by Hinojosa 1904, 529–30n3.
88. See Meyerson 1991, 18–33.
89. Ferrer i Mallol 1987, 88–90.
90. Monjo 2004, 59.
91. Ferrer i Mallol 1987, 90.
92. ACA, CR, Cartas Reales Diplomáticas, J II, c. 133, no. 79 (14 February 1326).
93. See Boswell 1978, 36.
94. As cited by Ehlers 2006, 98. See Burns 1990.
95. Catlos 2004, 400.
96. See, for example, Tierney 1963 and Ullman 1949.
97. Muñoz Jiménez 2003, 160–61.
98. Ray 2006, 7 and 178.
99. Finkelstein 1924, 336–47. Representatives appeared from communities throughout Catalonia and Valencia but not Aragon (no. 24). Other communities that allegedly could not attend "because of unavoidable accidents" wrote letters "making it clear that the work is pleasing to them" (no. 17).
100. Ibid., preamble and no. 19.
101. Ibid., nos. 5 (involvement in the Cort[e]s), 7 (against abusive tax collectors, who should not "cause anyone bodily pain"), and 10 (against indirect taxes).
102. Ibid., no. 10.
103. Ibid., nos. 19 and 11. The communities were also bound to take collective action against anyone deemed to be a *malsin* (no. 3).
104. Ibid., nos. 16 and 18.
105. Ibid., no. 17.
106. Ibid., no. 30.
107. Baer 1961–66, 1:210–11.

References

Unpublished Primary Sources
Archivo Ducal de Medinaceli (Seville) (ADM)
 [consulted at the Arxiu Montserrat
 Tarradellas i Macià (Poblet)]:
 Montcada.
Archivo Historico Nacional (Madrid) (AHN):
 Clero: Poblet;
 Órdenes Militares (OM).
Archivo Municipal de Fraga (Fraga):
 Pergaminos.
Arxiu Capitular de Lleida (Lleida) (ACL):
 Pergamins;
 Llibre vert.
Arxiu Capitular de Tortosa (Tortosa) (ACT):
 Cartularis 2, 4, 6, 8, 9, 9A;
 Pergamins.
Archivo de la Corona de Aragón (Barcelona)
 (ACA):
 Cancillería Real (CR):
  Pergaminos: Ramon Berenguer IV
   (RB IV), Alfons I (A I), Pere I
   (P I), Jaume I (J I), Pere II (P II),
   Alfons II (A II), Jaume II (J II),
   Extrainventario;
  Registros;
  Procesos en folio, legajo no. 126/2;
  Cartas Reales Diplomáticas: Jaume I
   (J I), Jaume II (J II).
 Gran Priorato de Cataluña (AGP), Órdenes
  Militares:
  Sección 1a—Pergaminos: Armario no. 4
   (Tortosa);
  Sección 2a—Códices: no. 115 (*Cartulari
   de Tortosa*).
Arxiu Històric Comarcal de les Terres del
 Ebre (Tortosa) (ACTE):
 Pergamins;
 Papers.
Arxiu Municipal de Lleida (Lleida) (AML):
 Fons Municipal: pergamins;
 Manuscrits: Registre 1372, *Llibre vert
  petit.*

Published Primary Sources
Abajo Martín, Teresa, ed. 1986. *Documentos
 de la catedral de Palencia (1035–
 1247).* Palencia: Ediciones J. M.
 Garrido Garrido.
Adler, Marcus Nathan, ed. and trans. 1983.
 *The Itinerary of Benjamin of Tudela:
 Travels in the Middle Ages.* Malibu,
 Calif.: Pangloss Press.

Altisent, Agustí, ed. 1993. *Diplomatari de Santa Maria de Poblet (960–1177)*. Barcelona: Abadia de Poblet and Generalitat de Catalunya.

Alturo i Perucho, Jesús, ed. 1985. *L'Arxiu antic de Santa Anna de Barcelona del 942 al 1200*. 3 vols. Barcelona: Fundació Noguera.

Alvira Cabrer, Martín, ed. 2010. *Pedro el Católico, Rey de Aragón y Conde de Barcelona (1196–1213): Documentos, testimonios y memoria histórica*. 6 vols. Fuentes históricas aragonesas 52. Zaragoza: Consejo Superior de Investigaciónes Científicas.

Aronius, Julius, ed. 1902. *Regesten zur Geschichte der Juden im Fränkischen und Deutschen Reiche bis zum Jahre 1273*. Berlin: Leonhard Simion.

Assis, Yom Tov, et al. 1991. *The Jews of Tortosa, 1373–1492: Regesta of Documents from the Archivo Histórico de Protocolos de Tarragona*. Sources for the History of the Jews in Spain 3. Jerusalem: Ginzei Am Olam.

Augustine. 2009. *The City of God*. Translated by Marcus Dods. Peabody, Mass.: Hendrickson.

Baer, Yitzhak [Fritz], ed. 1929. *Die Juden im Christlichen Spanien*. 2 vols. Berlin: Akademie-Verlag.

Barrau Dihigo, L., and J. Massó Torrents, eds. 1925. *Gesta comitum barcinonensium. Cròniques catalanes*. Barcelona: Institut d'Estudis Catalans.

Bastardas i Parera, Joan, ed. 1984. *Usatges de Barcelona: El codi a mitjan segle XII. Establiment del text llatí i edició de la versió catalana del manuscrit del segle XIII de l'Arxiu de la Corona d'Aragó de Barcelona*. Col·lecció textos i documents 6. Barcelona: Fundació Noguera.

Bisson, Thomas N., ed. 1984. *Fiscal Accounts of Catalonia Under the Early Count-Kings (1151–1213)*. 2 vols. Berkeley: University of California Press.

Bofarull y Mascaró, Próspero de, et al., eds. 1847–1973. *Colección de documentos inéditos del Archivo de la Corona de Aragón*. 42 vols. Barcelona: J. Eusebio Montfort.

Boretius, Alfred, and Victor Krause, eds. 1883. *Monumenta Germaniae Historica. Legum sectio II: Capitularia regum francorum I*. Hannover: Hahnsche Buchhandlung.

Burns, Robert I., ed. and trans. 1991. *Foundations of Crusader Valencia: Revolt and Recovery, 1257–1263*. Diplomatarium of the Crusader Kingdom of Valencia 2. Princeton: Princeton University Press.

———. 2001. *Transition in Crusader Valencia: Years of Triumph, 1264–1270*. Diplomatarium of the Crusader Kingdom of Valencia 3. Princeton: Princeton University Press.

Cabarte, Pedro, ed. 1624. *Fueros y observancias del reyno de Aragón. Fori quibus in iudiciis nec extra ad praesens non utimur*. Zaragoza.

Caffaro, Andrea. 1890. *Annali Genovesi di Caffaro e de suoi continuatori dal MXCIX al MCCXCIII*. Edited by Luigi Tommaso Belgrano. Fonti per la storia d'Itàlia 1. Genoa: Tipografia del R. Instituto Sordo-Muti.

Canellas López, Ángel, ed. 1961. "Colección diplomática de La Almunia de Doña Godina (1176–1395)." *Cuadernos de Historia Jeronimo Zurita* 12–13:191–354.

———. 1989. *Monumenta diplomatica aragonensia. Los cartularios de*

San Salvador de Zaragoza. 4 vols. Zaragoza: Ibercaja.

Caruana Gómez de Barreda, Jaime, ed. 1974. *El fuero latino de Teruel*. Teruel: Instituto de estudios turolenses.

Castro, Américo, and Federico de Onís, eds. 1916. *Los fueros leóneses de Zamora, Salamanca, Ledesma, y Alba de Tormes*. Madrid: Imprenta de los sucesores de Hernando.

Cingolani, Stefano M., ed. 2011. *Diplomatari de Pere el Gran: 1. Cartes i pergamins (1258–1285)*. Diplomataris 62. Barcelona: Fundació Noguera.

Colon, Germà, Arcadi Garcia, and Vicente García Edo, eds. 1980–2007. *Furs de València. Els nostres clàssics. Collecció A*. 11 vols. Barcelona: Editorial Barcino.

Cortes de los antiguos reinos de Aragón y de Valencia y Principado de Cataluña. 1896–1922. 27 vols. Madrid: Real Academia de la Historia.

Delaville le Roulx, J., ed. 1897. *Cartulaire général de l'ordre des Hospitaliers de S. Jean de Jérusalem (1100–1310)*. 3 vols. Paris: Ernest Leroux.

Desamparados Cabanes Pecourt, María de los, ed. 2009. *Documentos de Jaime I relacionados con Aragón*. Fuentes históricas aragonesas 50. Zaragoza: Consejo Superior de Investigaciones Científicas.

Dualde Serrano, Manuel, ed. 1950–67. *Fori antiqui Valentiae*. Madrid: Consejo Superior de Investigaciones Científicas.

Escribà i Bonastre, Gemma, ed. 1995. *The Jews in the Crown of Aragon: Regesta of the "Cartas Reales" in the Archivo de la Corona de Aragón*. Part 2, 1328–1492. Sources for the History of the Jews in Spain 5; Henk Schussheim Memorial Series. Jerusalem: Ginzei Am Olam, Central Archives for the History of the Jewish People.

Escribà i Bonastre, Gemma, and Maria Pilar Frago i Pérez, eds. 1992. *Documents dels jueus de Girona (1124–1595). Arxiu Històric de la Ciutat, Arxiu Diocesà de Girona*. Girona: Ajuntament de Girona.

Escribà i Bonastre, Gemma, and Maria Cinta Mañé, eds. 1993. *The Jews in the Crown of Aragon: Regesta of the "Cartas Reales" in the Archivo de la Corona de Aragón*. Part 1, 1066–1327. Sources for the History of the Jews in Spain 4; Henk Schussheim Memorial Series. Jerusalem: Ginzei Am Olam, Central Archives for the History of the Jewish People.

Fernández Flórez, José Antonio, et al., eds. 1976–99. *Colección diplomática del monasterio de Sahagún*. 7 vols. León: Centro de Estudios e Investigación San Isidoro.

Finke, Heinrich, ed. 1908–22. *Acta Aragonensia: Quellen zur Deutschen, Italienischen, Französichen, Spanischen, zur Kirchen- und Kulturgeschichte aus der Diplomatischen Korrespondenz Jaymes II (1291–1327)*. 3 vols. Berlin: W. Rothschild.

Font Rius, José María, ed. 1969–83. *Cartas de población y franquicia de Cataluña*. 2 vols. Madrid: Consejo Superior de Investigaciónes Científicas.

González Palencia, Ángel, and Inocenta González Palencia, ed. 1932. *El fuero latino de Albarracín (fragmentos)*. Madrid: Tip. de Archivos.

Gonzalvo i Bou, Gener, ed. 1994. *Les constitucions de pau i treva a Catalunya (segles XI–XIII)*. Textos jurídics catalans, Lleis i costums II/3. Barcelona: Generalitat de Catalunya, Departament de Justícia.

Gorosch, Max, ed. 1950. *El fuero de Teruel*. Stockholm: Almkvist and Wiksells.

Huici Miranda, Ambrosio, and María de los Desamparados Cabanes Pecourt, eds. 1976–88. *Documentos de Jaime I de Aragón*. 5 vols. Valencia: Anubar Ediciones.

Hyacinthe Albanés, Joseph, et al., eds. 1899. *Gallia christiana novissima: Histoire des archévêques, évêques, et abbayes de France. Marseilles (évêques, prévots, statuts)*. Valence: L'Imprimerie Valentinoise.

Imperiale de Sant'Angelo, Cesare, ed. 1938–42. *Codice diplomatico della Repubblica di Genova*. 3 vols. Rome: Tipografia del Senato.

Kagay, Donald J., ed. 2002. *The Customs of Catalonia Between Lords and Vassals by the Barcelona Canon, Pere Albert: A Practical Guide to Castle Feudalism in Medieval Spain*. Medieval and Renaissance Texts and Studies 243. Tempe: Arizona Center for Medieval and Renaissance Studies.

Kehr, Paul F., ed. 1926. *Papsturkunden in Spanien: Vorarbeiten zur Hispania Pontificia*. Vol. 1, *Katalanien*. Berlin: Weidmannsche Buchhandlung.

Klein, Elka, ed. 2004. *Hebrew Deeds of Catalan Jews (1117–1316)*. Publicacions de la Societat Catalana d'Estudis Hebraics 1; Girona Judaica 1. Barcelona: Societat Catalana d'Estudis Hebraics; Girona: Patronat Municipal Call de Girona.

Lévi-Provençal, E., ed. 1938. *La péninsule ibérique au moyen-âge d'après le Kitāb ar-rawḍ al-mi'ṭār fī ḫabar al-aḳṭār*. Leiden: E. J. Brill.

Mansi, G. D., et al., eds. 1901–27. *Sacrorum conciliorum: Nova et amplissima collectio*. 53 vols. Paris: H. Welter.

Mansilla, Demetrio, ed. 1954. *La documentación pontificia hasta Inocencio III (965–1216)*. Monumenta Hispaniae Vaticana, sección registros 1. Burgos: Ediciones Aldecoa.

Massip, Jesús, ed. 1996. *Costums de Tortosa*. Textos i documents 32. Barcelona: Fundació Noguera.

Miquel Rosell, Francisco, ed. 1945–47. *Liber feudorum maior. Cartulario real que se conserve en el Archivo de la Corona de Aragón*. 2 vols. Barcelona: Consejo Superior de Investigaciones Científicas.

Muñoz y Romero, Tomás, ed. 1847. *Colección de fueros municipales y cartas pueblas de l[o]s reinos de Castilla, León, Corona de Aragón y Navarra*. Vol. 1. Madrid: Imprenta de Don José María Alonso.

Pérez Martínez, Lorenzo, ed. 1977. "Corpus documental balear. Reinado de Jaime I." *Fontes Rerum Balearium* 1:1–112.

Pons i Guri, Josep M., ed. 1989. "Constitucions de Catalunya." In *Recull d'estudis d'història jurídica catalana*, 3:55–76. Textos i documents 38. Barcelona: Fundació Noguera.

Redondo Veintemillas, Guillermo, and Esteban Sarasa Sánchez, eds. 1999. *Libro de privilegios de Fraga y sus aldeas*. Facsimile ed. 2 vols. Zaragoza: Cortes de Aragón.

Régné, J. 1978. *History of the Jews in Aragon: Regesta and Documents, 1213–1327*. Edited by Yom Tov Assis. Jerusalem: Magnes Press.

Rovira i Ermengol, Josep, ed. 1933. *Usatges de Barcelona i Commemoracions de Pere Albert*. Barcelona: Editorial Barcino.

Salrach, Josep M., et al., eds. 1999. *Els pergamins de l'Arxiu Comtal de Barcelona de Ramon Borrell a*

Ramon Berenguer I. Barcelona: Fundació Noguera.

Sánchez Casabón, Ana I., ed. 1995. *Alfonso II Rey de Aragón, Conde de Barcelona y Marqués de Provenza: Documentos (1162–1196)*. Fuentes históricas aragonesas 23. Zaragoza: Institución Fernando el Católico.

Sarobe, Ramon, ed. 1998. *Col·lecció diplomàtica e la Casa del Temple de Gardeny (1070–1200)*. 2 vols. Diplomataris 16. Barcelona: Fundació Noguera.

Simonsohn, Shlomo. 1988. *The Apostolic See and the Jews: Documents, 492–1404*. Studies and Texts 94. Toronto: Pontifical Institute of Mediaeval Studies.

Soldevila, Ferran, ed. 1971. *Llibre dels feits del rei en Jaume o Crònica de Jaume I*. In *Les quatre grans cròniques*. Barcelona: Editorial Selecta.

Teulet, Alexandre, et al., eds. 1863–1909. *Layettes du trésor des chartes*. 5 vols. Paris: Henri Plon.

Tilander, Gunnar, ed. 1937. *Los fueros de Aragón según el manuscrito 458 de la Biblioteca Nacional de Madrid*. Lund: C. W. K. Gleerup.

———. 1956. *Vidal Mayor. Traducción aragonesa de la obra "In Excelsis Dei Thesauris de Vidal de Canellas."* 3 vols. Lund: Håkan Ohlssons Boktryckeri.

Toda, Eduardo, ed. 1938. *Cartulari de Poblet: Edició del manuscrit de Tarragona*. Barcelona: Institut d'Estudis Catalans.

Ubieto Arteta, Antonio, ed. 1951. *Colección diplomática de Pedro I de Aragón y Navarra*. Zaragoza: Consejo Superior de Investigaciones Científicas.

Udina Martorell, Frederic, ed. 1947. *El "Llibre Blanch" de Santas Creus: Cartulario del siglo XII*. Textos y estudios de la Corona de Aragón. Barcelona: Consejo Superior de Investigaciones Científicas.

Ureña y Smenjaud, Rafael de, et al., eds. 1935. *El fuero de Cuenca. Formas primitiva y sistemática: Texto latino, texto castellano y adaptación del fuero de Iznatoraf*. Madrid: Tipografía de Archivos.

Virgili, Antoni, ed. 1997a. *Diplomatari de la catedral de Tortosa (1062–1193)*. Diplomataris 11. Barcelona: Fundació Noguera.

———, ed. 2001a. *Diplomatari de la catedral de Tortosa (1193–1212)*. Diplomataris 25. Barcelona: Fundació Noguera.

Zurita, Jerónimo. 1967–77. *Anales de la Corona de Aragón*. Edited by Angel Canellas López. 8 vols. Zaragoza: Institución "Fernando el Católico."

Secondary Literature

Abulafia, David. 1994. *A Mediterranean Emporium: The Catalan Kingdom of Mallorca*. Cambridge: Cambridge University Press.

———. 2000. "The Servitude of Jews and Muslims in the Medieval Mediterranean." *Mélanges de l'École française de Rome—Moyen Âge* 112:687–714.

———. 2004. "'Nam iudei servi regis sunt, et semper fisco regio deputati': The Jews in the Municipal Fuero of Teruel (1176–1177)." In *Jews, Muslims, and Christians in and Around the Crown of Aragon*, edited by Harvey J. Hames, 97–123. The Medieval Mediterranean 52. Leiden: Brill.

Alanyà i Roig, Josep. 1996. *Besalú, vida i organització d'una juderia*. Besalú: Ajuntament de Besalú.

Almagro Basch, Martín. 1959–64. *Historia de Albarracín y su sierra*. Vols.

3–4. Teruel: Instituto de Estudios Terolenses.

Alvira Cabrer, Martín, and Damian Smith. 2006–7. "Política antiherética en la Corona de Aragón. Una carta inédita del Papa Inocencio III a la reina Sancha (1203)." *Acta Historica et Archaeologica Medievalia* 27–28:65–88.

Aragó Cabañas, Antonio M. 1962. "La institución 'baiulus regis' en Cataluña en la época de Alfonso el Casto." In *VII Congreso de Historia de la Corona de Aragón*, 3:137–42. Barcelona: [Diputación Provincial].

Arnold, Benjamin. 1991. *Princes and Territories in Medieval Germany*. Cambridge: Cambridge University Press.

Assis, Yom Tov. 1988. *The Jews of Santa Coloma de Queralt: An Economic and Demographic Case Study of a Community at the End of the Thirteenth Century*. Hispania Judaica 6. Jerusalem: Magnes Press.

———. 1997a. *The Golden Age of Aragonese Jewry: Community and Society in the Crown of Aragon, 1213–1327*. London: Littman Library of Jewish Civilization.

———. 1997b. *The Jewish Economy in the Medieval Crown of Aragon, 1213–1327: Money and Power*. Brill's Series in Jewish Studies 18. Leiden: Brill.

Aurell, Jaume. 2012. *Authoring the Past: Historiography, Autobiography, and Politics in Medieval Catalonia*. Chicago: University of Chicago Press.

Aurell, Martin. 1995. *Les noces du comte: Mariage et pouvoir en Catalogne (785–1213)*. Paris: Publications de la Sorbonne.

Baer, Yitzhak [Fritz]. 1913. *Studien zur Geschichte der Juden im Königreich Aragonien wahrend des 13. und 14. Jahrhunderts*. Historische Studien 106. Berlin: Ebering.

———. 1961–66. *A History of the Jews in Christian Spain*. 2 vols. Philadelphia: Jewish Publication Society of America

Balaguer, Anna M. 1999. *Història de la moneda dels comtats catalans*. Societat Catalana d'Estudis Numismàtics; Institut d'Estudis Catalans.

Balaguer, F. 1947. "Nuevas noticias de la aljama de Huesca." *Sefarad* 7:351–92.

Baldwin, John W. 1986. *The Government of Philip Augustus: Foundations of French Royal Power in the Middle Ages*. Berkeley: University of California Press.

Baron, Salo W. 1952–83. *A Social and Religious History of the Jews*. 2nd ed. 18 vols. New York: Columbia University Press.

Barrero García, Ana. 1976. "La familia de los *Fueros de Cuenca*." *Anuario de la Historia del Derecho Español* 46:713–26.

———. 1979. *El fuero de Teruel: Su historia, proceso de formación y reconstrucción critica de sus fuentes*. Madrid: Instituto de Estudios Turolenses.

Barthélemy, Dominique, and Stephen D. White. 1996. "Debate: The Feudal Revolution." *Past and Present* 152:196–223.

Barton, Thomas W. 2009. "Constructing a Diocese in a Post-conquest Landscape: A Comparative Approach to the Lay Possession of Tithes." *Journal of Medieval History* 35:1–33.

———. 2010. "Lords, Settlers, and Shifting Frontiers in Medieval Catalonia."

Journal of Medieval History 36:204–52.

———. 2011. "Muslims in Christian Countrysides: A Reassessment of *Exaricus* Tenures." *Medieval Encounters* 17:233–320.

———. 2012. "Jurisdictional Conflict, Strategies of Litigation, and Mechanisms of Compromise in Thirteenth-Century Tortosa." *Recerca* 14:201–48.

Bastardas i Parera, Joan. 1977. *Sobre la problemàtica dels Usatges de Barcelona*. Barcelona: Academia de Buenas Letras de Barcelona.

Bayerri, Enrique. 1933–60. *Historia de Tortosa y su comarca*. 8 vols. Tortosa: Imprenta Moderna de Algueró y Baiges.

Bellomo, Manlio. 1989. *L'Europa del diritto comune*. 4th ed. Rome: Il Cigno GG Edizioni.

Benito i Monclús, Pere. 2003. *Senyoria de la terra i tinença pagesa al comtat de Barcelona (segles XI–XIII)*. Barcelona: Consejo Superior de Investigaciones Científicas.

———. 2010. "Las crisis alimenticias en la Edad Media: Carácteres generales, distinciones y paradigmas interpretativos." In *Comer, beber, viver: Consumo y niveles de vida en la Edad Media hispánica. XXI Semana de Estudios Medievales*, edited by Esther López Ojeda, 123–58. Logroño: Instituto de Estudios Riojanos.

———. 2011. "Famines sans frontières en Occident avant la 'conjoncture de 1300': À propos d'une enquête en cours." In *Les disettes dans la conjoncture de 1300 en Méditerranée occidentale*, edited by Monique Bourin, John Drendel, and François Menant, 37–86. Collection de l'École française de Rome 450. Paris: Ecole française de Rome.

Bensch, Stephen. 1995. *Barcelona and Its Rulers, 1096–1291*. Cambridge Studies in Medieval Life and Thought, 4th ser., 26. Cambridge: Cambridge University Press.

———. 1996. "Three Peaces of Empúries (1189–1220)." *Anuario de Estudios Medievales* 26:583–603.

———. 2005. "Lordship and Coinage in Empúries, ca. 1080–ca. 1040." In *The Experience of Power in Medieval Europe, 950–1350*, edited by Robert F. Berkhofer III, Alan Cooper, and Adam Kosto, 73–92. Aldershot: Ashgate.

———. 2008. "A Baronial *Aljama*: The Jews of Empúries in the Thirteenth Century." *Jewish History* 22:19–51.

Berend, Nóra. 2001. *At the Gate of Christendom: Jews, Muslims, and 'Pagans' in Medieval Hungary*. Cambridge Studies in Medieval Life and Thought, 4th ser., 50. Cambridge: Cambridge University Press.

Berkhofer III, Robert F., Alan Cooper, and Adam Kosto, eds. 2005. *The Experience of Power in Medieval Europe, 950–1350*. Aldershot: Ashgate.

Bisson, Thomas N. 1986. *The Medieval Crown of Aragon: A Short History*. Oxford: Oxford University Press.

———. 1989a. "Feudalism in Twelfth-Century Catalonia." In Bisson 1989c, 153–78.

———. 1989b. "The Finances of the Young James I (1213–1228)." In Bisson 1989c, 351–91.

———. 1989c. *Medieval France and Her Pyrenean Neighbours: Studies in Early Institutional History*. Etudes présentées à la Commission internationale pour l'histoire des assemblées d'Etats 70. London: Hambledon Press.

———. 1989d. "The Organized Peace in Southern France and Catalonia (c. 1140–1233)." In Bisson 1989c, 215–36.

———. 1989e. "The Problem of Feudal Monarchy: Aragon, Catalonia, and France." In Bisson 1989c, 237–55.

———. 1989f. "Ramon de Caldes (c. 1135–1199): Dean of Barcelona and the King's Minister." In Bisson 1989c, 187–98.

———. 1989g. "The Rise of Catalonia: Identity, Power, and Ideology in a Twelfth-Century Society." In Bisson 1989c, 125–52.

———. 1989h. "Sur les origines du *monedatge*: Quelques textes inedits." In Bisson 1989c, 325–37.

———. 1989i. "An 'Unknown Charter' for Catalonia (1205)." In Bisson 1989c, 199–212.

———. 1994. "The 'Feudal Revolution.'" *Past and Present* 142:6–42.

———. 1996. "'Statebuilding' in the Medieval Crown of Aragón." In *El poder real de la Corona de Aragón (siglos XIV–XVI). Actas del XV° Congreso de Historia de la Corona de Aragón*, vol. I, pt. i, 141–58. Zaragoza: Gobierno de Aragón.

———. 2009. *The Crisis of the Twelfth Century: Power, Lordship, and the Origins of European Government*. Princeton: Princeton University Press.

Blasco Martínez, Asunción. 1991. "Los judíos del reino de Aragón: Balance de los estudios realizados y perspectivas." In *Actes: I. Col·loqui d'història dels jueus a la Corona d'Aragó*, 13–99. Quaderns de l'Institut 2. Lleida: Institut d'Estudis Ilerdencs.

Blumenkranz, Bernhard. 1960. *Juifs et chrétiens dans le monde occidental, 430–1096*. Paris: Mouton.

Bofarull, Francisco de. 1908. "Jaime I y los judíos." In *I Congrés d'Història de la Corona d'Aragó*, 2:819–943. Barcelona: Francisco Altés.

Bonnassie, Pierre. 1975–76. *La Catalogne du milieu du Xe a la fin du XIe siècle: Croissance et mutations d'une société*. 2 vols. Publications de l'Université de Toulouse–Le Mirail 29. Toulouse: A. Michel.

———. 1980. "Du Rhône à la Galice: Genèse et modalités du régime féodale." In *Structures féodales et féodalisme dans l'Occident méditerranéen (X^e–XIIIe siècles): Bilan et perspectives de recherches: École française de Rome, 10–13 octobre 1978*, 17–44. Collection de l'École française de Rome 44. Paris: École française de Rome.

Bönnen, Gerold. 2004. "Worms: The Jews Between the City, the Bishops, and the Crown." In *The Jews of Europe in the Middle Ages (Tenth to Fifteenth Centuries): Proceedings of the International Symposium Held at Speyer, 20–25 October 2002*, edited by Christoph Cluse, 449–58. Turnhout: Brepols.

Bos, Gerrit, et al., eds. 2010. *Medical Synonym Lists from Medieval Provence: Shem Tov ben Isaac of Tortosa, "Sefer Ha-Shimmush," Book 29. Part 1, Edition and Commentary of List 1 (Hebrew-Arabic-Romance/Latin)*. Leiden: Brill.

Boswell, John. 1978. *The Royal Treasure: Muslim Communities Under the Crown of Aragon in the Fourteenth Century*. New Haven: Yale University Press.

Brown, Peter. 2003. *The Rise of Western Christendom: Triumph and Diversity, A.D. 200–1000*. 2nd ed. London: Blackwell.

Burns, Robert I. 1973. *Islam Under the Crusaders: Colonial Survival in* the *Thirteenth-Century Kingdom of Valencia*. Princeton: Princeton University Press.

———. 1975. *Medieval Colonialism: Postcrusade Exploitation of Islamic Valencia*. Princeton: Princeton University Press.

———. 1984. *Muslims, Christians, and Jews in the Crusader Kingdom of Valencia: Societies in Symbiosis*. Cambridge: Cambridge University Press.

———. 1990. "Muslims in the Thirteenth-Century Realms of Aragon: Interaction and Reaction." In *Muslims Under Latin Rule, 1100–1300*, edited by James M. Powell, 57–102. Princeton: Princeton University Press.

———. 1995. "The *Guidaticum* Safe-Conduct in the Medieval Arago-Catalonia: A Mini-institution for Muslims, Christians, and Jews." *Medieval Encounters* 1:56–61.

———. 1996. *Jews in the Notarial Culture: Latinate Wills in Mediterranean Spain, 1250–1350*. Berkeley: University of California Press.

Büschgens, Andrea. 1995. *Die politischen Verträge Alfons' VIII. von Kastilien (1158–1214) mit Aragón-Katalonien und Navarra: Diplomatische Strategien und Konfliktlösung im mittelalterlichen Spanien*. Europäische Hochschulschriften, Reihe 3. Geschichte und ihre Hilfswissenschaften 678. Frankfurt am Main: P. Lang.

Carreras y Candi, Francesch. 1905. "Caciquisme polítich en lo segle XIII (Continuació)." *Boletín de la Real Academia de Buenas Letras de Barcelona* 5 (18): 63–79.

———. 1928. *L'Aljama de juhéus de Tortosa*. Real Academia de Buenas Letras de Barcelona Memoria 9.3. Barcelona: Imprenta la Renaxensa.

Caruana Gómez, Jaime. 1954. "Sobre el nacimiento de Alfonso II de Aragón." *Teruel* 11:5–32.

———. 1955. "Las adiciones al fuero de Teruel." *Anuario de Historia del Derecho Español* 25:681–702.

———. 1962. "Itinerario de Alfonso II de Aragón." *Estudios de Edad Media de la Corona de Aragón* 7:73–298.

Casanova Querol, Elisenda. 1991. "Estado de la cuestión sobre los judíos de Tortosa (XII–XIV)." In *Actes: I. Col·loqui d'història dels jueus a la Corona d'Aragó*, 393–400. Quaderns de l'Institut 2. Lleida: Institut d'Estudis Ilerdencs.

Catalunya Romànica. 1984–98. 27 vols. Barcelona: Fundació Enciclopèdia Catalana.

Catlos, Brian A. 2001–2. "Context and Convenience in the Crown of Aragon: Proposal for a Model of Interaction Between Ethno-religious Groups." *Revista d'Història Medieval* 12:259–68.

———. 2004. *The Victors and the Vanquished: Christians and Muslims of Catalonia and Aragon, 1050–1300*. Cambridge Studies in Medieval Life and Thought, 4th ser., 59. Cambridge: Cambridge University Press.

———. 2014. *Muslims of Medieval Latin Christendom, c. 1050–1614*. Cambridge: Cambridge University Press.

Cawsey, Suzanne F. 2002. *Kingship and Propaganda: Royal Eloquence and the Crown of Aragon, c. 1200–1450*. Oxford: Clarendon Press.

Celdrán Gomáriz, Pancracio, and Agustín Martínez. 2005. *Red de juderías de España: Caminos de Sefarad*. Alpedrete: Alymar.

Chazan, Robert. 1980. *Church, State, and Jew in the Middle Ages*. New York: Behrman House.

———. 2006. *The Jews of Medieval Western Christendom, 1000–1500*. Cambridge: Cambridge University Press.

Cheyette, Frederic. 1970. "Suum cuique tribuere." *French Historical Studies* 6 (3): 287–99.

Constable, Olivia Remie. 1996. *Trade and Traders in Muslim Spain: The Commercial Realignment of the Iberian Peninsula, 900–1500*. Cambridge Studies in Medieval Life and Thought, 4th ser., 24. Cambridge: Cambridge University Press.

———. 2003. *Housing the Stranger in the Mediterranean World: Lodging, Trade, and Travel in Late Antiquity and the Middle Ages*. Cambridge: Cambridge University Press.

———. 2010. "Regulating Religious Noise: The Council of Vienne, the Mosque Call, and Muslim Pilgrimage in the Late Medieval Mediterranean World." *Medieval Encounters* 16 (1): 64–95.

Corbella i Llobet, Ramon. 1984. *L'aljama de jueus de Vic*. Facsimile of 1909 edition. Vic: Publicacions del Patronat d'Estudis Ausonencs.

Crémieux, Adolphe. 1903. "Les juifs de Marseille au moyen âge." *Revue des Études Juives* 46:1–47, 246–68; 47:62–86, 243–61.

Curto, Albert. 1988–89. "La sinagoga del call jueu tortosí." *Calls* 3:29–34.

———. 1991. "El cementiri jueu de Tortosa." In *Actes: I. Col·loqui d'història dels jueus a la Corona d'Aragó*, 401–9. Quaderns de l'Institut 2. Lleida: Institut d'Estudis Ilerdencs.

———. 1993. "Recerques arqueològiques sobre la regió tortosina a l'època islàmica: Estat de la qüestió." In *La Ràpita Islàmica. Història institucional i altres estudis regionals. I Congrès de les Ràpites de l'Estat Espanyol*, edited by Mikel d'Epalza, 268–78. Sant Carles de la Ràpita: Institut d'Estudis Rapitencs.

———. 1999. "Topografia del call jueu de Tortosa." *Recerca* 3:9–24.

———. 2002. "Les comunitats jueves de Catalunya: L'àrea de Tortosa." In *La Catalunya jueva*, edited by Mariona Companys and Yom Tov Assis, 108–17. Barcelona: Ajuntament de Girona.

Daileader, Philip. 1999. "The Vanishing Consulates of Catalonia." *Speculum* 74 (1): 65–94.

———. 2000. *True Citizens: Violence, Memory, and Identity in the Medieval Community of Perpignan, 1162–1397*. The Medieval Mediterranean 25. Leiden: Brill.

———. 2006. "La coutume dans un pays aux trois religions: La Catalogne, 1228–1319." *Annales du Midi* 118 (255): 369–85.

Davis, Kathleen. 2008. *Periodization and Sovereignty: How Ideas of Feudalism and Secularization Govern the Politics of Time*. Philadelphia: University of Pennsylvania Press.

Degado Echeverría, Jesús. 1989. "'Vidal Mayor,' un libro de fueros de siglo XIII." In *Vidal Mayor, un libro de fueros del siglo XIII: Estudios*, 1:45–81. Huesca: Diputación Provincial de Huesca.

Díaz Esteban, Fernando. 1985. "Aspectos de la convivencia jurídica desde el punto de vista judío en la España medieval." In *Actas de II Congreso Internacional Encuentro de las Tres Culturas, 3–6 octubre 1983*, 105–16. Toledo: Ayuntamiento de Toledo.

Domingo, Dolors. 2007. *A la recerca d'Aurembiaix d'Urgell*. Lleida: Universitat de Lleida.

Domingo Grabiel, Anna. 1996. "Els límits del poder reial i senyorial: L'administració de la justícia sobre la població musulmana de la corona catalano-aragonesa (segle XIV)." In *El poder real de la Corona de Aragón (siglos XIV–XVI). Actas del XV° Congreso de Historia de la Corona de Aragón*, vol. 1, pt. ii, 159–71. Zaragoza: Gobierno de Aragón.

Doñate Sebastiá, José, and José Ramón Magdalena Nom de Déu. 1990. *Three Jewish Communities in Medieval Valencia: Castellon de la Plana, Burriana, Villarreal*. Jerusalem: Hebrew University.

Earenfight, Theresa. 2010. *The King's Other Body: María of Castile and the Crown of Aragon*. Philadelphia: University of Pennsylvania Press.

Ehlers, Benjamin. 2006. *Between Christians and Moriscos: Juan de Ribera and Religious Reform in Valencia, 1568–1614*. The Johns Hopkins University Studies in Historical and Political Science, 124th ser., 1. Baltimore: Johns Hopkins University Press.

Elukin, Jonathan. 2007. *Living Together, Living Apart: Rethinking Jewish-Christian Relations in the Middle Ages*. Princeton: Princeton University Press.

Emery, Richard W. 1959. *The Jews of Perpignan in the Thirteenth Century: An Economic Study Based on Notarial Records*. New York: Columbia University Press.

Epstein, Stephen. 1996. *Genoa and the Genoese, 958–1528*. Chapel Hill: University of North Carolina Press.

Esco, Carlos, Josep Giralt, and Philippe Sénac. 1988. *Arqueología islamica en la marca superior de Al-Andalus*. Zaragoza: Diputación de Huesca.

Fancy, Hussein A. 2013. "Theologies of Violence: The Recruitment of Muslim Soldiers by the Crown of Aragon." *Past and Present* 221:39–73.

Feliu, Eduard. 2002. "Cataluña no era Sefarad: Precisiones metodológicas." In *La Cataluña judía*, edited by Mariona Companys, 25–35. Barcelona: Àmbit.

Ferragud Domingo, Carmen. 2005. *Medicina i promoció social a la Baixa Edat Mitjana (Corona d'Aragó, 1350–1410)*. Estudios sobre la ciencia 36. Madrid: Consejo Superior de Investigaciones Científicas.

Ferran i Planas, Elisabet. 2006. *El jurista Pere Albert i les "Commemoracions."* Memòries de la Secció Històrico-arqueològica, 57. Barcelona: Institut d'Estudis Catalans.

Ferrer i Mallol, Maria Teresa. 1970–71. "El patrimoni reial i la recuperació dels senyorius jurisdiccionals en els estats catalano-aragonesos a la fi del segle XIV." *Anuario de Estudios Medievales* 7:351–492.

———. 1987. *Els sarraïns de la corona Catalano-aragonesa en el segle XIV: Segregació i discriminació*. Barcelona: Consell Superior d'Investigacions Científiques.

———. 1998–99. "The Muslim *Aljama* of Tortosa in the Late Middle Ages: Notes on Its Organisation." *Scripta Mediterranea* 19–20:143–64.

———. 2003. "L'aljama islàmica de Tortosa a la Baixa Edat Mitjana." *Recerca* 7:179–230.

Ferrer Navarro, Ramón. 1999. *Conquista y repoblación del Reino de Valencia*. Valencia: Promoción de Cultura Valenciana.

Fierro, Maribel. 1997. "Christian Success and Muslim Fear in Andalusī Writings During the Almoravid and Almohad Periods." In "Dhimmis and Others: Jews and Christians and the World of Classical Islam," edited by Uri Rubin and David J. Wasserstein, special issue, *Israel Oriental Studies* 17:155–78.

Finkelstein, Louis. 1924. *Jewish Self-Government in the Middle Ages*. New York: Jewish Theological Seminary.

Font Rius, José María. 1953. "La comarca de Tortosa a raíz de la Reconquista cristiana (1148). Notas sobre su fisonomía político-social." *Cuadernos de Historia de España* 19:104–28.

———. 1962. "El desarrollo general del derecho en los territorios de la Corona de Aragón (siglos XII–XIV)." In *VII Congreso de Historia de la Corona de Aragón*, 1:289–326. Barcelona: [Diputación Provincial].

———. 1985a. "La carta de seguridad de Ramón Berenguer IV a las morerias de Ascó y Ribera del Ebro (siglo XII)." In *Estudis sobre els drets i institucions locals en la Catalunya medieval. Col·lectanea de treballs del Professor Dr. Josep Mª Font i Rius amb motiu de la seva jubilació acadèmica*, 561–76. Barcelona: Universitat de Barcelona.

———. 1985b. "El procés de formació de les Costums de Tortosa." In *Estudis sobre els drets i institucions locals en la Catalunya medieval. Col·lectanea de treballs del Professor Dr. Josep Mª Font i Rius amb motiu de la seva jubilació acadèmica*, 141–61. Barcelona: Universitat de Barcelona.

Forey, A. J. 1973. *The Templars in the Corona de Aragón*. London: Oxford University Press.

Freedman, Paul H. 1979. "An Unsuccessful Attempt at Urban Organization in Twelfth-Century Catalonia." *Speculum* 54:479–91.

———. 1983. *The Diocese of Vic: Tradition and Regeneration*. New Brunswick: Rutgers University Press.

———. 1991. *The Origins of Peasant Servitude in Medieval Catalonia*. Cambridge: Cambridge University Press.

———. 2000. "Another Look at the Uprising of the Townsmen of Vic (1181–1183)." In "Homenatge al Dr. Manuel Riu i Riu," vol. 1, special issue, *Acta historica et archaeologica mediaevalia* 20/21:177–86.

———. 2002. "The Bishop of Tortosa's Rights over Alquézar According to a Letter of Pope Alexander III." *Recerca* 6:337–44.

———. 2010. "Rural Servitude and Legal Learning in Thirteenth-Century Catalonia." *Haskins Society Journal: Studies in Medieval History* 22:193–208.

Gampel, Benjamin. 2012. "Unless the Lord Watches Over the City: Joan of Aragon and His Jews, June–October 1391." In *New Perspectives on Jewish-Christian Relations*, edited by Elisheva Carlebach and Jacob J. Schacter, 65–89. Leiden: Brill.

García-Arenal, Mercedes. 1997. "Jewish Converts to Islam in the Muslim West." In "Dhimmis and Others: Jews and Christians and the World of Classical Islam," edited by Uri Rubin and David J. Wasserstein, special issue, *Israel Oriental Studies* 17:227–48.

García Biosca, Joan E., Josep Giralt, Ana Loriente, and Joan Martínez. 1998. "La gènesi dels espais urban andalusins (segles VIII–X): Tortosa, Lleida i Balaguer." In *L'Islam i Catalunya*, 137–65. Barcelona: Museu d'Història de Catalunya.

García-Guijarro Ramos, Luis. 2006. "The Aragonese Hospitaller Monastery of Sigena: Its Early Stages, 1188–c. 1210." In *Hospitaller Women in the Middle Ages*, edited by A. Luttrell and H. J. Nicholson, 113–52. Aldershot: Ashgate.

García i Sanz, Arcadi. 1979. "La concordança de les *Costums de Tortosa* i els *Furs de València*." In *Costums de Tortosa. Estudis*, edited by Javier Martínez Palacio, 287–325. Tortosa: Centre Associat de Tortosa.

———. 1987. "El dret històric dels països catalans, vist amb perspectiva de conjunt." *Revista de Catalunya* 9:55–68.

García Marsilla, Juan Vicente. 1993. "Puresa i negoci: El paper dels jueus en la producció i comercialització de queviures a la Corona d'Aragó." *Revista d'Història Medieval* 4:161–82.

Garcia-Oliver, Ferran. 1994. "De Perpinyà a Elx. Desenvolupament econòmic i geografia de les aljames." In *Xudeus e conversos na historia, actas do Congreso Internacional, Ribadavia, 14–17 de octubro de 1991*, 247–61. Santiago de Compostela: La Editorial de la Historia.

———. 2009. "Govern local i lluita política a les aljames de la Corona d'Aragó." In *Cristianos y judíos en contacto en la Edad Media: Polémica, conversión, dinero y convivencia*, edited by Flocel Sabaté and Claude Denjean, 707–31. De christianis et iudeis ad invicem 2. Lleida: Editorial Milenio.

———. 2011. *The Valley of the Six Mosques: Work and Life in Medieval Valldigna*. Turnhout: Brepols.

Glick, Thomas F. 1992. "Convivencia: An Introductory Note." In *Convivencia: Jews, Muslims, and Christians in Medieval Spain*, edited by Vivian B. Mann et al., 1–10. New York: Jewish Museum.

———. 2005. *Islamic and Christian Spain in the Early Middle Ages*. The Medieval and Early Modern Iberian World 27. 2nd ed. Leiden: Brill.

Goitein, S. D. 1967–93. *A Mediterranean Society: The Jewish Communities of the Arab World as Portrayed in the Documents of the Cairo Geniza*. 6 vols. Berkeley: University of California Press.

González Antón, Luis. 1975. *Las uniones aragonesas y las cortes del reino (1283–1301)*. 2 vols. Zaragoza: Consejo Superior de Investigaciones Científicas.

———. 1993. "Jaime II y la afirmación del poder monárquico en Aragón." *Aragón en la Edad Media* 10–11:388–96.

González Hurtebise, E. 1920. *Guía histórico-descriptiva del Archivo de la Corona de Aragón en Barcelona*. Madrid: Tip. de la Revista de Archivos, Bibliotecas y Museos.

Gonzalvo i Bou, Gener. 1990. "La pau i treva de l'any 1187 per al comtat d'Urgell i vescomtat d'Àger." *Ilerda* "Humanitats" 48:157–74.

———. 1996. "Els jueus i els *Usatges de Barcelona*." *Barcelona Quaderns d'Història* 2–3:117–24.

Gras i d'Esteva, Rafael. 1988. *Història de la Paeria*. Lleida: La Paeria.

Gual Camarena, Miguel. 1947–48. "Contribución al estudio de la territorialidad de los fueros de Valencia." *Estudios de Edad Media de la Corona de Aragón* 3:262–89.

———. 1967. "Peaje fluvial del Ebro (siglo XII)." *Estudios de Edad Media de la Corona de Aragón* 8:155–88.

Gudiol y Cunill, Josep. 1913. "Les bregues sobre lo senyoríu de Vich en el temps del rey Jaume I." In *Congrès d'Història de la Corona d'Aragó*, 1:194–218. Barcelona: Ayuntamiento de Barcelona.

Guichard, Pierre. 1990–91. *Les musulmans de Valence et la Reconquête: XIe–XIIIe siècles*. 2 vols. Damas: Institut français de Damas.

Guinot Rodríguez, Enric. 1986. *Feudalismo en expansión en el norte valenciano:*

Antecedentes y desarrollo del señorío de la Orden de Montesa. Siglos XIII y XIV. Castellón: Diputación de Castellón.

———. 1995. *Els límits del regne: El procès de formació territorial del país valencià medieval (1238–1500)*. Col·lecció politècnica 58. Valencia: Institució Valenciana d'Estudis i Investigació.

Haverkamp, Alfred. 1995. "The Jewish Quarters in German Towns During the Late Middle Ages." In *In and Out of the Ghetto: Jewish-Gentile Relations in Late Medieval and Early Modern Germany*, edited by R. Po-chia Hsia and Hartmut Lehmann, 13–28. New York: German Historical Institute.

Hinojosa, Eduardo de. 1904. "Mezquinos y exáricos. Datos para la historia de la servidumbre en Navarra y Aragón." In *Homenaje á D. Francisco Codera en su jubilación del profesorado. Estudios de erudición oriental*, 523–31. Zaragoza: M. Escar.

Huscroft, Richard. 2006. *Expulsion: England's Jewish Solution*. London: Tempus.

Iglesia Ferreirós, Aquilino. 1979. "Las Costums de Tortosa y los Fori/Furs de Valencia." In *Costums de Tortosa. Estudis*, edited by Javier Martínez Palacio, 121–286. Tortosa: Centre Associat de Tortosa.

Jenkins, Ernest E. 2012. *The Mediterranean World of Alfonso II and Peter II of Aragon (1162–1213)*. New York: Palgrave Macmillan.

Johnson, Cynthia. 2007. "Marriage Agreements from Twelfth-Century Southern France." In *To Have and to Hold: Marrying and Its Documentation in Western Christendom, 400–1600*, edited by Philip L. Reynolds and John Witte, Jr., 215–59. Cambridge: Cambridge University Press.

Jordan, William C. 1986. "Christian Excommunication of the Jews in the Middle Ages: A Restatement of the Issues." *Jewish History* 1:31–38.

———. 1989. *The French Monarchy and the Jews: From Philip Augustus to the Last Capetians*. Philadelphia: University of Pennsylvania Press.

———. 1997. "Home Again: The Jews in the Kingdom of France, 1315–1322." In *The Stranger in Medieval Society*, edited by F. R. P. Akehurst and Stephanie Cain Van D'Elden, 27–45. Minneapolis: University of Minnesota Press.

———. 1998. "Jews, Regalian Rights, and the Constitution in Medieval France." *Association of Jewish Studies Review* 23:1–16.

Kagay, Donald J. 1988. "Structures of Baronial Dissent and Revolt Under James I (1213–76)." *Mediaevistik* 1:61–85.

———. 1997. "Rebellion on Trial: The Aragonese Union and Its Uneasy Connection to Royal Law, 1265–1301." *Journal of Legal History* 18 (3): 30–43.

———. 1999. "*Princeps namque*: Defense of the Crown and the Birth of the Catalan State." *Mediterranean Studies* 8:66–72.

———. 2003. "The Treason of Center and Periphery: The Uncertain Contest of Government and Individual in the Medieval Crown of Aragon." *Mediterranean Studies* 12:17–35.

———. 2007a. "The King's Right Must Be Preferred to the Lord's: Sovereignty and Suzerainty in the Treatises of Pere Albert." In *War, Government, and Society in the Medieval Crown of Aragon*, article V, 693–703. Variorum Collected Studies Series CS861. Aldershot: Ashgate.

———. 2007b. "The Line Between Memoir and History: James I of Aragon and the *Llibre dels Feyts*." In *War, Government, and Society in the Medieval Crown of Aragon*, article XII, 165–76. Variorum Collected Studies Series CS861. Aldershot: Ashgate.

Kantorowicz, Ernst Hartwig. 1957. *The King's Two Bodies: A Study in Mediaeval Political Theology*. Princeton: Princeton University Press.

Kelleher, Marie A. 2010. *Measure of Woman: Law and Female Identity in the Crown of Aragon*. Philadelphia: University of Pennsylvania Press.

Kisch, Guido. 1970. *The Jews of Medieval Germany: A Study of Their Social and Legal Status*. 2nd ed. New York: Ktav.

———. 1978. *Forschungen zur Rechts-und Sozialgeschichte der Juden in Deutschland während des Mittelalters*. Sigmaringen: Jan Thorbecke Verlag.

———. 1979. *Jewry-Law in Medieval Germany: Laws and Court Decisions Concerning Jews*. New York: American Academy for Jewish Research.

Klein, Elka. 2005. "Good Servants, Bad Lords: The Abuse of Authority by Jewish Bailiffs in the Medieval Crown of Aragon." In *The Experience of Power in Medieval Europe, 950–1350*, edited by Robert F. Berkhofer III, Alan Cooper, and Adam Kosto, 59–72. Aldershot: Ashgate.

———. 2006. *Jews, Christian Society, and Royal Power in Medieval Barcelona*. Ann Arbor: University of Michigan Press.

Kosto, Adam J. 2001a. "The *Liber feudorum maior* and the Counts of Barcelona: The Cartulary as an Expression of Power." *Journal of Medieval History* 27:1–22.

———. 2001b. "The Limited Impact of the *Usatges de Barcelona* in Twelfth-Century Catalonia." *Traditio* 56:53–88.

———. 2001c. *Making Agreements in Medieval Catalonia: Power, Order, and the Written Word, 1000–1200*. Cambridge Studies in Medieval Life and Thought, 4th ser., 51. Cambridge: Cambridge University Press.

Lacarra, José María. 1981. "Introducción al estudio de los mudéjares aragoneses." In *Actas del I° Simposio Internacional de Mudejarismo*, 17–28. Madrid: Consejo Superior de Investigaciones Científicas and Diputación Provincial de Teruel.

Lalinde Abadía, Jesús. 1963a. *La gobernación general en la Corona de Aragón*. Zaragoza: Institución "Fernando el Católico."

———. 1963b. "Los pactos matrimoniales catalanes (esquema histórico)." *Anuario de la Historia del Derecho Español* 33:133–266.

———. 1966. *La jurisdicción real inferior en Cataluña ("corts, veguers, batlles")*. Seminario de Arqueología e Historia de la Ciudad 14. Barcelona: Ayuntamiento de Barcelona.

———. 1967. "El 'curia' o 'cort' (una magistratura medieval mediterránea)." *Anuario de Estudios Medievales* 4:168–297.

Langmuir, Gavin I. 1990a. "'Iudei nostri' and the Beginning of Capetian Legislation." In *Toward a Definition of Antisemitism*, 137–66. Berkeley: University of California Press.

———. 1990b. "'Tanquam Servi': The Change in Jewish Status in French Law About 1200." In *Toward a Definition of Antisemitism*, 167–94. Berkeley: University of California Press.

Lapeña Paúl, A. I. 1999. "Estudio histórico del *Libro de privilegios de Fraga y sus aldeas* y su época." In *Libro de privilegios de Fraga y sus aldeas*, edited by Guillermo Redondo Veintemillas and Esteban Sarasa Sánchez, 2:11–65. Facsimile ed. Zaragoza: Cortes de Aragón.

León Tello, Pilar. 1989. "La estancia de judíos en castillos." *Anuario de Estudios Medievales* 19:451–67.

Linder, Amnon. 2008. "The Legal Status of the Jews in the Roman Empire." In *The Cambridge History of Judaism*, vol. 4, *The Late Roman-Rabbinic Period*, 128–73. Cambridge: Cambridge University Press.

Linehan, Peter. 1971. *The Spanish Church and the Papacy in the Thirteenth Century*. Cambridge Studies in Medieval Life and Thought, 3rd ser., 4. Cambridge: Cambridge University Press.

Lladonosa Pujol, Josep. 1962. "Proyección urbana de Lérida durante el reinado de Alfonso el Casto." In *VII Congreso de Historia de la Corona de Aragón*, 2:195–205. Barcelona: [Diputación Provincial].

———. 1972–74. *Història de Lleida*. Tàrrega: F. Camps Calmet.

Llop Jordana, Irene. 1999. *Jewish Moneylenders from Vic According to the "Liber Judeorum": 1341–1354*. Jerusalem: Hebrew University of Jerusalem.

———. 2006. "L'aljama de jueus de Vic al segle XIII: Orígens i consolidació de l'aljama (1231–1315)." Ph.D. diss., Universitat de Barcelona.

López Elum, Pedro. 1998. *Los orígenes de los Furs de València y de las Cortes en el siglo XIII*. Valencia: Pedro López Elum.

Lourie, Elena. 1990a. "Anatomy of Ambivalence: Muslims Under the Crown of Aragon in the Late Thirteenth Century." In *Crusade and Colonisation: Muslims, Christians, and Jews in Medieval Aragon*, article VII, 1–77. Variorum Collected Studies Series CS317. Aldershot: Ashgate.

———. 1990b. "Mafiosi and Malsines: Violence, Fear, and Faction in the Jewish Aljamas of Valencia in the Fourteenth Century." In *Crusade and Colonisation: Muslims, Christians, and Jews in Medieval Aragon*, article XII, 69–102. Aldershot: Ashgate.

Maíz Chacón, Jorge. 2010. *Los judíos de Baleares en la baja Edad Media: Economía y política*. Oleiros: Netbiblo.

María, Ramón de. 1943. "Don Poncio de Torrella y el asedio de Peñíscola." *Boletín de la Sociedad Castellonense de Cultura* 18:271–74.

Martínez Palacio, Javier. 1979. *Costums de Tortosa. Estudis*. Tortosa: Centre Associat de Tortosa.

Masiá de Ros, Angeles. 1949. "La cuestión de los límites entre Aragón y Cataluña: Ribagorza y Fraga en tiempos de Jaime II." *Boletín de la Real Academia de Buenas Letras de Barcelona* 22:161–81.

Massip, Jesús. 1984a. "Les *Constitucions de Catalunya* de l'arxiu de la ciutat de Tortosa." *Revista de Llengua i Dret* 4:125–34.

———. 1984b. *La gestació de les Costums de Tortosa*. Tortosa: Consell Intercomarcal de les Terres de l'Ebre.

———. 1995. *Inventari de l'Arxiu Històric de Tortosa*. 2 vols. Tarragona: Diputació de Tarragona.

Maya, Cynthia. 1997. "A Medieval City in Transition: The Tortosa Frontier,

1148–1294." Ph.D. diss., University of California, Los Angeles.

———. 1999. "Conquest and Pragmatism: Jew and Muslim in Post-conquest Tortosa." *Al-Masaq* 11:15–25.

McCrank, Lawrence. 1993. "Documenting Reconquest and Reform: The Growth of the Archives in the Medieval Crown of Aragon." *American Archivist* 56:256–318.

Meyerson, Mark D. 1991. *The Muslims of Valencia in the Age of Fernando and Isabel: Between Coexistence and Crusade.* Berkeley: University of California Press.

———. 2004a. *A Jewish Renaissance in Fifteenth-Century Spain.* Princeton: Princeton University Press.

———. 2004b. *Jews in an Iberian Frontier Kingdom: Society, Economy, and Politics in Morvedre, 1248–1391.* The Medieval and Early Modern Iberian World 20. Leiden: Brill.

Milton, Gregory. 2012. *Market Power: Lordship, Society, and Economy in Medieval Catalonia (1276–1313).* New York: Palgrave MacMillan.

Miravall, Ramon E. 1973. *El call jueu de Tortosa, l'any 1149.* Barcelona: Rafael Dalmau.

———. 1999. *Madīna Turtūxa: Introducció a la Tortosa islàmica.* Tortosa: Dertosa.

———. 2000. "La comunitat jueva de Tortosa i la seva carta de seguretat." In *Les cartes de població cristiana i de seguretat de jueus i sarraïns de Tortosa (1148/1149),* edited by Josep Serrano Daura, 85–104. Barcelona: Universitat Internacional de Catalunya.

Miret y Sans, Joaquín. 1904a. "La carta de franquicias otorgada por el Conde de Barcelona a los judíos de Tortosa." In *Homenaje a D. Francisco Codera en su jubilación del profesorado. Estudios de erudición oriental,* 199–205. Zaragoza: Mariano Escar.

———. 1904b. "Itinerario del Rey Alfonso I de Cataluña, II en Aragón." *Boletín de la Real Academia de Buenas Letras de Barcelona* 4 (15): 389–423; 4 (16): 437–74.

———. 1905–6. "Itinerario del Rey Pedro I de Cataluña, II en Aragón." *Boletín de la Real Academia de Buenas Letras de Barcelona* 5 (18): 79–87; 5 (19): 151–60; 5 (20): 238–49; 6 (21): 265–84; 6 (22): 365–87; 6 (23): 435–50; 6 (24): 497–519.

———. 1918. *Itinerari de Jaume I, "el Conqueridor."* Barcelona: Institut d'Estudis Catalans.

Monjo, Marta. 2004. *Sarraïns sota el domini feudal: La baronia d'Aitona al segle XV.* Lleida: Universitat de Lleida.

Montagut Estragués, Tomàs de. 1993. "La recepción del derecho feudal común en Cataluña (notas para su estudio)." In *Estudios sobre renta, fiscalidad y finanzas en la Cataluña bajomedieval,* edited by Manuel Sánchez Martínez, 153–75. Madrid: Consejo Superior de Investigaciones Científicas.

Morales Arrizabalaga, Jesús. 2007. *Fueros y libertades del Reino de Aragón: De su formación medieval a la crisis preconstitucional (1076–1800).* Zaragoza: Rolde de Estudios Aragoneses.

Motis Dolader, Miguel Ángel. 1990. *Los judíos en Aragón en la Edad Media (siglos XIII–XV).* Colección Mariano de Pano y Ruata 5. Zaragoza: Caja de Ahorros de la Immaculada.

———. 2005. *Los judíos de Teruel en la Edad Media.* Teruel: Instituto de Estudios Turolenses.

Mundill, Robin R. 1998. *England's Jewish Solution: Experiment and Expulsion,*

1262–1290. Cambridge Studies in Medieval Life and Thought, 4th ser., 37. Cambridge: Cambridge University Press.

———. 2010. *The King's Jews: Money, Massacre, and Exodus in Medieval England*. London: Continuum.

Mundó, Anascari M. 1979. "El pacte de Cazola del 1179 i el 'Liber feudorum maior': Notes paleogràfiques i diplomàtiques." In *Jaime I y su época. X Congreso de Historia de la Corona de Aragón*, 1:119–29. Zaragoza: Institución "Fernando el Católico."

Muñoz Jiménez, Isabel. 2003. "Juderías de realengo y juderías de señorío: La judería de Calatayud." In *Juderías y sinagogas de la Sefarad medieval. XI Curso de Cultura Hispanojudía y Serfardí de la Universidad de Castilla–La Mancha*, edited by Eloy Benito Ruano et al., 158–88. Cuenca: Ediciones de la Universidad de Castilla–La Mancha.

Muntner, Süssmann. 1957. "R. Shem Tov Ben Isaac of Tortosa about the Life of the European Jewish Doctor and His Ethics." In *Sinai Jubilee Volume*, edited by Yehudah Lev Hakohen Maimon, 321–27. Jerusalem: Mossad Harav Kook.

Mutgé i Vives, Josefa. 1992. *L'aljama sarraïna de Lleida a l'edat mitjana: Aproximació a la seva història*. Barcelona: Consejo Superior de Investigaciones Científicas.

Nelson, Janet. 1994. "Kingship and Empire in the Carolingian World." In *Carolingian Culture: Emulation and Innovation*, edited by Rosamond McKitterick, 52–87. Cambridge: Cambridge University Press.

Neuman, Abraham A. 1942. *The Jews in Spain: Their Social, Political, and Cultural Life During the Middle Ages*. 2 vols. Philadelphia: Jewish Publication Society of America.

Niermeyer, J. F. 1997. *Mediae latinitatis lexicon minus*. Leiden: E. J. Brill.

Nirenberg, David. 1996. *Communities of Violence: The Persecution of Minorities in the Middle Ages*. Princeton: Princeton University Press.

O'Brien, Bruce R. 1999. *God's Peace and the King's Peace: The Laws of Edward the Confessor*. Philadelphia: University of Pennsylvania Press.

O'Callaghan, Joseph F. 2003. *Reconquest and Crusade in Medieval Spain*. Philadelphia: University of Pennsylvania Press.

O'Connor, Isabel. 2005. "The Mudejars and the Local Courts: Justice in Action." *Journal of Islamic Studies* 16 (3): 332–56.

O'Hanlon, Rosalind. 2000. "Recovering the Subject: *Subaltern Studies* and Histories of Resistance in Colonial South Asia." In *Mapping Subaltern Studies and the Postcolonial*, edited by Vinayak Chaturvedi, 72–115. London: Verso.

Oliver, Bienvenido. 1876–81. *Historia del derecho de Cataluña, Mallorca, y Valencia*. Madrid: M. Ginesta.

Orti Gost, Pere. 2001. "La primera articulación del estado feudal en Cataluña a través de un impuesto: El bovaje (ss. XII–XIII)." *Hispania* 61 (3): 967–98.

Pagarolas, Laurea. 1984. *La comanda del Temple de Tortosa: Primer periode (1148–1213)*. Tortosa: Dertosa.

———. 1999. *Els Templers de les terres de l'Ebre (Tortosa) de Jaume I fins a l'abolició de l'Orde (1213–1312)*. 2 vols. Tarragona: Diputació Provincial de Tarragona.

Pano y Ruata, Mariano de. 1943. *La santa reina Doña Sancha, hermana hospitalaria, fundadora del monasterio de Sijena.* Zaragoza: Berdejo Casanal.

Pastor y Lluis, Federico. 1917. "Disposición de 1297 para el juramento de los judíos de Tortosa." *Boletín de la Real Academia de Buenas Letras de Barcelona* 17 (68): 302–3.

Pennington, Kenneth. 1993. *The Prince and the Law, 1200–1600: Sovereignty and Rights in the Western Legal Tradition.* Berkeley: University of California Press.

Pérez, Joseph. 2007. *History of a Tragedy: The Expulsion of the Jews from Spain.* Translated by Lysa Hochroth. Urbana: University of Illinois Press.

Piles Ros, L. 1990. "El final de la aljama de los judíos de Burriana." *Sefarad* 50:129–66.

Pladevall i Font, Antoni. 1966. "Els senescals dels comtes de Barcelona durant el segle XI." *Anuario de Estudios Medievales* 3:111–30.

Planas, Silvia, and Manuel Forcano. 2009. *Història de la Catalunya jueva: Vida i mort de les comunitats jueves de la Catalunya medieval.* Barcelona: Àmbit and Ajuntament de Girona.

Poulet, André. 1993. "Capetian Women and the Regency: The Genesis of a Vocation." In *Medieval Queenship,* edited by John Carmi Parsons, 93–116. New York: St. Martin's Press.

Powers, James. 1985. "Two Warrior-Kings and Their Municipal Militias: The Townsman-Soldier in Law and Life." In *The Worlds of Alfonso the Learned and James the Conqueror: Intellect and Force in the Middle Ages,* edited by Robert I. Burns, 95–129. Princeton: Princeton University Press.

Ray, Jonathan. 2004. "Royal Authority and the Jewish Community: The Crown Rabbi in Medieval Spain and Portugal." In *Jewish Religious Leadership: Image and Reality,* edited by Jack Wertheimer, 307–31. New York: Jewish Theological Seminary.

———. 2005. "Beyond Tolerance and Persecution: Reassessing Our Approach to *Convivencia.*" *Jewish Social Studies* 11 (2): 1–18.

———. 2006. *The Sephardic Frontier: The Reconquista and the Jewish Community in Medieval Iberia.* Ithaca: Cornell University Press.

———. 2010. "The Jew in the Text: What Christian Charters Tell Us About Medieval Jewish Society." *Medieval Encounters* 16:243–67.

———. 2013. *After Expulsion: 1492 and the Making of Sephardic Jewry.* New York: New York University Press.

Reuther, Timothy, Chris Wickham, and Thomas N. Bisson. 1997. "Debate: The Feudal Revolution." *Past and Present* 155:177–225.

Riera i Sans, Jaume. 1987. "Les llicències reials per predicar als jueus i als sarraïns (segles XIII–XV)." *Calls* 2:113–43.

———. 2000. *Retalls de la vida dels jueus: Barcelona, 1301–Besalú, 1325.* Barcelona: Rafael Dalmau.

———. 2006. *Els poders públics i les sinagogues: Segles XIII–XV.* Girona: Ajuntament de Girona.

———. 2009. "Jaime y los judíos de Cataluña." In *La sociedad en Aragón y Cataluña en el reinado de Jaime I,* edited by Esteban Sarasa Sánchez, 135–55. Zaragoza: Diputación de Zaragoza.

Riu y Cabanas, Ramon. 1892. "Aljama hebrea de Solsona." *Boletín de la Real Academia de la Historia* 21:20–24.

Rodón Binué, Eulalia. 1957. *El lenguaje ténico del feudalismo en el siglo XI en Cataluña: Contribución al estudio del latín medieval.* Barcelona: Escuela de Filología.

Rodríguez-Bernal, Francesc. 2010. *Els vescomtes de Cardona al segle XII: Una història a través dels seus testaments.* El Comtat d'Urgell 7. Lleida: Edicions de la Universitat de Lleida; Institut d'Estudis Ilerdencs.

Romano, David. 1977. "Sobrejunterías de Aragón en 1279–1283." In *Homenaje a don José M. Lacarra en su jubilación del profesorado*, 2:329–51. Zaragoza: Anubar Ediciones.

———. 1983. *Judíos al servicio de Pedro el Grande de Aragón (1276–1285).* Barcelona: Universitat de Barcelona.

———. 1991a. "Característiques dels jueus en relació amb els cristians en els estats hispànics." In *De historia judía hispánica*, 475–90. Col·lecció Homenatges 6. Barcelona: Universitat de Barcelona.

———. 1991b. "Els jueus de Lleida." In *Actes: I. Col·loqui d'història dels jueus a la Corona d'Aragó*, 99–138. Quaderns de l'Institut 2. Lleida: Institut d'Estudis Ilerdencs.

Roth, Norman. 1994. *Jews, Visigoths, and Muslims in Medieval Spain: Cooperation and Conflict.* Medieval Iberian Peninsula 10. Leiden: E. J. Brill.

———. 1995. "The Civic Status of the Jew in Medieval Spain." In *Iberia and the Mediterranean World of the Middle Ages: Studies in Honor of Robert I. Burns, S.J.*, edited by Larry J. Simon, 1:139–62. The Medieval Mediterranean 4. Leiden: Brill.

———, ed. 2003. *Medieval Jewish Civilization: An Encyclopedia.* New York: Routledge.

Rowe, Nina. 2011. *The Jew, the Cathedral, and the Medieval City: Synagoga and Ecclesia in the Thirteenth Century.* Cambridge: Cambridge University Press.

Ruiz, Teofilo. 1985. "Unsacred Monarchy: The Kings of Castile in the Late Middle Ages." In *Rites of Power: Symbolism, Ritual, and Politics Since the Middle Ages*, edited by Sean Wilentz, 109–44. Philadelphia: University of Pennsylvania Press.

———. 2004. *From Heaven to Earth: The Reordering of Castilian Society, 1150–1350.* Princeton: Princeton University Press.

Sabaté, Flocel. 1995. "Discurs i estratègies del poder reial a la Catalunya al segle XIV." *Anuario de Estudios Medievales* 25 (2): 617–46.

———. 1996. "El poder reial entre el poder municipal i el poder baronial a la Catalunya del segle XIV." In *El poder real de la Corona de Aragón (siglos XIV–XVI). Actas del XV° Congreso de Historia de la Corona de Aragón*, vol. 1. pt. ii, 327–42. Zaragoza: Gobierno de Aragón.

———. 1997. *El territori de la Catalunya medieval: Percepció de l'espai i divisió territorial al llarg de l'Edat Mitjana.* Publicacions de la Fundació Salvador Vives Casajuana 123. Barcelona: Fundació Salvador Vives i Casajuana.

———. 2003. *Història de Lleida.* Vol. 2, *Alta Edat Mitjana.* Lleida: Pagès.

———. 2011. "Poder i territori durant el regnat de Jaume I. Catalunya i Aragó." In *Jaume I. Commemoració del naixement de Jaume I*, edited by M. Teresa Ferrer i Mallol, 1:61–130. Memòries de la Secció Històrico-Arqueològica 91–92. Barcelona: Institut d'Estudis Catalans.

Salarrullana de Dios, José. 1989a. "La aljama de judíos de Fraga." In *Estudios históricos acerca de la ciudad de Fraga*, 2:15–108. Fraga: Ayuntamiento de Fraga.

———. 1989b. "Fronteras o límites de Aragón y Cataluña en los tiempos medievales." In *Estudios históricos acerca de la ciudad de Fraga,* 1:119–78. Colección Urganda 4. Fraga: Ayuntamiento de Fraga.

———. 1989c. "El señorío o la honor de Fraga bajo los Moncadas." In *Estudios históricos acerca de la ciudad de Fraga,* 2:315–76. Colección Urganda 5. Fraga: Ayuntamiento de Fraga.

Salleras, Joaquín, and Ramón Espinosa. 1986. *Los Montcada de Fraga: La historia de un señorío catalán en tierras de Aragón.* Fraga: Ayuntamiento de Fraga.

Salrach, Josep M. 1987. *El procès de feudalització (segles III–XII).* Historia de Catalunya 2. Barcelona: Edicions 62.

Sánchez Martínez, Manuel. 2005. "The Invocation of *Princeps namque* in 1368 and Its Repercussions for the City of Barcelona." In *The Hundred Years War: A Wider Focus,* edited by L. J. Andrew Villalon and Donald J. Kagay, 297–329. History of Warfare 25. Leiden: Brill.

Sánchez Real, José. 1951. "La judería de Tarragona." *Sefarad* 11:339–48.

Sanpere y Miquel, Salvador. 1910. *Minoría de Jaime I. Vindicación del procurador Conde Sancho, años 1213–1219.* Barcelona: Imprenta de Francisco Altés.

Sapir Abulafia, Anna. 2011. *Christian-Jewish Relations, 1000–1300: Jews in the Service of Medieval Christendom.* Harlow: Pearson.

Secall i Güell, Gabriel. 1983. *Les jueries medievals tarragonines.* Estudis vallencs 14. Valls: Institut d'Estudis Vallencs.

Segura y Valls, Juan. 1879. *Historia de la villa de Santa Coloma de Queralt.* Barcelona: Imprenta de Vicente Magriñá.

Sénac, Philippe. 2000. *La frontière et les hommes (VIIIe–XIIe siècle): Le peuplement musulman au nord de l'Ebre et les débuts de la reconquête aragonais.* Paris: Maisonneuve et Larose.

Septimus, Bernard. 1979. "Piety and Power in Thirteenth-Century Catalonia." *Studies in Medieval Jewish History and Literature* 1:197–230.

Serrano Daura, Josep. 1997. *El conflicte catalanoaragonès pel territori de la Ribera d'Ebre i de la Terra Alta, en els segles XIII i XIV.* Ascó: Ajuntament d'Ascó.

———, ed. 2000a. *Les cartes de població cristiana i de seguretat de jueus i sarraïns de Tortosa (1148/1149).* Barcelona: Universitat Internacional de Catalunya.

———. 2000b. *Senyoriu i municipi a la Catalunya Nova (segles XII–XIX): Comandes de Miravet, d'Orta, d'Ascó i de Vilalba i baronies de Flix i d'Entença.* 2 vols. Col·lecció Estudis 25. Barcelona: Fundació Noguera.

———. 2006. "La coexistència de les comunitats cristiana, jueva i sarraïna a Tortosa a la baixa edat mitjana." *Revista de Dret Històric Català* 6:173–93.

Serra Vilaró, Joan. 1962–68. *Història de Cardona.* 4 vols. Tarragona: Sugrañes Hnos.

Shatzmiller, Joseph. 1994. *Jews, Medicine, and Medieval Society.* Berkeley: University of California Press.

Shideler, John. 1981. "Les tactiques politiques des Montcada seigneurs de Vic du début du XIIIe siècle." *Ausa* 9:329–42.

———. 1983. *A Medieval Catalan Noble Family: The Montcadas, 1000–1230.* Publications of the Center for Medieval and Renaissance Studies 20. Berkeley: University of California Press.

Shoval, Ilan. 2004. "'Servi regis' Re-examined: On the Significance of the Earliest Appearance of the Term in Aragon, 1176." *Hispania Judaica Bulletin* 4:22–69.

Simonsohn, Shlomo. 1991. *The Apostolic See and the Jews: History*. Studies and Texts 109. Toronto: Pontifical Institute of Mediaeval Studies.

Singer, Isidore, et al., eds. 1908. *The Jewish Encyclopedia: A Descriptive Record of the History, Religion, Literature, and Customs of the Jewish People from the Earliest Times to the Present Day*. 12 vols. New York: Funk and Wagnalls.

Smith, Damian. 2004. *Innocent III and the Crown of Aragon: The Limits of Papal Authority*. Burlington, Vt.: Ashgate.

Soifer, Maya. 2007. "The Jews of the 'Milky Way': Jewish-Christian Relations and Royal Power in Northern Castile-León (ca. 1050 to 1371)." Ph.D. diss., Princeton University.

———. 2009. "Beyond *Convivencia*: Critical Reflections on the Historiography of Interfaith Relations in Christian Spain." *Journal of Medieval Iberian Studies* 1:19–35.

Soifer Irish, Maya. 2013a. "The Castilian Monarchy and the Jews (Eleventh to Thirteenth Centuries)." In *Center and Periphery: Studies in Power in the Medieval World in Honor of William Chester Jordan*, edited by Katherine L. Jansen, G. Geltner, and Anne E. Lester, 39–50. Later Medieval Europe 2. Leiden: Brill.

———. 2013b. "*Tamquam domino proprio*: Contesting Ecclesiastical Lordship over Jews in Thirteenth-Century Castile." *Medieval Encounters* 19:534–56.

Soldevila, Ferran. 1962. *Història de Catalunya*. 2nd ed. Barcelona: Emporium.

———. 1968. *Els primers temps de Jaume I*. Barcelona: Institut d'Estudis Catalans.

Stein, Peter. 1999. *Roman Law in European History*. Cambridge: Cambridge University Press.

Stacey, Robert. 2001. "Jewish Christians in Twelfth-Century England: Some Dynamics of a Changing Relationship." In *Jews and Christians in Twelfth-Century Europe*, edited by Michael Signer and John Van Engen, 340–54. Notre Dame Conferences in Medieval Studies 10. Notre Dame: Notre Dame University Press.

Stow, Kenneth. 1992. *Alienated Minority: The Jews of Medieval Latin Europe*. Cambridge: Harvard University Press.

———. 2007a. "The '1007 Anonymous' and Papal Sovereignty: Jewish Perceptions of the Papacy and Papal Policy in the High Middle Ages." In *Popes, Church, and Jews in the Middle Ages: Confrontation and Response*, article IV, 1–81. Variorum Collected Studies Series CS876. Aldershot: Ashgate.

———. 2007b. "Papal and Royal Attitudes Toward Jewish Lending in the Thirteenth Century." In *Popes, Church, and Jews in the Middle Ages: Confrontation and Response*, article III, 161–84. Variorum Collected Studies Series CS876. Aldershot: Ashgate.

Strayer, Joseph R. 1971. "Defense of the Realm and Royal Power in France." In *Medieval Statecraft and the Perspectives of History: Essays by Joseph R. Strayer*, edited by John F. Benton and Thomas N. Bisson, 380–423. Princeton: Princeton University Press.

Támaro, Eduardo. 1894. "Los judíos en Manresa." In *An Inquiry into the Sources of the History of the Jews in Spain*, edited by Joseph Jacobs, 155–58. London: David Nutt.

Tierney, Brian. 1963. "'The Prince Is Not Bound by the Laws.' Accursius and the Origins of the Modern State." *Comparative Studies in Society and History* 5:378–400.

Tilander, Gunnar. 1933. "El fuero latino de Albarracín." *Revista de Filología Española* 20:278–87.

Tolan, John. 1999. "Une 'convivencia' bien précaire: Le place des juifs et des musulmans dans les sociétés chrétiennes ibérique au Moyen Âge." In *La tolérance: Colloque international de Nantes, mai 1998*, edited by Guy Saupin et al., 385–94. Rennes: Presses universitaires de Rennes.

Torró, Josep. 1999. *El naixement d'una colònia: Dominació i resistència a la frontera valenciana (1238–1276)*. Valencia: Universitat de València.

Turull i Rubinat, Max, and Oriol Oleart. 2000. *Història del dret espanyol*. Barcelona: Universitat de Barcelona.

Ubieto Arteta, Antonio. 1975. *Orígenes del Reino de Valencia: Cuestiones cronológicas sobre su reconquista*. 2 vols. Colección "Obras de investigación" 12. Valencia: Anubar.

———. 1983. *Historia de Aragón*. Vol. 3, *Divisiones administrativas*. Zaragoza: Anubar Ediciones.

Udina Martorell, Frederic. 1986. *Guía histórica y descriptiva del Archivo de la Corona de Aragón*. Madrid: Ministerio de Cultura.

Ullmann, Walter. 1949. "The Development of the Medieval Idea of Sovereignty." *English Historical Review* 64:1–33.

Vanlandingham, Marta. 2002. *Transforming the State: King, Court, and Political Culture in the Realms of Aragon (1213–1387)*. The Medieval Mediterranean World 42. Leiden: Brill.

Vargas, Michael A. 2011. *Taming a Brood of Vipers: Conflict and Change in Fourteenth-Century Dominican Convents*. The Medieval and Early Modern Iberian World 42. Leiden: Brill.

Ventura, Jordi. 1960. *Pere el Catòlic i Simó de Montfort*. Barcelona: Aedos.

Vidal Franquet, Jacobo. 2008. *Les obres de la ciutat: L'activitat constructiva i urbanística de la universitat de Tortosa a la baixa edat mitjana*. Biblioteca "Abat Oliba" 282. Barcelona: Publicacions de l'Abadia de Montserrat.

Vidal Mayor, un libro de fueros del siglo XIII: Estudios. 1989. 2 vols. Huesca: Diputación Provincial de Huesca.

Villanueva, Jaime, et al. 1803–52. *Viage literario á las iglesias de España*. 22 vols. Madrid: Imprenta Real.

Virgili, Antoni. 1997b. "Acerca del quinto templario. La Orden del Temple y los Condes de Barcelona en la conquista de Al-Andalus." *Anuario de Estudios Medievales* 27 (2): 775–802.

———. 2001b. "'Ad detrimentum Yspanie': La conquesta de Ṭurṭūša i la formació de la societat feudal (1148–1200)*. Barcelona: Universitat Autònoma de Barcelona.

———. 2009. "*Angli cum multis aliis alienigenis*: Crusade Settlers in Tortosa (Second Half of the Twelfth Century)." *Journal of Medieval History* 35 (3): 297–312.

Vose, Robin. 2009. *Dominicans, Muslims, and Jews in the Medieval Crown of Aragon*. Cambridge Studies in

Medieval Life and Thought, 4th ser., 74. Cambridge: Cambridge University Press.

Watt, J. A. 1991. "The Jews, the Law, and the Church: The Concept of Jewish Serfdom in Thirteenth-Century England." In *The Church and Sovereignty, c. 590–1918: Essays in Honour of Michael Wilks*, edited by Diana Wood, 153–72. Studies in Church History: Subsidia 9. Oxford: Basil Blackwell.

Willoweit, Dietmar. 1988. "Vom Königsschutz zur Kammerknechtschaft. Anmerkungen zum Rechtsstatus der Juden im Hochmittelalter." In *Geschichte und Kultur des Judentums: Eine Vorlesungsreihe an der Julius-Maximilians-Universität, Würzburg*, edited by Karlheinz Müller and Klaus Wittstadt, 71–89. Quellen und Forschungen zur Geschichte des Bistums und Hochstifts Würzburg 38. Würzburg: Kommissionsverlag F. Schöningh.

Ziegler, Joseph. 1992. "Reflections on the Jewry Oath in the Middle Ages." In *Christianity and Judaism: Papers Read at the 1991 Summer Meeting and the 1992 Winter Meeting of the Ecclesiastical History Society*, edited by Diana Wood, 209–20. Studies in Church History 29. Oxford: Oxford University Press.

———. 2003. "Jewish Oath." In *Medieval Jewish Civilization: An Encyclopedia*, edited by Norman Roth, 483–87. New York: Routledge.

Zimmermann, Michel. 1988. "Le concept de Marca Hispanica et l'importance de la frontière dans la formation de la Catalogne." In *La Marche supérieure d'Al-Andalus et l'occident chrétien*, edited by Philippe Sénac, 29–48. Publications de la Casa de Velázquez. Série Archéologie 15. Madrid: Casa de Valázquez.

———. 1993. "Le rôle de la frontière dans la formation de la Catalogne (IX–XIIème siècle)." In *Las sociedades de frontera en la España medieval. Aragón en la Edad Media: Sesiones de trabajo. II seminario de historia medieval*, 7–29. Zaragoza: Universidad de Zaragoza.

Index

d'Abbeville, Jean, 68–69, 72
abbot of Valldigna, 1–4
Abecimfa, Alazar, 236 n. 29
Abenbruc, Salamó, 77
Abinbentalcan, Aser, 163
Abulafia, David, 5
Açavella, Abraham, 1–3, 207
Açday, Naci, 167
adelantats (also *adelantados*)
    duties of, 77–78, 103
    fiscal functions of, 78, 103
    presence of, in Tortosa, 172
    required to swear oath of maledictions, 177–78, 180–81, 182, 246 n. 58
    responsibility of, regarding flood damage, 182, 183–86
    right to elect, 103, 105-6, 145, 196
    right to elect, granted to Calatayud, 73–74, 98
    system of, throughout Catalonia, 77–78, 167–68
Aeça, Azmet, 1–3
Aitona, 204, 205–6, 208–9
Alaçar, David, 156–57
Albala, Jahuda, 126

Albaney, Azac, 109–10
Albarine, Abrahim, 105
Albarracín, 205
Alcañíz, 149–50, 173, 241 n. 39
Alcohen, Mosse, 126
Alconstantini, Mosse, 76, 227 n. 93
Alconstantini, Salamó, 76, 77
Alexander II (pope), 6
Alfons I
    and the *Gesta Comitum Barchinonensium* (*Deeds of the Counts of Barcelona*), 8
    borrowing by, 38–42
    creation and modification of Peace and Truce under, 9, 58, 59, 60, 69
    and declining royal authority over Tortosa, 53
    fiscal crisis under, 47
    and the *Fuero de Teruel*, 5
    grants exemption on commerce levies, 34
    jurisdiction of, over Tortosa's Jews, 42–46
    last will and testament of, 47
    and leveraging of Tortosa, 40–42

Alfons I (*continued*)
    and the *Liber feudorum maior* (*Great Book of the Fiefs*), 8
    policies and administrative strategies of, 8, 38
    and protection of Jews in Tortosa, 42–45, 88
    and rates of visitation to Tortosa and Lleida, 66–67
    and receipt of homage from men of Tortosa, 42, 107
    and Sancha of Castile, 47
    system of toll collection under, 34–35
    withdrawal of, from lordship over Tortosa, 40

Alfons II
    and *collecta* of Tortosa, 151, 152
    and counts of Empúries, 203
    crown initiatives under, 144
    and jurisdiction over Fraga, 199–200, 202
    renegotiation under and Corts of 1283, 153–56
    and retention of position of rabbi of the Jews of Aragon, 77
    royal visitations under, 226 n. 57
    and Templar commander of Alcañíz, 241 n. 39

Alfons III
    confirmation of Montcada family's lordship over Fraga by, 249 n. 35
    and jurisdiction over Fraga, 202–3

Alfonso VII of Castile-León, 12–13, 45–46, 78
Alfonso X (of Castile-León), 78, 152
aljama(s), Jewish, 15, 16, 18, 20, 21, 43, 74, 76, 77, 78, 93, 95, 97–98, 101, 102, 103, 105–6, 113, 117, 122, 123, 124, 125, 126, 129, 132, 135, 136, 143–44, 145–46, 147, 148, 149–52, 155–56, 158, 159, 164, 165, 167, 169, 172–73, 174, 175–76, 177–79, 181, 183–84, 192–93, 194, 195, 198–199, 202–3, 206, 212, 218 n. 101, 221 n. 95
aljama(s), Muslim, 48, 85–86, 166, 175, 182, 185, 208, 235 n. 25

Almohac, Ali, 50
Alzira, 1, 206–7, 238 n. 73
Amelii, Bernat, 65
Almuli, Jucef, 126
Amposta, 67, 133, 238 n. 67
Anastasius IV (pope), 190
Aquinas, Thomas, 6
Aragon (region)
    collecta of Tortosa as pertaining to, 149–50
    collecta of Lleida as pertaining to, 151
    communal rights for Jews in, 146
    general judge or rabbi of the Jews of, 77
    Hospitaller rights over Jews and Muslims in, 163
    Jewish oath in, 176
Assis, Yom Tov, 10–11, 16
Astruc, Maimó, 195
Astruc, Vidal, 195, 249 n. 34
d'Asús, Haió, 36–37
Augustine, 6
Aurell, Jaume, 8
"autonomy by default," 18, 73, 84, 102, 147, 165
"autonomy by design," 18, 73, 103, 145–146, 149, 165, 174
Avinachura, Azac, 157
Avinahole, Abobacher, *alcaydus*, 85–86
Avincara, Mosse, 109–10
Avinzabarra, Jafias, 104–5, 236 n. 29

Baer, Yitzhak, 12, 33, 213
bailiff(s) (of monarchy)
    activity and powers of, 41, 43, 48, 85–86, 123
    dismissal of Jewish, 140
    efforts by monarchy to enlarge powers of, 129–30
    involvement of, in upholding peace legislation, 60–61
    Jaume requests right to maintain, in Tortosa, resident, 56–57
    restrictions to office of, 56–57, 81–82, 103, 239 n. 2
    return of royal, 66–67, 121–28, 136

royal administration in Tortosa without, 139–43
withdrawal of dedicated royal, in Tortosa, 65
bailiff(s) (of Templar Order), 39, 41, 56, 87, 94, 108, 121
bailiff(s) (of Montcada family), 45, 87, 107–12
bailiff(s) (of joint seigniorial regime), 121–22
bailiff(s) general (of Valencia), 1–2, 12
Al-Bakrī, 34
Banyeres (castle), 91–93, 99–101, 229 n. 34. *See also* fortified refuges, for Jews
Barcelona (town)
    bishop of, 225 n. 32
    collaboration of Jews in, 211
    Corts held at, 59, 68, 70, 111, 131, 153–55
    customary laws of, applied to Tortosa or other lordships, 16, 27–28, 112, 147, 166, 176
    Jewish communal organization in, as observed by Klein, 7, 11, 18, 27, 90, 164, 236 n. 27
    migration of Jews to, 244 n. 29, 247–48 n. 77
    paers of, 228 n. 98
    privileges awarded to Jewish community of, 71, 74, 98, 104, 105
    and relief for frontier Tortosa, 37
    royal authority over, 20
    royal household in, 105
    royal officials in, 142, 148, 162
    royal visitations to, 226 n. 57
    subsidy responsibilities of Jewish *aljama* of, 122, 129, 150–52, 195, 211, 237 nn. 48,49
Barcelona (county), 8
baths, in Tortosa
    administration of, 113, 233–34 n. 110
    right to use, included in the *Consuetudines* and *Costums*, 116, 233 n. 101
Benifassà, 49, 223 n. 125
ben Isaac, Shem Tov, 89–90
Benjamin of Tudela, 34
ben Saruq, Menaḥem, 25
Bensch, Stephen, 18, 23, 105, 165, 203–4

Berenguer, Ramon IV
    administative strategy, 26, 28–29, 53
    establishes Jewish community at Tortosa, 19, 25–26, 28, 31, 33
    grants individual Jewish privileges, 43–44
    issues Muslim charter of security, 25, 34–35
    Jewish policy of, 29–31
    territorial expansion and governance under, 7–8
Besalú, 103, 104, 105, 122, 129, 218 n. 91
Bisson, Thomas, 7, 8, 26, 64, 161, 162, 172
Blanche (of Champagne), Countess, 191
Blasco Martínez, Asunción, 15
Boniface VIII (pope), 205
Bonsenyor, 134
Bonsenyor, Vidal de, 239 n. 75, 247 n. 77
Boswell, John, 15
bovatge, 39, 59, 60, 124, 134, 139
Burns, Robert I., 17–18, 124

Calatayud
    privileges awarded to Jews of (1229), 73–74 97–98, 104, 146, 230 n. 54
    administration of Jewish oath in, 177
Calixtus II (pope), 6
Cap, Isaac, 206
Cardona, Esteve de, 142
Cardona, Guillem de, 68
Cardona, Viscount of, 145
Carreras y Candi, Francesch, 246 n. 63
Carta de la Paeria (1275), 118, 169, 234 n. 117
Carta del sagrament (1297), 177
Castejón de la Puente, castle of, 39
Castellet, Romeu de, 141
Catalonia
    application of *Usatges de Barcelona* in, 9, 111
    communal rights for Jews in, 145–46
    crown's emergency measures regarding Jews and Muslims during famine in, 72
    end of Jewish officialdom in, 140
    feudalism in, 10
    general legal conditions in, 131, 154

Catalonia *(continued)*
  Jewish oath throughout, 176–180
  legal circumstances of Jews in, 59, 77–78, 102, 147–48, 159
  Lleida's affiliation with, 151
  market for Jewish settlers in, 27
  noble opposition to the crown in, 51, 131
  peace constitutions governing, 58–63, 69–70
  procurator of, 61
  royal authority and administration in, 26, 42, 58, 72, 77–78, 161, 169, 174–75
  and Sepharad, 229 n. 29
  standardized system of *adelantats* in, 168
  subsidy demands for Jewish *aljamas* of, 150, 151
  territorial limits of, 63, 149
  Tortosa's affiliation with, 149–51
Catlos, Brian, 18–19
Cavalleria, Jafuda de la (bailiff), 76
Celestine III (pope), 222 n. 110
Ceret, Guillem de (local officer in Tortosa), 181–82
Cervera
  Corts held at (1202), 59–60
  receipt of Lleida's Jewish privileges by, 175
Cervera, Guillem (IV) de
  as administrative co-lord in Tortosa, 50
  granted lordship over Tortosa and Benifallet, 48–49
  participation in Corts under Jaume I, 69
  receives fiefs in vicinity of Tortosa according to the *Usatges de Barcelona*, 232 n. 92
  as royal ally and creditor, 51
  as royal lieutenant, 65, 93, 94
  and transfer of his rights to Tortosa to the Templars, 51–52, 65, 85
Charles II of Anjou, 190

Cheyette, Frederic, 126
Choen (land owner), 36–37
Christian-Jewish relations
  in Perpignan, 116–17
  in Tortosa, 117
  in wider Crown of Aragon, 5–6
Cogdez, Azac avi, 43–44
Cohen, Jucef, 142
collecta(s) (groupings of Jewish communities for tax assessment)
  of Girona-Besalú, 103–4, 122
  inconsistencies in system of, 149–51
  role of Jewish officers in administering, 78, 103, 145
  tax evasion and, 149–51
  Tortosa as head of new, 173, 241 n. 44
Commemoracions (Customs of Catalonia), 73, 131, 143, 155, 237 n. 57
Constitucions de Catalunya, 178–80, 204, 238 n. 59
Consuetudines Dertuse civitatis, 114–18, 176, 178
conversion, laws regarding, of Jews and Muslims, 72
convivencia, 18, 164–65, 218 n. 97. *See also* micro-*convivencia*
Costums de Tortosa, 114–18, 146, 166–67, 169–70, 176–80, 184, 229 n. 21, 230 n. 60, 233 n. 101, 234 nn. 117, 118, 238 n. 59, 239 n. 2, 243 n. 21
Crown of Aragon
  composition, location, and political formation of, 4, 7
  extent of royal jurisdiction within, 7–10, 161–63
  Jewish communal identity within, 211–13
  jurisdiction over Jews in, as compared with other kingdoms, 5–7, 15, 46, 159, 165, 189–93, 210
  litigation involving Jews within, 180
  political circumstances of, 138, 153, 157–58, 205, 209
  seigniorial privileges to Jews in, 97

servi regis principle in, 5, 10, 12, 14, 158
use of multiple judicial forums by subjects in, 113, 186, 195
customary laws. *See* individual law codes by title

Daileader, Philip, 18, 117
debt. *See also* moneylending
  of crown under Alfons I, 38–47, 221 n. 72
  of crown under Pere I, 47–51
  of crown under Jaume I, 53, 61–63, 121, 123, 132–33, 162, 197
  of French crown, 14
  of municipality of Tortosa, 101
Delmas, Sebastià, 142
dominium
  baronial, in France, 13
  held by the Templars elsewhere, 157
  held by the Templars in Tortosa, 40–41, 43–44, 46, 110
  seigniorial, in Tortosa, 52, 83
Dona, widow of Azac, 43–44, 88
Douai, Pierre de, 61
dower, of Sancha of Castile, 47
Durfort, Guillem, 224 n. 30

Ebro River, 31, 34–35, 133, 150, 181, 228 n. 13, 246 n. 60
Ebro Valley, 18, 35, 38–42, 47, 66, 138, 204, 238 n. 66
ecclesiastical jurisdiction over Jews, 189–93
Edward I (of England), 13
Edward the Confessor (of England), 12
elite Jews, in Tortosa. *See also* Jews, elite
  education of, 89–90
  exemption of, 43–45
  identification of, 90–91
Elukin, Jonathan, 23
Empúries
  activity of independent counts of, vis-à-vis royal policy-making, 8, 69, 70–71, 105–6
  conflict with the crown over autonomy of, 203–4
  Jewish policy elaborated by counts of, 18, 23, 71, 95, 165–66, 193
Escandarani, Mosse, 141
ethnoreligious groups
  in Lleida, 167–68
  membership within, 125
  methodology of scholarship on, 10–11, 18, 22–23, 57, 164–65, 171, 224 n. 5, 233 n. 102, 233 n. 107
  positioning in Tortosa's urban landscape, 32
  as regulated in the *Costums de Tortosa*, 114–19
  relations of, 19, 30, 91, 107–8, 113–14, 180, 188, 248 n. 78
exemptions. *See* taxation, exemption from

Fancy, Hussein, 216 n. 22
Fernando IV (of Castile-León), 190–91
Foix, Count of, 145
Folch, Ramon, 194–95
fortified refuges, for Jews, 87–88, 91–93
Fourth Lateran Council (1215), 68–69, 191, 226 n. 62
Fraga, 196–203, 241 n. 47
Frederick I Barbarossa (of German Empire), 190
Frederick II (of German Empire), 190
Freedman, Paul, 10, 60
Fuero de Calatalifa, 12–13
Fuero de Teruel, 5, 7, 10–13, 15, 30, 43, 45, 59, 70, 74, 205, 217 nn. 52, 60, 218 n. 80
Fueros de Aragón, 131, 205, 245 n. 45, 250 n. 48
Fueros de Cuenca, 45, 217 n. 52
Furs de València, 2, 3, 12, 70, 75, 114, 176, 207, 239 n. 2

Gesta Comitum Barchinonensium (Deeds of the Counts of Barcelona), 8
Girona
  bishop of, 70
  Corts held at, 72, 176

Girona (*continued*)
    mandates concerning Jewish community of, 148, 204
    payments of tribute by Jewish community of, 129, 237 n. 49
    privileges and exemptions awarded to Jewish community of, 71, 74, 103, 104–5, 122, 144
Gonzalvo i Bou, Gener, 29
Gregory IX (pope), 190
Guardia, Arnau, 142
Guardia, Ramon de (Montcada bailiff), 109–10
guidatge (also *guidaticum* and *carta guidatici*; license of safe passage), 80, 95, 104–5, 124, 125, 236 n. 29

hierarchy, disputes over Tortosa's seigniorial, 106–9
Holy Week violence against Jews, 144
homicide, punishments for, 29–30, 169, 212
Honorius III (pope), 191
Hospitallers, 106, 133, 163–64, 227 n. 77
Hug IV (of Empúries), Count, 69
Huesca, Cortes held at (1247), 72, 205

Ibn Adret, Salomon (rabbi), 14
Al-Idrīsī, Muhammad, 34
Innocent III (pope), 62, 222 n. 110
ius commune, 111, 131, 238 n. 59
ius maletractandi (right of mistreatment), 9, 69

Jaume I
    appoints Naci Açday as crown rabbi of Lleida, 167
    and campaign to capture Penyíscola, 66, 89,
    borrowing by, 62, 63–64, 105, 121, 123, 125, 132–33, 162–63
    competition of, with Tortosa's seigniorial regime, 95–99
    convoking of Cort(e)s by or under, 59, 61, 62, 63, 64, 66, 68, 69, 70–73, 102, 108, 111, 131, 135, 140, 176, 205
    development and diffusion of royal policies under, 68–78
    evolution of Jewish policy under, 59, 62–64, 68–77
    on fiscal policies of Alfons and Pere, 53, 63, 225 n. 33
    governmental activity through minority of, 61–64
    installation and activity of royal bailiff in Tortosa under, 120, 122–28, 135–36
    intervention of, in Tortosa's seigniorial administration, 64–68, 78–81, 94, 103–5, 125–26, 135–37, 170–71
    and Jewish oath-taking rituals, 176
    and jurisdiction over Fraga, 196–97
    manipulates Perpignan's customary laws, 174–75
    Pere II builds on tactics of, 139
    pervasiveness of royal governance under, 11
    policies and administrative strategies of, 8
    and pursuit of rights to a bailiff in seigniorial Tortosa, 55–58, 136
    rates of visitation by, 66–67
    requires Jews to repay debts owed by deceased royal bailiff, 162–63
    retreats from use of *ius commune* in courts, 111
    treatment of seigniorial autonomies under, 10
Jaume II
    administration of Tortosa by, 158–59, 173–74
    alters statutes in the *Vidal Mayor* and *Fueros de Aragón*, 205
    appeals for exclusive right to exercise criminal jurisdiction, 204–5
    assigns charter of donation to abbots of Valldigna, 3
    concedes income from Aitona to Ot de Montcada, 209
    and court case regarding responsibility for flood damage in Tortosa, 184–85

and Jewish oath-taking rituals, 178
and jurisdiction over Fraga, 200, 202
and jurisdiction over Vic, 194
licenses migration of Jews from Lleida
    to Aitona, 206
reduces office of rabbi or judge of Jews
    of Aragon, 77
and royal acquisition of Tortosa,
    157–58
Jewish *call* (quarter), in Fraga, 201
Jewish *call* (quarter), new, of Tortosa
    collaboration with old Jewish *call*, 101
    expansion of, 100–101, 228 n. 11
    positioning and characteristics of,
        99–100, 230 n. 58
Jewish *call* (quarter), old, of Tortosa
    collaboration of, with new Jewish *call*,
        101
    demographics of, 90
    flood damage in, 181–84
    under Jewish charter, 88, 90
    openness to non-Jewish property own-
        ership, 31, 91
    positioning and characteristics of,
        31–32, 99–100
Jewish charter(s)
    ad hoc, 75
    and alteration under seigniorial admin-
        istration in Tortosa, 88, 94
    awarded to Calatayud, Mallorca,
        Valencia, Barcelona, and Girona,
        73–76
    conditions and intentions of, for
        Tortosa, 27–37, 103–4, 166, 183
    issued to Tortosa by Ramon Berenguer
        IV, 25–26, 74
    and Tortosa's physical environment,
        31–33
    of Tortosa's seigniorial regime (1228),
        87–95, 99
Jews
    accommodation and protection of, as
        advocated by theologians and
        jurists, 21
    administration of, in accordance with
        customary regulations, 153–55

as citizens under *Consuetudines Dertuse
    civitatis* and *Costums de Tortosa*,
    115–18
as community members, 22–23,
    218–19 n. 109
court procedures for cases involving,
    147–48
desire an analog to the Cort(e)s, 211
ecclesiastical jurisdiction over, 189–93
elite, 18, 43–44, 45, 76–77, 89–91,
    121–25, 140, 173, 195, 210,
    232 n. 88, 236 n. 27
implications of royal acquisition for,
    172–75
implications of seigniorial acquisition
    for, 42–46, 84–87, 87–88, 101–2,
    107
impressions of, concerning royal
    administration, 81, 144–45,
    149–51
impressions of, concerning seigniorial
    administration, 81, 113
involvement of, in legal dispute
    between lords and citizens in
    Tortosa, 112–14
judgment of legal cases involving, 22,
    76–77, 78, 80, 100–2, 108–10,
    113, 115, 117–118, 122, 126–27, 131,
    142, 145–46, 147–48, 154, 156–57,
    166–70, 172, 176–86, 190–91,
    192–93, 194–95, 200, 206, 207
methodological approaches to the study
    of, 21–23, 164–65
obligation of, to use municipal court,
    in Tortosa, 22, 74, 80, 108, 113–14,
    117–18, 146, 147, 166–67, 169,
    170, 176–77, 179
obligation of, to use seigniorial court, in
    Solsona, 194
organization and representation desired
    by, in mid-fourteenth century,
    211–13
and political development of Crown of
    Aragon, 4–10
in positions of authority under Pere II,
    140

Jews (*continued*)
    presence of, in Tortosa during Andalusi period, 25–26, 33
    relocation of, to or from royal lands, 13, 72, 104, 179, 205–6, 212–13, 244 n. 29
    regulations concerning the conversion of, 72
    required to pay tribute. *See* subsidies; taxation
    responsibility of, to repair flood damage in Tortosa, 182–86
    role of, in development and jurisdictional history of Tortosa, 164–65
    as royal administrators, 122–26, 147–48
    royal regulations concerning, under Jaume I. *See* Jaume I
    sequestering of, during Holy Week, 144
    settlement of, in Tortosa, 32–33
    standardization of communal conditions of, 210–11
    and willingness to collaborate with monarchy, 147
Joan I, 169–70, 204, 243 nn. 18,19
Jordan, William Chester, 13, 126
jurisdiction. *See* royal governance and jurisdiction; seigniorial administration; seigniorial authority

Kagay, Donald J., 237 n. 57
kashrut (Jewish religious dietary laws), 33
Klein, Elka, 7, 11, 18, 23, 77–78, 90, 164, 165
Kosto, Adam, 9

land ownership
    decline of royal, in Tortosa, 64–65
    Jewish, in Tortosa, 32–33, 36–37, 88
    in Jewish quarter, 91
    Muslim, in Tortosa, 31–32, 33
lèse majesté (crime of violating majesty), 69, 75, 79
Liber feudorum maior (*Great Book of the Fiefs*), 8, 38, 58
Lleida
    Andalusi principality of, 7
    bishop of, 112, 234 n. 111
    citizens of, 121
    consulate in, 61
    diocese of, 72
    Corts held at (1214), 61, 224 n. 8
    judicial framework of, 167
    lack of Jewish and Muslim settlement charters for, 167
    migration of Jews from, 206, 244 n. 29
    officials based in, 65, 116, 142, 199, 209
    privileges given to, 167–68, 175
    property rights of Montcada family in, 196–97
    restrictions of wheat sales in, 72
    rise of, as royal administrative center, 66, 197
    royal property or incomes in, 41, 231 n. 73, 236 n. 29
    royal visitations to, 66–68, 226 n. 57
    as source of foodstuffs for Tortosa, 37
    subsidy responsibilities of, 122, 129, 149, 151, 237 n. 48, 250 n. 59
    vicariate of, 199, 241 n. 47
lleuda (commerce levy), 34, 37, 40, 42, 61, 108, 109, 124, 157
loans. *See also* debt
    collection of by Jews, facilitated by the crown, 1, 105, 125, 126, 133, 141, 148, 198, 206–7
    confiscation of improper Jewish, 72, 135–36
    held by Jews, 72, 105, 125, 133, 141, 181–82, 191
    regulations concerning, by the crown, 74, 148, 174–75, 198
Louis IX (of France), 13
Luna, Lope Ferrench de, 203

Maimó, Abraham, 121, 122
Maimó, Jafias, 125–26, 135
Mallorca, 72, 74, 229 n. 22
malsins (Jewish informers), 125, 196, 212, 235 n. 26, 251 n. 103
Marcus, Ivan, 23
Margalida, Dona, 110
Marseille, 89–90, 190

Martí (Infant), 207
merum et mixtum imperium (also *mixt o mer imperi*; criminal and civil justice), 3, 12, 131, 154, 157, 204–5, 237 n. 56, 250–51 n. 71
Meyerson, Mark, 123
micro-*convivencia(s)*
   defined, 19
   diversification of, 23–24, 84, 168
   of Lleida, 168
   of Tortosa, 84, 86–87, 101, 106, 114–19, 165–66, 175, 187
   of Tortosa, as compared with other cases, 233 n. 108
   persistence of, 187
   role of non-royal authorities in developing, 14, 189
migration. *See* Jews; Muslims (Andalusis); Muslims (resident; *mudéjares*)
miscegenation laws, 114, 118, 234 n. 116
moneylending. *See* debt; loans
Monjo, Marta, 208–9
Montcada, Guillem (II) de (lord of Fraga) (d.
   and jurisdiction over Fraga, 196, 199, 200–201
   and royal acquisition of Tortosa, 157
Montcada, Ot de (baron of Aitona), 208, 209
Montcada, Ramon (II) de (lord of Tortosa) (d. 1229)
   consents to renewal of Jews' privileges in Tortosa, 45
   and development and diffusion of royal policies under Jaume I, 69, 71
   exerts control over the office of *zalmedina* in Tortosa, 86
   and imposition and collection of levies, 35, 48, 152–53
   and seigniorial administration of Tortosa, 50, 86
   and seigniorial disputes, 106–7
   supports Jaume I's peace initiatives, 64
Montcada, Ramon (III) de (lord of Tortosa and Fraga) (d. ca. 1286)
   and accessibility of Banyeres, 93
   and enforcement of crown initiatives, 146
   exerts control over the office of *zalmedina* in Tortosa, 109
   and imposition and collection of levies, 152–53
   and lordship over Fraga, 197, 198
   and opposition to royal bailiff in Tortosa, 127–28
   and seigniorial disputes, 107–12
Montcada family
   and administration of Tortosa, 19, 40, 50, 83–84, 87, 107, 222 n. 110
   and disputes with Templars over Tortosa's administration, 84, 106–12
   hereditary rights over local offices in Tortosa, 61, 65, 86, 109, 146, 228 n. 6
   and jurisdiction over Aitona, 206
   and jurisdiction over Fraga, 196–97, 199–201
   and jurisdiction over Vic, 193–94
   and tradition of service to the crown, 134, 146
Montpellier, 72, 75–76, 89, 225 n. 32
Morales Arrizabalaga, Jesús, 73
Mordofay, Açim, 235 n. 21
Mordofay, Muschet, 124, 235 n. 21, 238 n. 62
morería (Muslim quarter), 32, 100, 108, 109, 184, 208, 219–20 n. 27, 220 n. 32
Morlans, Rotlan de, 36
Morvedre
   Jewish bailiffs in, 123, 134, 234–35 n. 11
   as member of Valencian *collecta*, 151
Motis Dolader, Miguel, 15
Muslim charter of security (Tortosa), 27, 34–35, 166
Muslims (Andalusi)
   calculus made by surrendering, in Tortosa, 28
   flight of elite, 31–32
   potential for migration of, 27
   shipyards and walls established by, in Tortosa, 31
   trading by, 33–34

Muslims (resident; *mudéjares*)
    accommodation and protection of, 21
    as community members, 22–23
    conversion of, 72
    as borrowers, 1
    as creditors, 62–63
    elite, 31–32, 85–86
    excluded from citizenship clause in *Consuetudines*, 115–16
    excluded from exemption on commerce levies, 34
    influence of provisions of protection over, 69
    Jaume I's policy shift regarding, 59
    judgment of cases between, 109
    relocation of, to or from royal lands, 27–28, 205, 208–9
    renegotiation of jurisdictional rights over, 154–55
    responsibility of, to repair flood damage, 184, 185
    restrictions on the mobility of, in the *Vidal Mayor*, 205
    revolts by, 121
    rights of, in Lleida, 167
    royal jurisdiction over, 12–13
    and seigniorial administration of Tortosa, 84–86
    status of, under *Consuetudines Dertuse civitatis*, 117–18
    in Tortosa, 31–32, 33

Neuman, Abraham, 17
nobility
    Aragonese, 61, 48, 73, 131, 251 n. 76
    capitalizes on crown's need for support, 153, 198
    Catalan, 60–61, 131, 145, 195
    French, 13–14
    loses prerogatives to crown by means of *convenientiae*, 9
    promotion of the *Usatges de Barcelona* by, 111–12
    revolts by, 130–31, 145, 203, 237–38 n. 57

oath-taking
    acts of, 61, 131, 135
    disputing over Jewish, 176–81, 183
    Muslim, 234 n. 118
    procedures for, 5, 70, 72, 118, 176–78, 179, 180–81, 184, 234 n. 118, 239 n. 79, 245 nn. 41,45
Ordinance of Melun (1230), 13–14

paers, 61, 77–78, 118, 140–41, 228 n. 98, 236 n. 34, 239 n. 5, 248 n. 78
Palencia, 46, 190–91
Peace and Truce
    assemblies and constitutions establishing, 8–9, 16, 56, 58–59, 60, 61, 63, 69, 204, 224 n. 8, 225 n. 37, 241 n. 38
    enlargement of, through Jaume's reign, 59–63, 69, 79
    monarchy's responsibility to defend, 30, 49, 61, 65, 69, 131, 143, 153, 155
peace, with Muslims, 62
pedatge (commerce levy), 34, 37, 56, 61, 124
Pedro I (of Aragon), 45
Pedrola, 203
Penyíscola, 64, 66, 123–24, 133, 157, 235 nn. 20,21, 236 n. 29, 238 n. 67
Pere Albert, 73, 131, 143, 154, 227 n. 83
Pere de Queralt, 16
Pere de Trilles, 198–99
Pere I
    adjudicates dispute between Templars and citizens of Tortosa, 47
    authorizes consular regime in Lleida, 167
    borrowing by, 50–51
    confirms donation of Tortosa to Templars, 48
    confirms exemption to heirs of *alfaquim* of Tortosa, 44
    death of, 61, 83
    exempts Hospitaller domains from taxation, 163–64
    exempts Muslim family in Tortosa, 50, 65

grants lordship over Tortosa and
     Benifallet to Guillem (IV) de
     Cervera, 48–51
as heir of Alfons I, 47–48
interaction of, with Jews and Muslims
     of Calatayud, 97–98
moves away from direct lordship over
     Tortosa, 38, 56, 64, 171
offers Tortosa economic relief package,
     37
Peace and Truce established by, 59–60,
     61–62, 63, 69
policies and administrative strategies
     of, 8
potential for interaction of, with elite
     Jews in seigniorial Tortosa, 45
protection of non-Christians under, 59
and rates of visitation to Tortosa and
     Lleida, 66–67
reallocates Tortosa to Templar Order,
     51–52
reduces tithe obligations in Tortosa,
     35–36
and Sancha of Castile, 47–49
secures possession of Jews and
     Muslims in Hospitaller domains,
     163–64
and seigniorial authority over Tortosa,
     53–54
taxation imposed by, 61
Pere II
     applies *Fueros de Aragón* to non-noble
          citizens of Fraga, 250 n. 48
     attempts to administer Tortosa, 139–43
     borrowing by, 133
     collection of Jewish subsidies under,
          151
     convokes Cort(e)s, 153, 155, 159
     and Corts of 1283, 153–57
     creates office of rabbi or judge of Jews
          of Aragon, 77
     crown initiatives regarding Jews under,
          143–49
     demands subsidy from Jews of Solsona,
          195

eliminates system of Jewish bailiffs,
     140
and jurisdiction over Jews of Fraga,
     197–99
manages Jewish oath-taking rituals,
     176–77
and service of Astruc Xixó, 133
Pere III
     confirms charter of donation to
          Valldigna, 3
     confirms Tortosa's customary privileges,
          170
     convokes Cort(e)s, 209
     defends regalians rights to Jews,
          192–93
     pervasiveness of royal governance
          under, 12
     restores domains in Valencia to seignio-
          rial control, 209
     stance of, concerning pervasiveness of
          royal governance, 12
Perpignan
     citizenship of Jews in, 116–17
     consulate in, 61
     customary laws in, 174–75
Philip (II) Augustus (of France), 13
Philip IV (of France), 14
policy diffusion. *See also* royal policies
     under Jaume I, 68–78
     under seigniorial administration,
          84–87, 119
     of *servi regis* provision, 11, 217 n. 52
Ponç de Menescal, 107, 231 n. 76
Ponç Hug (III) of Empúries (count), 71, 95,
     105–6
Ponç Hug (IV) of Empúries (count), 203
Portella, Içmael de, 77
postat (*potestas*) (ruler or power-holder),
     29–30, 74, 111, 171, 204
potestas (feudal right), 111, 197, 199, 202
Prats, Berenguer de (bishop of Tortosa),
     185–86, 247–48 n. 77
Princeps namque, 131, 155–56, 242 n. 61
prohoms (*probi homines*) (leading men), 79,
     114, 133, 140–41, 156, 243 n. 19

questia, 48, 49, 61, 103, 108, 116, 121, 124, 128–30, 159, 195

Ravaya, Jucef, 198
Ray, Jonathan, 17–18, 20, 21, 91, 172
Raymond VI of Toulouse (count), 190
Regine, Maimo, 220 n. 38
Remolins (Tortosa)
    artisanal production and commerce in, 89
    establishment of new Jewish *call* within, 99–101
    location and characteristics of, 31–33, 88, 99, 220 n. 28, 229 n. 21
    positioning of *morería* within, 219–20 n. 27
Riera i Sans, Jaume, 15–16
roads, protection over public, 69, 79
Robi, Samuel (bailiff), 140, 240 n. 20
Roman legal material and principles. See also *ius commune*
    opposition to, by nobility, 111, 131
    influence of, on customary legal collections in Crown of Aragon, 29, 72, 131, 143, 238 n. 59
    use of, by Jaume I to promote royal authority, 79–80, 130–31
royal acquisition of Tortosa
    circumstances motivating, 157–58
    implications of, 170–75, 186–87
    royal policy-making following, 157–59, 175–86
    transfers enacting, 157
royal administrative advances
    conflict with the seigniorial regime due to, 128–32
    crown motives behind, 135–37
    empowered by the installation of a royal bailiff, 121–28
    and exemptions and privileges, 78–81, 95–96
    and Jewish taxation, 149–53
    political setbacks impeding, 153–57
    strategies intended to carry out, 132–35, 139–49

royal governance and jurisdiction
    competitive policy-making intended to further, 95–98
    as defined by the *Commemoracions* of Pere Albert, 73, 131
    as defined by the *Furs de València*, 75
    expansion of, 68–78, 202–4
    innovation in the face of, by the seigniorial administration, 87–99, 102–6, 194, 195
    limitations on, 204–13
    obstruction of, in Valldigna, 1–4
    opposed by Templars, 110–11
    promotion of, in Tortosa, 55–56, 79–81, 121–24, 139–46, 155–56
    seigniorial administration and transition to, 157–60
royal policies. *See also* policy diffusion
    imposed on *aljamas* of Tortosa, 144–47
    maintained and applied by lords, 84–87
    and seigniorial policy making, 102–6, 147–48
royal visitations, 65–67, 103–5, 128, 226 n. 57
royal withdrawal from Tortosa
    circumstances motivating, 38–40
    transfers enacting, 40–53

Sabaté, Flocel, 10
Sancha of Castile (queen), 47–49, 52–53, 85–86, 97, 222 n. 110
Sanç of Provence (count), 61, 62
Santa Coloma de Queralt, 16
Santes Creus, 40
segregation, 31, 88, 91–93
seigniorial administration, 83–84. *See also* seigniorial authority
    changes to *calls* under, 99–102
    continuity under, 84–87
    crown initiatives forced upon, 140–48
    implications of, 162–70
    innovation under, in Tortosa, 87–95
    and Jewish evasion of royal subsidies in Tortosa, 150–53
    local customary conditions under, in Tortosa, 114–19

policy-making under, 102–6
and royal acquisition of Tortosa, 157–158
royal intervention and competitive initiatives under, in Tortosa, 95–99
royal taxation attempts under, 121–32, 149–53, 155–56
seigniorial disputes and developments in, 106–14
seigniorial authority. *See also dominium*; seigniorial administration
   as advantageous for Jews, 152–53, 165, 172–73
   assumption of, over Tortosa, 19–20, 38–42, 46–53
   challenges by citizens to, in Tortosa, 47, 79, 85
   challenges by monarchy to, 2–3, 8, 15, 78–80
   disputes among lords concerning, in Tortosa, 106–14
   limitations on royal authority by, under Jaume I, 55–57
   over Jews, 14–15, 20, 81, 193–204, 212–13
   pervasiveness of, 10, 20
   respect of, shown by the monarchy, 75
self-defense
   of Jews in Fraga, 196
   of Jews in Banyeres (Tortosa), 91
   of nobles in Catalonia, 131
self-determination, Jewish, 90–91, 148–49, 165, 183, 213
self-governance, Christian, 85, 113
self-governance, Jewish, 73–74, 77–78, 97–99, 102–103, 105–6, 147–48, 167–68, 172, 177, 196
servi regis provision, 5, 7, 11–12, 21, 30, 43, 45, 59, 74, 117, 130, 137, 154–55, 205, 210
Sestrica, 208
Shatzmiller, Joseph, 89
Sicut iudeis (Calixtus II), 6
Siscar, Arnau de (queen's lieutenant), 48
Soifer Irish, Maya, 78, 152, 217 n. 61, 222 n. 101

Solsona, 194–95
subsidies. *See* taxation
subvicar
   as recipient of royal overtures, 142
   as seigniorial appointee, 239 n. 9
synagogue
   ability of lord to license new, in Fraga, 201
   construction of new, in Tortosa, 92–93, 100–102, 122
   preaching by friars in, 144
   performance of Jewish oath in, 176, 177
   right of Jewish *aljama* to restrict access to, 174
   as symbol of Judaism, 6

Tahuell, Omar, 192–93
Tarazona, 97
Tarragona
   archbishop of, 159, 225 n. 32
   ecclesiastical *parlament* held at (1235), 72
   Jewish community of, 33
   monarchy's regalian possession of Jews in, 159
   and relief for frontier Tortosa, 37
   restrictions on wheat sales in, 72
   as subject to *supravicaria* of Tortosa, 159
tasca, 79
taxation
   as source of conflict among Tortosa's seigniorial regime, 107–9
   evasion of, 150–52, 155–56, 172–73, 210–11, 232 n. 88, 244 n. 29
   exemption from, 28, 34, 35–36, 37, 43–44, 50, 56, 61, 86, 95–96, 121, 124–25, 158, 163, 190
   in Fraga, 198–99, 201, 202
   and Jewish self-governance, 73, 78, 103, 147
   of Jews, 103, 116, 122–23, 125, 127, 129–30, 149–150, 190, 195, 198–99, 202, 212
   and opposition by lords, 60, 127–30, 136–37, 159

INDEX 289

taxation (*continued*)
- participation of Jews in municipal, in Tortosa, 114, 115–116
- policies of Pierre de Douai regarding, 61
- as a regalian preserve, 5
- by royal administration, 123, 127, 148, 155, 173–74, 195, 198–99, 202, 212
- royal rights of, in Tortosa, 40, 48, 57, 129
- by seigniorial administration, in Tortosa, 67–68, 108, 121, 128–29
- and the *servi regis* principle, 75–76, 137
- transfers of royal rights of, 45

Templars
- and accumulation of property in lower Ebro region, 19–20, 28–29, 38–42, 47–53
- and administrative concord with Jaume I (1247), 55–58, 136
- entrusted with management of crown's finances under Jaume I, 62, 63–64
- jurisdiction of, over non-Christians, 107–13
- and lordship over Tortosa, 22
- resists royal administrative advances, 129–31
- response of, to installment of royal bailiff, 127–28
- and royal acquisition of Tortosa, 157
- and seigniorial disputes, 106–9
- style of administration of, as lords of Tortosa, 84–87
- as Tortosa's chief jurisdictional lord, 106–8, 109
- use of *Usatges de Barcelona* to justify lordship by, 30, 110–12

tithes
- collection of, by see of Tortosa, 89
- concord over, between see of Tortosa and Templars (1185), 42
- donation of, by Alfonso VII of Castile-León, 45–46
- from Jews and Muslims, 97, 192
- owed to Templars, repaid by crown, 68
- reduced under Pere I, 35–36

Tortosa
- during Andalusi period, 7, 25, 33–34, 35
- bishop of, 36, 48, 64, 66, 89, 116, 173–74, 185–86, 191, 192, 219 n. 14, 227 n. 77, 247–48 n. 77, 248 n. 17
- case study of, 4, 19–21
- as Catalonian, Valencian, or Aragonese town, 149–51
- Christian settlement charter for, 27–28
- conquest and settlement of, 7, 19–20, 25–26, 31–33
- Corts of 1225 held at, 63–64, 66, 71, 108
- customary legal conditions in, 27, 114–19, 169–70, 176–81, 182–84, 186–87, 232 n. 97
- decline of property holdings and administrative presence of monarchy in, 38–42, 46–53, 55–58
- economic and demographic conditions in, 28, 29, 33–37
- elite Jewish culture in, 89–91
- establishment of *supravicaria* in, 159
- flooding in, 181–82, 246 n. 60
- frontier conditions of, 35–37
- Jewish *call* of. *See* Jewish *call*, new, of Tortosa; Jewish *call*, old, of Tortosa
- Jewish privileges issued for, 21, 25–26, 27–31, 87–95, 99–102, 104–5, 166, 183, 187
- Jewish society in pre-conquest period in, 25–26, 33
- micro-*convivencia* in, 106–7, 114–19, 164–66, 168, 187, 233 n. 108
- Muslim privileges issued for, 25, 27, 31, 34, 166
- office of vicar in. *See* vicar
- population growth of Jewish community in, 89–90
- public spaces in, as defined by the *Costums de Tortosa*, 183–84

290 INDEX

reduction of monarchy's contact with, 64–68
retained Andalusi infrastructure in, 31–32
royal authority and administration in. *See* royal policies; royal governance and administration; royal withdrawal from Tortosa
seigniorial regime of. *See* seigniorial regime; seigniorial authority
synagogues in, 92, 93, 100–1, 122, 144, 174, 177
taxation of. *See* taxation

trade
infrastructure in Tortosa, 89
in the pre-conquest lower Ebro region, 33–34
in the post-conquest lower Ebro region, 34–35, 133, 158
regulations regarding, 30

Treaty of Corbeil (1258), 122

universitas (municipal collective)
of Fraga, 197, 199, 201–2
Jewish and Muslim membership in, elsewhere in Europe, 218–19 n. 109

universitas of Tortosa
and conflict with seigniorial regime, 79–80, 96, 102, 113, 158, 168, 232 n. 97
and dispute over Jewish oath-taking regulations, 176–81
Jewish and Muslim membership in, as defined by the *Consuetudines* and *Costums de Tortosa*, 115–17, 233 n. 107
and jurisdiction over Jews, as compared with other towns, 233 n. 108
and liability for repairing flood damage, 181–85, 246 n. 65, 247 n. 74
and local customary laws, 112–13, 114–19, 147
under royal administration, 168–69, 175

Urgell, Count of, 34
Urgell (county), 8, 72, 216 n. 32

Usatges de Barcelona
as applied to community of Mallorca, 74
as applied to lordship over Fraga, 197
as applied to lordships held by Guillem de Cervera, 232 n. 92
creation and content of, 7–8, 73, 237 n. 57
impact of, in Catalonia, 9
Princeps namque clause of, 131, 155–56, 242 n. 61
promoted by Catalan nobility, 111
references to, 232 n. 90
royal (comital) control of Jews, as defined by, 29–30
seigniorial authority over Jews sanctioned by, 15, 111
and seigniorial administration of Tortosa, 110–12
used to guide royal governance and policy-making, 29, 42, 56, 58–59, 73, 131, 143, 154, 204, 232 n. 94, 241 n. 55
used to bolster seigniorial authority, 59–60, 171

Valencia (town)
as Andalusi commercial center, 35
privileges awarded to Jewish community of, 74, 75–76
subsidy responsibilities of Jewish *aljama* of, 122

Valencia (kingdom)
alleged jurisdiction of crown and royal officials over, 1–3, 11–12, 72, 75
collecta of Tortosa as pertaining to, 150–51
frontier castles in, 51
Jewish officials in, 76, 123–24
Jewish residents of, 126
legal unification of. *See Furs de València*
managing Muslims of, 121–22

Valencia (kingdom) (*continued*)
    nobility of, 209
    subsidy responsibilities of Jewish *aljamas* within, 129
    trade within or by merchants from, 105, 128
    warfare and diplomacy with Muslim, 62, 64, 66, 68, 89
Valldigna, 1–4, 46, 191, 206, 207–8
Vic, 61, 193–94
vicar
    activity of, as local official in Tortosa, 110, 118
    as recipient of royal overtures, in seigniorial Tortosa, 133, 141, 144
    role of, in upholding provisions of peace legislation, 60–61
    role of, in presiding over municipal court, 79, 140, 146, 178, 184, 233 n. 103, 248 n. 78
    as royal official, 65, 140–41, 159, 175, 199, 225 n. 49, 241 n. 47, 242 n. 74, 244 n. 30
    as seigniorial appointee, in Tortosa, 65, 127, 146, 239 n. 2
Vidal Mayor, 72–73, 205, 251 n. 76

wine grapes, 92

Xixó, Abrahim, 91, 101, 124

Xixó, Astruc
    as backer of new synagogue, 100–101
    career of, as royal bailiff of Tortosa, 120–21, 122–28, 231 n. 84, 234–35 n. 11, 235 nn. 16,19, 236 n. 27, 238 n. 66, 240 n. 20
    death and estate of, 142
    exemptions and protections for family of, 124–25, 135
    influence beyond Tortosa, 124, 132, 235 n. 20, 236 nn. 27,29
    as instrument of royal power, 127, 142–43
    and Jewish community, 132–34, 140, 172
    later career of, 132–35, 238 n. 67, 239–40 n. 14
    legacy of, 135–36, 139–40
    as litigant, 142
    as money-lender, 141, 235 n. 19
    and seigniorial opposition, 127–28
    and repayment of outstanding debts, 141
    as royal creditor, 122, 123, 124–25, 239 n. 2

zalmedina (magistrate), 86, 94, 109, 167, 228 n. 6
Zaragoza, 37, 76, 77
Ziegler, Joseph, 176

www.ingramcontent.com/pod-product-compliance
Lightning Source LLC
Chambersburg PA
CBHW021355290426
44108CB00010B/250